The Path of a Genocide

The Path of a Genocide

The Rwanda Crisis from Uganda to Zaire

edited by
Howard Adelman & Astri Suhrke

Transaction Publishers
New Brunswick (U.S.A.) and London (U.K.)

Second printing 2000
Copyright © 1999 by Transaction Publishers, New Brunswick, New Jersey.

Library of Congress Catalog Number: 98-47757
ISBN: 1-56000-382-0 (cloth); 0-7658-0768-8 (paper)
Printed in the United States of America

Library of Congress Cataloging-in-Publication Data

The path of a genocide : the Rwanda crisis from Uganda to Zaire / edited by
    Howard Adelman and Astri Suhrke.
        p. cm.
    Includes bibliographical references and index.
    ISBN 1-56000-382-0 (cloth); 0-7658-0768-8 (paper)
    1. Rwanda—Politics and government.   2. Genocide—Rwanda—History—20th century. 3. Rwanda—Foreign relations.   I. Adelman, Howard,
1938–   II. Suhrke, Astri..

DT450.435.P385   1999
320.967571—dc21   98-47757

Contents

Part III: Peacekeeping

Acknowledgments

This book developed out of an evaluation study initiated in 1995 by the Nordic countries, eventually sponsored by nineteen countries and eighteen international agencies, to assess international emergency assistance to Rwanda during and after the genocide of 1994. The sponsors of the study wanted to understand the role of the international community in managing the conflict and what knowledge was available beforehand of the impending genocide. The editors of this volume were requested to write the latter study, which was published as: *Early Warning and Conflict Management: Genocide in Rwanda* (henceforth, the Report), which constituted Study II of the five volume *Evaluation of Emergency Assistance to Rwanda* (Copenhagen 1996). Without the assistance of numerous persons in governments, NGOs, international agencies, and academia around the world, neither the report nor this book would have been possible.

The core of this volume consists of a selection from the set of specialized studies that were commissioned and used as resource materials for the 1996 Report. The studies contain a wealth of valuable information which could not be included in the Report, but which deserve publication in their own right, particularly in light of the continuing and justified focus on the genocide as evidenced by the genocide trials, the 1997 Belgian and 1998 French inquiries, and continuing media attention. Most of the authors of those studies kindly agreed to revise their manuscripts for this published volume. New chapters were added as the Central African disaster unfolded.

To help contributors keep up with the rapidly developing events and weld their different perspectives into a coherent volume, the United States Institute of Peace provided financial assistance to hold a conference in December of 1996. This meeting brought together most of the chapter authors for the first time, while additional experts and policymakers served as commentators. The U.S. Committee for Refugees kindly made its meeting facilities in Washington available, and research staff at the York University Centre for Refugee Studies, especially two post-doctoral fellows, Susanne Schmeidl and Kurt Mills, organized the workshop. Graduate students at York University, funded by a grant from the Social Sciences and Humanities Research Council of Canada—particularly Tammy Stone and Gerry Butts—helped prepare the glossaries, bibliography, and the manuscript for publication.

The Norwegian Ministry of Foreign Affairs, which co-sponsored the original evaluation, provided additional assistance to develop the book manuscript and enable the two editors to have a long working session on an island in Pointe au Baril, Ontario during the summer of 1997. As initiator and principal sponsor of the Rwanda evaluation, the Danish Foreign Ministry provided financial assistance to enable copies of this volume to be distributed widely in Africa. We are particularly grateful to Niels Dabelstein of DANIDA for his patience, good humor, and sustained support.

Finally, we wish to repeat the acknowledgment given to our families in our 1996 Report: "We would like to thank our spouses and children who had to put up with an intense travelling schedule, and our absence even when physically present as we struggled to dispassionately dissect a human catastrophe."

H.A., A.S.
Toronto and Bergen
1998

Preface

Howard Adelman
Astri Suhrke

Dramatic changes that carry hope as well as despair have unfolded in sub-Sahara Africa in the 1990s. In the richest and largest country, South Africa, Nelson Mandela came to power in 1994; apartheid ended just as the genocide in Rwanda was underway. In 1997, in the second largest country of Africa, rich in mineral wealth, a thirty-two-year-old kleptocracy was overthrown in Zaire.[1] In the north, there are new rulers and signs of enduring peace in Ethiopia and Eritrea.

This book focuses on the Great Lakes region of Africa, where events have been swift and at times devastating. After a decade of war, repression, and the most horrific genocide in the latter half of this century,[2] new and loosely allied regimes have replaced old-style dictatorships. But they have all come to power with—or on—waves of violence. The change of regime in Zaire was, in many ways, the last spasm of a conflict in which the Rwanda genocide three years earlier was the centerpiece. Since the genocide, dramatic changes have taken place: the continuation of the genocide against the Banyarwanda in Zaire by the ex-FAR and *Interahamwe* who controlled the camps in Zaire;[3] the July 1996 coup in Burundi; the outbreak of civil war in Zaire, initially targeting the ex-FAR and *Interahamwe*; the subsequent mass repatriation of refugees from Zaire in November 1996 triggered by that conflict, and the mass repatriation of refugees from Tanzania in December; the aborted Canadian-led humanitarian peacekeeping mission on behalf of the refugees during that same period; the defeat by the Laurent-Desirè Kabila-led Alliance des Forces Dèmocratiques pour la Libèration du Congo-Zaire (AFDL) and the creation of the Democratic Republic of Congo (DRC) as the successor state to the Mobutu-led government of Zaire that fell. This manuscript was completed before the current Rwandese government involvement in Zaire/Congo had been established and before the issue of the number and extent of massacres of Hutu in Zaire/Congo had been sorted out.

The genocide itself had roots in an earlier conflict that began in Uganda in a now-familiar pattern. Refugees became agents as well as victims of violence; the refugee warriors[4] sought security for themselves by resorting to military means to attain power and to secure their membership in the state. In their quest, civilian members of that community were targeted by other communities that felt threatened. Violence, once initiated, generated reprisals against "the other" side. In Rwanda, those reprisals and the response to perceived and actual threats reached a totally different order when extremists within the Hutu community targeted the whole of the Tutsi population in Rwanda for extermination. The genocidists won the war against the civilian population, but lost against the invading Tutsi-dominated refugee army. They themselves became refugees in Zaire.

An effort was made to begin the cycle again as the defeated army and militias from refugee camps in Zaire targeted civilian members of the local society and conducted raids back into Rwanda.[5] With the backing of the new governments in Rwanda and Uganda, groups in the local populations rose up and drove out the militants. By the spring of 1998, the cycle of violence had yet to run its course in Burundi or, for that matter, in Rwanda or Uganda. For example, the violence continues with extremist terrorist attacks in the Gisenyi and Ruhengeri préfectures, and sometimes overzealous responses by the overwhelmingly Tutsi-dominated Rwandese army. Indeed, the most critical question in the Great Lakes Region at present is whether the governments and their adversaries can break free from this heritage. Otherwise the new leaders in Uganda, Rwanda, and the DRC will continue to be confronted by dissident communities and militant refugees, disaffected by regimes which they do not believe represent them. The dissidents will seek revenge, security and power by using violent means to overthrow those regimes. When that quest is matched by repression and targeted killings, a new cycle in the spiral of violence begins.

By examining the decade (1986–1997) of conflict which brackets the Rwanda crisis, this book provides important background to current conflicts in the region. First and foremost, however, it is a study of the international involvement and responses to the genocide. The contributors include a collection of specialist scholars from Uganda, Rwanda, Zaire (DRC), Ethiopia, Norway, Britain, France, Canada, and the United States. They provide detailed background and analysis of regional forces that fueled the Rwanda conflict. They also document how and why the international community failed to stop or significantly mitigate the genocide.

The genesis of this study originated in the dilemma of the international community providing development and relief assistance only to witness a new spiral of violence and larger refugee flows. Soon after the genocide, nineteen donor countries and seventeen multilateral organizations, international agencies, and international NGOs[6] pooled their efforts in an unprecedented effort to sponsor an in-depth study that went beyond the relatively straightforward task of evaluating whether aid was delivered effectively and efficiently. The study looked at the history of the violence and what the international community knew in advance, as well as what action had been taken to prevent the crisis.

In the preparation of that report, a number of original, in-depth studies were commissioned from scholars to examine various aspects of the problem. With the completion of the Rwanda study, the Canadian International Development Agency (CIDA) requested a follow-up study by Howard Adelman and his colleagues at York University on early warning and conflict management in Zaire. Further, Astri Suhrke was asked to testify for the parliamentary inquiry in Belgium which provided additional access to documentation. Based on both the original and additional material, this enabled the best of the specialized studies undertaken in preparation for both reports to be selected and edited, with additional material added to provide a regional focus for this volume narrating over a decade of horror culminating in genocide as well as radical change.

The quality and originality of the research included in the general narrative is sufficient in itself to have justified this volume and to make the material available to scholars of the region. However, no account covering such a large area and so many players could be expected to be comprehensive. While each study in this volume focuses on one dimension of the Rwanda conflict, together they progressively tell the story of how the genocide unfolded and how the world responded. For example, although chapter 10 by Livingston and Eachus, "Rwanda: U.S. Policy and Television Coverage," focuses on the role of television in shaping U.S. public opinion and foreign policy, other significant inputs into that policy—the shadow of Somalia, for example—are assumed rather than examined and analyzed, and the marginal status of Rwanda in American foreign policy during most of this period is referred to in other chapters.

In addition to omissions, in telling a story with different chapters written by different authors, inevitably there will be overlap and redundancy. We have edited the contributions to eliminate redundancy where it was merely repetitive. However, when the analysis was central to that section of the tale, we have allowed for repetition, as would have happened even if a single author had written the entire book. For example, Jones includes coverage of the role of the OAU in the chapter on the Arusha Accords, while Tekle in the previous chapter has already described the role of the OAU in the overall crisis. The difference is that Jones examines Arusha from a global angle and the perspective of a case study of preventive diplomacy, while Tekle's analysis was more about the role of regional institutions, in this case an intergovernmental organization dealing with all of Africa. Similarly, Jones mentions and summarizes the French role at Arusha, while Callamard in the following chapter documents it in detail. Thus, we have permitted overlap where different perspectives fill out or were crucial to the story, but eliminated it where it is simply repetitive. This process was helped by the generous contribution of the United States Institute for Peace, which allowed most of the authors to come together in Washington to discuss their different contributions and then re-edit their material to take into account the comments received and the perceptions of others.

Nevertheless, the present collection of studies, we believe, has significance beyond the region and the specialized areas on which the original Rwanda study focused. Together they provide a narrative of a period which has witnessed not only a seismic change in central Africa, but also a radical reexamination of the involvement of states and international actors in humanitarian issues. After all, the U.N. Security Council accepted a responsibility to assist in protecting civilians in Rwanda, but withdrew most of its peace keepers shortly after the genocide began. When the U.N. reversed itself, the new forces were deployed so tardily that the genocide was completed before the arrival of the peace keepers.

This volume is also relevant in light of the fact that France withdrew its support for the 1966 Report after examining the draft, and the U.N. Secretariat surprisingly attacked the factual accuracy of the final report (surprising in light of the numerous opportunities to offer corrections to drafts provided to the Secretariat). More particularly, the then Secretary-General, through his spokesperson, argued that the information about the planned genocide was passed onto the Security Council,[7] contrary to the conclusions of our study. Full publication of the scholarship

behind the report is necessary to allow independent scholars to determine for themselves the quality of the work. The chapters on France
and on peacekeeping are, therefore, not only relevant to depicting the
French and U.N. roles in Rwanda, but as a corrective to the U.N. official account of its role prior to and during the genocide as depicted (we
allege misleadingly) in the U.N. publication, *The United Nations and
Rwanda 1993–1996* (New York: U.N. Publications, 1996).

The analyses of the deeper roots of the genocide in this collection
are valuable for comparative studies of genocide and ethnic violence
as well. The volume also offers a diachronically broad perspective in
contrast to the tendency in political science to treat the conclusion of a
peace agreement as the end of a conflict. This case study demonstrates
that peace accords may be just a stage in the cycle of violence, and a
very fragile one at that. In fact, the peace agreement may itself become
a catalyst for violence for those who reject the peace, as happened in
Rwanda.

This collection also attempts to overcome the dichotomy prevalent
in the social sciences between domestic and foreign affairs, between
internal and external forces. Though the focus of the volume is the role
of international actors in a region of conflict, the local context and the
close interaction between internal and external forces are critical to
understanding the role of the latter. Moreover, as refugees and political
actors move across national borders but remain active players in their
home country—a feature that continues to characterize conflict in the
Great Lakes region—new alliances develop. The distinction between
"external" and "internal" is further blurred.[8] On another level, local
developments can be critically affected even by the expectations of
external assistance, or failure to render such aid, as was evident in
Rwanda on the eve of the genocide.

Though we are boastful about the value and importance of this
volume, based on the studies themselves, we are no longer sanguine
about the prospects that we can learn from the past in order to chart a
more peaceful future. The studies themselves have made us far more
cautious about the ability to translate scholarship into effective action. Too many times even the conclusions of studies are simply used
to reinforce the preconceptions of policy makers already in place.
The most we can hope is that this in-depth analysis will add to the
entire spectrum of studies of both successes and failures in international affairs, and, further, that some policy makers *might* draw valuable lessons from it.

With all the bravura about the breadth and depth of this volume and its value as scholarship, as well as some degree of modesty about its utility for policy makers, it is the past that hangs as a very heavy cloud over what is put forth as detached scholarship; the genocide in Rwanda dominates the volume. The centrality of that genocide makes detached scholarship difficult, and almost impossible for those directly affected by the genocide. The chapter on extremism in Rwanda by Joan Kakwenzire and Dixon Kamukama was self-consciously written by a partnership of a Tutsi and a Bairu, the Ugandan equivalent of a Hutu, with direct input from two other local scholars, a Tutsi and a Bairu, respectively, in an effort to ensure objectivity in spite of the pain suffered by the Tutsi authors by the loss of many relatives. Similarly, the deeply conflicting and impassioned views held by French observers and policy makers on France's role cannot help but be reflected in the analysis of Agnes Callamard and Gérard Prunier in their respective chapters.

The methodology and approach of this volume raises other issues. Conventional wisdom holds that the end of the Cold War represented a watershed in world affairs. Without underestimating the importance of the fall of the Berlin Wall, particularly for Europe, this volume suggests that the changes ostensibly brought about by the end of the Cold War and its importance to global events were overrated. Rwanda was strategically marginal to the superpower rivalry during the Cold War, and remained of marginal significance to the lone superpower afterwards. The point emerges starkly because the acute phase of the conflict—set off by the RPF invasion of Rwanda—started shortly after the fall of the Berlin Wall, although the timing was coincidental.

In reality, conflict in the Great Lakes Region was influenced by the external logic of older rivalries, especially competition between erstwhile European imperial allies. That rivalry was barely submerged during the Cold War and subsequently resurfaced. Often referred to as "the Fashoda syndrome" in France (see Prunier's chapter), the contest was over language and cultural domination. As it turned out, the attempt to protect and promote French culture in the region against the advancing Anglophone sphere not only failed, but the old, client regimes of France were replaced by leaders who converted the international language of their countries from unilingual French states to bilingual English/French states. The language conversion in Rwanda and Zaire reflected not simply dependency on English-speaking Uganda by the RPF in Rwanda, and dependency on Rwanda by the Alliance in the DRC. The new leaders are relatively efficient, rational, and pragmatic in comparison to their predecessors. With that realism, they accepted English as the language of technology and global communication. The new regimes represent a breed of African "post post-independence" leaders who are not being primarily indebted to extra-regional states in achieving power. African governments, for better or worse, have become the prime agents of change in the region.

The new leaders combine the loyalty of an ethnic cohort with a rhetorical dedication to state rather than ethnic nationalism. This pragmatic rationality fits well with their acceptance of market force economics, in spite of the Marxist rhetoric in their past. But the new modernism still has to deal with the conundrum of multiethnic states where it is difficult to repress ethnicity in favour of a renewed national identity, particularly when the minority ethnic group holds most positions of power.

It is hard to envision how these regimes will overcome their access to power through violence and the grasping of the levers of power by groups disproportionately dominated by members of one ethnic group when they achieved victory. Power sharing based on ethnicity does not seem to be a meaningful term to the new victors. How can power seized through violence establish a government subject to the rule of law? Further, in these conditions, how can a political culture develop that is accountable to the people as sovereign? Both processes are a prerequisite for building a democratic state. An effort is being made to define everyone as primarily a citizen of the state—as Ugandans, Rwandans, Congolese. But everyone is conscious of their own ethnic membership and the fact that the governments in the respective countries are not representative of the various ethnic cultures in the country. The challenge is particularly acute for the minority rulers of Rwanda who cannot forget—nor should they be expected to forget—the trauma of the genocide committed against their people and moderate Hutu.

Given these developments and the relative autonomy of the actions that brought about the present situation, talk of devolution of responsibility for humanitarian intervention and peacekeeping seems ironic, for devolution presumes that power and authority originally reside at the centre and are delegated down to the regions. In the dramatic events from Uganda through Rwanda to Congo in the last decade of this century, power exercised locally was the primary determinant of the results, even though outside assistance was provided to the different sides throughout the conflict. More importantly, the international community emerged as a paper tiger even in the face of ill-equipped and relatively poorly trained local forces.

The examination of that paper tiger is the main focus of the book. In the current context of discussions of early warning, preventive diplomacy, peacekeeping, and peace building, this collection of essays constitutes a detailed case study of the worst case of international failure in the 1990s. It is essential to understand why the international community fails to act when needed, mandated, and required by international norms and agreements. In the current inability of the U.N. or even regional states to stop the accelerating number of massacres in Burundi, this text should be required reading by scholars, peace keepers, and policy makers concerned with these issues. Similarly, all the policy dilemmas raised by the Rwandan case—from early warning to humanitarian assistance—have a Zairean or Congo sequel.

For example, the original study that we undertook on early warning and conflict management in Rwanda recommended improvements in the early warning system as an important ingredient for prevention. In the Zaire crisis, there were ample warnings that if the international community did not disarm the ex-FAR and militias encamped in eastern Zaire, a new round of violence would result. Further, in contrast to the distorted and inadequate media coverage of the build-up and execution of the Rwandan genocide, coverage on Zaire was relatively well-informed, assisted enormously by the information provided by the U.N. IRIN service that was established after the genocide. But the necessary actions were not taken. When decisions were made in late 1996 to intervene, it was only to provide the refugees with humanitarian aid, and even this was pre-empted by local forces and lack of cooperation from Rwanda. For some, this purportedly proves that one aspect of the problem is *not* a failure in early warning.

But early warning is not just the provision of accurate and critical information. It is the analysis of that information to enable strategic choices to be made. Often, however, strategic choices are made axiomatically on the basis of key political values, with inadequate intelligence data being brought in during the early stages of decision-making. Fuller information is collected only afterwards when the policy has to be implemented. This seems to have been the case with the Canadian decision to launch a humanitarian mission to Zaire in November 1996. The initiative was caught between the competing views of the Americans and the French, the former resisting any intervention and advocating (and supporting?) the rebels, while the latter allegedly hoped that a humanitarian intervention would use the guise of humanitarianism to place foreign troops in a position to effectively block the rebel advance.

Without early warning in this broader sense, that is early warning which is not just information and the setting off of alarms, but which allows facts to be analysed within a policy context to develop coherent and realistic policy options, the policy lacked an adequate foundation for decision-making. As a result, well-intentioned humanitarian missions are misconceived and have to be aborted. In fact, it was the rebel-Alliance attacks on the camps which separated the militants from the rest of the refugees and provided the catalyst for large-scale repatriation which the international community had heretofore failed to bring off.

Another recurrent theme during this decade of conflict is exile refugee communities transforming themselves into "refugee warriors," invading their home countries using the host country as a base and setting a pattern of violence. In the worst case, a state which was attacked responded with massacres of civilians and eventually a genocide. For the international community, the activities of "refugee warrior" communities pose operational and legal-moral questions that have become intertwined.

The UNHCR has both a moral and a legal responsibility to assist and protect refugees, and to promote durable solutions, the foremost being repatriation. But in the face of the fears of the refugees about returning, and the intimidation by the militants who also fostered those fears, the UNHCR was unable to facilitate significant repatriation. Further, the aid agencies have to provide assistance and aid in the refugee camps in a situation in which refugees have used their camps as military bases and skimmed part of donor proceeds to finance their military operations. Refugee camps have been used as sanctuaries for armed units, including genocidal killers, launching attacks against local populations and across the border. When those camps are attacked, the international community in general, and U.N. agencies in particular, have been unable to protect the refugees or even manage to ensure the supply of humanitarian assistance for women and children who typically constitute the majority in such camps. All the painful dilemmas raised by these kinds of situations have been experienced by aid agencies operating in the Great Lakes region during the last decade of conflict. When large-scale repatriation of Rwandese (Hutu) from eastern Zaire took place in late 1996 to bring about a permanent solution, it was largely as a result of action by local players and, to some degree, in opposition to the policies advocated by many international humanitarian organizations.

Though the issues of refugee warriors, refugee protection and repatriation, early warning, humanitarian intervention and conflict management are all themes in this volume, the genocide in Rwanda remains the centrepiece. The authors' goal is not to cast blame, but to explain the international failure of the international community to intervene and prevent or mitigate the genocide in a situation in which the forces perpetrating the genocide were relatively weak and ill-equipped with the tools of violence. The U.N. had been invited to play a role, had agreed to do so, and had ready access to the area of conflict. (U.N. peace keepers controlled the airport in Kigali throughout the whole Rwandese massacre.) Nevertheless a genocide occurred in which the vast majority of the resident Tutsi and moderate Hutu population of Rwanda, usually estimated at 800,000 but perhaps a million or more, were slaughtered by low-tech means, mainly machetes, in a three month centrally organized operation that proceeded with twice the efficiency of the Nazi Holocaust of the Jews. This occurred while people in North America and Europe were watching *Schindler's List* on their movie screens and leaving the theatre profoundly moved, vowing that such genocides should never again occur.

After the genocide was over in Rwanda, the killings did not stop. The locale merely shifted to Zaire. The genocidists who had fled to Zaire expanded their murderous mayhem targeting the Banyamulenge in Zaire, triggering the civil war in that country. In the process of the rebels defeating both the genocidists and overthrowing the dictatorship of Mobutu, they massacred Hutu refugees. Throughout, the rebels were strongly supported by the RPF government in Rwanda, dominated by the Tutsi community which had turned from victim to power-broker.

What can we learn about the seeds of exclusion, extremism and genocide from such horrendous cycles of violence and revenge, and what can be done to prevent their recurrence? This is the central question posed by this volume.

Notes

1. The name "Zaire" will be used when referring to the country when it was called by that name; otherwise its new name, the Democratic Republic of Congo (DRC), will be used.
2. The editors were privileged to have been selected to write the second report: *Early Warning and Conflict Management: Genocide in Rwanda* (Copenhagen: DANIDA, 1996) which constituted Study II of *The Evaluation of Emergency Assistance to Rwanda,* which was sponsored by nineteen countries and eighteen international agencies and NGOs.
3. Some reputable scholars argue that the fights between the genocidists and the Banymulenge or Banyarwanda in Zaire are but part of a long history of feuds between local politicians and the Banyamulenge, including residents of Tutsi

origin and Rwandese refugees from the 1959–1962 revolution and struggle for independence in Rwanda. We have a different interpretation of the massacres at Masisi. They are not simply the continuation of past disputes over who or who is not Zairean, but a continuation of the genocide led by the ex-FAR and interahamwe from Rwanda living in refugee camps in Zaire. These conclusions are drawn from interviews with some of the 4000 Masisi who crossed into Rwanda on 13 April 1996, and another 4,000 who were waiting to cross. The conclusions were confirmed when another 2,000 prepared to cross on 29 April 1996. This does not mean that the local Hunde were not involved, but the instigators and main perpetrators were the extremist Hutus from Rwanda.

4. For a more detailed analysis of the conception of refugee warriors and the problems and solutions in various settings, cf. Zolberg, Ari, Astri Suhrke, and Sergio Aguayo, *Escape from Violence: Conflict and the Refugee Crisis in the Developing World*, New York: Oxford University Press, 1989. For additional elaborations of the problem, cf. Astri Suhrke, "A Crisis Diminished: Refugees in the Developing World," *International Journal*, XLVIII:2, Spring 1993, 215–39; Howard Adelman, "Refugees, the Right of Return and the Peace Process," *Economics of Peace in the Middle East*, Bashir Al Khadra, ed., Yarmouk University, 1995; Howard Adelman, "Modernity, Globalization, Refugees and Displacement," in Alastair Ager, ed., *Refugees, Contemporary Perspectives on the Experience of Forced Migration*, London: Cassell Publishers, 1998; and Howard Adelman, "Crimes of Government as Causes of Mass Migration," in Alex P. Schmid, ed., *Migration and Crime*, Milan: ISPAC, 1997.

5. There were more than raids. On 3 March 1996, mortar attacks were launched on the central market of Cyangugu in the first use of heavy weapons since the end of the war in Rwanda in 1994.

6. The countries of the OECD were actually represented by their nineteen bilateral donor agencies, who, with the European Commission and the secretariat of the Development Assistance Committee of the OECD, nine multilateral agencies and U.N. departments, the International Committee of the Red Cross (ICRC) and the International Federation of the Red Cross and Red Crescent Societies (IFRC), and five international NGOs and NGO umbrella organizations, formed a Steering Committee to supervise the research and writing of the report. The report emerged in five volumes published by DANIDA in Copenhagen in 1996.

7. Unsuccessfully, "(T)he chair of the Steering Committee sought clarification (in the event unsuccessfully) of the 'factual inaccuracies' alleged by the U.N. Spokesperson and the Under-Secretary General for Humanitarian Affairs." *The Joint Evaluation of Emergency Assistance to Rwanda: A Review of Follow-up and Impact Fifteen Months After Publication*, Copenhagen: DANIDA, June 12, 1997, 8–9.

8. Cf. Marie Bernard-Meunier, Assistant Deputy Minister for Global Issues in the Department of Foreign Affairs and International Trade (DFAIT) in Ottawa, Canada, in her Foreword to the *Proceedings—Conflict Prevention: African Perspective*, for the International Francophone Meeting, Ottawa, September, 1995. Perhaps unintentionally, she confused the contrast between inter- and intrastate conflicts with the conclusion that intrastate conflicts are confined within the boundaries of a single state. She said: "The fact that these conflicts occur within single states distinguishes them from the interstate confrontations in the Cold war era." (p. 8) This slip was made even though the conference itself noted that, "in Africa, in addition to creating problems within countries, tension and conflict contribute to regional instability because of the porous nature of boundaries." *Summary of Proceedings*, 11.

Text of the January 11, 1994 Cable

94/422 1/2

23:52z

JB
ku

CNR 12

REC'D

OUTGOING CODE CABLE

JAN 11 1994

DATE: 11 JANUARY 1994   HIR 17

TO: BARIL\DPKO\UNATIONS NEW YORK	FROM: DALLAIRE UNAMIR\KIGALI
FAX NO:MOST IMMEDIATE-CODE CABLE-212-963-9852 INMARSAT:	FAX NO: 011-250-84273
SUBJECT:REQUEST FOR PROTECTION FOR INFORMANT	
ATTN: MGEN BARIL	ROOM NO.2052
TOTAL NUMBER OF TRANSMITTED PAGES INCLUDING THIS ONE: 2	

1.   FORCE COMMANDER PUT IN CONTACT WITH INFORMANT BY VERY VERY
IMPORTANT GOVERNMENT POLITICIAN.   INFORMANT IS A TOP LEVEL
TRAINER IN THE CADRE OF INTERHAMWE-ARMED MILITIA OF MRND.

2.   HE INFORMED US HE WAS IN CHARGE OF LAST SATURDAYS
DEMONSTRATIONS WHICH AIMS WERE TO TARGET DEPUTIES OF OPPOSITION
PARTIES COMING TO CEREMONIES AND BELGIAN SOLDIERS.   THEY HOPED TO
PROVOKE THE RPF BN TO ENGAGE (BEING FIRED UPON) THE DEMONSTRATORS
AND PROVOKE A CIVIL WAR.   DEPUTIES WERE TO BE ASSASSINATED UPON
ENTRY OR EXIT FROM PARLIAMENT.   BELGIAN TROOPS WERE TO BE
PROVOKED AND IF BELGIANS SOLDIERS RESORTED TO FORCE A NUMBER OF
THEM WERE TO BE KILLED AND THUS GUARANTEE BELGIAN WITHDRAWAL FROM
RWANDA.

3.   INFORMANT CONFIRMED 48 RGF PARA CDO AND A FEW MEMBERS OF THE
GENDARMERIE PARTICIPATED IN DEMONSTRATIONS IN PLAIN CLOTHES.
ALSO AT LEAST ONE MINISTER OF THE MRND AND THE SOUS-PREFECT OF
KIGALI WERE IN THE DEMONSTRATION.   RGF AND INTERHAMWE PROVIDED
RADIO COMMUNICATIONS.

4.   INFORMANT IS A FORMER SECURITY MEMBER OF THE PRESIDENT.   HE
ALSO STATED HE IS PAID RF150,000 PER MONTH BY THE MRND PARTY TO
TRAIN INTERHAMWE.   DIRECT LINK IS TO CHIEF OF STAFF RGF AND
PRESIDENT OF THE MRND FOR FINANCIAL AND MATERIAL SUPPORT.

5.   INTERHAMWE HAS TRAINED 1700 MEN IN RGF MILITARY CAMPS
OUTSIDE THE CAPITAL.   THE 1700 ARE SCATTERED IN GROUPS OF 40
THROUGHOUT KIGALI.   SINCE UNAMIR DEPLOYED HE HAS TRAINED 300
PERSONNEL IN THREE WEEK TRAINING SESSIONS AT RGF CAMPS.   TRAINING

FOCUS WAS DISCIPLINE, WEAPONS, EXPLOSIVES, CLOSE COMBAT AND TACTICS.

6.   PRINCIPAL AIM OF INTERHAMWE IN THE PAST WAS TO PROTECT KIGALI FROM RPF. SINCE UNAMIR MANDATE HE HAS BEEN ORDERED TO REGISTER ALL TUTSI IN KIGALI. HE SUSPECTS IT IS FOR THEIR EXTERMINATION. EXAMPLE HE GAVE WAS THAT IN 20 MINUTES HIS PERSONNEL COULD KILL UP TO 1000 TUTSIS.

7.   INFORMANT STATES HE DISAGREES WITH ANTI-TUTSI EXTERMINATION. HE SUPPORTS OPPOSITION TO RPF BUT CANNOT SUPPORT KILLING OF INNOCENT PERSONS. HE ALSO STATED THAT HE BELIEVES THE PRESIDENT DOES NOT HAVE FULL CONTROL OVER ALL ELEMENTS OF HIS OLD PARTY\FACTION.

8.   INFORMANT IS PREPARED TO PROVIDE LOCATION OF MAJOR WEAPONS CACHE WITH AT LEAST 135 WEAPONS. HE ALREADY HAS DISTRIBUTED 110 WEAPONS INCLUDING 35 WITH AMMUNITION AND CAN GIVE US DETAILS OF THEIR LOCATION. TYPE OF WEAPONS ARE G3 AND AK47 PROVIDED BY RGF. HE WAS READY TO GO TO THE ARMS CACHE TONIGHT-IF WE GAVE HIM THE FOLLOWING GUARANTEE. HE REQUESTS THAT HE AND HIS FAMILY (HIS WIFE AND FOUR CHILDREN) BE PLACED UNDER OUR PROTECTION.

9.   IT IS OUR INTENTION TO TAKE ACTION WITHIN THE NEXT 36 HOURS WITH A POSSIBLE H HR OF WEDNESDAY AT DAWN (LOCAL). INFORMANT STATES THAT HOSTILITIES MAY COMMENCE AGAIN IF POLITICAL DEADLOCK ENDS. VIOLENCE COULD TAKE PLACE DAY OF THE CEREMONIES OR THE DAY AFTER. THEREFORE WEDNESDAY WILL GIVE GREATEST CHANCE OF SUCCESS AND ALSO BE MOST TIMELY TO PROVIDE SIGNIFICANT INPUT TO ON-GOING POLITICAL NEGOTIATIONS.

10. IT IS RECOMMENDED THE INFORMANT BE GRANTED PROTECTION AND EVACUATED OUT OF RWANDA. THIS HQ DOES NOT HAVE PREVIOUS UN EXPERIENCE IN SUCH MATTERS AND URGENTLY REQUESTS GUIDANCE. NO CONTACT HAS AS YET BEEN MADE TO ANY EMBASSY IN ORDER TO INQUIRE IF THEY ARE PREPARED TO PROTECT HIM FOR A PERIOD OF TIME BY GRANTING DIPLOMATIC IMMUNITY IN THEIR EMBASSY IN KIGALI BEFORE MOVING HIM AND HIS FAMILY OUT OF THE COUNTRY.

11. FORCE COMMANDER WILL BE MEETING WITH THE VERY VERY IMPORTANT POLITICAL PERSON TOMORROW MORNING IN ORDER TO ENSURE THAT THIS INDIVIDUAL IS CONSCIOUS OF ALL PARAMETERS OF HIS INVOLVEMENT. FORCE COMMANDER DOES HAVE CERTAIN RESERVATIONS ON THE SUDDENNESS OF THE CHANGE OF HEART OF THE INFORMANT TO COME CLEAN WITH THIS INFORMATION. RECCE OF ARMED CACHE AND DETAILED PLANNING OF RAID TO GO ON LATE TOMORROW. POSSIBILITY OF A TRAP NOT FULLY EXCLUDED, AS THIS MAY BE A SET-UP AGAINST THE VERY VERY IMPORTANT POLITICAL PERSON. FORCE COMMANDER TO INFORM SRSG FIRST THING IN MORNING TO ENSURE HIS SUPPORT.

13. PEUX CE QUE VEUX. ALLONS-Y.

MAP 1
Great Lakes Region

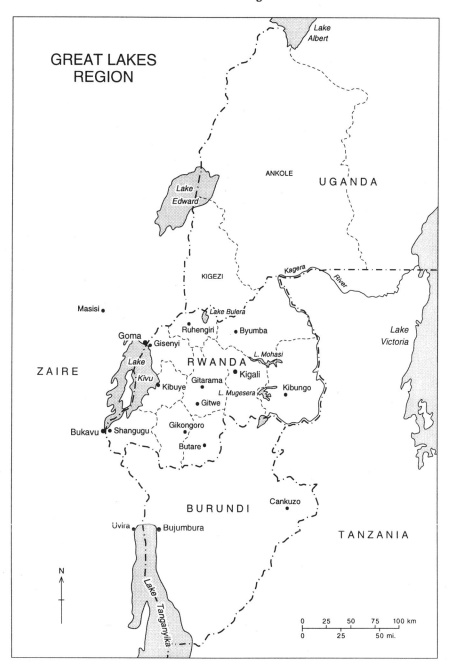

MAP 2
Rwanda: Refugee and Displaced Populations. 31 March 1995

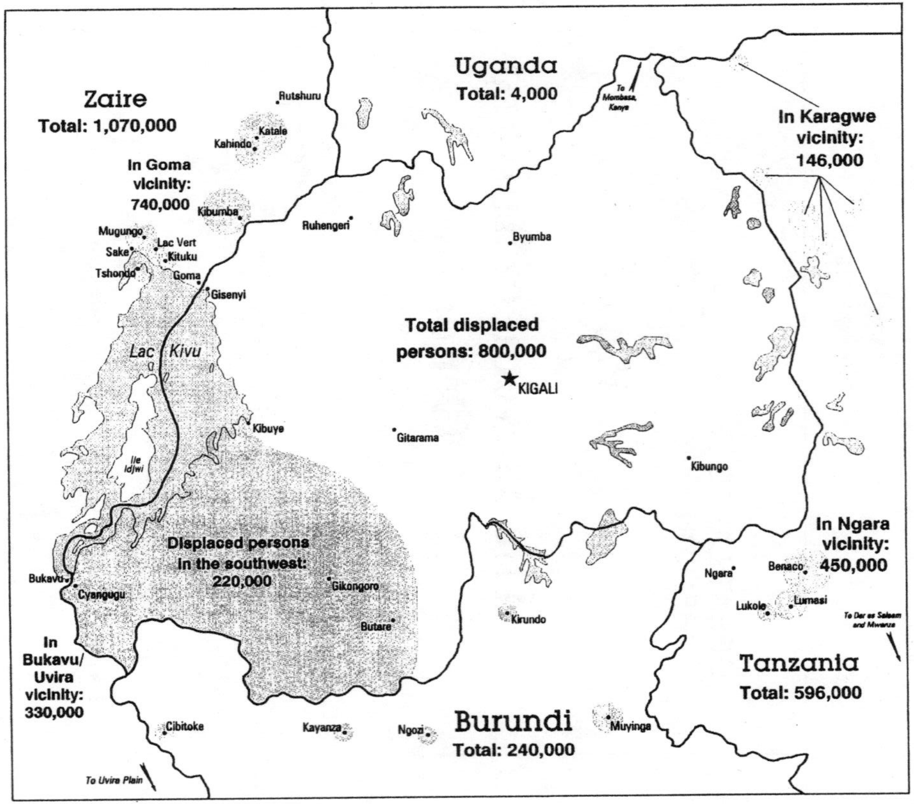

Uganda
Total: 4,000

In Karagwe vicinity: 146,000

In Ngara vicinity: 450,000

Benaco
Lumasi
Lukole
Ngara

Tanzania
Total: 596,000

Kibungo

Byumba

Total displaced persons: 800,000

★ KIGALI

Gitarama

Muyinga

Kirundo

Burundi
Total: 240,000

Ngozi

Kayanza

Displaced persons in the southwest: 220,000

Gikongoro
Butare

Kibuye

Cibitoke

Lac Kivu

Ile Idjwi

Zaire
Total: 1,070,000

In Goma vicinity: 740,000

Rutshuru
Kahindo
Kibumba
Katale
Mugunga
Lac Vert
Saka
Kituku
Tshondo
Goma
Gisenyi

Ruhengeri

Cyangugu
Bukavu

In Bukavu/Uvira vicinity: 330,000

To Uvira Plain

To Mombasa Kenya

To Dar es Salaam and Mwanza

Part I

The Movement Towards Genocide

1

Rwandese Refugees and Immigrants in Uganda

Ogenga Otunnu

This chapter analyzes the politics of exile and the treatment of Rwandese immigrants and refugees in Uganda. The first part sketches the ethnic connections between the peoples of Rwanda and Uganda from the pre-colonial period until German colonial rule and then traces the movement of Rwandese immigrants into Uganda and their reception up to the pre-independence period in Rwanda. The second part examines the movement of refugees from Rwanda into Uganda and their reception during the first Obote regime. The third part extends the analysis into the Idi Amin and second Obote regimes until Museveni achieved power in Uganda in 1984.

Pre-Independence Rwandese Immigration into Uganda

The Tutsi in Rwanda had an historical relationship with Banyarwanda and related peoples in Uganda. Between the sixteenth and nineteenth centuries, a number of centralized states emerged in the region, including Mpororo, inhabited mainly by the Bahororo, and encompassing most of the counties of Western Ankole and most of Kigezi district in contemporary Uganda and a portion of northern Rwanda. The ruling house of the Mpororo had close cultural and kinship ties with the ruling houses of Ankole (Hima). and Rwanda (Tutsi). When Mpororo disintegrated, some of its principalities were subsequently annexed by the Ankole state and the Rwanda state, and the rest were later forcibly merged into the Ankole and Kigezi districts of Uganda by the British colonial regime.[1]

3

Between the sixteenth and the nineteenth centuries, another central-ized state in the region, Rwanda, extended its sphere of political influ-ence to a portion of Ankole in Uganda based on the pre-existing kinship networks between the ruling houses of the two states, and intermar-riages between the two politically relevant ethnic groups in Rwanda and Ankole: the Tutsi and the Hima. In the nineteenth century, Rwanda extended its nominal hegemony to Bufumbira, most of the present day Kabale (Kigezi). and Kisoro (Bufumbira). districts of Uganda. Rwanda's hegemony was nominal in these areas because the Chiga, who were numerically the dominant group in Kigezi, put up a determined and protracted resistance against centralized autocracy and foreign rule. The extended distance from the citadel of imperial power made it difficult to directly and effectively administer the territories from Rwanda (Edel 1957, 1–5; Mateke 1970; Hopkins 1970; Brazier 1968; Rutanga 1983, 229–49).

The territorial expansion of the pre-colonial states of Mpororo, Ankole, and Rwanda had encouraged ethnic alliances, especially be-tween the Tutsi (Rwanda). and the Hima (Ankole), as well as ethnic counter alliances among the politically subservient ethnic groups, es-pecially between the Hutu (Rwanda). and the Hiru (Ankole). [also called Bairu—editors]. These alliances blurred ethnic differences between the Tutsi and the Hima, on the one hand, and between the Hutu and the Hiru, on the other. They also increased conflict and confrontation between members of the two camps. Secondly, although the shifting frontiers of the pre-colonial territorial states remained porous, the frontiers cut across some related families, compounds, and nationalities, complicating the question of national identity, na-tional allegiance and citizenship.

Pre-colonial alliances and conflicts were greatly exacerbated during European colonial rule when Rwanda and Burundi came under the ambit of German colonial hegemony, Uganda became a possession of the British, and the Congo (now the Democratic Republic of Congo), was colonized by the Belgians. The delimitation of national boundaries shifted from time to time depending on the quality of available topo-graphical information, administrative, political, and economic impera-tives, and cut across some families and ethnic groups. For example, the Anglo-Belgian Protocol of 14 February 1914, brought part of the Mufumbiro region and the Kigeatuczi district (Kabale), under British rule so that the Bafumbira, a subgroup of the Banyarwanda, found them-selves in Uganda, Rwanda, and the Congo.[2]

After the First World War, when German colonial control was re-placed by the Belgium trusteeship under the League of Nations, the economic policy of the new administration increasingly emphasized the production of cash crops and state conscripted labor for developing infrastructure, and imposed relatively heavy taxation. This policy led to loss of fertile land to cash crop production, food scarcity, and conflict over the unevenly distributed and scarce land. These problems, exacerbated by high human and cattle population density, led to waves of mass migration of Rwandese to Uganda from the 1920s to the 1950s. The overwhelming majority of the immigrants, numbering some 200,000, were Hutu. They settled in Buganda, Kigezi, Ankole, Busoga, and Bunyoro, where they worked in agriculture, construction, local governments, industries, ginning, brick works, cattle keeping, forestry, and fishing (Richards 1952, 17–118; Essack 1993, 23; Mamdani 1977, 149, 154, 155).

The Initial Rwandese Refugee Movements into Uganda

Between 1952 and 1959, when the Belgian political reforms threatened the intermediary position of the Tutsi oligarchy in the colonial state and provided some limited autonomous political space to the Hutu, which challenged the privileged position of the Tutsi, political violence between the Tutsi and the Hutu escalated (Lemarchand 1970, 81, 83, 146, 149, 150–54, 157–63, 167–71, 173, 177–78, 192). When, in September 1961, the *Parti du Mouvement de l'Emancipation Hutu* (PARMEHUTU), the political party of the *Mouvement Democratique Rwandis*, won a landslide victory in the U.N.-supervised legislative elections, another wave of political violence followed that claimed many lives and forced hundreds of thousands of Tutsi and their cattle to seek refuge in Uganda, Tanzania, Burundi, and Congo.

At the time that some of them arrived in Kigezi and Ankole, the colonial government in Uganda had been attempting a number of initiatives to address acute problems: contain the political violence and political instability in many parts of Uganda, especially in Buganda, Bugishu, Bukedi, and Toro (the Bakonjo and Baamba territories);[3] control cattle disease in the country;[4] complete the program to eradicate tsetse flies from western Uganda; and control the effects of the Mau Mau revolt spilling from Kenya into Uganda by implementing the 1954 ordinance against the Mau Mau.[5]

Given these problems, the colonial government initially declared that Rwandese refugees in Kigezi and Ankole districts were illegal immigrants. When the government received information from the Belgians that tens of thousands of Tutsi, with thousands of cattle, were contemplating fleeing to Uganda, the government hastily enacted rules which specifically prohibited the Tutsi from entering Uganda.[6] Those refugees that had arrived between November and 3 December 1959 were either confined to the quarantine area near the border or were forcibly repatriated.[7]

These measures infuriated some African members of the Legislative Council so much that they demanded that the government explain the rationale of the policy of refugee deterrence. The government offered the following reasons: there was no political persecution in Rwanda; the Tutsi who were fleeing Rwanda were either misinformed about the political situation or were political criminals; it was impossible to accommodate such a large number of illegal immigrants with their cattle anywhere in the country, particularly since western Uganda was already overstocked, over grazed, lacked water, and had not been totally reclaimed from the tsetse fly; and that the cattle that the Tutsi brought with them were diseased and would spread cattle disease in the country.[8]

This policy received the backing of some African members of the Legislative Council from Kigezi and Ankole.[9] They pointed out to the government that it was morally unacceptable for a regime that itself had a profound legitimization crisis to deny asylum to the Tutsi when, without consulting Ugandans, it resettled some Polish, Italian, German, Austrian, Romanian, Bulgarian, Hungarian, and Yugoslav refugees in the country during and after the Second World War.[10] Thus,[11] on 29 February 1960, A. M. Obote introduced a motion in the Council: "Revocation of the Batutsi Immigrants Rule," explaining:

The reign of terror was so bad that the people of Ruanda wanted to seek safety somewhere. A number of them decided to seek refuge in Uganda. But I wish the House to know that they did not come as ordinary immigrants; they were running away from acts of violence which were the rule of the day in their country. They thought that peace could be obtained in Uganda and that the people would welcome them. Indeed, these people are kinsmen of the people of Ankole, of Uganda, and the only thing that any one of them could do was to go to a fellow brother to seek for his safety.... And this time there seems to be no reason whatsoever why the Government of Uganda should not have sympathized with the case of the Batutsi.... I am pleading for the whole of the Batutsi tribe [sic] who came to Uganda to seek for safety. I am pleading for the principle of offering asylum to people in need of it; and I am pleading for the case of people who are now being ruled by another race. I am pleading on behalf of the people of Uganda.... I ask the Uganda Government not to think very much of what other evidence they have received from the Belgian Government.... I want the door to be opened to these people to come to Uganda.[12]

However, the majority of the African members of the Council opposed it. The motion was defeated.[13]

When Uganda obtained self-government in 1961, more Tutsi refugees fled to the country and other neighboring states (Lemarchand 1970, 150–51, 160, 196). Some of the refugees who registered with the government were immediately resettled in two reception centers: Kamwezi in Rukiga county (Kigezi District) and Kizinga in Rwampara county (Ankole district). Most of the refugees, however, settled spontaneously with relatives and friends in Kigezi and Ankole (Uganda Protectorate 1961, especially: 1–23).

While more Tutsi refugees were fleeing to Uganda, a group of Tutsi refugee warriors, the *Inyenzi*, invaded Rwanda in July 1961 and May 1962. The invasions generated political instability in Western Uganda, and prompted the government in May of 1962 to warn the refugees against using the country as a military base to attack Rwanda.

> Firm discipline is absolutely necessary if these refugees are to be made to behave in a manner which does not prejudice relations between Uganda and her neighbors. It is important that the Uganda government should begin to look outside her boundaries and not take decisions based only on possible political repercussions within Uganda itself...even though...the government may alienate certain sections of the community within Uganda. (cited in Lemarchand 1970, 208)

The government followed the warning with action; it expelled twenty-four Tutsi refugees for their involvement in *Inyenzi* armed invasions. In a further attempt to contain the insecurity caused by the refugee warriors near the Uganda-Rwanda border, the government relocated the refugees from Nakivale to the Ibuga refugee settlement. Despite these measures, refugee warriors, including those from Congo and Sudan, continued to carry out cross-border invasions against their home countries. In July 1963, the activities of the refugee warriors forced the Prime Minister, Obote, to warn them against cross-border invasions:

> I wish to make it clear that I will not tolerate this sort of activity.... We have no intention within the context of the Addis Ababa spirit and Charter of allowing Uganda to be used as a base for any attacks or subversion against any African state.... If [our] hospitality is abused, and refugees use or attempt to use Uganda as a base to attack our neighbors, we shall have no alternative but to withdraw the protection we granted to these people. (Lemarchand 1970, 208)

Rwandese refugee warriors were not the only target. The government issued a warning that was directed specifically at Sudanese refugee warriors: "If the Sudanese wish to settle down in a new life here they are welcome. But if they come here merely to use Uganda as a springboard for attacks and subversion against a friendly neighboring government, they are jeopardizing our international relations and reputation. We are not going to allow that to happen." (*Weekly News*, Dar es Salaam, 8 November, 1963:3, cited in Sekiki 1972, 11–12). This was followed by the arrest of some leaders of the southern Sudanese refugees, including J. H. Oduho of the Sudanese African National Union (SANU), and the relocation of some of the refugees from Moyo to Ibuga.[14]

The invasions by the Tutsi refugee warriors, however, continued, and they provoked the largest backlash at the same time as more anti-Tutsi political violence erupted in Rwanda. As a result, more Tutsi fled to Uganda. According to the Minister of Community Development, L. Kalule-Settala, 7,652 Rwandese refugees arrived in the country between May and September 1962. These refugees, together with those who had preceded them, were resettled in Ankole District: 8,000 cattle owners were resettled south of Lake Nakivali; 11,000 non-cattle owners were resettled in the Oruchinga Valley; and 4,000 non-cattle owners were kept in the Oruchinga Relief Camp awaiting resettlement in the Oruchinga Valley. At that time, the number of Rwandese refugees who had registered with the government was 23,000. An estimated 10,000 unregistered Rwandese refugees had settled spontaneously with relatives and friends in the Kigezi and Ankole Districts (Uganda Protectorate, 1962, 438–39). According to the 1962/1963 Government's Annual Report, some 10,000 Rwandese refugees crossed into Uganda, bringing the total number of registered Rwandese refugees to about 40,000. The report also indicated that "of all the Rwanda refugees in the country more than half were women and children. About a third of the refugees are cattle-owners and a total of approximately 30,000 head of cattle were brought in Uganda by these refugees" (Uganda Government 1964, 32).

As many more refugees fled to Uganda, the government established more reception centers: Nakivale Refugee Settlement in Ishingiro county, Ankole (1962); Oruchinga Valley refugee Settlement near Nakivale (1963); the Ibunga Refugee Settlement in Bunyagabu county, Toro district (1963); Kahunge, Rwamwanja, and Kaka settlements in Toro district (1964); and the Kyangwali Refugee settlement in Bunyoro district (1966). (See tables 1, 2 and 3.)[15]

The presence of such a large number of refugees presented a considerable humanitarian responsibility for the government. Initially, the

TABLE 1.1
Total Number of Refugees Living in Uganda
January 1, 1966 to January 1, 1967

Group of refugees	Number on	Number on
Area of settlement	1.1.1966	1.1.1967
1. **Rwandese**		
a). Oruchinga	12,500	11,500
b). Nakivale	6,500	8,009
c). Kahunge	5,500	6,793
d). Ibuga	800	717
e). Rwamanja	2,600	2,500
f). Kyaka	2,000	1,956
g). Kinyara	3,500	2,820
Sub-Total	33,400	34,295
2. **Sudanese**	17,050	10,981
3. **Congolese**	3,100	1,576
Total	53,560	46,852
B. Outside Settlements.		
1. **Rwandese**	32,000	34,000
2. **Sudanese**	27,000	44,000
3. **Congolese**	25,000	32,000
Total	**84,000**	**110,000**

Source: Progress Report on Refugee Situation in Uganda. March, 1967 (deposited at the Refugee Studies Programme, Oxford University).

TABLE 1.2
Number of Refugees in Uganda in 1969 and 1970

Year	Number
Rwandese	
1969	70500
1970	71000
Sudanese	
1969	71500
1970	71500
Zaireans	
1969	34000
1970	34500

Source: US Committee for Refugees.

TABLE 1.3
Size of Settlements and Allocation of Land in 1969

Settlement	Sq. Miles	Acres per Family
Kahunge	72	10
Rwamwanja	54	10
*Ibuga	16	10
Kyaka	—	—
Oruchinga	13	10
**Kyangwali	50	10
Nakivale	40	10

Source: World Alliance of YMCA, "Report of visits to the Refugee Settlements of Uganda made by the YMCA African Refugee Secretary, 27/11/1969" (deposited at the Refugee Studies Programme, Oxford University).
* The total land was 24 sq. miles. Out of this, 8 sq. miles were allocated to the National Youth Service.
** When Kinyara was closed down, the refugees were transferred to Kyangwali.

government was quite generous to the refugees because it thought that they would not stay in the country for long. However, when it became clear that most of the refugees were going to stay in the country indefinitely, hospitality fatigue set in and generosity gradually turned into hostility. This change of attitude towards the refugees was partly influenced by the financial, security, and political problems resulting from the presence and activities of the refugees. Thus, commenting on the challenges of meeting the needs of the refugees, Dorothea Hunter of Oxfam made the following observations in her report of August-September, 1968:

> My observations concern only refugees in Uganda, whose total number is now 163,000, an enormous burden for a country of only 7.9 million people.... Last year I had the impression that Government still hoped that many, if not most of them would return home. However, despite the setting up of the Special Fund For Voluntary Repatriation, the provisions for which were to be executed between all the Governments concerned, the obvious lack of enthusiasm in taking up this opportunity among the refugees themselves has now convinced Government that the majority of them are determined to remain in the country if they possibly can. This conclusion has been reached only now, at a time when the UNHCR's responsibility for the refugees is beginning to be phased out. Government is therefore now faced with the responsibility for some 50,000 refugees spread about in 12 settlements, quite apart from any problem which might arise among the remaining 113,000 understood to be living outside the camps.[16]

Other related factors also contributed to the compassion fatigue—

the growing economic crisis in the country as well as the growing hostility from the host communities that stemmed from the perception that the government was able to help the refugees but could not meet the basic socioeconomic needs of its own people.

The growing hostility towards the refugees and the government, and the inability of the international community to share adequately the responsibility of assisting the refugees, forced the government to threaten mass expulsion of the refugees. For example, as early as March 1964, the Minister of Information, Nekyon, told the OAU conference in Lagos that "Uganda has no alternative...but to send some of these people away, unless Uganda received help" (*Africa Research Bulletin*, March 1964:37A). He also claimed that most of the assistance that the government provided to Rwandese refugees "had been spent...on the purchase of arms. Refugees were even selling the food given to them...in order to send money to their King. They had abused Uganda's hospitality by forming groups to invade Rwanda to overthrow the Government" (ibid). The government also complained that some of the refugees were using refugee camps to recruit rebels to attack their home governments. Such activities, it insisted, made it extremely difficult to provide security to the host communities and innocent refugees (Uganda Government 1964, 32–33).

The threat to expel the refugees prompted some international organizations and agencies, such as the Oxford Committee for Famine Relief, the Red Cross, Save the Children Fund, YMCA, Oxfam, and the United Nations High Commissioner for Refugees (UNHCR), to provide more assistance to the refugees. The organizations, especially Oxfam, also contemplated initiating an integrated rural community development program to provide common services to both the refugee and the host community. The program was also expected to integrate the refugees into the host communities and reduce anti-refugee sentiments. However, both the assistance and the proposed community development program failed to relieve the government from providing most of the basic needs of the refugees. It also failed to reduce the growing anti-refugee sentiments in the country and the crisis of legitimacy of the regime that resulted from the hostility.

During this period, relations between the government and Tutsi refugees further deteriorated. This was caused by the political activities of President and Kabaka (King) E. Mutesa and the deposed Umwami (King) of Rwanda, Kigeri IV. To begin with, when the latter was deposed after the elections in Rwanda, he fled to Buganda, where he was

Mutesa's guest. Relations between the two leaders were strengthened by the close collaboration between their parties: Mutesa's Kabaka Yekka (Kabaka Alone) and Kigeri's Abadehemuka. This collaboration—which grew during the period of violent conflict over land (the Lost Counties referendum) in Buganda, the collapse of the alliance between Obote's Uganda People's Congress (UPC), and Mutesa's Kabaka Yekka, and the Cold War in the Congo (the Congo Crisis) that destabilized Uganda—suggested to Obote that the two "kings" and their parties were conspiring to topple him. Furthermore, the collaboration between Mutesa and Kigeri encouraged insurgency activities by Tutsi refugee warriors against Rwanda. Since the insurgencies were sponsored from Uganda with the tacit approval of Mutesa, Uganda was in direct violation of the Charter of the OAU which prohibited a member state from supporting subversive activities against another member state.[17]

Another factor that accounted for the deterioration of relations between the government and Tutsi refugees was the pressure exerted on the former by Hutu immigrants. The immigrants demanded that the government stop Tutsi refugee warriors from causing political instability in Uganda and Rwanda. This demand could not be ignored because the immigrants constituted the overwhelming majority of the 378,656 Rwandese immigrants and refugees in Uganda in 1964 (Uganda Government 1965,18–19). Some Tutsi refugees, who were highly placed in Obote's government, including Frank Kalimuzo, joined the Hutu to pressure the regime to clamp down on the refugees (Lemarchand 1970, 206–07). This pressure, compounded by the insecurity caused by the refugees, forced the government to expel the deposed Umwami, Kigeri IV, from the country (Lemarchand 1970, 209). It also prompted the government to amend the law on aliens. This law made it an offense for anyone to harbor a refugee without the permission of the government, required refugees to stay in designated refugee settlements, and gave the Director of Refugees the power to deport any refugee who violated the law or did not meet the refugee determination criteria (*Africa Research Bulletin*, 1–31 December 1964: 203C-204A; Kiapi, 1993:10–13).

During this period, the UNHCR also exerted pressure on the states hosting Tutsi refugees to control the political and military activities of the refugee warriors. This measure was intended to prevent the refugee warriors from provoking more violence against the Tutsi in Rwanda. If the Hutu-dominated government in Kigali was not provoked by the refugee warriors, the UNHCR seemed to reason, no more Tutsi would flee the country. Such a development would make it a bit easier for the agency and the host countries to protect and assist the refugees (Lemarchand 1970, 209–27; Essack 1993, 6). In fact, it had become impossible for the UNHCR and the host countries to protect the refugees because of the insecurity that the refugee warriors caused in the host communities; the host communities in all the neighboring countries were attacking the refugees for taking land, jobs, and social services from the indigenous population. The growing anti-Tutsi sentiments in the host communities further suggested to the UNHCR the need to prevent more Tutsi from becoming refugees. For the UNHCR, the best way to do so was to prevent the refugee warriors from invading their country of origin. (Richards 1952, 196).

This measure, however, did not reduce the growing anti-Rwandese sentiments in Uganda. In Buganda, for example, many Baganda peasants complained bitterly that immigrants and refugees took their land and demanded the expulsion of the refugees and immigrants. Similarly, Rwandese refugees continued to face discrimination and violence in Ankole. To begin with, in the 1920s, the majority of Hutu immigrants were accommodated in Ankole by their cousins, the Bairu. This was followed by the arrival of tens of thousands of Tutsi refugees. The presence of the Tutsi, however, provoked anti-Tutsi sentiments in the area. A number of factors accounted for this development. First, the Tutsi had oppressed and exploited the cousins of the Bairu, the Hutu, for centuries. The Bairu, as such, did not want the persecutors of their cousins to settle in Ankole. Secondly, the arrival of Tutsi refugees in the 1950s and 1960s coincided with increased power struggles between the Hima and Bairu in Ankole (Karugire 1993, 73–74). One of the strategies the Hima employed to maintain their waning hegemony over the Bairu was to recruit their cousins, the Tutsi, to swell their ranks. This strategy brought Tutsi refugees into the power struggles in Ankole. Thirdly, the alliance between the predominantly Catholic Tutsi and the Catholic-dominated Democratic Party (DP) in Ankole turned some Banyankole members of the UPC, who were predominantly Protestants, against the Tutsi. These factors pressured the local UPC establishment in Ankole to ask the government to enforce the law of the land by keeping the refugees out of local and national politics. Some Banyankole, both Hima and Bairu, also demanded that the refugees be relocated from Ankole because they were taking away land, jobs, and social services from the host communities (Helle-valle 1989, 145–46, 155).

This pressure coincided with the growing political violence and economic crisis in the country: mass unemployment, the imposition of the state of emergency in Buganda and in the Baamba-Bakonjo territories of Toro, the death of Mutesa in exile in England, the abortive assassination of Obote on 9 December 1969, the detention of hundreds of Obote's political opponents, the imposition of a one-party state, and the unveiling of Obote's Common Man's Charter which, among other things, advocated a policy of Ugandanization of employment and land ownership. This meant that refugees could not be legally employed or own land. To keep the refugees out of both the local and national politics, the government proposed to provide them with identity cards. However, this policy was overtaken by the Amin coup of January 1971. Despite the fact that the policy was never implemented, Tutsi refugees considered Obote and the UPC—though both had vigorously advocated for the rights of the refugees to asylum and protection in Uganda during the period of decolonization—enemies (International Commission of Jurists 1977, 5; Otunnu 1994, 3–14; Nabuguzi 1993, 25).

Rwandese Refugees under Idi Amin and the Restored Obote Regimes

After Idi Amin came to power, relations between the Amin regime and the refugee population, Rwandese refugees included, were very cordial. This reflected the fact that the regime needed some refugees to join the army and the death squads (drawn from the State Research Bureau, the Public Safety Unit, the Marines, and Military Police Anti-Corruption and the Anti-Smuggling Units) because it had become quite skeptical about the loyalty and dedication of Ugandans in the army and death squads. To encourage the refugees to join the forces, Amin invited the deposed Umwami of Rwanda, Kigeri IV, to Uganda. The presence of the Umwani and the close ties Amin developed with him encouraged more Tutsi refugees to join the forces. Tutsi refugees, like refugees from southern Sudan and eastern Zaire (the Democratic Republic of Congo), also joined the forces to secure good jobs, acquire wealth, and receive security.

Being loyal and dedicated to the regime of terror meant terrorizing, raping, detaining, and murdering perceived opponents of the government. Accumulating wealth in the lawless, violent, and chronically underdeveloped society also meant that the refugees had to do what many Ugandans were doing to acquire wealth and land: unleash terror against segments of the society. The result was that the terrorized and chronically poor Ugandans turned more decidedly against the refugee population. Hostility towards the refugees also escalated because many Ugandans felt that they were being treated as second-class citizens in their own country. For example, when some of the Sudanese refugees, who had not repatriated following the 1972 Addis Ababa Agreement, continued to grab land and terrorize people in East Acoli in 1976 and 1977, the people of Mucwini and Madi Opei massacred some of them. This massacre, which highlighted the growing anti-refugee sentiments throughout the country, was carried out with the support of some high-ranking Ugandan soldiers who were opposed to the presence of the refugees in the forces.[18]

The regime also promoted anti-refugee sentiments in the country by publicly blaming the refugees for the prevailing economic and political crises, in 1978, blaming refugees from Rwanda, Zaire, Somalia, Kenya, Burundi, Sudan, and Ethiopia for sabotaging government efforts to address economic and political problems. The refugees were then ordered to register with the government, remain confined to designated camps, and refrain from supporting insurgency activities.[19] The orders were never carried out because the pronouncements were intended to achieve a number of related objectives: suggest to the majority of Ugandans that the regime shared their disapproval of the brutality of the refugees, erroneously implying that the regime was not the principal author of the terror; provide a popular and vulnerable scapegoat that could be blamed for the severe socioeconomic and political crises in the country, thereby allowing the refugees to join the long lists of individuals and groups that were being blamed—Obote, the Asians, the insurgents, Zionists, Britain, Tanzania, and the apartheid regime in southern Africa; prevent the refugees from employing unsanctioned terror against the population; and to maintain contact with, and receive international assistance from, the international community through agencies such as the UNHCR, Oxfam, YMCA, the Red Cross, and the International University Exchange Fund.[20] These contacts and the assistance were particularly important because the regime faced a severe economic crisis at home and a profound legitimization deficit on the international front.

Immediately after the overthrow of the Amin regime, anti-Rwandese sentiments escalated partly as a result of the presence of some refugees in the Uganda Liberation Army (UNLA) who formed an important part of the 10,000 soldiers who were recruited by the Minister of Defense, Yoweri, Museveni.[21] The refugees joined the army primarily to acquire adequate military training for a future war against the Hutu-dominated regime in Rwanda. The recruitment of Tutsi refugees for the purpose of attacking Rwanda was encouraged by the Rwanda Alliance for National Unity (RANU). which was formed in June 1979. Many Tutsi refugees in the UNLA, including those who would later become leading members of the Rwanda Patriotic Army (RPA), Chris Bunyenyezi, Sam Kaka, Fred Rwigyema, Dr. Peter Bayingana, and Paul Kagame, belonged to RANU. Some of the refugees joined the UNLA to protect their people against reprisals for the activities of those refugees who worked for the Amin regime. There were those who, like many Ugandans, joined the army to earn a living. The only way the refugees could stay in the army was by disguising their national identity. This was not extremely difficult because many of them were born in Uganda and had acquired Kiganda, Kiga, and Banyankole names. Furthermore, the refugees had the physical features of the indigenous Banyarwanda, Banyankole, and the Bakiga. Staying in the army also required them to protect and enhance the power of their leader, Museveni.[22]

Some of the refugees, like other members of Museveni's and Obote's armies in Ankole, unleashed terror against the Muslims in the area. The objective of the terror was to punish those Muslims who prevented Museveni's Front for National Salvation (Fronasa) and Obote's Kikosi Maalum armed groups from gaining support in the area during the uncoordinated and hastily executed invasions against the Amin regime.[23] The refugees, as a part of the Fronasa, also waged a war of supremacy against Obote's Kikosi Maalum faction of the UNLA in Ankole. For example, the massacre of many people in Ankole, including over 100 Muslims in Busenyi in June 1979, was attributed in part to the power struggle between Museveni's Fronasa and Obote's Kikosi Maalum factions of the UNLA. The involvement of the refugees in these clashes provoked more hostility towards them.

Anti-Rwandese sentiments further escalated during the 1980 election when political opponents of Museveni, in Ankole and elsewhere in the country, constantly referred to him as a Rwandese refugee, and the Uganda Patriotic Movement (Museveni's party) and the Fronasa as Rwandese organizations.[24] Hostility toward the refugees also grew following the involvement of some Tutsi refugees in the armed struggle against the Obote regime. For example, the refugees were involved in the raid on the Kabamba Army Training School on 16 March 1981; the ambush of the military convoy that killed 70 UNLA soldiers at Kawanda on 16 March 1981; and the ambush of a civilian bus, twenty-six miles from Kampala on Bombo road, in which forty unarmed civilians were killed.[25] These incidents, among others, induced the regime and UPC functionaries to target Rwandese refugees in the army and elsewhere for reprisals. The more the Popular Resistance Army (PRA, later the National Resistance Army—NRA) intensified its armed struggle, the more the regime and the UPC functionaries terrorized Rwandese refugees. The more the refugees were persecuted, the more they fled and joined the NRA. The more they joined the NRA, the more their increased presence in the NRA tended to confirm the claim that the NRA was a Tutsi organization.[26]

In the Luwero Triangle (Luwero, Mukono and Mpigi districts), Rwandese refugees were also persecuted because some Baganda, who had always blamed immigrants and refugees for grabbing their land since the colonial era, felt that Museveni and his "fellow" Rwandese had brought untold sufferings upon them by waging armed insurgencies from the area.[27] According to these Baganda, Museveni waged the war from the Luwero Triangle because of the presence of Tutsi refugees in the area, the strategic and topographical location of the area, and the socioeconomic and political significance of the area to the country (Helle-Valle 1989, 133; Watson 1991, 6).

Some Baganda turned against the refugees because of the terror tactics that the NRA employed to recruit the Baganda into its ranks, and to eliminate opposition to its presence in the Luwero Triangle. For instance, Lance-Sera Muwanga claimed that some members of the NRA, disguised in army and police uniforms, terrorized and murdered many Baganda in order to drive them into its camp (Muwanga 1983, 20–22; Muwanga and Gombya 1986, 20). Lance-Sera Muwanga and H. Gombya highlighted another factor that increased anti-Rwandese sentiment in Buganda: the atrocities committed by the NRA's death squad or the "Black Bombers" against the Baganda commanders of the NRA, such as Seguya Bona and Kaggwa Bandi, who were regarded as potential opponents of Museveni.[28]

Another factor that sustained anti-Rwandese sentiment in Luwero was the flight of the Rwandese "laborers" into the NRA. The flight meant the loss of cheap labor in the area. The situation got worse when the former laborers, as some Baganda referred to the refugees, returned and violently demanded food and unpaid service from their former employers. The demand the refugees placed on their former hosts was particularly annoying to the Baganda who regarded the refugees as inferior to them.[29]

The violent territorial rivalries between the two main insurgency groups in Buganda, the predominantly Baganda Uganda Freedom Army (UFA) and the Banyankole-Rwandese NRA, took the form of both an "ethnic" war and a war between the leaders of the two groups. For example, the leader of the UFA, Dr. A. Kayira, reported that after the UFA attacked Lubiri barracks in February 1982, it was ambushed and disarmed by the NRA. Later when Museveni invited the leadership of UFA to the NRA command post in Luwero, Kayira claimed, "There were no less than 50 fresh heads at a quick count. We found Museveni and the NRA soldiers inside the ring of human heads. He told us while pointing at the heads: 'You see those heads? That is how I deal with those who do not agree with me.'"[30]

Throughout this period, political violence against the refugees was largely concentrated in Ankole, primarily a direct outcome of decades of conflict over land, jobs, and social services between the host communities and the refugees. The situation got worse when the UPM, including its leader, lost the elections and subsequently launched a guerrilla war against the Obote regime in 1981. According to the Banyankole, the refugees stole cattle from the host communities to feed the insurgents.[31]

Another factor that contributed to the persecution of Tutsi refugees in Ankole was the pressure exerted on the Banyankole to publicly denounce the NRA. This pressure came mainly from two prominent Banyankole ministers and very close associates of Obote: Chris Rwakasisi and Major Edward Rurangaranga.[32] The pressure was intended to reduce the limited support the NRA enjoyed in Ankole. It was also aimed at suggesting to the country and the rest of the world that the NRA enjoyed only the support of Rwandese refugees, not the support of Ugandans (Clay n.d.,1, 3).

Internal rivalries between two UPC camps in Ankole, the "scientists" and the "syndicate," also contributed to the persecution of the refugees. The former comprised highly educated, soft-spoken, and diplomatic leaders of UPC. The most prominent members of this camp were three government ministers: Dr. Adonia Tiberonda, Dr. E. Rwanyarare, and E. Kamutu. This camp believed that the best way to protect the Banyankole from being treated as bandits or terrorists was to isolate and condemn Museveni and the armed refugees for the ensuing political violence in Buganda (Clay n.d., 7).

The "syndicate," on the other hand, was led by two powerful, ruthless and ambitious Banyankole cabinet ministers: Rwakasisi and Rurangaranga. This group was engaged in power rivalry with the scientists over the future leadership of UPC. In order to prove its unwavering loyalty to Obote and increase its limited support in Ankole, the group advocated the eviction of Rwandese refugees from Ankole. This proposition was presented by the two ministers—who had been in violent conflict with Museveni since the 1978–1979 war against the Amin regime (Uganda Government 1994, 31) —as an extension of the counterinsurgency against the NRA. The eviction was also expected to free some land and property which the camp could distribute to enlarge its political support in Ankole.[33]

The decision by the syndicate to evict the refugees was strengthened by the growing anti-Rwandese sentiments in Ankole and the intensification of insurgencies in Buganda which induced Obote to issue a warning to the refugees on January 11, 1982:

> Most atrocities during Amin's era were committed by refugees.... [M]any refugees voted in the December 1980 general elections.... Refugees have been found to flirt with terrorists in the Luwero District and are responsible for the unrest there.... Some refugees have proved a liability to the nation.... If refugees, particularly those from Rwanda, do not reciprocate our hospitality...Ugandans may order their government to build camps for them.... Alternatively, we shall tell them to go...[34]

A month later, the Minister of Culture and Community Development began to enforce the Control Alien Refugee Act (Chapter 64 of the Laws of Uganda, 1964) that required refugees to live in designated refugee settlements.[35] Next, in October 1982, the Mbarara District Council, which was closely allied to the syndicate, issued a memorandum to the government urging the eviction of the refugees, or, in its language "regrouping" the refugees in designated settlements. It also accused the refugees of the following:

- Committing atrocities against Ugandans during the Amin regime;
- thwarting the liberation efforts in 1972;
- exterminating innocent and prominent traders out of business jealousy;
- grabbing land from (and sometimes at pain of death of) citizens;
- perpetrating cattle thefts and the killings of the owners of the cattle, especially after the general elections in 1980;
- killing innumerable head of cattle even as late as the second half of October 1982;
- collaborating with Amin's forces against the liberation forces in 1979;
- campaigning, registering and voting in the 1980 elections;
- joining Museveni's camp in the bush immediately after the elections. (Clay n.d. 51)

These developments set the stage for the massacre and evictions of Rwandese refugees which began immediately after the memorandum was circulated in October 1982. The areas which were gripped by this terror were Mbarara, Rakai, and Masaka.[36] By November 1982, an estimated 40,000 Rwandese refugees had been evicted from the southern part of Mbarara district. The refugees fled to Rwanda. An estimated 4,000 refugees were trapped at Marema Hill, on the Uganda side of the Uganda-Rwanda border. During the evictions, some thirty-seven refugees were reported to have been killed by some Banyankole UPC functionaries and National Security Agency (NASA). officers. It was estimated that some 45,000 head of cattle were confiscated from the refugees. In December 1983, an estimated 19,000 Rwandese refugees were evicted from Rakai District, east of Mbarara District. Some of the refugees sought refuge in Mbarara town and in the less turbulent refugee camps, including the Nakivale. During the campaign against the refugees, a few Ugandans who were declared "Rwandese refugees" by their local opponents in Ankole were also evicted from their homes.[37]

A number of possible explanations may be advanced for the discrepancy. First, far fewer refugees fled Uganda. Second, most of those who

TABLE 1.4
Refugees in Uganda, 1981–1985

Year	Country of Origin	Number
1981	Rwanda	80,000
	Sudan	500
	Zaire	32,000
1982	Rwanda	80,000
	Sudan	500
	Zaire	32,000
1983	Rwanda	80,350
	Sudan	590
	Zaire	31,350
1984	Rwanda	80,350
	Sudan	590
	Zaire	31,350
1985	Rwanda	118,000
	Sudan	590
	Zaire	31,350

Sources: UNHCR, *Refugees*, 1981–1985.

TABLE 1.5
Ugandan Refugees, 1981–1985

Year	Country of Asylum	Number
1981	Kenya	1,050
	Zaire	115,000
	Sudan	110,000
1982	Kenya	1,800
	Zaire	60,000
	Sudan	170,000
	Rwanda (Banyarwanda)	44,000
1983	Kenya	2,354
	Zaire	270,000
	Sudan	200,000
	Tanzania (Banyarwanda)	10,000
	Rwanda (Banyarwanda)	31,000
1984	Kenya	3,875
	Zaire	30,800
	Sudan	200,000
	Tanzania (Banyarwanda)	2,500
	Rwanda (Banyarwanda)	30,400
1985	Kenya	4,158
	Zaire	17,000
	Sudan	250,000
	Rwanda (Banyarwanda)	3,200

Sources: UNHCR, *Refugees,* 1981–1985; Office of the United Nations High Commissioner for Refugees, *Report on UNHCR Assistance Activities,* 1981–1985.

fled were Ugandan Banyarwanda. The problem with this explanation is that existing evidence, including that offered by Nabuguzi, suggests that those who claimed to be Ugandan Banyarwanda were Rwandese refugees who made the claim in order to avoid persecution in Rwanda. Third, there were at least 40,000 unregistered Rwandese refugees in Uganda. In this instance, those who fled were unregistered Rwandese refugees. Finally, the UNHCR and the US Committee for Refugees did not adjust the number of Rwandese refugees who did not flee Uganda. It is important to bear in mind that the numbers game in refugee studies depends on why, how, when and by whom the counting was done. It also depends on who was counted. For example, if the refugees are counted to attract more international assistance or to embarrass a regime, the number may be deliberately inflated.

The evictions provoked enormous international condemnation.[38] In a desperate attempt to calm the international outcry, the regime denied any involvement in the persecution of the refugees. It also claimed that what had been presented by international human rights organizations— the UNHCR, the US Committee for Refugees and Cultural Survival— as persecution of the Banyarwanda, was generally a nonviolent operation aimed at improving the administration and protection of the refugees. The limited violence that occurred, it further claimed, resulted from clashes between the host communities and the refugees over land and unlawful activities of some of the refugees. The official explanation, however, did not convince the international community.[39]

The influx of Tutsi refugees into Rwanda that resulted from the evictions/*refoulement* made the Hutu-dominated regime of Juvenal Habyarimana extremely nervous. A number of reasons accounted for this reaction. First, the forced repatriation of tens of thousands of the refugees took the regime by surprise. Secondly, the regime suspected that the returnees were supporters of RANU and NRA. This perception was influenced by the fact that some of the leading members of RANU, such as Chris Bunyenyezi, Sam Kaka, Fred Rwigyema, Dr. Peter Bayingana, and Paul Kagame, were also prominent members of the NRA.[40] Thirdly, it expected the remaining tens of thousands of Tutsi refugees to join the forced repatriation. Fourthly, the influx undermined the regime policy that denied the refugees the right to return to their home country.[41] This political anxiety made the Habyarimana regime confine the returnees to isolated and heavily guarded camps. It also forced the government to close the Rwanda-Uganda border. Thereafter, it justified its repatriation deterrence policy by claiming that most of the refugees were Ugandans, not Rwandese. Although the claim was misleading, it was supported by the Tutsi returnees who were too scared to admit to the Hutu-dominated regime that they were Rwandese. Uganda, on the other hand, insisted that those who had fled to Rwanda and the border area were Rwandese refugees. The unwillingness of the two governments to recognize their displaced citizens, left the refugees without asylum and without a state to call their own.[42]

The crisis and the international pressure that accompanied the persecution of Tutsi refugees prompted the two governments to hold a joint ministerial committee meeting from 22–27 October 1982. The meeting took place at Gabiro in Rwanda. The committee examined: the root causes of the refugee crisis; measures taken by the two governments to resolve the crisis; the question of nationality of the refugees;

and durable solutions to the refugee crisis. At the end of the meeting, the parties agreed on the following:

1. The Government of Uganda accepts the responsibility for the Rwandese people still in Uganda and to keep refugees in designated areas in accordance with recognized international laws and procedures;
2. The Governments of Rwanda and Uganda agree to maintain law and order at their common border;
3. The Rwanda Government undertakes to expedite and fully examine applications of Rwandese refugees in Uganda for voluntary repatriation;
4. The two Governments agree to the necessity of identifying the nationalities of the refugees who have recently arrived in Rwanda. The Rwanda Government agrees to the reabsorption of those who have been identified as Rwandese nationals, and the Uganda Government undertakes to examine the possibility of compensating those who might have left their property in Uganda;
5. Uganda Government agrees that the identified Ugandan nationals shall be recognized as Ugandan refugees in Rwanda and Uganda accepts to examine their applications for voluntary repatriation in accordance with international laws applicable to refugees;
6. The joint Rwanda-Uganda ministerial committee recommends that the two Governments continue direct negotiations relating to the Rwandese nationals and refugees still in Uganda with a view of finding a permanent solution; and
7. In view of the urgency and importance of this matter, the joint committee recommends to the two Governments to implement these recommendations as soon as it is possible.[43]

The agreement, however, was not implemented in time to relieve the plight of the refugees (*Africa Research Bulletin,* 1-31 January 1983:6699C). The delay prompted another joint ministerial meeting, organized by the UNHCR from 6 to 8 March 1983. The meeting took place in Kabale in Uganda. At the meeting, the two government delegations agreed to abide by international conventions and instruments governing the treatment of refugees in their territories, and to formulate guidelines to determine the status of the affected persons. Thereafter, the governments began to screen the affected population for status.[44] However, as the US Committee for Refugee noted, progress in resolving the crisis remained interminably slow.[45]

The political violence against the Rwandese had a number of other significant implications. First, it eroded the international legitimacy of the Obote regime. Indeed, it was not until December 1984 that the government managed to salvage its international image. The development of December took place when some of the fleeing members of the NRA kidnapped some 1,500 Baganda, mostly women and children, and took them to Kyaka I and Kyaka II refugee camps. Rather than attack the refugee camps, where the NRA insurgents were hiding, the government discussed the matter with representatives of International Non-governmental Organizations (NGOs) which were observing the screening of those displaced by the evictions. The government also consulted with Western governments on how to handle the situation. After the NGOs and Western governments had verified the incident, they asked the government to provide a safe passage for the NRA to leave the camps without causing bloodshed. The government accepted the advice. By default, the tactic that the NRA employed suggested to some Western governments that it was quite possible that the evictions were partly provoked by the NRA to discredit the government.[46]

Secondly, it escalated and sustained hostility between the refugees and the host communities in Ankole and Buganda. Thirdly, it suggested to some of the refugees that it was less traumatic to join the NRA than to be persecuted in the camps. The result was that many more refugees joined the NRA. Finally, the exodus of more refugees into the NRA reproduced and sustained the image of the NRA as a predominantly Rwandese armed opposition group. This image, in turn, generated and sustained violence against the refugees.[47]

A pattern was set in which the refugees, in order to protect themselves, either attempted to return to their home country by force of arms, or joined military forces in their host country, only to see their insecurity increased as this act alone aroused the hostility of the host population. This pattern would reach its culmination when they fused the two processes and joined the Ugandan military as a means to launch a military invasion to return to Rwanda.

Notes

1. Karugire (1989) 44; Lemarchand (1970) 18; Jo Helle-valle (1989) 115. The former Ankole District comprises three districts: Busenyi, Mbarara, and Ntungamo. The former Kigezi District is now the Kabale District. See *Constitution of the Republic of Uganda, 1995*: 172–73.
2. See, for example, McEwen (1971); Uganda Protectorate (1956) 82–84, 92–96; Edel (1957); Mateke (1970). On factors that determined how Uganda's borders were drawn, see Stigand (1968) 230–34; Barber (1965). Mr. A. G. Bazanyamaso, for example, told the Legislative Council on 29 February 1959, that "when these boundaries were demarcated they passed through some villages, cutting them into two halves, one half coming into Uganda and the other half remaining within Ruanda-Urundi. Cf. Uganda Protectorate (1960)169. See also, the statement is-

sued by Dr. Obote following the eviction of Banyarwanda in 1982: "[W]e have five neighbors with whom Uganda has good relations to all of them. The Uganda border was drawn before independence. We inherited a border which cut across tribes, clans, and even families. It is, therefore, important that when we describe a person from a border district in terms of a tribe, that we are extremely careful in the use of our language. Relatives of Ugandans on both sides of the border remain relatives despite being citizens of different states. In this age of the rule of law, any action we take must be in conformity with the law of Uganda, international law, charters and conventions to which Uganda is a party..." Cited in Bugingo 4.

3. See Uganda Protectorate, *Report of the Commission of Inquiry into the Disturbances in Uganda during April 1949*, especially: 16–17, 21–23, 31–65, 71–101; *Report of the Commission appointed to Review Boundary between the Districts of Bugishu and Bukedi*. Entebbe: Government Printer, 1962; *Report of Inquiry into Disturbances in the Eastern Province, 1960*. Entebbe: Government Printer, March 1962, especially:14–15; *Proceedings of the Legislative Council*. Entebbe: Government Printer, September, 1959:159–72; Uganda Government, *Report of the Commission of Inquiry into the Recent Disturbances Amongst the Baamba and Bakonjo People of Toro*. Entebbe: Government Printer, 1962; Mengo, Department of Information, *Buganda's Independence, 1960*, Ghai (1970) 755–70.

4. The policy dated back to 1902 when the government enacted *The Cattle Disease Ordinance of 1902*. This ordinance was later reinforced by *The Cattle Disease (Amendment) Ordinance of 1913* and *The Cattle Disease Ordinance (Control Ordinance)* of June 23, 1954. See Uganda Protectorate, *The Cattle Disease Ordinance, 1902; The Cattle Disease (Amendment) Ordinance, 1913*. CO 612/6.

5. See Uganda Protectorate, *An Ordinance to Make Provision for the Registration of Persons of the Kikuyu Tribe of Kenya, 22 February, 1954*. CO 684/9. For useful information on the Mau Mau revolt or revolution see Kitching (1980) 25–311; Kanogo (1987)125–78.

6. Many of the Tutsi who were fleeing into Uganda were associated with the conservative Tutsi party, the *Union Nationale Rwandaise* (UNAR), which received financial and diplomatic support from the Communist countries in the U.N. Trusteeship Council. It is possible that the ties that the UNAR had with some Communist states during the Cold War in the 1950s and UNAR's vigorous campaign for immediate independence influenced the anti-Tutsi policy that was formulated by the colonial regime in Uganda. See Prunier (1995) 47–48. For details on the rules, cf. *The Aliens (Batutsi Immigrants) Rules, 1959* (Legal Notice No. 311 of 1959), Uganda Protectorate, *Proceedings of the Legislative Council*. Entebbe: The Government Printer, 29 February 1960: 164, 170. Evolution of refugee policies is highlighted by the following legislation: Uganda Protectorate, *The Refugees (Control and Expulsion) Ordinance, 1947*. CO 684/6; Uganda Protectorate, *An Ordinance to make Further and Better Provision for Regulation of Immigration into the Protectorate, No. 33 of 1947*. CO 684/6; Uganda Protectorate, *An Ordinance to amend the Immigration (Control. Ordinance, 1947, No. 18 of 1949*. CO 684/7; Uganda Protectorate, *An Ordinance to provide for the Registration and Control of Aliens, No. 23 of 1949*. CO 684/7; Uganda Protectorate, *An Ordinance to amend the Immigration (Control) Ordinance, No. 8 of 1953*. CO 684/9; Uganda Protectorate, *An Ordinance to Amend the Immigration (Control) Ordinance, No. 7 of 1954*. CO 684/9. See also Kiapi (1993)1–2.

7. See contribution to debates on Tutsi immigrants by the Chief Secretary, in Uganda Protectorate, *Proceedings of the Legislative Council*, 1959. Entebbe: Government Printer, 1960:170–73. See also Kiapi (1993) 9.

8. See the contribution to the debates by the Chief Secretary, Sir Charles Hartwell, and the Minister of Natural Resources, A. B. Killick, in Uganda Protectorate, *Proceedings of the Legislative Council*, 1959: 170–73, 190–93.

9. They included J. Bikangaga and C. B. Katiti. Obote, W. W. K. Nadiope, J. K. Babiiha, A. G. Bazsanyamoso and C. J. Obwangor.

10. See contribution to the debates by A. G. Bazanyamaso in Uganda Protectorate, *Proceedings of the Legislative Council*, 1959: 170. Some 7,000 Polish refugees, mainly women and children, were resettled in Nyabyeya (Masindi District) and Koja (Mpunge, Mukono District) between 1942 and 1945. Italian POWs were resettled in Jinja and Italian civil internees were resettled in Entebbe. Most of the Italians were brought from Eritrea, Ethiopia, and Somali land. Some Germans, Austrians, Romanians, Bulgarians, Yugoslavs, Hungarians, and stateless Jews were settled at the Arapai camps, near Soroti. See Lwanga-Lunyiigo (1993).

11. Obote's contribution on this motion will be cited in detail because it captured the position of the majority of the African representatives. It also provides a good background for understanding the political persecution that the Tutsi would face in Uganda.

12. See contribution to the debates by Obote in Uganda Protectorate, *Proceedings of the Legislative Council*, 1959:164–66.

13. Those who voted for the motion were: A. M. Obote, J. K. Babiiha, A. G. Bazanyamoso, C. B. Katiti, B. K. Kirya, G. B. K. Magezi, Mrs. M. I. Mitha, Y. B. Mugoma, W. W. K. Nadiope, M. M. Ngobi, P. L. Oola, C. J. Obwangor, G. Oda, W. W. Rwetsiba, and J. S. Visana. Those who voted against the motion were: Lt.-Col. A. A. Baerlin, Mr. T. B. Bazarrabusa, Mr. W. L. Bell, Mr. J. Bikangaga, Mr. D. V. Broadhead-Williams, Mr. G. D. Cannon, Major. A. S. Din, Mr. C. R. Donald, Mr. H. P. Foxon, Mrs. W. H. L. Gordon, Mr. I. D. Hunter, Professor K. Ingham, Mr. H. K. Jaffer, Mr. M.S. Kiingi, the Minister of Works, Mr. S. w. Kulubya, Mr. J. Lokolimoi, Mrs. F. A. Lubega, Mr. J. W. Lwamfa, Mr. M. Mugwanya, Mr. D. J. K. Nabeta, Mrs. S. Ntiro, Mr. P. C. Ofwono, Mr. G. W. Oguli, Mr. A. Opwa, Dr. T. D'Souza, Mr. M. J. Starforth, and Mr. J. V. Wild. Two members declined to vote: J. M. Madhvani and C. K. Patel. See Uganda Protectorate, *Proceedings of the Legislative Council*, 1959: 195–56.

14. See Sekiki (1972) 12–13; Uganda Protectorate (1962) 515–75; *Africa Research Bulletin*, 1–31 August 1968: 1155A; Otunnu (1994):4–5, 7–8.

15. See Helle-Valle (1989) 138–40; Mushemeza (1993) 21. Details have only been reproduced for the Rwandese refugees.

16. Dorothea Hunter, "Report of Visits in East Africa, August-September 1968," (deposited at the Refugee Studies Programme, Oxford University): 1. See also, Assistant Director of Refugees in the Ministry of Culture and Community Development, S. K. Katenta Apuli, "Proposed Request for Assistance for Refugee Settlements, 22 May 1969" (deposited at the Refugee Studies Programme, Oxford University): 1–4; The Adviser on Zonal Rural Development, Oxfam, T. F. Betts, "Request Settlement in Uganda, 18 August 1967" (deposited at the Refugee Studies Programme, Oxford University); L. Capplelletti (U.N. Deputy Resident Representative, UNDP), A. T. Nielsen (Representative, UNHCR.). and T. F. Betts (Adviser on Zonal Rural Development, Oxfam), "Memorandum: Sudanese Refugees—Uganda, Kampala, 25 June 1969" (deposited at the Refugee Studies Programme, Oxford University): 1–4; T. F. Betts, "Sudanese Refugees—Northern Uganda, 21 June 1969" (deposited at the Refugee Studies Programme, Oxford University): 1–2; M. Harper (Field Director, Oxfam), "UGA 16A/8901—Sudanese Refugees in Uganda, 30 May 1969" (deposited at the Refugee Studies Programme, Oxford University):1–6; African Refugee Secre-

tary, World Alliance of YMCA, "Report of Visits to the Refugee Settlements of Uganda, 27 November 1969" (deposited at the Refugee Studies Programme, Oxford University); S. K. Katenta Apuli, Ministry of Culture and Community Development, "Request for Assistance in Refugee Settlements, 23 May 1969" (deposited at the Refugee Studies Programme, Oxford University).

17. See Mutesa (1967) 168–70; Mutesa (1966) 10–11; Obote (1970) 35; Lemarchand (1970):208–09; E. Nabuguzi (1993)18. About the Congo crisis, See, for example, Hempstone (1962) 3–230; Kabongo (1986) 27–50. The Aims and Principles of the OAU Charter declare the sovereign equality of all member states; non-interference in the internal affairs of a member state; respect for the sovereignty and territorial integrity of each member state; and condemn subversive activities on the part of a member state. See, for example, Ajala (1974) 65.

18. For opposition to the regime from a section of the army, see *Africa Research Bulletin*, 1–31 July 1973:2919AB; *Africa Research Bulletin*, 1–31 August 1973:2958c; *Africa Research Bulletin*, 1–31 December 1973:307C. For a discussion about the Addis Ababa Agreement, see Zolberg, et al (1989). 52–53.

19. See *Africa Research Bulletin*, 1–31 January 1978:4705C; *New York Times*, 1 January 1, 1978:6.

20. For the various assistance that the international organizations and agencies provided, see International University Exchange Fund, "Project No. 71/72 LS UGA. 8 (A): Agreement between UNHCR and IORD. Nairobi, 28 February 1978" (deposited at the Refugee Studies Programme, Oxford University); Jimmy, "Transfer of Refugees—Uganda. TFB/JB No. 72/7. Kampala, 8 January 1972" (deposited at the Refugee Studies Programme, Oxford University); T. B. Betts, "Evaluation of Sites Proposed for Resettlement of Refugees: Report Prepared for Uganda Government by Special UNDP/FAO/WHO Mission., February 1972" (deposited at the Refugee Studies Programme, Oxford University); "Agreement between the Uganda Government and the United Nations High Commission for Refugees. Project No. 71-72/LS/UGA. 8(A)" (deposited at the Refugee Studies Programme, Oxford University).

21. According to UNLF Anti-Dictatorship, *The New Military Dictators*. Mbale, 1980: 11, Y. Museveni's army comprised over 8,000 troops in the UNLA by September 1979. In *Selected Articles on the Uganda Resistance War*. Second Edition. Kampala: NRM Publication, 1986: 6, Museveni handed over 10,000 of his troops to the UNLA by June 1979.

22. Essack (1993) 19, 36, 45; Rwanda Patriotic Front, "Background to Genocide" (deposited at the Refugee Studies Programme, Oxford University), June 1994: 7–8; Watson (1991) 13; Museveni (1992) 125; Uganda Government (1994) 31.

23. See, for example, Museveni, *Selected Articles on the Uganda Resistance War*: 4–5; *Daily Nation*, 12 Friday 1971; *Daily Nation*, 28 January 1971:1; *Daily Nation*, Saturday, 13 February 1971:1; "Sudan: the South and Uganda," *Africa Confidential*, 13, 8 (21 April 1972):1–2.

24. See Essack (1993) 6, 19, 45; Rwandese Patriotic Front, "Rwanda: Background to the Genocide,":7–8; "Colonel 'Cries' as he tells inside story of NRA war," *The Monitor*, Kampala, Wednesday, 25–27 January 1995:1, 28; *The Monitor*, Friday, 9 November 1993:13; Uganda Democratic Alliance, "An Open Letter to His Excellency, Yoweri Museveni, 6 February 1989":4; Uganda People's Front, "Who is Yoweri Museveni, his attitudes and views?," Kampala, February 1988; N. Kabukol, "The Challenge of a New Generation: Recolonization of Uganda," Kampala, 1991:11–14; "Rwandese Refugee Army overruns Garrison," *Weekly Topic*, Kampala, 12 October 1990:1; "Rwanda/Uganda: A Violent Homecoming," *Africa Confidential*, 31, 20: 12 October 1990; Watson (1991) 9, 13; Uganda

Democratic Coalition, *US Coaxed into Training Rwanda Rebels*. 1, 1 (August 1991):3–4.

25. See Museveni (1992) 134–36; Uganda Government (1994) 35; Amnesty International, *Uganda: Several Hundred Political Prisoners*. 21 August 1981:1; "Uganda," *Africa Report* (May-June 1981):36; *Africa Research Bulletin*, 1–31 March 1981:5993C; *Africa Research Bulletin*, 1–31 March 1981:5998C-59998A; A. M. Obote, "Notes on Concealment of Genocide in Uganda, 1990":49–59; "Uganda: Straining at the Edges," *Africa Confidential*, 31, 21 (1990):6; Essack (1993) 36; *Africa Research Bulletin*, 1–31 March 1981:5998C-5999A.

26. See *Africa Research Bulletin*, 1–31 January 1983:6712C; *New York Times*, 25 January 1983:1, 5; "Uganda: Opposition Wins and Losses," *Africa Confidential*, 24, 7 (30 March 1983): n.p; Watson (1991) 10; *Africa Research Bulletin*, 1–31 March 1981:5998C-5999A; Museveni (1992) 122–25, 134–36; Nabuguzi (1993) 19.

27. The attitudes of some Baganda towards immigrants and refugees are highlighted in Richards (1952) 161, 196–97.

28. According to them, the Black Bombers were led by Matiya Kyaligonza, Patrick Kalegeya, Pekos Kuteesa, Mark Mugenyi, and Dampa (nicknamed Hitler). Muwanga and Gombya (1991) 22.

29. See Muwanga and Gombya (1991) 22; Obote, "Notes on Concealment of Genocide in Uganda": 50; Muwanga (1983) 20–22. For works that discuss Buganda feelings of superiority towards immigrants and refugees, see Richards (1952) 161.

30. Muwanga and Gombya (1991) 21. See also, Obote, "Notes on Concealment of Genocide in Uganda": 51–52; "Uganda: the Opposition Tangle," *Africa Confidential*, 23, 16 (4 August 1982).

31. See "Uganda Straining at the Edges," *Africa Confidential*, 31, 21 (1990): 6; Helle-Valle (1989) 164–77; Clay (n.d.) 7. Museveni lost the parliamentary election to a DP candidate who was also his brother-in-law, Sam Kutesa.

32. Obote ("Notes on Concealment of Genocide in Uganda": 20) mentioned the close ties between Obote and the two ministers during the 1978–1979 war.

33. Interviews with some prominent UPC leaders in Mbarara, Kisoro, and Bushenyi, June 1984 and August, 1993; Clay (n.d.) 164–77.

34. *Uganda Times*, Kampala, 11 January 1982, cited in Clay (n.d.) 33. Refugees have always been blamed for abusing the hospitality of Uganda. For example, in 1990, the Vice-Chairman of the National Resistance Movement, Moses Kigongo, did just that. See Essack (1993): 6.

35. This law is exhaustively discussed by Kiapi (1993) 9–19.

36. Clay, ibid. This wave of violence erupted while Obote was in Italy, and the minister in charge of refugees, Dr. James Rwanyarare, was attending an international meeting in Geneva.

37. See Watson (1991) 10–11; High Commissioner for Refugees, "Uganda," *Report on UNHCR assistance activities in 1982-1983 and proposed voluntary funds programmes and budget for 1984*: 129; Clay (n.d.) 34–48. According to Nabuguzi (1993) 19, the refugees who fled to Rwanda found themselves confined to camps and only survived persecution by claiming to be Ugandan Banyarwanda. According to the data provided by the UNHCR, at least 40,000 Banyarwanda, most of them Rwandese refugees, fled to Rwanda in 1982. Yet, the same source, as seen in tables 1.5 and 1.6, do not document any change in the numbers of Rwandese refugees in Uganda.

38. See *Africa Research Bulletin*, 1–31 October 1982:6613C-6614A; *New York Times*, 10 October 1982: 10; *New York Times*, 12 October 1982: 12.

39. See Clay (n.d.) 36; *Africa Research Bulletin*, 1–31 October 1982:6614A.
40. See Essack (1993) 19, 45; "Colonel cries as he tells his story of the NRA war," *The Monitor*, Wednesday, January 25–27, 1995: 1, 28.
41. On the violation of the right of the refugees to return to their homeland, see Amnesty International, *Rwanda: Persecution of Tutsi Minority and Repression of Government Critics, 1990–1992* (May 1992): 4–5; Human Rights Watch (1992) 7; Watson (1991) 13; Museveni (1992) 122–23; "Rwanda Refugee Availed passports," *New Vision*, Kampala, Thursday, September 2, 1993: 1–2.
42. See, for example, Nabuguzi (1993) 19; *Africa Research Bulletin*, 1–31 October 1982:6614B; High Commissioner for Refugees, Uganda: *Report on UNHCR assistance activities in 1982–1983 and proposed voluntary funds programmes and budget for 1984*, 129.
43. *Africa Research Bulletin*, 1–31 October 1982:6614B. See also, High Commissioner for Refugees, "Uganda": *Report on UNHCR Assistance*: 129; Clay (n.d) 61.
44. High Commissioner for Refugees, "Uganda," *Report on UNHCR assistance activities in 1982–1983 and proposed voluntary funds programmes and budget for 1984*: 129; Clay (n.d.) 61–62.
45. US Committee for Refugees, *World Refugee Survey, 1984*: 7. See also, *Africa Research Bulletin*, 1–31 March 1983: 6762A-C.
46. See "Uganda: the Fall of President Obote," *Africa Contemporary Record*, 1984–1985: B 399.
47. See Human Rights Watch Arms Project (1994) *Arming Rwanda:* 8; Helle-Valle (1989) 164–77.

2

An Historical Analysis of the Invasion by the Rwanda Patriotic Army (RPA)

Ogenga Otunnu

In late 1989, a group of RPA refugee warriors carried out an abortive armed invasion of Rwanda. After its defeat by the Rwandan army, the RPA hastily returned to its military base inside Uganda. On 1 October 1990, an estimated 10,000 well-armed refugee warriors of the RPA, led by Major General Rwigyema, carried out another invasion of Rwanda. The overwhelming majority of the invaders were, at least until the invasion, active members of Lieutenant General Museveni's National Resistance Army (NRA) in Uganda. The invasion provoked a protracted civil war in Rwanda.

What accounted for the emergence of the RPA? How did it develop into a credible military force? Why did the warriors invade Rwanda in 1989 and 1990? What role did Uganda play in the 1990 invasion? Could Uganda have halted the invasion? This chapter examines the RPA's preparation for the Rwanda invasion following Museveni's victory in Uganda. It also discusses the factors that influenced the timing of the 1990 invasion and Ugandans' response to that invasion.

The Museveni Victory and the RPA's Preparation for the Invasion

Immediately after the NRA seized power in Uganda on 25 January 1986, it embarked upon a massive military recruitment campaign that drew from friendly areas in western and southern Uganda. By 1990, the NRA comprised over 200,000 soldiers. The recruitment was driven by the need to secure eastern and northern Uganda, where the regime

31

had a severe legitimacy crisis. It was also an important part of a military preparation designed to allow the regime to withstand the possible disintegration of its military alliance with combatants from Uganda and West Nile. The Rwandese refugees saw the recruitment as a means to enlist more refugees into the NRA for future armed struggles in Rwanda (Watson 1991, 13; Museveni 1992, 124; Human Rights Watch Arms Project 1994, 8).

According RPA/NRA leader Major Dr. Bayingana, the recruitment of refugees had to be carried out without causing suspicion in Rwanda and Uganda. He explained: "We preferred to have every member of the RPA in his mother NRA unit from where he or she could join the zero hour of 'exodus.'... Besides, we did not want to embarrass President Museveni, whom many of us greatly admire." Also, he further noted: "[W]e were very much concerned with the success of the NRA first" (Essack 1993, 20).[1]

In order to protect the regime, the Rwandese in the NRA participated in the counter-insurgencies in Acholi, Teso, Lango, Kasese, and West Nile. The refugees viewed these operations as the most practical military training they could acquire for future armed struggle in Rwanda. However, their participation generated more anti-Rwandese sentiments in Uganda. For instance, during the northern and eastern campaigns, a Muganda NRA officer observed that the Rwandese

> are always excited to fight against the rebels. Most of the time they are able to find and kill hundreds of rebels in areas where there are no rebels.... This is not necessarily a bad military strategy because it strikes terror among the ordinary people and discourages them from supporting the rebels. The only problem we have with these people is that they do not obey our command. For example, a private does not listen to a major who is not a Rwandese.... They do not trust us...they think we will ally with the Acholi.... This lack of trust explains why some Baganda who were members of the Uganda Federal Army were murdered by the Rwandese in Lowero and now in Acholi. (Author's interview, Kampala, 1989)

A Verona Father, who taught for many years in Gulu, highlighted some causes of anti-Rwandese sentiments in the area:

> These people (some of them are Ugandans) are quite excited about the armed conflict in Acholi...almost anybody they see during their operation they shoot at or cut with their machetes or bayonets. These Rwandese use the most unacceptable counter-insurgency strategies; they herd women, children and old people into houses and set the houses on fire; they rape women in the presence of their male relatives, and at times, they force the male relatives to sleep with those women after they [the soldiers] have exhausted their sexual desire.... These people are determined to spread *slim* [HIV] to the Acholi. I also witnessed them mutilate

unarmed people, including school children, from the Holy Rosary primary school. Some of these people had taken refuge at the Cathedral.... The irony, however, is that the surviving victims are often paraded by the soldiers or government functionaries before a group of reporters, and asked to expose those who mutilated them. Naturally, they say that the rebels did it. The rebels are also involved in these dirty acts of killing and mutilating people who collaborate with the government.... People lost all their belongings to these soldiers and the rebels. I have been told by kind Rwandese officers (and there are many who are better than Ugandans in the NRA) that thousands of head of cattle confiscated from here will help them in another war.... Now we hear that Museveni wants to resettle the Rwandese in Acholi and Lango. People are worried about the news because they do not want to share their land with these people. (Author's interview, Gulu, 1988)

Similar counter-insurgency strategies were employed in other insecure areas of Uganda. For example, under the leadership of the Commanding Officer of the 306th Brigade in Teso, Chris Bunyenyezi, and Brigade Commander, Tom Kyaligonza, hundreds of unarmed civilians were massacred. A further estimated 200,000 were kept in what the *Church Times* (London) described as "concentration camps" (9 March 1990). In Teso, many cattle were also confiscated by the army.

A number of important observations can be made. First, the majority of the Rwandese in the NRA received their military training while fighting counter-insurgency wars in Uganda. A few of them, including Paul Kagame, were sent by the Museveni regime for military training to places such as the United States, Britain, North Korea and Canada (*New Vision*: Kampala, 6 June, 1994). Second, the atrocities committed by the NRA during the counter-insurgencies provoked a tornado of anti-Rwandese sentiment in the country. Ironically, non-Rwandese members of the NRA who committed similar atrocities during the wars were hardly blamed by those who bitterly complained against the Rwandese (Watson 1991, 13). Third, the persistent complaints of discrimination and disappointment by Baganda officers in the NRA promoted anti-Rwandese sentiment in the NRA. Also, as in Buganda and Ankole, anti-Rwandese sentiment in the rest of the country resulted from a protracted struggle over land, jobs, social services and political power (Essack 1993, 6; *Monitor*: 28 June 1995: 1–9). Fourth, the Rwandese were able to conceal their military plans because most high-ranking officers in the NRA held similar positions in the RPA; they were also in charge of security and intelligence matters in the country. For example, the leadership of the Rwandese in the NRA included: Major General Rwigyema (Deputy Commander of the NRA), the then Deputy Minister of Defence, Major Paul Kagame (Head of Intelligence and Counter-Intelligence), Major Dr. Peter Baingaina (Head of NRA Medical

Services), Major Chris Bunyenzi (Commanding Officer of the NRA's 306th Brigade), Major Sam Kaka (Commanding Officer, Military Police), Lieutenant Colonel Wasswa, Major Stephen Ndugate, Captain Kitare, and Lieutenant Byegyeka (Watson 1991, 13; *Africa Confidential*: 12 Oct. 1990). Finally, the growing tension, discrimination and hostility faced by the refugees in Uganda created further incentives to launch the invasion and to ogranize public fundraising, hold RANU (later RPF) conferences at Makere University and other places in Kampala as early as 1987 (Prunier 1995, 72–73).

The Timing of the Invasion

A number of closely related factors accounted for the timing of the invasion. First, the escalation of anti-Rwandese sentiment, especially from the areas that benefitted most from the overthrow of the UNLA terror, Buganda and Ankole, sent a clear message to the RPA: mobilize and invade while you still have access to military, economic, and political resources of Uganda (Watson 1993, 9). The new Uganda Investment Code prohibited aliens from owning land and increases the pressure for an immediate armed struggle against Rwanda (ibid. 14; *Monitor*: 14–18 Jan. 1994).

Another influential factor was the growing internal power rivalry and frustration within the RPA. Power rivalry and disagreements over military strategies split the RPA into two main warring camps. The first camp was led by Major Dr. Banyingana and included influential officers such as Charles Kabanda and Major Chris Bunyenyezi. This group maintained that the RPA and its political wing, the Rwanda Patriotic Front (RPF), should be led by Banyingana, who was better educated and more articulate than Rwigyema. In an attempt to boost their position, Banyingana embarked on extensive international tours to recruit Rwandese into the RPF and to mobilize military and financial support for an armed struggle against Rwanda. During the tours, Banyingana began to act as the overall leader of the RPF. This camp was so impatient with the protracted peace negotiations between the RPA/RPF and the Rwandan government that it was determined to rush the armed struggle. Thus, in late 1989, supporters of this camp launched an abortive invasion of Rwanda (Essack 1993, 34–35).

The second, more powerful camp was lead by Major General Rwigyema, the official leader of the RPF/RPA. This faction had easy access to government and private sector resources. It was also supported by the most powerful RPA/NRA officers, including Major Kagame and Colonel Wasswa. According to C. Watson, the group respond to the challenge of its legitimacy by intimidating and imprisoning any Rwandese in Uganda, including those in the NRA/RPA, who disagreed with its politics and military strategies:

> From November 1989 to June 1990, Banyarwanda refugee Major Paul Kagame was acting head of the NRA's military intelligence. He is alleged to have used its resources to intimidate dissenters within the RPF, some of whom wanted and attempted a small, abortive invasion in 1989, as well as refugees who did not favor an armed return or who had relations with the Rwandese state. Some were imprisoned (Watson 1991, 13).

The two camp rivalries became so feverish that each camp contemplated an invasion to enhance its position at its rival's expense. The rush to forestall any possible military initiative by the other competitor made the camps realize that further delays would erode the RPA's strength and expose some of its military strategies to the government in Kigali. Indeed, it is commonly believed that the violent power rivalry later led to the mysterious deaths of Rwigyema, Banyingana, Bunyenyezi, and at least sixty members of the Banyingana camp (Essack 1993, 34–35; Watson 1991, 14).[2]

The timing of the invasion was also influenced by a host of affairs internal to Rwanda: conflict between the north and south and power struggles among the northerners; the effects of the 1980 "Equilibrium Policy"; the harrowing effects of the Structural Adjustment Policies of the International Monetary Fund (IMF) and World Bank; famines; increased government crackdown upon opponents; and the flight of some prominent businessmen and government functionaries into the RPF/RPA. These crises convinced the RPA that the regime in Kigali was resting on shallow political soil. If the regime were attacked militarily, the RPA/RPF reasoned, more regime instability and terror would be provoked. Increased regime terror, in turn, would facilitate the collapse of the regime under fire. If the armed invasion did not lead to total disintegration of the beleaguered and disorganized regime, it further reasoned, it could force President Habyarimana to make a politically fatal compromise with the armed opposition (Essack 1993, 4, 9, 18).

The Rwandan government's response to the impending invasion also influenced the timing. The abortive 1989 RPA invasion, the visible presence of high-ranking Rwandese in the NRA, and the frantic fund-raising activities by the RPA/RPF in Uganda suggested to the Rwandan government that an organized invasion was but a matter of time. This forced the Rwandan government to mobilize military support from its allies, including Egypt, France, and Zaire. The regime also began to expand its militia and standing army. These responses sent an unequivocal message to the RPA: invade while you still stand a good chance of destabilizing the government or stay in Uganda and disintegrate into oblivion. The RPA chose the former option and moved hastily toward a military campaign (Essack 1993, 6).

The timing of the invasion was also influenced by the parallel strategy pursued by Kigali: a negotiated settlement with the RPF/RPA, a vigorous campaign to exploit and manipulate anti-Rwandese sentiment in the NRA, and the rivalry in the RPA. It thus engaged in a protracted negotiated settlement and sent large sums of money to some NRA/RPA officers. These officers were expected to collaborate with Kigali, intensify the power struggle in the RPA, and eliminate some of the RPA/NRA officers; among those targeted were Rwigyema and Banyingana. When the former learned of the plot, he identified the officers on Kigali's payroll to President Museveni (Essack 33). The news of the plot created panic in the RPA, which forced contemplation of an early invasion. As RPA chief Kagame noted, "if the leaders...like Rwigyema and Banyigana had died at the hands of Habyarimana agents in Kampala...then the armed struggle would have been delayed" (Essack 34).

The slow pace and extended length of the negotiations with Habyarimana also influenced the timing of the invasion. The regime reluctantly and gradually became accommodating to RPA/RPF demands (Watson, 13). However, some members of the RPA, especially those who subscribed to Museveni's justification of total war against repressive regimes (Prunier 1995, 68), felt the negotiations were taking too long and that Habyarimana's concessions were inadequate. They felt the RPA would not meet its political and military objectives of removing Habyarimana from power. Thus, Kagame noted that the negotiations "needed a long time which we could not survive, given the rate of intrigues which was being formed by Habyarimana's gang of four NRA officers" (quoted in Essack, 33).

The result was that the "war party" in the RPA/RPF exerted pressure for an early invasion, which would induce the Habyarimana regime to offer better concessions more quickly. These would allow the RPA/RPF to join, then topple, the government. A section of the war party was also determined to launch its own invasion of Rwanda, should the leadership of the RPA decide to listen to the "peace party" and postpone the invasion (Interview by author, Toronto, 1991).

The RPA's military training, and the near-decisive military victory it scored against the insurgents in the north and east of Uganda also influenced the timing of the invasion. Indeed, as soon as the RPA achieved most of its counter-insurgency objectives, it began to speed up plans for the invasion of Rwanda. However, since no one knew how long the proposed war would take—especially after the decisive loss during the 1989 invasion—and because of the Habyarimana regime's continued mobilization, the RPA decided to have some of its members remain in the NRA. This was intended to protect the Museveni regime against its armed and unarmed political opponents. It was also hoped that those members of the RPA who would remain in the NRA would provide vital military and political support for an armed campaign against Rwanda (*Information Digest*: March 1995, 2). As Bayingana put it, after three months of planning, the question was how, not when "to evacuate" RPA troops from the NRA for the invasion (Watson, 13).

Another factor was Museveni's attempt to demobilize some members of the NRA/RPA. This decision was partly the result of the NRA's military victory against the insurgents, and the growing domestic and international pressure to demobilize some of the 100,000 soldiers. The army consumed at least 37 percent of the country's official budget (*Information Digest*: 2). Among those short-listed for demobilization were Rwandese refugees, both members and non-members of the RPA. Though the technical process of demobilization or Reduction-in-Force (RIF) did not start before 1992, the political rumors associated with the impending process spread like a wild bush fire. This caused enormous uncertainty, tension, anxiety, and a feeling of betrayal among Rwandese refugees in the NRA; a situation that was compounded by the rumor that most marked for demobilization were Ugandans, not Rwandese. Another version of the rumor had it that the Rwandese to be demobilized were already demobilizing for an armed struggle in Rwanda. This again meant that the majority demobilized would be Ugandans. Anti-Rwandese sentiment in the NRA was fired by these rumors. Faced by this hostility, and the belief that the package for demobilization and re-integration was inadequate, some RPA members exerted more pressure on the leadership to speed preparation for the invasion. Since these soldiers had almost unlimited access to NRA military hardware, and were increasingly restless, the leadership had to respond accordingly in order to avoid a serious organizational dilemma.

The absence of the strongman, President Habyarimana, from Rwanda at a time of increased internal instability and uncertainty in the country also provided bait for the RPA to invade Rwanda while he was away. According to the RPA, the invasion would easily disorganize the divided cabinet and the poorly trained Rwandan army. Museveni's absence also made it easier to mobilize the RPA/NRA for the invasion, while at the same time protecting him from criticism, especially from OAU member states, of any direct involvement in the invasion (Watson, 13).

Museveni's attempts to stem antiregime *cum* anti-Rwandese sentiments in the country also contributed to the timing of the invasion (*Africa Confidential*: 26 Oct 1990, 4–6). These sentiments logically responded to the enormous power the regime gave Rwandese refugees in the NRA, Internal Security Organization (ISO), External Security Organization (ESO), and government. For example, some leading members of the DP from Buganda condemned Museveni, whom they described as a Tutsi refugee, for the Tutsi domination of the country. By presenting Museveni as a Tutsi refugee, the politicians destroyed any lingering distinction between antiregime and anti-Rwandese sentiments. In part, the politicians destroyed the distinction in order to disguise their opposition to the regime as opposition to arrogance and domination by the refugees (*Monitor*: 28–30 June 1995, 9).

The refugees' rapid accumulation of land also contributed to antiregime *cum* antirefugee sentiments. For example, during the August 1990 debate in the National Resistance Council (NRC), Ugandans of competing political persuasions blamed the government for giving refugees land and encouraging them to terrorize Ugandans. The clashes between the refugees and the host community at Mowogola ranches in Ankole, among other, was mentioned as an example of the terror that the refugees continued to unleash against Ugandans (ibid).

Faced with growing opposition, the regime decided to "remove" some "visible" Rwandese refugees, including Major General Rwegyema, from the NRA and government. Although these refugees retained their influence and privileges, the regime expected their publicized removal to vitiate its legitimacy crisis, especially in Buganda, Kigezi, and Ankole. However, the measure generated its own contradiction: it sent an unintended message to some of the RPA in the NRA that other stakeholders were capable of forcing Museveni to remove them. This created restlessness, confusion and frustration, which, in turn, generated more pressure to invade before the RPA became a spent force. The measure created a further problem for the regime insofar as its political opponents insisted that both the government and the army remained in the hands of Rwandese refugees.

This "removal strategy" raised at least two critical and related questions for the regime: How many should be removed, and at what cost? These questions were difficult because the removal of a handful of Rwandese refugees had not stemmed the tide of antiregime *cum* anti-Rwandese sentiments in the country. Further, if the government removed many refugees, the rest could desert immediately and disorderly, causing serious security and foreign policy problems. Early warning signals also indicated that mass removal would cause anxiety among the remainder to skyrocket and would possibly result in an immediate and uncoordinated invasion of Rwanda. In the end, increased restlessness in the RPA, factional rivalries in the RPA/NRA and the infiltration of the RPA/NRA by Habyarimana's agents sent a clear message to the government: the invasion is inevitable and will happen soon. The question then became how to control and disguise the exodus and impending invasion. It was important to disguise these activities since they violated the OAU at a time when Museveni sat in the chair. The strategy was now for Museveni to play a double game of "allowing Rwigyema to build his expeditionary army while professing friendship with his neighbors" (*Africa Confidential*: 28 Sept. 1990, 4).

Another thesis, however, dismisses these factors as determinants regarding the timing of the invasion. According to this viewpoint, Museveni and the leaders of the RPA/RPF in the NRA/NRM and government had been planning the invasion since 1986. One of invasion's objectives was to end the suffering of the Tutsi, Museveni's ethnic group. Thus, it was the urgent need to liberate Museveni's people that determined the amount of military, financial, and political support that the regime devoted to the mission (ibid: 22 March 1991: 6). Despite the fact that there was an urgent need to end the growing persecution of the Tutsi in Rwanda, Uganda, and eastern Zaire, it is unclear how much weight this noble desire exerted on the timing of the invasion.

A related perspective suggests that the timing was based on Museveni's belief that the Rwandan regime was too weak to survive an organized armed invasion by the seasoned RPA/NRA veterans of the wars in Luwero, Acholi, West Nile, Teso, and Kasese. According to this school, the invasion was spurred by Museveni's vaulting ambition to create a Tutsi dynasty in Uganda, Rwanda, Burundi, and Zaire. This dynasty would allow Museveni to achieve a number of objectives: liberation of his people in the region; hegemony of his people in the region; fulfilment of his promise to the RANU (now RPA/RPF); reward the Tutsi in Burundi and eastern Zaire for the military, political, and economic assistance provided during the war against the Obote and Okello regimes; enable him to stage a comeback to power in Uganda in the event of a coup or multiparty victory; protect his regime, especially from the growing opposition in Buganda, Kasese, and Bundibugyo; and make him kingmaker in the region, partly by destabilizing, if not overthrowing the regimes in Kenya, Zaire, and Sudan.

Although it was true that Museveni repeatedly told the regime in Kigali that the refugee warriors were better trained than the Rwandan army, it is unclear that this consideration played a prominent role in the timing of the invasion. Similarly, while it is true that Tutsi in Burundi, Uganda, and eastern Zaire supported Museveni in the early 1980s in the hope of receiving some rewards, there is no evidence to suggest that a Tutsi dynasty was the expected or intended award. Indeed, such a strategy could not have envisaged the creation of a Tutsi dynasty be-cause Museveni remained diametrically opposed to such a political system, which would endanger his regime by uniting regional opposi-tion against it. This claim seems rather to be based on the fact that the Tutsi are in power in Rwanda and Burundi; that the Tutsi in Rwanda, Burundi, Uganda, and Zaire played a leading role in the war against Mobutu; and the questionable contention that Uganda is ruled by the Tutsi. Perhaps the perspective is quite persuasive with regard to the threat Museveni faced, especially in Buganda and from the strategic but conflict-laden alliance between the UPC and the DP. This threat could have persuaded Museveni to demobilize the refugee warriors not only to reduce the threat but also to create a military base which could be called upon in time of need.

The claim that Museveni wants to become a kingmaker in the Great Lakes region seems based on the following: the assistance he gave the Tutsi to seize power in Rwanda; the allegation that the current Rwandan government—which works closely with Museveni—is opposed to any form of economic, military, or political embargo against the Tutsi regime in Burundi; the leading role that the Rwandan and Ugandan (and, to some degree, Burundi) governments played in Mobutu's overthrow; and the increased influence and power of the Tutsi in the Laurent Kabila regime (Democratic Republic of Congo). The claim is also based on the fact that Museveni has provided military and political support to the John Garang faction of the Sudan People's Liberation Army (SPLA) and the Mwakenya armed opposition group that wants to topple the regime in Kenya. One major shortcoming of this claim is that it refuses to acknowledge the fact that Kenya, Sudan, and Zaire also provided assistance to anti-Museveni forces. Yet, like Uganda, the three countries denied supporting such groups. The assertion further ignores the fact that Museveni's prominence in the region is partly a result of his unmatched political and military competence (*Africa Confidential*: 26 Oct 1990: 1).

Yet another perspective maintains that the timing of the invasion was determined by the reluctance of the international community to intervene in armed conflict in Africa; this was certainly true after the Somalia tragedy. According to this view, Museveni and the RPA/RPF leadership determined that it was better to invade while the international community was suffering from humanitarian fatigue; demonstrating what can be called an insensitivity syndrome; undergoing a crisis in formulating a coherent, coordinated, and feasible post-Cold War policy; and suffering from their own legitimacy crises on the domestic front at the same time as the Eastern European crises dominated the news. This perspective was supported by the RPA/RPF expectation that western governments would only express concern to Uganda following the planned invasion, particularly since Uganda was being paraded through Africa by the IMF and World Bank as a success story of the Structural Adjustment Policies (SAP). Diplomatic words of concern would be issued only to Uganda because, while Kenya, Malawi, Zambia, and Zaire were being demonized for violations of human rights and their unwillingness to practice multiparty democracy, Uganda was being shielded from such pressure by human rights and refugee advocates, scholars, journalists, and western donors (*Africa Confidential*: 28 Sept 1990, 2). This interpretation further maintains that Museveni knew from his close friend, Lynda Chalker (British Minister of Overseas Development), that Britain was relying upon him to kick the French out of the Great Lakes region of Africa. The perspective concludes that Museveni also counted on American acquiescence, since the US was counting on him to dislodge the regime of terror in Khartoum and to check the spread of Islamic Fundamentalism in the Great Lakes region (*New Federalist*: 9 June, 1997).

In any event, by early 1990, the momentum toward the invasion was irreversible. It was reported that at least 20,000 Tutsi refugees disappeared from refugee settlements, including Kyaka. By August, there were numerous reports of cattle confiscation by the RPA/NRA. For example, some 1,200 head of cattle were reported confiscated at Mawogola in Ankole by the same group. The cattle reported to be slaughtered, smoked, and preserved to feed the refugee warriors during the planned invasion (*Weekly Topic*: 12 Oct 1990, 7).

The RPA/RPF purportedly planned the invasion to take place while both Museveni and Habyarimana were in the USA (Essack, 32–33). It was also planned to coincide with preparations for independence celebrations in Uganda, which were often accompanied by troop deployments, a good disguise for troop movements toward Rwanda (*Africa Confidential*, ibid.). Between July and September 1990, the RPA began to mobilize for the war. The soldiers were sent to Mbarara and news about the mobilization circulated freely in Kampala among the general public, foreign diplomats, and journalists (*Arming*: 19). A few days before the invasion, thousands of NRA/NRP soldiers arrived in Mbarara from places as far as Arua, Gulu, Kitgum, Soroti, Kampala, Entebbe, and Jinja. In order to contain the growing public anxiety, Rwigyema told the inquisitive on-lookers at Mbarara that "he was taking the troops to prepare for celebrations on October 9, Uganda's Independence Day" (Watson, 14). The explanation, however, was contradicted by some NRA/RPA soldiers who were so excited that they told the public about the invasion. On 1 October, Rwigyema led an estimated 10,000 soldiers into Rwanda (ibid.).

Ugandan Involvement in the Invasion

The incident raised questions about the involvement of Uganda in the invasion. According to the Habyarimana regime, the invasion was carried out by Uganda. It supported its position by noting that the invasion was led by the NRA. Furthermore, during and after the invasion the NRA/RPA moved freely between Uganda and Rwanda. It also pointed to the presence of non-Rwandese members of the NRA in the invasion. Thus, the Chief of Staff of the Rwandan Army, Colonel Deogratias Nsabimana, told the Human Rights Watch Arms Project (HRWAP) that "the involvement of Uganda in this conflict is evident. The attack came from there, and also we know that it was conducted and led by NRA military officers (HRWAP. 6) The Habyarimana regime also supported its claim by presenting some NRA official documents, vehicles, weapons and Prisoners of War (POWs) that it had captured during the invasion (Essack, 10). The regime further claimed that between 1986 and 1994, the RPA was harbored, trained, financed, and equipped by Uganda (*Monitor*: 26 Nov 1991, 11).

The views put forward by the regime in Rwanda regarding Uganda's roles in the invasion received some support from the Human Rights Watch Arms Project. For example, it noted that "Uganda provided weapons, munitions and other military supplies to RPF. These included munitions, automatic rifles, mortars, artillery and Soviet-designed katyusha multiple rocket system." It further observed that "Uganda allowed the rebel movement to use its territory as a sanctuary for the planning of attacks, stockpiling of weapons, raising of funds and movement of troops" (HRWAP, 6). The HRWAP supported its position by quoting a senior NRA officer:

> A senior NRA operations officer told the Arms Project that Uganda has supported the RPF throughout the conflict. The officer said that after the failure of the RPF's October 1990 invasion, the NRA provided even heavier weaponry including artillery. The officer said that throughout the conflict, the NRA provided a steady stream of ammunition, food and logistical supplies, and that the two armies shared intelligence information. (ibid.)

The HRWAP reinforced its claim by pointing out that the news of the mobilization was such common knowledge in Uganda that it was practically impossible for the regime not to have known about it. Also, the movements of thousands of soldiers with heavy weapons from different parts of the country to Mbarara and the Kabale could have not taken place without the tacit approval of the regime. Similarly, HRWAP insisted that the invasion was not a conspiracy by the RPA:

> The Arms Project finds this claim [conspiracy] not credible. Many journalists, diplomats and other observers told the Arms Project that the fact of the invasion was common knowledge in Kampala and other locations throughout Uganda, as thousands of soon-to-be RPA members bid farewell to relatives and friends.... Moreover, while military intelligence may have been under the control of the alleged conspirators, Uganda has a separate Internal Security Organization (ISO) with several thousand agents that was created precisely to prevent renegade or conspiratorial activity within the NRA. That the ISO could have been entirely uninformed of both the conspiracy and its execution is not credible.... Finally, movements in preparation for the invasion were efficient, but not especially rapid. Diplomats and Western military observers say that troops, trucks and weapons left Kampala together in the local football stadium in Kabale, 300 kilometers southwest of Kampala and 20 kilometers north of Rwandan border. This movement began on September 29, 1990, two days prior to the October 1, invasion. There is no evidence that any NRA or other Ugandan authorities challenged this alleged mass defection of troops. (ibid: 19–20)

The participation of the non-Rwandese members of NRA in the invasion also raised questions about Uganda's direct involvement in the war. Two broad categories of Ugandan NRA members participated. The first group were bodyguards of senior NRA/NPA officers who accompanied them under the assumption that they were still active members of the NRA. Some were so attached to the officers that they would have chosen to participate in the invasion even if they had been given the choice to remain in their respective NRA units in Uganda. For many reasons, the majority of these guards did not return to Uganda (*Weekly Topic*: 19 Oct 1990). The second group were Ugandan soldiers who were given marching orders to an unknown destination, which turned out to be Mbarara, Kabale, and then Rwanda. One Ugandan sargeant noted that "it is not uncommon for soldiers, especially those of the lower ranks, not to know where they are going or what mission they will be asked to undertake.... In keeping with acceptable military conduct, we were ordered to fight, and we fought" (author's interview: Kampala, 1994).

Based on overwhelming evidence linking Uganda to the invasion, HRWAP concluded that it:

> finds a high degree of institutional complicity between the NRA and the RPF. At the very least, Uganda and its leaders are responsible for allowing military renegades to plan and execute the invasion of a sovereign state with Ugandan weapons, launched from Uganda. The arms project also believes that there is credible evidence that the Ugandan government allowed the RPF to move arms, logistical supplies and troops across Ugandan soil, and provided direct military support to the RPF in the force of arms, ammunition, and military equipment. (HRWAP, 21)

The Uganda government, however, has consistently denied any involvement in the invasion. According to President Museveni:

> he first heard of the invasion at 5 a.m. in his hotel in New York when he was telephoned by Maj. Gen. Mugisha Muntu, the Army Commander, who told him that perhaps 14 Banyrwanda army officers had deserted. He immediately contacted Habyarimana who was sleeping on the floor below and informed him of the possible danger. "I would like to make it very clear that we did not know about the desertion of these boys nor would we support it," he said. "If we were asleep, why did they not also defeat them before they crossed the border?...We cannot keep soldiers on standby indefinitely for an unconfirmed report." (*New Vision*: 11 Oct 1990)[3]

In his address to Makere University in June 1991, Museveni reinforced his claim by suggesting that the mobilization and invasion were the outcome of a Rwandese conspiracy in the NRA:

> in October last year, the Banyarwanda in our army conspired and went into Rwanda and started to cause trouble there. Some people have asked the question: "How could so many people go without the government being aware with of it?" But there is an English word called conspiracy—I think we have all heard of it. The truth of the matter is that these people conspired, took us by surprise and went to Rwanda, which was not particularly difficult. (Museveni, 123)

Museveni also denied that his government supported the RPA either financially or militarily. He argued that the RPA stole arms from the NRA: "[T]hose who were in the army were able to run away with their guns because each soldier stays with his gun. Other weapons and equipment were stolen by the deserters" (2). This official line was echoed by many government officials, including the Vice-Chairman of NRM, Moses Kigongo; who went further and condemned the refugees for abusing the hospitality they enjoyed in Uganda for three decades (Essack, 6).

The detailed position of the Uganda government is as follows:

1. The Government of Uganda was not aware of the refugees' intentions to invade Rwanda. However, there have always been rumors of such plans which the Government has shared with the Government of Rwanda. The refugees always denied these rumors.
2. The problem of the Rwandese refugees has been a long-standing one.
3. The President of Uganda informed the President of Rwanda as soon as desertions were detected in the NRA and the two Presidents have since met twice on this subject.
4. The President of Uganda is still prepared to promote a dialogue between the Rwandese refugees living in Uganda and the Government of Rwanda. The issue of refugees is not of Uganda's own making.
5. The issue of the Rwandese refugees is not confined to Uganda, but it obtains in other countries such as Zaire, Tanzania and Burundi.
6. The Government of Uganda regrets these developments but should in no way be held responsible for what has happened.
7. Meanwhile the following immediate measures have been undertaken by the Government of Uganda:
    (a) All possible entrances and exits of the Uganda-Rwanda border have been sealed by Uganda troops.;
    (b) There will be no assistance to the attackers from the Ugandan side;
    (c) The Uganda Government will not allow the refugees to retreat into Uganda;
    (d) Those who come back will be arrested, charged and tried in accordance with their status;
    (e) There will be regular meetings of the Heads of State of Uganda and Rwanda;
    (f) Intensified efforts will be undertaken by the two Presidents to resolve the issue of Rwandese refugees politically and peacefully through meetings between the two Presidents, and through Ministerial Committees.[4]

Museveni insisted that Uganda's involvement in the Rwanda crisis was to be seen only in terms of her tireless efforts to persuade the RPA and Rwandan government to resolve their disputes peacefully. He also reminded the international community of his efforts to organize and attend regional conferences to designed to deal with the Rwandan refugee problem (Essack, 41). Uganda's role in the Rwanda crisis was that of peace broker, not war monger.

These explanations nonetheless rest on shaky ground. For example, the public pronouncement that the government would punish returning NRA deserters was consistently contradicted:

> RPF officers who led and organized the conspiracy, including the former head of the NRA military intelligence and now top RPF commander Paul Kagame, travelled frequently and openly to Kampala to meet with foreign diplomats, reporters and RPF supporters within the NRA. These visits and meetings in Kampala took place throughout the three year war, as late as 1993. Rather than arrest the organizers of this alleged act of high treason, Ugandan authorities greeted them repeatedly...On several occasions throughout the war, journalists, diplomats and international military observers say that wholesale numbers of RPF troops operating in organized units have crossed back into Uganda, and have camped in border areas for months. Despite their claims that ex-NRA soldiers in the RPF would face charges "punishable by death," Ugandan authorities made no effort to arrest, deter, or otherwise control these RPF forces. (HRWAP, 21)[5]

Responses to the Invasion in Uganda

The Ugandan reactions to the Rwandan invasion were mixed, reflecting the nature of past and present relationships between the Rwandese and the Ugandans. The reactions can be usefully grouped into a number of related categories, the first of which comprised those who were very close to the Rwandese. This group maintained that the refugees had legitimate and conscionable reasons to return home with dignity. Accordingly, this group applauded the RPA's victory. There were, however, some in this group who did not want to see the refugees repatriated; partly because they continued to benefit from their close ties with the refugees. Another section embraced the repatriation because of expected economic benefits to be gained in Rwanda after the refugees' victory (author's interview of a prominent DP leader, London, April 1994).

The second category comprised those unfriendly to the refugees. They also applauded the invasion, seeing it as a humane way of getting rid of "the Rwandese refugees who had become a social and political scourge...[who] had infiltrated the entire political, social and economic fabric of the Ugandan community" (Essack, 5). This group demanded immediate repatriation of the Rwandese after the invasion, and for the immediate cessation of all diplomatic, economic, and military assistance to the RPF/RPA. This group comprised the majority of Ugandans, who saw repatriation as a viable response to the country's land, employment, economic, and political problems (*Africa Con*: 22 March 1991, 6).

The third category comprised those unfriendly to the refugees *and* the invasion. This group believed the invasion to be financed and largely supported by the Ugandan government. They felt that the war was not in Uganda's national interest; that it represented little other than an expansion of the "Tutsi confederacy" which would entrench the group's colonization and exploitation of Uganda.

The fourth group initially supported the invasion on the grounds that it would lead to repatriation of the refugees. However, they became hostile when some of the refugees were allegedly parachuted in to register and vote in the Assembly elections. The *Weekly Topic* reported on 26 November:

> Tension is mounting in many parts of the country where ethnic Banyarwanda have settled with more and more local authorities barring them from registering as voters in the forthcoming Constituent Assembly [elections]. The controversy which started in Kabale last week is spreading to Buganda districts of Masaka and Mpigi where either side is insisting on their position. At the same time a cross section of people...called for the suspension of the registration exercise until the issue of citizenship has been clarified.

The fifth category comprised those who hated the Rwandese because the invasion, RPA mobilization and armed confrontation caused the loss of their peoples' lives and property. Though found throughout the country, this group was concentrated in Kigezi, where armed engagement occurred. Some tried to get compensation from the government. The *Monitor* reported in its 28–30 June 1995 issue that "about 82 families, which lost relatives during the RPF war against the Rwandese government, have appealed to President Yoweri Kaguta Museveni for assistance" (7).

The final group feared that the growing anti-Rwandese sentiments stirred by the invasion, coupled with the strong Rwandese presence in the government, would have deleterious effects for them because they resembled the Tutsi. This group occupies the Kisoro District (Bufumbira). In an attempt to avoid persecution, they declared to the country that they are no longer Banyarwanda, but Bufumbira. A. Ruzinda, who is closely linked to this group, summarized their predicament:

> There is a general belief that every Munyrwanda is either an immigrant alien or an alien refugee. This has led to the violation of the rights of the Banyarwanda citizens to the extent that the people of Kisoro District would rather be called Bufumbira in order to escape the suspicion, persecution, hatred, ridicule and discrimination that quite often goes with being called a Munyarwanda. (*New Vision*: 14–18 Jan. 1994, 1–2)

Conclusion

A few observations can be highlighted. First the persistent persecution of the Tutsi in the Great Lakes region since 1959 paved the way for the formation of the RPA. Second, the RAP's emergence as a dominant military force was directly related to the military victory and tenure of the NRA in Uganda; indeed, most leaders of the RPA held similar positions in the NRA. Third, many factors influenced the invasion of Rwanda, including (though not exclusively): discrimination and alienation in the NRA; factionalism in the RPA; Museveni's political survival strategies; and the prevailing economic, political, and humanitarian climate in the post-Cold War regional and international arena. Fourth, there is considerable evidence that the mobilization for the invasion was public knowledge in Uganda. This in turn suggests that President Museveni's regime was almost certainly aware of it as well. The existing evidence also indicates that the regime trained, provided sanctuary, arms, logistical support, political, and diplomatic assistance to the RPA throughout the period of military engagement in Rwanda.

The invasion intensified anti-Rwandese sentiments in Uganda to their boiling point. It was thus not surprising that the inhabitants of the Kisoro district consciously changed their ethnic identification to avoid association with the Rwandese. The legitimacy crisis the invasion caused for the Museveni regime strongly suggests that Rwandan refugees will likely face persecution in Uganda when the President loses power. Finally, any regime in Uganda that is hostile to the Rwandese will likely shorten the life span of the RPA/RPF in Rwanda.

Notes

1. In the same interview, Dr. Bayingana claimed that our people "increasingly saw the need to master military science if we were ever to overthrow the Rwanda dictatorship. Accordingly, when the NRA launched an armed struggle, for us we also saw the opportunity for individual training and actually participating in order to get experience without raising the eyebrows of both the NRA leadership and Rwanda government" (Essack 1993, 19).
2. After Rwigyema's death, Major Paul Kagame, who was in the USA on a joint Uganda-American military training program, returned to Uganda and proceeded to northern Rwanda to assume the leadership of the RPA. Since Kagame had been actively involved in the power struggle, his assumption of leadership did not eliminate hostility between the camps. Indeed, the Banyigana camp and other dissenters were effectively, and at times brutally, silenced (see Human Rights Watch Arms Project 1994, 9).
3. In September 1996, at the Kigali conference where the internationally sponsored Adelman/Suhrke report was discussed, many government representatives

(including the Ugandan ambassador) vociferously denied that Uganda knew of the invasion. As proof, a Rwandese RPF official testified that he had personally phoned to tell Museveni of the invasion at 11:00 P.M. This report is conspicuous for several reasons. First, why would an RPF official phone Museveni in New York to tell him of the invasion? How would he know where to find Museveni? Second, he testified to calling at 11:00 P.M.; if this is Ugandan time, it is over twelve hours before the 5:00 A.M. time when Museveni claimed to learn of the invasion. Why would Museveni wait so long before informing Habyarimana? Third, the officer claimed he told Museveni about the *invasion*, while Museveni maintained that he was aware only of the desertions. Finally, the statement directly contradicts Museveni's claim that he learned the news from General Muntu.

4. See briefing given by the Minister of State for Foreign and Regional Affairs, Hon. David Omara-Atubo to Diplomatic Representatives Resident in Kampala on 4 October 1990, 1.

5. See also *New Vision,* 10 October 1994: 28. The paper reported that one of the so-called deserters, the Vice President and Minister of Defence, Paul Kagame, was Museveni's guest during Uganda's 32nd independence celebration (cf. *Sunday Vision,* Vol. III, 1, 8 Jan. 1995). The paper illustrated that it has been "established that Rwandese Vice-President Maj. Gen. Paul Kagame and top officials of the RPF, who left Uganda to attack their country in October 1990, are still holding Ugandan passports. The passport control officer, Mr. O.B. Muchandara, teasingly told the journalists that 'these people have not yet returned our guns, so how do you expect them to surrender the passports? I even don't know which passport General Kagame used when he visited Uganda last October.... [A]sk customs agents at the border.... We don't know who has gone back, who is a Munyarwanda because these people applied for passports as citizens of Uganda.'"

3

The Role of Zaire in the Rwandese Conflict

Shally B. Gachuruzi

Introduction: Zaire and the Great Lakes Region

The strong influence of Zaire in the Great Lakes Region (Uganda, Rwanda, Burundi, and Zaire) has always been a feature of the political landscape of the region. These four countries share geographical boundaries, culture, and three of them share a colonial history. Until 1960, Rwanda, Burundi, and Zaire were all under the same colonial administration. Zaire, by far the largest, in fact, the second in size in Africa, and the richest of the four in natural resources and people, became independent before Rwanda and Burundi, two of the smallest but most densely populated countries in Africa. With the independence of Zaire in 1960, Rwandese and Burundians who were in Zaïre became Zaireans. For five years, until 1965, Zaire adopted and preached a policy of noninterference in the internal affairs of Rwanda and Burundi, but that did not last.

When President Mobutu came to power in November 1965, Zaire's position of noninterference in the internal affairs of other countries changed. Mobutu supported the opposition to the Rwandese government and trained the opposition top cadres, such as Bisengimana Rwema, his former cabinet director. By contrast, he maintained a cordial relationship with the first President of Burundi, Michel Micombero, who was his personal friend. When Juvénal Habyarimana took power in Rwanda (1973), President Mobutu supported the new Rwandese regime, but then opposed President Bagaza, who overthrew his cousin, President Michel Micombero of Burundi, in a 1976 coup.

This chapter depicts the role played by the Zairean government in the Rwandese crisis, but only after providing the demographic, political, and economic background on the Banyarwanda[1] in Zaire, which includes both Hutu and Tutsi. The first section examines the demography of the region of Zaire occupied by the Banyarwanda, their native-born cousins and other ethnic groups. The paper then describes the political culture of the Banyarwanda and their economic (and political) role within Zaire. Only then does the chapter return to the relationship between Zaire and Rwanda until the RPF invasion of Rwanda.

The Demography of the Kivu Region

The Kivu region, located on the Eastern side of Zaire, shares borders with Rwanda, Burundi, Uganda, and Tanzania.[2] It is the most over-populated region in Zaire with 8 million people, representing one-fifth of the Zairean population, almost the equivalent of the Rwandese population prior to the genocide of 1994.

In addition to Hutu and Tutsi and their ethnic cousins, the North and South Kivu regions, where the majority of both the old Rwandese refugees (1959–1962) and the 1994 more recent mass migration of refugees were sheltered, are occupied by the following ethnic groups: Nandé, Hundé, Nyanga, Hauw, Shi, Rega, Fuleru, Vira, and Bembe. The Hutu and Tutsi constitute almost 40 percent of the population of the province. The Hutu are the second largest ethnic group in this region and are mostly farmers. The Tutsi, a minority, are usually cattle herders.

The history of the Banyarwandese migration to Zaire dates back to the sixteenth century. The King of Rwanda attempted to extend his power base in the Kivu region, which was already inhabited by indigenous Banyarwanda called Banyabwisha. Having conquered the region, he planted Bivumu "power trees" and put his representatives in Busanza, Jomba, Rugari, Gisigari, Kamuronsi, and Gishari. The Rwandese Kingdom thus extended further than the present border in North Kivu. However, the current boundaries became fixed after the First World War in 1926, and the Rwandese Kings lost the region previously conquered in Zaïre.

The Belgian colonists favored the Rwandan occupation of Masisi in North Kivu, arguing that Rwanda was overpopulated and therefore that the Rwandese needed the extra territory. The criterion of overpopulation was determined by the size of cattle herds rather than the number of people living in a particular area. Hutu and Tutsi, totaling about 6,000 families by 1944,[3] were sent to Masisi, not only to cultivate the fertile lands, but also as labor to replace the indigenous population whose lands were expropriated by the colonialists. As a result, the indigenous population not only refused to work for the colonialists, but, with the exception of their historical cousins, the Banyabwisha, resented the migration of Banyarwanda, leaving a legacy of suspicion between the Banyarwanda and the Nandé, Hundé, and Nyanga.

Additional migratory waves into Zaire followed, first in 1959, during the Rwandese revolution, and again in 1962, at the time of Rwandese independence. This last wave comprised more than 50,000 Tutsi refugees who located mainly in Nyamitaba, Goma, Bibwe, Ihura, and Bugabo. Braeckman (1994, 318) wrote,

> ...at the time of independence the influx of refugees added, along with past migrations and the Rwandan revolution in 1959–1960, more than 50,000 mostly Tutsi refugees, that crossed the Zairan frontier.

The Political Situation of the Banyarwanda

During the first republic of Zaire (1960–1965), the political situation of Zaireans of Rwandese extraction was stable. Their representation in the provincial government was significant: they served as ministers and members of the provincial parliament. However, at the local level, especially in the Masisi district where they constituted a majority (+85 percent), the Banyarwanda lacked representation.

Then, in 1964, in elections ostensibly held in order to provide representational equity in all the important positions at the local level, the Banyarwanda won in Masisi. The provincial governor, however, canceled these elections because he was antagonistic toward the Banyarwanda. As a result, the "Kanyarwanda," a war between Banyarwanda and Bahundé, broke out in Masisi in 1964 and lasted until 1965. The Governor sent a military force to quell the rebellion, and many Banyarwanda were killed.

Since that time, the relationship between the Banyarwanda and the indigenous population, with the exception of the Banyabwisha, has been characterized by tension ready to explode into a civil war. The hostility against the Banyarwanda, and against the Tutsi in particular, remained very strong. The Banyarwanda were accused of usurping power in Zaïre, and of profiting from the country's wealth to a greater degree than the indigenous population. According to Braeckman,

> their relative economic success, dynamism, and sheer numbers weakened the local populations—the Hundés, Nyangas, Nandés—who felt inferior on their own soil. During the national conference, quite a few grievances were aired by the

natives, who reproached individuals of questionable nationality (who straddled the fence and presented themselves as Zairans while all the while supporting the FPR on the Tutsi issue) and accused them of taking over their best lands. The Tutsis of Goma withdrew and were blamed for sending their children to rejoin the Front while the Hutus showed themselves to be more sensitive to the major ethnic propaganda campaign coming from Kigali. (Braeckman, 1994: 319)

During the fifteen years of the second republic (1965–1980), the political situation in Zaire in general, and in Kivu in particular, remained calm. Bisengimana Rwema, the Director of the Zairean Presidential cabinet from 1970 to 1980, played an important role in this respect, taking care of the interests of Tutsi. Even though Banyarwanda occupied important posts at the administrative level, they did not hold senior political positions. However, during the elections which followed this period of relative tranquillity, Hundé candidates, who later became members of parliament, indulged in irregularities and were accused of rigging the elections. Consequently, the postelection period was characterized by waves of protests, all of which were quickly but violently quelled.

The antagonistic relationship between the Banyarwanda and other ethnic groups reached a breaking point when, in 1981, Zaireans of Rwandese extraction lost their Zairean citizenship by the cancellation of the law of 5 January 1972, which had recognized Zairean citizenship for most Banyarwanda. That law had stated that

"Zairan, are all persons one of whose ancestors is or was a member of one of the tribes established in the territory of the Republic of Zaire by the very latest 15 November 1908 and as they are modified by later agreements." Article 15 states that "natives of Rwanda-Urundi who had settled in the province of Kivu prior to the 1st of January 1960 and who continued to reside since that time in the Republic of Zaire until the time this law takes effect, obtained Zairan nationality on 30 June 1960."

However, on 29 June, 1981, the Zairean parliament passed a law explicitly canceling the citizenship rights for the Banyarwanda in Kivu, except for the native Banyabwisha. Since then, the Banyarwanda have not been allowed to vote. Even for the period when they could vote, they were ineligible to run for political office.

More recent events have both exacerbated, and been the outcome of, ethnic tensions that have been ongoing since 1964. For example, in 1993, in the Walikale and Masisi zones, North Kivu, in the Eastern part of Zaire, Nyanga-Hundé launched a surprise attack against the Banyarwanda. After one day of killings, the Banyarwanda stopped the attack and quickly inflicted a defeat on the aggressors, but not without a large number of deaths (as many as 7,000, according to Braeckman 1994) and the creation of many refugees.

Even though many observers claim that the major cause of this ethnic conflict arose from the Banyarwanda's disregard of the traditional authority in trying to put in place their own structures, the real reasons were that, on the one hand, the indigenous people were jealous of the Banyarwanda success in business, and, on the other hand, ethnic conflict and violence was stimulated and used by the Zairean regime to deflect criticism and legitimize its political power. Even though the Zairean government, in dismissing Kalumbo and Bamwisho, the governor and vice-governor, respectively, of the North Kivu region during this period, tried to disassociate itself from the ethnic conflict and violence, the government did nothing to punish the vice-governor, Bamwisho (Nyanga), who was the principal instigator of the attack against the Banyarwanda. After Bisengimana Rwema retired from office, Tutsi in the 1980s and 1990s no longer occupied major political positions in Zaire and, what is worse, lacked a powerful protector.

Even though the Banyarwanda won the military battle, at great cost, they lost the subsequent political war. The battle ended with the violent repression of Banyarwanda, the same result as the war of Kanyarwanda discussed earlier. While the President of Zaire may have forsaken assisting the Tutsi to recover power in Rwanda, the Tutsi in Zaire never forgot the project, hoping that one day they would return home. These events reinforced that desire. The loss of Zairean citizenship, political power, rights, and the protection of the state kept reinforcing the motivation of the Tutsi to recover their Rwandese citizenship even though they wielded economic power in Zaire.

The Economic Power of Zairean Banyarwanda and the Rwandese Crisis

As already stated, many Banyarwanda, particularly the Tutsi, were financially successful in business in Zaire.[4] All Zairo-Rwandese entrepreneurs were—and continue to be—engaged in different areas of business in addition to being cattle breeders. This conforms with Rwandese tradition: ownership of large herds of cattle and sheep and the employment of hired workers, servants and courtiers are long-standing symbols of prestige and social status.

Even though they themselves could not hold political office, the economic power of these entrepreneurs implicitly conferred upon them a degree of political power. They had a network of powerful colleagues, and were called upon for consultations with those who held political office. Consequently, to some degree, they were able to influence political decisions, particularly in economic matters. Links to political power are very helpful in succeeding in business in Zaire. Political support can either allow entrepreneurs to advance, or be a cause of their failure. Some even argued that political connections were the *sine qua non* without which one could not achieve economic success. For Bayart (1989), the relationship with the government allowed individuals to become rich and to acquire social status at the local, regional, and national levels. There certainly tended to be a direct correlation between wealth and political power.

The Tutsi, like other Zairean businessmen, understood the dynamics of the system. They fostered relationships with Zairean politicians and acquired access to government privileges. Indeed, during the second republic (since 1965), the symbiotic relationship between the government and the business community grew. This was possible due to a covert network among government agents and businessmen.[5]

However, it would be a mistake to think that entrepreneurs cannot achieve success without government connections. McGaffey's research (1987) on Nandé traders who succeeded in business without government connections supported this conclusion. But once wealth had been acquired, successful businessmen were "integrated" into the "circles of power."

Even though Braeckman (1994) argued that the Rwandan Patriotic Front (RPF) was supported financially by the Rwandese diaspora in Canada and the United States, there is evidence that most of the support came from the Tutsi of Zaire. Further, the Tutsi in Zaire provided recruits. For example, in 1990, Zairo-Rwandese recruited and trained new Rwanda Patriotic Front (RPF) soldiers in Bibwe,[6] North Kivu, Zaire. In 1993, a ship with a load of weapons, owned by a Zairo-Rwandese and destined for the Rwanda Patriotic Front (RPF) soldiers, was apprehended by Zairean security forces; it was later released without explanation.

Concerning financial support by Tutsi in Zaire, Reyntjens (1994:148) wrote that

> during the first two years of the war, the refugee communities contributed nearly $2 million and some wealthy sympathizers made considerable individual efforts.

All these examples provide evidence of the involvement of Zairean Tutsi in the Rwandese crisis. However, there was one important difference between the situation among the Banyarwanda in Zaire and those in Rwanda at this time. In contrast to the atmosphere of hostility between Rwandese Hutu and Tutsi, the Hutu and the Tutsi of Zaire, prior to the genocide and the flight of Hutu refugees into Zaire, had been very united. During the 1964 "Kanyarwanda" war between the Banyarwanda of Zaire and the Bahundé, as well as during the 1993 crisis when the Nyanga and Hundé attacked them, Hutu and Tutsi of Zaire acted together in fighting the indigenous population. Amongst the Zairean Banyarwanda could be found an intense spirit of cooperation. For example, traders did not ask for a written statement as testimony of debt; rather they relied on trust. If an abuse of trust occurred, the abuser was not sent to court. The person would be judged by a family council which was constituted of both Hutu and Tutsi. Also, interethnic marriages flourished between the two groups, and traditional ceremonies, such as births, funerals, ancestor reverences, and other communal events, brought Hutu and Tutsi together. There was ample evidence that the Banyarwanda in Zaire got along well and enjoyed a very positive relationship quite separately from their need for a united front when they faced a hostile indigenous population.

Rwandese-Zairean Relations

However, the economic power, which translated itself into a degree of political power, and the friendship with the local Hutu were all for naught when the Rwandese Hutu refugees, led by the well-armed ex-FAR and interahamwe, arrived in 1994 following the genocide in Rwanda. The Tutsi in Zaire themselves became targets of violence, attacks and ethnic cleansing. The Hutu refugees seemed to have the tacit and probably overt support of the government. Even though communal solidarity had become part of everyday existence, and reflected a consolidation of the socioeconomic structure, ethnic cohesion could not survive the presence and actions of well-armed extremist Hutu.

The relations between the Hutu extremists from Rwanda and the government of Zaire had a history, for there was a cooperation accord between Rwanda and Zaire. Claiming to be the guarantor of peace in the region, in 1979, the Zairean President initiated the creation of the "*Communauté Economique des Pays des Grands Lacs*" (CPGL), which included Burundi, Rwanda, and Zaire. This organization (CPGL), the creation of which was ratified in 1985 by the three member countries, was more a political or symbolic arrangement than an economic one. It purported to prevent military confrontations between member countries, and stood for noninterference in the internal affairs of each of the members by any other member.

In 1985, Zaire and Rwanda concluded an additional accord which provided for common security services, the sharing of security information, military cooperation and interdiction of opposition movements on each other's territory. This accord was used to justify the arrest of Zaireans in Rwanda. It also explained why the authorities of the former Rwandese government could find refuge in Zaire after the genocide in Rwanda.

According to some interpreters, the cooperation went even deeper; even though Habyarimana seemed to be in control of the political situation in Rwanda during his term in office, important decisions were actually being made after consulting "big brother," President Mobutu.

> Didn't the latter always support and counsel, didn't he also act as "mediator," even if he had generally suggested to his neighbor that he present a strong face for the FPR, and not allow Westerners to strong-arm him? (Braeckman, 1994: 172)

When, in 1990, the Rwanda Patriotic Front (RPF) attacked Rwanda, in keeping with the military cooperation between Rwanda and Zaire, the Zairean government sent elite troops to quell the rebellion. The Zairean army fought beside French[7] and Rwandese soldiers; together they initially stopped the Rwanda Patriotic Front (RPF). The Zairean army was not paid by either the Zairean government or the Rwandese government for their involvement in the battle against the Rwanda Patriotic Front (RPF). Zairean soldiers engaged in systematic pillage and the rape of women and teenagers. Given their propensity for destruction, at the request of Habyarimana, Zairean troops were sent home after the RPF incursion had been halted. They left Rwanda with trucks laden with looted goods such as televisions and other electronic and electrical appliances (Braeckman 1994, 72).

Paradoxically, while Zairean troops were fighting in Rwanda, new Rwanda Patriotic Front (RPF) recruits were being trained in Bibwe/North Kivu. Members of the Zairean parliament denounced Zairean involvement in the war, arguing also against the President's tacit approval of military training on Zairean territory. What seemed initially to be a defeat suffered by the RPF largely at the hands of the Zairean troops, was actually the beginning of the end, not only of the government in Rwanda, but of the Mobutu regime itself. The victory of the Zairean army over the Rwandese rebels in Rwanda in 1990 would be the last battle they would win, in fact, the last battle in which they acted as an effective fighting force.

Notes

1. The term *Banyarwanda* refers to Zairean Hutu and Tutsi who were in Zaire until 30 June, 1960. It also includes Rwandese Tutsi and Burundian Hutu refugees sheltered in Zaïre. This term does not include the Banyabwisha who are Zairean natives. The Banyarwanda in Africa in 1994 before the genocide were distributed as follows: Burundi—5,831,000; Rwanda—7,903,00; Uganda—1,200,000; Zaire—4,000,000 for a total Banyarwanda population of 18,934,000 (Cf. *Universal World Atlas*, Maplewood, New Jersey, 1994).

2. In 1990, the region was split into three distinct provinces: North Kivu, South Kivu, and Maniema.

3. The numbers that came grew from 354 families in 1937 to 629 in 1938, 1,453 in 1940, 1,931 in 1941, 2,169 in 1942, 3,718 in 1943, 6,050 in 1944, and 6,173 in 1945 (Jewsiewicki 1984, 47).

4. For example, the Bisengimana family during the Mobutu regime came to own more than half of Idjwi island on Lake Kivu. They engaged in cattle ranching and also control led the Zairean computer market. The millionaire, Maro, controlled the telephone market. Haga bred cattle and owned a large share of Zaïre's hotel business, including one of the most prestigious hotels in Zaire. As well, Haga also controlled the Zairean automobile market. Kaku, the leader of the stock breeders organization in Kivu, owned almost half the cattle stock in Masisi. Zayo, also a stock breeder, was in both the hotel and the coffee business.

5. Alain and Edgar Hazoumé (1988, 41) wrote:

   The average consumer, totally marginalized, is in no way encouraged to participate in national economic development. It is not so much his weaker income that causes him to undertake nothing , but the paralyzing impression that all the economic cogs are selfishly appropriated. This is why Africans think that they cannot make their fortune without being directly or indirectly served by political power. They are not altogether wrong, because it is difficult to see, since independence, the fortunes that have been able to accumulate independently of political instances. It seems, on the contrary, that the best springboard for starting a business…is a symbiosis with political authority.

6. Bibwe is situated in the Masisi zone, North Kivu, where the majority of the population consists of Rwandan refugees from the 1959–1962 period.

7. See Callamard's chapter and Prunier (1995), who would interpret this description of the French role as an overstatement [eds.].

4

The Development and Consolidation of Extremist Forces in Rwanda 1990-1994

Joan Kakwenzire and Dixon Kamukama[1]

Political Party Formation

On the eve of the invasion by the RPA/F, Rwanda appeared quiet; the opposition in the country seemed to have become resigned to being forever ruled by the Habyarimana party—the MRND—practically the only political party in the country. The single party system was a product of the history of multypartyism prior to independence and the process of achieving that independence.

The history of political parties in Rwanda exemplifies ethnic cleavage primarily rather than nationalism or ideology. Parties, prior to independence and after, were formed along "ethnic" lines first and then ideology or personalities. The independence struggles in Rwanda were at first marked by the formation of movements aimed at the abolition of "class" privileges and preferential access to jobs, as well as creating opportunities for education for all and ultimately inaugurating genuine independence (Amaza, 1995). Grégoire Kayibanda created MSM, the *Mouvement Social Mahutu*. The Tutsi had concentrated their major political efforts on the royalist party, the National Rwandese Union (UNAR—*Union Nationale Rwandaise*), a pro-Monarchist anti-Belgian political party which emerged in 1959 largely supported by Tutsi to push for independence.

However, the Belgians misrepresented these struggles to mean that Tutsi organizations sought to dominate the Hutu majority even though some of these organizations crisscrossed Hutu-Tutsi cleavages. By 1959, the Belgians had completely fallen out with the Tutsi. To counter the assertiveness of the UNAR, in 1959 the Belgians persuaded Grégoire Kayibanda, who would become the first President of independent Rwanda, to convert his Hutu movement, MSM, into the *Parti du Mouvement de L'Emancipation de Bahutu* (PARMEHUTU). PARMEHUTU, as its name suggests, was a party which aimed at emancipating the Hutu from the alleged perpetual feudal oppression of the Tutsi. With the formation of the PARMEHUTU, the independence struggle in Rwanda took a new turn and became a Tutsi-Hutu struggle. Other political parties formed during that period also had an ethnic inclination even though two parties tried to rise above ethnicity. APROSOMA (*Association pour la Promotion Sociale de la Masse*— Association for the Social Promotion of the Masses), a primarily Hutu political party, was started in the November 1957 by Joseph Gitera. RADER (*la Rassemblement Démocratique Rwandais*, the Rwandese Democratic Union) was formed in October of 1959 by Chief Bwanakweri, supported by moderate Tutsi and backed by Belgium to counter the royalist Tutsi *independentist* UNAR. With political growth concentrated in ethnic-based political associations, the ground was prepared for subsequent ethnic extremism.

What exacerbated extremism was the hand lent to the Hutu by the Belgians to ensure Hutu domination of the Tutsi (Amaza 1995; Africa Rights 1994). After the mysterious and abrupt death of King Mutara Rudahigwa III of Rwanda in Burundi in July 1959, the Belgians spearheaded the abrupt and violent end of Tutsi rule in Rwanda. In the infamous revolution of 1959 which began on 1 November 1959, thousands were massacred, thousands more fled the country, and over 20,000 were displaced internally (Watson 1991, 4). Watson (as well as others— Kamukama 1993) recognized that ethnic conflict was aggravated by the Belgian intervention in Rwanda politics and the subsequent crackdown on Tutsi. By 1960 Belgian favoritism against the Tutsi was full blown. Watson provides as an example the arrests in November 1959. After some order had been established following the initial fighting, 919 Tutsi as compared to only 312 Hutu were arrested and charged with causing public disorder.

The ethnic vendetta continued after independence, this time with exiled Tutsi, mostly nonmonarchist, causing most of the disturbances. The leftist Tutsi had formed a clandestine guerillalike organization, the *Inyenzi* (cockroaches), which sought to force the government to permit the Tutsi return to Rwanda. Though eventually effectively destroyed by 1964, between 1961 and 1966, largely from bases in Burundi, *Inyenzi* launched ten fierce attacks against the PARMEHUTU regime (Watson 1991). In the December 1963 surprise attack, when the invaders from Burundi got almost as far as Kigali, they were not only beaten back, but a pogrom against Tutsi led to the execution of Prosper Bwanakweri (leader of RADER), the slaughter of 10,000, and the flight of tens of thousands of additional Tutsi into exile. Thus, ethnicization of the internal Rwandese political struggles led to a war waged literally by "outsiders" against the "insiders" which then further reverberated on the insiders in turn. The internal tension, with its external counterpart in violent conflict, and its reflection in turn in internal repression, would be repeated with much greater devastation decades later.

Amaza (1995) noted that the "ethnicization" also opened avenues for further imperialist repenetration into Rwandan affairs. Since the Rwandese—in their struggle for independence—failed to rise against the Belgians on a united front, they allowed colonialists to step in as arbitrators in post-colonial Rwandan problems. The neocolonialists were able to exploit this situation. The annihilation policy of the Kayibanda regime against the Tutsi political elites and the opposition political parties aggravated the situation. Parties, like the UNAR, APROSOMA, and RADER, were banned, resulting in a one-party dictatorship, even though the results of the communal elections in June and July of 1960 overwhelmingly favored PARMEHUTU which won 2,390 of the 3,125 positions, the remaining positions divided almost equally among APROSOMA, RADER, and independent candidates, with UNAR humiliated with only fifty-six positions. From the new *bourgmestres* who had replaced the traditional chiefs as head of the communes in the 1960 elections, 160 in 229 communes were PARMEHUTU. A huge majority was not sufficient; a monopoly was demanded. But this move was not made immediately.

On 28 January 1961, Kayibanda organized the meeting of bourgmestres and municipal councilors in Gitarama to declare a sovereign Democratic Republic of Rwanda, though independence would not be formally granted until 1 July 1962. A national legislature had to be created. In the 25 September 1991 elections, PARMEHUTU won almost 80 percent of the seats, virtually monopolizing Hutu representation since most of the opposition seats went to UNAR which now became the main representatives of the Tutsi internally, thereby fixing the Tutsi-Hutu divide as well as forming the ground for a one party monopoly. As the U.N. Trusteeship Commission Report of March 1961 had described the situation, a racial dictatorship of one party had been created.

The subsequent annihilation of the opposition Hutu as well as Tutsi parties meant that the single-party dictatorship had to devour its own insiders—the Hutu. Kayibanda surrounded himself with Hutu supporters mainly from his home base in Gitarama as well as the Butare (Astrida) area. This alienated him from the northern Hutu who felt that they had been isolated from the system. The political stance shifted from an "ethnic" to a regional basis for the concentration of power and the distribution of oppression. In response to his political isolation and using the massacres of Hutu by the Tutsi leaders in Burundi in the spring of 1972 as either a catalyst or an excuse, Kayibanda began persecuting the Tutsi anew, rigidly enforcing the 9 percent quota for Tutsi in higher education, government, or even private employment. The result of this witch hunt backfired when the "people's" committees began to attack the authorities as well as the Tutsi.

To restore peace, Major General Juvénal Habyarimana, a former Minister of Defense and Head of the National Guard, staged a bloodless coup on 5 July 1973 in which the northern Hutu conspired and toppled the Kayibanda establishment (Amaza 1995, 8). The coup in itself helps to demystify the long standing perception of the Rwanda crisis as a result of "age-old hatred of the Hutu for Tutsi," since the 1973 coup exhibited a house divided against itself (Hutu against Hutu).

Habyarimana did not help the situation. He simply perpetuated and consolidated the interethnic and intraethnic divide/divisions in Rwanda. For instance, like Kayibanda, he established a single party dictatorship under MRND, a party he helped to found in 1975. The single party stuck with its extremist policy of *equilibre ethnique et régional* (ethnic and regional equilibrium) which was used as a basis for the distribution of resources and opportunities. Though Habyarimana ended the coercive persecution of the Tutsi, the policy continued to operate on a quota system (ratio) according to the population size of each "tribe" The MRND also possessed a very strong intelligence system which it used to further the interests of the Habyarimana regime.

That intelligence system was very useful in aborting the attempted April 1980 coup of Colonel Théoneste Lizinde, a Hutu and Security Chief from the northern district of Bugoyi, the rival to Habyarimana's home base in Gisenyi. Lizinde had been used by Habyarimana to kill dozens associated with the former Kayibanda regime. Arrested with others and jailed for over a decade, Lizinde was freed in 1991 by the RPF in the offensive and capture of Ruhengeri. He was then recruited to join the RPF.

By the end of his rule, Habyarimana's regional and later family politics, led to his almost total reliance on "kinsmen" from the northern region to perpetuate himself in power. The nucleus of his support was mainly his home area of Gisenyi. Determined to maintain their power, they are believed to have eliminated rival allies, such as Colonel Stanislas Mayuya in 1988, and critical opponents such as the journalist, Father Silvio Sindambiwe, and a member of the opposition in Parliament from Butare, Félecula Nyiramutarambira. This explains why the first victims of Hutu extremist genocide in 1994 were mostly Hutu from Central and Southern Rwanda regions (see Africa Rights, 1994).

By the time of the RPF invasion of Rwanda, the Central Command in the country had been shaken. The Habyarimana regime, which had entrenched itself politically through its party, the MRND, found out that it was not only being challenged by the military invasion of the RPA, but also by opposition from the newly formed political parties, journalists, the international community, and other organizations of groups or individuals. Something had to be done to save the regime. In the attempt to fortify their hitherto unchallenged social, political, and economic position, the seeds of extremism developed in the colonial period in the ethnicization of politics were now being sown in the narrow regional clanism that saw all outsiders as threats to their monopoly on power.

However, on the surface, events seemed more promising. While at face value, the situation in Rwanda on the eve of the invasion appears to have been quite normal (the Rwanda National Bank at the time provided figures that showed that inflation was running at a negligible 1.7 percent), underneath flowed two currents, one a political/military threat from outside, and the other an economic/political one from within.

The 1986 National Resistance Movement (NRM) takeover in Uganda was to have important political implications for Rwanda. Most of the young men and women who had participated in the Uganda guerilla war were Banyarwanda refugees living in Uganda. Some of them acquired very high ranks and positions in both the government and the army. This was one of the first "shock wave" messages to the rigid regime of Habyarimana. For the first time, he saw in these young soldiers in Uganda a possible formidable opposition force against him. This probably explains why on 27 July 1987, the Central Committee of the MRND issued a declaration announcing that it would not allow the immigration of large numbers of Rwandan refugees, offering the excuse that the country's economy was incapable of sustaining increased numbers. The announcement was made at this time because the Habyarimana regime feared that Rwanda's refugees would want to return home no matter the means and that the Rwanda refugee group in Uganda would be the first group that would want to return. Habyarimana's visit to Uganda in February 1988 to discuss the problem of refugees brought him much closer to one of the real problems his regime was facing.

Secondly, political tension was slowly mounting within the country as well. The economic crisis facing the country, to which the President personally admitted on 16 June 1987 by appointing a management committee for the crisis, added to the pressure on the regime. Coffee prices, the main export crop which financed the government, collapsed in 1986. The World Bank and IMF were forcing a SAP, a structural adjustment program, on Rwanda, severely cutting the dole available to his supporters. The pressure to maintain the monopoly on power thus increased.

At the same time, a few incidents in the early 1990s demonstrated the increasing political tension as well as the increasing boldness of the opposition. There were signed petitions by intellectuals in August of 1990 demanding moves towards democratization. On 7 September 1990, when Pope Paul visited Rwanda, the President declared what could be seen as graded amnesty for convicted prisoners in the country, graded, because all but the political prisoners were pardoned. Habyarimana could not bear the thought of his political opponents being out of prison.

One year later, the situation had changed dramatically internally as well as externally. The RPF had invaded on 1 October 1990 which had spurred the opposition significantly. Though the invasion was initially followed by a wave of arrests and murders, the opposition in fact became emboldened. The initial reaction of the government was to use force to counter any move against it. However, pressure from the international community demanded that the Rwanda government open up the democratic process in the country. So while the government forces faced external politico-military pressure from the RPA and the international community, internal pressure, especially from the multipartyists, increased.

By early 1991, the Habyarimana government realized the futility of using force in sorting out the political mess in the country. This partly explains why the government accepted the process of peace talks and the many cease fires with the RPF. On the home front, the government adopted a positive policy towards the opposition. In the first week of March, for example, the government announced the release of 1,500 prisoners who had been accused of being supporters and sympathizers with the RPF. Those that had been sentenced to death would not be executed. On 14 March, President Habyarimana announced the establishment of amnesty centers at Kinigi, Cyanika, Rwempasha, and Kaniga. RPA fighters were given fifteen days to report to these respective locations.

Though earlier on the President had promised political reforms in the country as a verbal gesture, on 10 April 1991, a commission, that had been put in place to prepare a political reform program, actually recommended that the President institute reforms: modify the 1978 constitution, abolish the single-party system, and create the post of Prime Minister. These were presented by the President to his cabinet on 21 April. On 28 April President Habyarimana presented the same political reform recommendations to his MRND extraordinary congress. At this meeting, the party changed its name to the *Mouvement Républicain National pour la Democratie et le Développement* (MRNDD) from the *Mouvement Révolutionnaire National pour le Développement* (MRND), a symbolically important change.

At the same time, political parties were reconstituted or founded openly: UPR, the *Union du Peuple Rwandais*, the Rwandan People's Union, a political party established in Brussels on 9 November 1990 by Silas Mayjambere; MDR, the *Mouvement Démocratique Républicain*, the Democratic Republican Movement, founded in March 1991 as the successor to the first President, Grégoire Kayibanda's MDR-PARMAHUTU, which became the main opposition party; PSD, the *Parti Social Démocrate*, the Social Democratic Party, in April/May which became the second largest opposition party; PL the *Parti Libéral*, the Liberal Party, that same spring led by Justin Mugenzi, the third largest opposition party with many Tutsi and business-minded members; and PDC, *Parti Démocrate Chrétien*, the Christian Democratic Party, the smallest of the four opposition parties to the Habyarimana regime, also founded in 1991 and led by Nayinzira Nepomuscen.

The arrest of three editors were, however, the most telling. The editor of *Ijambo*, founded in 1990, François Xavier, was detained in May and charged with slandering military officers and demoralizing the army. On 3 July 1991, Vincent Rwabukwisi, an editor of the newly founded bimonthly newspaper (*Kanguka*), was arrested on charges of subversion and endangering state security for allegedly working in collusion with Rwandan refugees living abroad; the government asked that he be given a sentence of twenty years in prison. Three days later, another editor, Hassan Ngeze of *Kangura*, a rabid pro-Hutu paper, was also arrested on charges of subversion and endangering state security for threatening relations with Burundi when he wrote in one of his columns that 70 percent of Rwanda's wealth was in the hands of the minority Tutsi. While Ngeze's arrest could be interpreted as a strong point favoring the Habyarimana regime—indicating fairness in suppressing both Tutsi and Hutu opposition and a regime that could not reject the will of the people of Rwanda—the arrest indicated both an intimidation and a public relations exercise.[2] All three editors were let out in September without even being tried.

Habyarimana's March 1990 promise of a move towards multipartyism and democracy to mollify the French appeared—but only appeared— to be in the process of realization. To understand why it was not fulfilled, we have to return to the political/military threat from outside.

The Extremist Response to Internal Reforms and the Invasion by the RPF

The invasion by the RPF on 1 October 1990 did not make the tense political atmosphere any lighter; the president/government now had to contain both internal and external pressures. While the seemingly positive attitude to political reform was taking place, not everyone in the country was happy about these changes. Probably even those announcing them might not have been committed to them. People, especially those from the North, and including MRNDD sycophants who had for long benefitted from the monolithic regime of Habyarimana, were not happy to see "bread falling from their hands." The army too, was divided, and this resulted in mutiny on 1 May 1991. At the same time, the beneficiaries of the regime started making maneuvers on how to continue the system even in the face of new political reforms.

On the surface, however, the reforms seemed in the process of institutionalization. On 7 May, the National Assembly discussed the new political reform recommendations and resolved to develop a new law on political parties and to write a new constitution reflective of a multiparty system. The President was reported to have warned against formation of parties based on ethnicity, as had been the case in the past, but eventually the Assembly determined to allow the formation of sectarian parties provided they had an open membership.

President Habyarimana on 10 June 1991, after many consultations and with mounting pressure from different sides, signed a new constitution legalizing multiple political parties, putting in place the post of a Prime Minister as head of government business and reducing the powers of the President. At the same time he signed a law that set out rules by which parties would function. A new chapter appeared to have been opened in the political history of Rwanda. The practice would show whether this indeed was a new chapter.

By August 1991, about twelve new political parties were operating in the country, not only the MDR, the PSD, the PL, the PDC, and the MRNDD, but also seven smaller parties instigated by Habyarimana as possibly a deliberate attempt to make a sham of multipartyism. The most notorious of these small parties was yet to appear on the scene. The extremist Hutu CDR, *Coalition pour la Défense de la République*, Coalition for the Defense of the Republic was founded in 1992 and led by Martin Bukyana.

While the image painted by the political reforms appeared positive, the reality was different; the political atmosphere was still tense with fear and suspicion. This was not the first time multipartyism operated in Rwanda. The central question remained whether these parties would improve the political situation or not. More specifically, what role did they have in acting to check extremism or in the development of the extremist ideology? A brief examination of the history and performance of political parties in Rwanda might help throw some light on what the performance of these new parties would be.

Political Subversion

This was reflected in the preparations which the Habyarimana regime made to defend their political (and economic) power. The strategy with respect to political parties had three tracks. First, this preparedness included the infiltration of the opposition political parties by agents of the regime so as to water down the intentions of some of these parties and create extremist Hutu factions within them: it was no wonder that some of the parties, that started as formidable opposition parties, eventually relapsed to the "the old time religion" of worshipping the MRND which had monopolized power since 1975. Secondly, it involved creating a myriad of small "opposition" parties that were really alternative fronts for Habyarimana. Thirdly, the CDR (Coalition For the Defense of the Republic) was a creation of Habyarimana and his supporters to give an impression that MRNDD was relatively moderate at the same time as the regime justified the creation of the party as a testimony to its own dedication to multiparty democracy, though Parliament at one stage rejected this political party because of its ethnic stance. The party's Manifesto clearly shows (p.8) that this was a sectarian party based on an extremist ideology. Mr. Martin Bucyana, its President, on the occasion of the official acceptance of the party, was reported to have said, "We are convinced that the unity of the Bahutu will stop violence and will bring the excess ambitions of the minority Tutsi to their acceptable level" (Human Rights Report Oct. 1994).

Inculcation of the Philosophy of Extremism

One general observation about political parties is that most of their manifestos preached progress and development of Rwanda. However, as noted above, the CDR preached open hostility towards those prepared to deal with that opposition—be it real or imagined—and branded them as enemies. The philosophy of extremism was, in fact, rooted in the MRND and was considered to be the "best" way to face the challenge caused by the rebirth of political party activities in the country which once again brought into the country the element of opposition and challenge to the repressive and choking decades old authority of the MRND. While the new political parties did not represent the old scenario as it was at the time of independence when political party formations strictly followed ethnic cleavages, an almost similar pattern was followed by the main opposition party, the MDR. But even more telling was the regionalism of that and other parties. The MDR had its base of support in the center and south of the country as did the PSD which was backed by many involved in inter-marriages. Further, for the first time, the regime was openly challenged by individuals or groups of individuals that Habyarimana viewed as a formidable force against his hitherto unchallenged power. Political party leaders like Faustin Rucogoza of the MDR, and Fredrick Nsamwambaho of PSD, were strong personalities that commanded great respect and popularity countrywide. The Habyarimana regime and its MRND had the greatest support from the northern parts of the country and itself was riven not only by moderate and extremist factions, but by those same factions regionally based in Gisenyi and Ruhengeri respectively. So while the preindependence political party formations divided the country primarily along ethnic lines, the new parties of the 1990s divided the country along regional and personal lines as well.

The challenges were met by a strong resistance from the party in power. Supporters of the regime were determined not to let such new challenges go by unchecked, preparing the ground for the institutionalizing of extremism initially through the use of propaganda, misinformation, indoctrination, politicization of ethnicity, and the militarization of politics. With these in place, extremism had taken root. The next step was to consolidate it.

Consolidation of Extremism

The invasion of Rwanda by the RPF/A crystallized a process that had slowly been developing prior to this invasion. On the surface, the regime was bending to accommodate the internal opposition and the threats from the invading RPF. But this only reinforced the sense that extremism was the only force that the regime could employ in order to save itself from falling.

While there were many different ways in which extremism as a political weapon was consolidated, we can group them under two main themes: the politicization of ethnicity and the militarization of politics. As noted above, ethnicity in Rwanda was a weapon that the colonial regime used to justify its presence in the country. Rwanda was so politicized at the time of independence that the country was split politically into two sharply divided groups of Banyarwanda: Bahutu and Batutsi. The country went into a civil war because of this ethnic factor in 1959, and the subsequent regimes of Kayibanda and Habyarimana did very little to de-ethnicize politics in Rwanda. The result was that at the time of the RPF/A invasion of the country, erroneous signals regarding the enemy of Rwanda (*inyangarwanda*) had been sent. A mistaken identification of the problem of Rwanda was made when the regime of Habyarimana pointed an accusing finger at the Batutsi as the greatest enemy of the country. Ethnicity was highly politicized.[3]

> Ethnically based political parties...failed to conceive of a post-colonial state other than an ethnically discriminatory one...either in favor of "Hutu majority" or organized as a "Constitutional Tutsi monarchy." Parties...capable of organizing on an anti ethnic basis and of being sites of a democratic prescription in the post-colonial state were overwhelmed by others and circumstances much as the absence of an independently organized working class movement. (Wamba-Dia-Wamba 1994)

Further, the absence or weakness of civil society organizations incarnating emancipatory politics (worker's peoples' committees for political independence, etc.) which would recognize the multiplicity of the people of Rwanda and weaken the ethnic forces was fatal (Wamba-dia-Wamba 1994, 13). Thus, ethnicity in the country at the time of independence and after became a political issue. It is no wonder that the policy of using the ethnic identity cards, that had been introduced by the colonial administration, continued to be used, especially during the Habyarimana era.

With the Tutsi out of power at the time of independence, their image as the "overlords" in Rwanda never left the political scene in Rwanda. Both the Kayibanda and the Habyarimana regimes used the "Tutsi over-lord image" to consolidate power for their own Hutu group. This ethnicity issue was not only politicized, but militarized and radicalized when the Tutsi in exile attempted to recapture power by force (the Inyenzi invasions of 1961–66). These invasions not only radicalized politics in Rwanda, but were used by different regionally-based Hutu groups to compete over which party could be most "purely" the defenders of the Hutu, thus reinforcing divisions within the Hutu camp while reifying the anti-Tutsi identity of both. This division took the form of regional divisions (North versus South), which eventually led to the coup that toppled the Kayibanda regime (Wamba-Dia-Wamba 1994).

The Habyarimana regime thus made no attempts to redress this ethnic problem. At the level of ideology, racism was propagated among Rwandan youth at school, through radio and theater. In school, the history syllabus painted the Tutsi as natural enemies of the Hutu, and projected the sectarian PARMEHUTU party as a national salvation force. This systematic preaching of racial ideology served to keep alive racial hatred at a time when opportunities existed for national reconciliation.

The post-independence ruling cliques went further than simple indoctrination. Though the Habyarimana regime initially stopped the pogroms against the Tutsi, it also made their plight worse by enforcing the policy of ethnic ratios and introducing regional quotas with the hope of correcting the inherited ethnic and regional imbalance of disproportionate numbers of Tutsi and Hutu southerners in the professions and higher education. They introduced racism in state organs and made it official state policy. Based on fictitious statistics, the ruling clique allocated educational and employment opportunities on a quota system. The Hutu were officially allowed 90 percent of educational and employment opportunities, while the Tutsi and Twa got only 9 percent and 1 percent respectively. Further, to "re-balance," a disproportionate number of the Hutu places went to northerners, and a disproportionate number of northern spaces went to those from Gisenyi. This was the system officially called "ethnic balance" (or equilibre ethnique). The policy, in fact, created much more regional and ethnic animosity than had ever been known in the country. This will partly explain why, in Habyarimana's propaganda machinery, and later on in the killings, his target groups were both the Batutsi (generally), whom he saw as his immediate and number one enemies, and members of the opposition, most of them Bahutu from the South.

Further, to facilitate the operation of this policy of official discrimination, the state continued the colonial practice of ethnic identity cards. This meant that a person could be identified quickly as a Mututsi or Muhutu by mere glancing at his or her identity card. However, even if someone carried a Hutu ethnic identity card, but was known in his local commune as a Tutsi, that individual was treated as a Tutsi since he could not obtain the required letters for entry into higher education and hence the professions.

But even this system of "ethnic balance" did not apply in all spheres of national life. In the armed forces, for example, only Hutu were allowed to serve. After over three decades of post-independence, Rwanda had only one Tutsi army officer. Further, to maintain the "purity" of the Rwandan military, no army officer was allowed to marry a Tutsi woman. Such was the scale of state sponsored racism.

However, before the RPF/A invasion in 1990, the "ethnic thing" had somehow become less of a political issue. Part of the explanation emerges from the fact that between 1968 to the mid 1980s the threat of refugee (Batutsi) invasion had greatly decreased. Hutu extremism, which had increased when there was the threat from the Batutsi, was for sometime contained, especially with the strong MRND in control. The majority of the party's strong men were men and women from Habyarimana's family (relatives) in the north, (members of what they termed AKAZU, meaning a small house), who, in their attempts to consolidate their regime, turned to regionalism as their instrument of political control and cultivated an image of people in the south as the enemy. The "ethnic thing" had in a way created a certain consciousness which made the Batutsi look at the Bahutu as "the other group" and the oppressors. This "Otherness", be it from the regional angle of the ethnic factor, was an important factor in the creation and consolidation of extremism.

The 1990 RPF/A invasion gave the Habyarimana regime the opportunity to reawaken the ethnic consciousness in Rwanda, a consciousness that viewed the invader/the enemy as being the Batutsi. Extremism, which did not begin with the invasion, was now reinforced and slowly began to consolidate. The MRND, which had monopolized power for long time, had never faced a sociopolitical crisis as the one brought about by this invasion; the regime had to ensure that it employed all manner of political maneuvers to ensure the security of their regime. One of the methods Habyarimana employed was to strengthen his sectarian policies through an ideology he called "UNION OF THE BAHUTU" whose aim was to work up the Bahutu against the Batutsi. Some of the methods employed in their attempts to save the regime included the use of propaganda, misinformation, assassinations, intimidation which, when put together, formed a strong basis for the consolidation of extremism. Alan Zarembo has made a pertinent observation that partly explains why most African leaders (and Habyarimana in particular) were not willing either to be democratic or to relinquish power.

> Colonial regimes taught Africans bad lessons in government. First, people came to believe that political power is the only source of wealth. The state dictates who prospers. Second, political entrepreneurs learned that manipulating ethnic identity is an effective way to stay in control. (Zarembo 1994)

These methods of Habyarimana were used to exclude possible challengers to his monolithic regime. As a leader, he had many followers who believed in him and in whatever he said. His followers had actually given him the title UMUBYEYI—which literally means the parent, the provider and the one above everything. This kind of belief in an individual is dangerous, and was bound to cause problems in the country.

Propaganda and Misinformation as Instruments in the Consolidation of Extremism

In 1992, a commission set up by the Rwanda Government to define the real enemy of Rwanda, reported on 21 September 1992. The enemy was defined as:

> Tutsi inside or outside Rwanda who are extremist and nostalgic for power...who want to take power in Rwanda by force. (Minister de la Defend Nationale "Definition et identification de l'ennemi," 21 September 1992)

The signal being sent to all people of Rwanda (read Hutu) was that the enemy was Tutsi. The report was meant to incite the Hutu, who now had the backing of the government, to deal a blow to this "enemy."

A program of misinforming the general populace and spreading ethnic hatred through any means available was set in place.

A few examples can be cited here to show seeds of animosity that were being sown by MRNDD propagandists while extremism took root. On 10 December 1990, in its 6th Edition, *Kangura*, (which literally means wake them up), a newsletter owned by Habyarimana's principal private secretary, Col. Elie Sagatwa, and the army chief of staff, Col. Serubuga, issued what they termed "Ten Commandments." These "Commandments" were supposed to appeal to and guide the supporters of the Habyarimana regime in how to deal with their "enemy," the Tutsi. It also provided a philosophy to justify why those in power should stay in power. Among those commandments, the following really helped in working up some elements among the Bahutu into becoming extremists:

1. Every strategic point, be they political, administration, military and security, must be entrusted to Bahutu.
2. The education sector (pupils, students, teachers) must be majority Hutu.
3. Rwandese Armed Forces must be exclusively Hutu; the experience of October war has taught us a lesson; no military person should marry a Tutsi woman.
4. The Bahutu should stop having mercy on Batutsi.
5. The Bahutu, wherever they are, must have unity, solidarity and be preoccupied by the fate of their Hutu brothers. The Bahutu, both inside and outside Rwanda, must constantly look for friends and allies for the Hutu cause, starting with our Hutu brothers, must constantly counteract the Tutsi propaganda, and must be firm and vigilant against their common enemy the Batutsi.
6. The 1959 social revolution, the 1961 referendum, and the Hutu Ideology must be taught to every Muhutu and at all levels. Every Muhutu must spread this ideology widely. We shall consider as a traitor any Muhutu who persecutes his Muhutu brother for having read, spread and taught this Ideology (Ondoga Ori Amaza 1995).

The pursuit of the policies based on the "Ten Commandments" philosophy eventually paved the way for the massacres that erupted in Rwanda, especially after Habyarimana's death. People had been fed an unhealthy diet of an ideology based on ethnicity. Ethnic emotions have often empowered a people collectively to perform acts of unbelievable cruelty and savagery.

Another piece of the propaganda literature that transformed peoples' emotions into extremism was an official pamphlet titled, "The Whole Truth of the October 1990 War Imposed Upon Rwanda by Aggressors from Uganda Armed Forces." This paper, targeted towards the whole nation, described the motive of the RPF/A invasion as wanting to set up an extended Tutsi-Hima Kingdom in the Bantu area of the Lake region, and compared the RPF/A to the historical genocidal regimes of Hitler of Germany and Pol Pot of Cambodia (Kigali, Afrepadem, and Leon Mugesera, March 1991).

The psychological preparation of the population of Rwanda towards extremism continued, especially through newspapers and the radio. Fiery speeches by prominent persons in society and deliberately organized meetings prepared for the killings. Rwanda is quite a literate country with over 69 percent of the people able to read and write. It was, therefore, easy for the propagandist and exponents of ethnicity to reach the general populace. There were in all about twenty extremist newspapers that were used as the mouthpieces of the regime, especially beginning in 1990. Among these, the most notorious ones were: *Umurwanashyaka, Umurangi, Interahamwe, Echo des Mille Collines, Ijambo, Kangura, La Midaille Nyiramachibiri,* and *Kangura International.*

Another media device that was used by the regime to prepare the population psychologically was radio. The state-owned radio carried a message of hatred and extremism, but nothing compared to Radio Television Libre des Mille Collins (RTLM), a privately owned radio whose directors were mostly members of the AKAZU, licensed for broadcast on 4 April 1993, and exclusively intended to prepare people's minds for genocide while it broadcast the most popular music. This FM radio, which broadcast propaganda and misinformation, had the state as its patron; for example, the station had an uninterrupted power supply newsprint in a time of shortages, the bills for which were paid for by the state.

Journalists on RTLM, among them, Gihigi Gaspard, member of CDR, Habimana Katano, member of MRND(D), and Bemeriki Valerie, member of CDR, spent all day broadcasting intoxicating propaganda based on ethnicity. This was an effective tool of preparation for extremism since it reached all peasants in the country.

Another related example of radio used to propagate the message of ethnicity and extremism occurred when Ferdinand Nahimana, Director of the Rwanda Office of Information (ORINFOR), and founder member of CDR and RTLM radio, broadcast a "communique" on Radio Rwanda, purportedly issued by a Human Rights Activists group based in Nairobi. This "communique" allegedly issued on March 1992 claimed that a plot by Tutsi who wanted to kill prominent Hutu in the country had been unearthed. This broadcast, which was repeated five times, was aimed not only at creating animosity of the Hutu against the Tutsi, but was also intended to make the Tutsi in Rwanda feel guilty and intimidated. The effect of such a broadcast was really far reaching; it was not only heard by the Tutsi, whom it psychologically undermined, but by the majority Hutu population on whom the effect cannot be mistaken.

In the same theme of psychologically working of the population towards extremism, important persons issued statements that ensured that extremism was indeed consolidated. Among such persons was Léon Mugesera, a graduate from Rwanda and Canada, Vice-President of the Gisenyi MRNDD, ideologue of extremism and a man of considerable repute. In his famous speech of 22 November 1992 at an MRND meeting in Gisenyi, he not only declared all other political parties, other than MRND and CDR, accomplices of the enemies of Rwanda, but advocated extermination of these accomplices of the RPF.

> You cell members, work together, watch over intruders in your cell, suppress them. Do anything you can so that nobody sneaks out.... The fatal mistake that we made in 1959...is that we let them (Tutsi) out of the country. Their homeland is Ethiopia through a short-cut, i.e., River Nyabarongo. I want to insist on that point; we must effectively react..." (Wilson Rutayisire 1995, 11)

In a similar manner, on 6 December 1990, *Kangura* published an article written by the Hutu community living abroad entitled, "Appeal to the Conscience of Bahutu." In its conclusion, the article appealed to all Bahutu to accept as their own the "Ten Commandments." It continued, "[I]t is high time for us to wake up, to deepen our consideration and to be aware of a new ideology, the ideology of the Bahutu which consists of defending all that was granted by the Revolution of 1959 and that of the referendum of the 25 September 1961" (*Kangura* Vol.6, 1990).

These messages indeed had the effect they were intended to have. Taking Léon's message for example: when the massacres started, the machete was the main implement in the genocide, and bodies were put in the Kagera River which at one point joins the Nile which flows towards the north (Ethiopia—"the Tutsi homeland"). The poor peasants had taken in the message; they became a fertile ground for extremism. The speech of Leon Mugesera also shows the impunity with which these perpetrators of crimes carried on their game unimpeded. Under a sober government, Mugesera would have been convicted for inciting violence.

Militarization

The second phase in the consolidation of extremism that eventually led to genocide was the militarization of ethnicity. This phase was no longer one of talking, but of arming and training militia in the name of saving the regime. In reality, the militia were not only intended to save the regime, but to be implementers of the racist ideology of Hutu versus Tutsi. The key to this direction was the expansion of the army, re-equipping it with more sophisticated killer weapons, the training of paramilitary groups, and arming some sections of the population.

According to Human Rights Watch (Jan 1994), at the time the RPF launched their attack in October 1990, Rwanda had an army of only 5,000 men, equipped with light arms including Belgian-made FAL, German-made G3 and AK automatic rifles. It also had eight 812 mm mortars, six 57 mm antitank guns, French 83 mm Blindicide rocket launchers, 12 French AML-60 armored cars, and 16 French M. armored personnel carriers. By the time the war ended, the army had expanded to at least 30,000 strong, armed with a wide range of heavier guns and weaponry. This flood of heavier arms and weapons systems contributed to thousands of civilian casualties and the displacement of hundreds of thousands more. France, Egypt, and South Africa have been singled out as the suppliers of this arsenal. With all this strength, the impunity of the armed forces to commit crime increased. Military operations (which were in reality massacre operations), especially those carried out by the Presidential Guard, became the order of the day. It was this same army, which was being trained and equipped by the French that in turn trained the militia and youth wingers of the MRND and CDR in extremist killer tactics. The Presidential Guard was actually part of the army that was created after the 1990 invasion. Its composition actually points to its extremist character; it was made up of exclusively Hutu extremists from the home area of Habyarimana and his wife. It was the regime's most trusted section of the army.

Intensive military training was started in different parts of the country. Among the areas of training were: Nyungwe and Gashwati forests, Rusumo, Mugesera, and Sake, all in Kibungo Prefecture. Another training camp was at Bugarama in Changungu prefecture. Other significant ones were at Nyandungu, Mutara, and Gako. In these training camps, youth wingers, especially the *Interahamwe* and Impuzamugambi--youth wingers of CDR--received training. The *Interahamwe*, who were a notorious and most feared civilian terrorist group, was an armed youth wing of the MRND created in 1992 with the sole aim of terrorizing the perceived enemies of the regime. They were later joined by the Impuzamugambi. Interestingly, they—like the army—were divided into sections, each with a particular "assignment" to accomplish. The activities of these militia groups were usually coordinated by the army. Ironically, the Commander of the *Interahamwe*, Robert Kajuga, who turned out to be a notorious extremist killer, whose targets were Tutsi, was himself of Tutsi ancestry. His extremism could have been an overreaction to prove to the regime that had him in power, that his was an unwavering commitment.

In 1993, these groups intensified their terror, often putting up roadblocks to trap their targets. At times they raided homes and staged massive propaganda demonstrations in Kigali streets. It was these groups that later committed atrocities in the Bugesera and other areas.

Other than the training, there were various secret meetings at which details of genocide plans were made. Some of these meetings include those held on 17 November 1993, presided over by the then Chief of Staff, Col. Deogratius Nsabimana at Byumba. The following day, at Remera in Kigali, Joseph Nzirorera—then Secretary General of MRND—convened another meeting whose objective was to map out ways of eliminating all Batutsi and those opposed to the segregation ideology. Concrete plans were made to deploy militia in Kigali, Gitarama, Nyanza, and Bugesera, areas mostly inhabited by Tutsi. Another known meeting was presided over by Habyarimana himself at his Robero Hotel on 20 November 1993. At this meeting, issues dealing with logistics to be used by the killers—like the distribution of weapons such as guns, grenades, knives, pangas, axes, and the provision of transport—were discussed. Extremism was not only consolidating, but plans were being drawn up to implement that extremist ideology. But the final stage—that of implementation of these plans—was yet to come.

This stage of the implementation was directly linked to the Arusha Peace talks to which the extremists were opposed. They referred to them as "jokes." With the diplomatic pressure at Arusha and the readiness and determination of the RPF to bring order in Rwanda (a fact that Habyarimana was well aware of), it was feared in the extremist circles that Habyarimana would give in to this pressure. This is why implementation of the final Arusha agreement was delayed. If the agreement was implemented, the long held genocide plan of the extremists would never succeed. While the truth of the shooting down of the plane carrying Habyarimana and the President of Burundi on 6 April 1994 has not yet been established, all accusing fingers point to these extremists as the ones that decided to get rid of Habyarimana who seemed to be getting in their way. Extremism had turned on and devoured its own leader.

The killing of Habyarimana unleashed the wave of killing that saw thousands massacred within hours of the downing of the plane. The killings seemed to follow a deliberate pattern designed by the killers before the incident of 6 April. The killers went after not only Tutsi, but any other person they thought was against them, be they Hutu or Tutsi. Top members of opposition parties were especially targeted. Vice President Agatha Uwilingiyimana and her family were merely the most prominent victims. Within two weeks of the outburst of this blood bath, about one quarter million people had been killed. The well-worked-out plan of the extremists had indeed come to fruition.

One cannot help but conclude that extremism and genocide had indeed been planned when one looks at the utterance of Col. Théoneste Bagosora immediately after the shooting down of the plane. He accused Belgian troops within the U.N. peace keepers as the plotters of the incident that killed Habyarimana, a diversionary measure not only to sew confusion but to provide less of a motive for the RPF to make a concerted push for Kigali and "disturb" their plan. If Bagosora had pointed an accusing finger at the RPA, the RPF might have descended on Kigali as quickly as possible, not only to save their counterparts who had earlier arrived in Kigali under the Arusha Treaty arrangement, but also to save the Tutsi and other Hutu moderates whom they always saw as easy targets of the Habyarimana regime.

A lady survivor, Christine, who testified before a conference on Genocide organized in Kigali 5 November 1995 said the plan to wipe out a section of the people of Rwanda had been hatched a long time before the plane crash.[4] She testified to the effect that the state-owned radio station issued announcements immediately after the crash, to the effect that people should not leave their houses. This made the people easy targets since they were found in their houses. Her whole family had been found at home; all her children, husband, and other relatives were killed. They had been fooled into the carefully laid trap of the extremist killers. Since misinformation was one of the tools of the killers, they made it appear—even when massacres had begun in the countryside—as if this was just something small happening only in Kigali and the surrounding area. They used their propaganda machinery effectively. This explains why people ran to upcountry areas hoping that they would be safe, not knowing of the roadblocks and other terrorist acts that waited them; they walked into their death traps.

Agnes Mukeshimana (seventeen years old) and Emmanuel Ntabonvura (fourteen years old), both Tutsi survivors of the genocide at Mugombwa in Muganza in the southern borders of Rwanda with Burundi, where 26,000 bodies have been collected, also told stories of the preparations of the killers. The two young people said they smelled danger when, weeks before the general massacres began, they started hearing their neighbors and "friends" referring to them as "snakes." They also pointed to the fact that their neighbors, mostly Hutu who had always drunk and eaten with them, had for weeks before the genocide refused to share anything in common with them.[5] Agnes also told us of suspicious secret meetings restricted to Hutu that were always called by Emmanuel Ndayambaje, the bourgmestre of the area. Indeed, when massacres started, she had observed that it was Ndayambaje, now in prison in Belgium, who directed the killings.

The massacres did not stop until after the RPF had taken over the government. By then the toll of the extremism numbered about one million people. Extremism in the genocide in Rwanda was carefully planned, grew, developed and was consolidated, growing in a culture of impunity, especially in post-colonial Rwanda. The impunity with which massacres of innocent people were carried out in 1959 continued in 1963, then in 1973, 1991, and 1992. In all these circumstances, the perpetrators of these crimes against humanity were not brought before the law to face justice. So the extremist killers in the 1994 genocide were actually continuing a culture of impunity that started decades ago; they had come to learn that there was nothing wrong with killing any perceived enemy—after all, if you did, nothing would happen to you especially since this killing was state engineered and sanctioned. This is the culture that guided the extremism that climaxed in the genocide of 1994 in Rwanda.

The Role of the International Community in Fostering Extremism

An important factor to consider in apportioning blame in the genocide is the fact that the responsibility was in some cases direct and in some cases indirect. The responsibility can be assessed not only by what one did, but also in terms of what one failed to do. While this is a subject that has been variously treated in detail elsewhere (see Agnes

Callamard, Ogenga Otunnu, Gérard Prunier, Bruce Jones, and others), it serves our purposes to highlight some issues on the subject. A few examples here will suffice.

France in the Carnage

Of all the foreign forces that have been implicated in the creation and development of extremism in Rwanda, France has particularly been identified as a country that propped up the dictatorial regime of Habyarimana; France logistically supported the extremist army of the regime, directly trained extremists, and in some instances French troops were accused of being directly involved in the mistreatment and killing of the citizens of Rwanda (*Rwandese Review,* April 1993:5–7). France, therefore, has a moral and legal responsibility in the genocide.

France's connection with Rwanda goes back to colonial times. Though France was not the official colonial power in Rwanda, French presence and influence was felt through their Catholic missionaries in the country who greatly impacted the making of the official colonial policies in Rwanda. Eventually, French became the national language in Rwanda, and therefore part of Francophone Africa. Overall, there is a symbolic relation that France nurtures with its former colonies; this is what leads her to providing military and financial aid to a network of countries that fall under her direct or indirect influence. In all these former colonies, especially in Francophone Africa, their relationship with France has been characterized by what John Darnton of New York Times service has called "a Faustian bargain": "…allow in French technocrats to run state enterprises and companies, trade mainly with the mother country, and sign a military assistance pact and you will be secure. France will prop up your economy by giving you the African Franc which is supported by the French treasury, and rush its army to your side if trouble develops" (*New York Times* 27/4/94).

That "Faustian bargain" has indeed characterized France's relations with Rwanda. Her interest and presence in Rwanda did not so much come to the fore until 1975, two years after Habyarimana took over power from Kayibanda. Mr. Habyarimana signed a military cooperation agreement with France. Indeed, when the RPF/A started the war against the regime, France rushed in combat troops, mortars, and artillery to help the government. Although the government of France later said these forces were for the purpose of protecting French and other foreign nationals in Rwanda, reports were received of these troops coming into direct combat against the RPF/A advances. In some of their areas of operation, not a single French citizen lived there, yet the argument advanced had been that the French Military presence could be explained by their need to protect their nationals in Rwanda (*Human Rights Watch Arms Project*, January 1994). The French also were involved in instructing the militias and the regular army in the use of some of the arms they brought (*Rwandese Review*, April 93:5–7).[6] This same source notes that during the days of genocide, while the extremist militias and government troops hunted down their perceived enemies, the French troops interrogated those captured just before they met their death. Some RPA sources also told of how, during the combat, they were able to eliminate the man operating the artillery gun, a French Legionnaire (RPF/A anonymous).

The leaders of France and Rwanda also had very close family ties— Mitterand of France and Habyarimana were friends, but their sons, Jean Christophe Mitterand and Jean Pierre Habyarimana, were not only closer friends, but that friendship was consolidated further by business dealings. The two camps used political power in their countries in order to boost and protect their respective economic interests. The *Rwanda Review* (2:3, 1993) ran a letter from Mitterand to Habyarimana, a letter that was not only both personal and official, but also talked about the interests of France in Rwanda. There is also an indication that Jean C. Mitterand was one of the biggest arms dealer in Rwanda. It was therefore in the interest of France that there should be use for the arms France was ready to supply to Rwanda, arms that eventually ended in the arms of the hands of the extremist killers.

All these point to the fact that France bears a degree of responsibility for the extremist massacres that befell the country in 1994. Even if France had not been involved in the arming, training, and indirect combat on the side of the government, the failure of France to denounce loudly and unequivocally the crimes against humanity in Rwanda is itself questionable. France had a military presence in Bagesera and Bagogwe, where the initial massacres took place, yet they never publicly or otherwise denounced these killings, or even chose to investigate them. Quite the reverse—France continued training the regime's forces in Central Africa and in France.

At the height of the killings, France sent in her troops in an operation code named Opération Turquoise. This was supposed to be a humanitarian operation—a force of intervention to stop the genocide and save the survivors by creating "safe havens" or "no war" zones. This would have been a welcome gesture on the part of France, especially knowing that they had spent months watching "their students"—the Rwandese extremists—committing offenses, without France raising a finger. Though some lives were saved, interestingly, however, the areas under the jurisdiction of Opération Turquoise—Kibuye, Cyangungu, and Gikongoro—where there was no war fought, were after the war found to be among the worst hit areas; they were areas with the greatest physical destruction as well as enormous numbers of lives lost. The biggest question becomes, what happened to these "safe areas"? Were the French the ones who destroyed them or did they stand by as the militias and government troops wrecked havoc?

Another glaring factor pointing to French complicity in the extremist genocide lies in the fact that after the death of Habyarimana and the beginning of genocide in Rwanda, a new government was announced in Kigali, a government made up of men and women that are mentioned among the 400 or so leaders of the genocide. France knew these people very well. The vast majority of the victims of genocide were killed after this government had come into power, a government that came into power in spite of the Arusha Peace Accords that called for power sharing, which had not been implemented. While all the world waited and watched events unfolding in Rwanda, and some condemned the killings, France became the first government to recognize the extremist government led by Theodor Sindikubwabo (among others) against the protests from abroad of Faustin Twagiramungu, the Prime Minister designate under the Arusha Accords, and in spite of Sindikubwabo's personal instigation of the genocide in Butare.

The greater sense of "French Nationalism" or (Imperialism?) led France to want to have her Francophone interests protected. After all the invading RPF/A was largely made up of men and women with an Anglophone background; their success would mean supplanting the French in Rwanda. On the other hand, the personal ties between the Mitterand and Habyarimana families, and the economic dealings that they had would draw the French into the conflict. Prunier's chapter in this book, "Operation Turquoise—a Humanitarian escape from a political dead end," cites Jean C. Mitterand, son of President Mitterand, after receiving a call in Brussels from Habyarimana wanting to know whether French troops would come to his help, commenting (in the presence of the author), "We'll send him a few boys, old man Habyarimana. We'll get him out of trouble. In any case, in two, months it will all be over." All these point to those strong family ties, standing military agreements, as well as economic and language interests that brought France into the conflict.

The Church

One of the institutions that have been implicated in the extremist killings in Rwanda is the church. Rwanda is a highly religious country; about 90 percent of the population are Christians. However, some church leaders—bishops, priests, and nuns—were among those whose hands are soiled with blood of those that were massacred by the Habyarimana regime and its even more extremist successor. The killers were overwhelmingly Christians, as are the vast majority of the 80,000 or so people awaiting trial for the genocide.

The church's involvement in the politics of Rwanda goes back to colonial times, when church leaders became the vanguards of divisive politics in the country. Just like the colonial masters did, the church—especially the Catholic Church—first threw its support behind the Tutsi. At the time of independence, they switched sides to support the Hutu and accused the Tutsi of being oppressors. The story of church's involvement in divisive politics in Rwanda is very well documented by Ian Linden (*Church and Revolution in Rwanda*, 1977). Names of missionaries like Monseigneur Classe, Monsieur Mortehan, and Cardinal Lavigerie are particularly associated with divisive colonial church politics that sowed the seeds of hatred in Rwanda.

It is against this background that the church's involvement in the development of extremism in Rwanda in the 1990s can be understood. However, while we stress the church's involvement—especially the individuals in these churches—we should also note that during this same period of suffering, there were wonderful acts of heroism, sacrifice, and even martyrdom, performed by some members of the same church; more than one-hundred church men and women died at the hands of extremists.

Usually, the church plays an important role in uniting people. It socializes them and intercedes and cares for them in times of need. There is a bond, therefore, that grows between the leaders of the church and their followers; this bond entails respect, trust, and reverence for the church and their followers. The church, therefore, becomes a haven of peace and protection. Indeed, when the massacres started, the only place people felt were safe were churches. Thousands of people fled to church buildings, but unfortunately it was in these same places that thousands of people met their death. At a church in Mugombwa in Muganza Commune there are 26,000 bodies, some collected from the surroundings areas, but most of them from the church at Mugombwa. According to Ntabonvura Emmanuel (a fourteen-year-old boy) interviewed at Mugombwa on 2 November 1995, many people who had run from different areas had gathered inside the church for protection. The extremists did not respect the church; they threw grenades in the crowd inside the church, and there were virtually no survivors. The church at Mugombwa is one of many such churches countrywide where thousands perished.

The top church leaders, like the Anglican Bishop of Kigali and his Catholic counterparts, played a big role in the development of extremism. Bishop Nsthamihigo (Bishop of Kigali) now lives in exile in Nairobi in spite of the call for all persons living in exile to return. During a visit of the Archbishop Cary of Canterbury to Rwanda, he informed Bishop Nsthamihigo that if he knew he did not have any questions to answer on the genocide, he could safely return home, but the Bishop chose not to return.

Church leaders were very close to political power in the Habyarimana regime. Hugh McCullum, a Canadian journalist, calls the relationship between the church and the regime, "an umbilical relationship" (*New Vision* May 24, 1995). He gives the example of the Catholic Archbishop, Vincent Nsengiyumva, who was a prominent member of the MRND. Such a Bishop not only participated in and identified with partisan politics, thus dividing up his own laity, but knowingly identified with the MRND with all its sectarian and extremist policies. Other senior Catholic and Anglican priests are known to have had "hot lines" to Habyarimana's palace, and drove luxurious cars provided by the state.

In return, these leaders of the church dutifully repaid the regime. In this respect they failed to provide for their people in the hour of need. They could not preach against the injustice of the regime nor did they warn the people of the impending danger. The church should have assumed its role as the conscience of the people. Even in the last hours when the extremists were killing people, these church leaders never let the people know that the situation was so bad that the walls of the churches could offer little protection, though, ironically, it was in Kabgayi that over 90 percent of the refugees were saved, but Archbishop Nsengiyumva, together with two other Bishops (including the liberal Bishop Thadée Nsengiyumva) and ten priests, were killed in June 1994 by an irate RPF soldier who accused them of complicity in the genocide. The soldier purportedly committed the murders out of anger and grief and not because of a policy of revenge by the RPF.[7] He was actually later pursued in order to be brought to justice.

The church involvement in the history of Rwanda has mostly been negative; the policies of the church during the colonial times were closely identified with those of "divide and rule" of the colonial governments. Indeed Monseigneur Classe and Cardinal Lavigerie are remembered in Rwandese historiography as apostles of sectarianism; the church became the social arm of colonialism. At the time of independence, this church was not decolonized; the new leaders tended to carry on with the policies of their forerunners. It was no wonder, therefore, that some of the leaders of the church were involved in the extremist acts that engulfed Rwanda in April 1994. On the other hand, for the many that never actively participated in the genocide, the blame leveled against them is that they largely failed to meet their expected role in society; they never warned the people or they fooled them into thinking they would offer them protection.

Belgium

Belgium and France are the two countries that have been Rwanda's traditional assistance providers and trading partners. Belgium took over from the Germans as the new colonial masters until Rwanda attained independence. So, the social political and economic policies of Rwanda, like those of any other former colony, were largely shaped by the Belgians. The indirect rule policy, the policy of "Ethnic" Identity Cards and many others, were all created by the Belgian colonial authorities. And for our purposes—and as noted earlier—ethnicization of politics and, therefore, the polarization of Rwanda society into two camps of Batutsi and Bahutu, was the architectural work of the Belgians. Their role in the 1959 "Revolution," where thousands of Tutsi were massacred, is well documented (Rutayisire, 1995:5) Wilson Rutayisire continues to observe that in the same "Revolution" when PARMEHUTU activists started massacring people, they were supported by ground and airborne units of the Belgian armed forces. Their contradictory and opportunistic policies started the mass bloodletting in Rwanda. Their legacy continued in post-colonial Rwanda.

As for their (Belgian) part in the recent extremism, it was only an indirect one stemming from the Belgian role in sewing many of the seeds of animosity in the country, but continuing in post-colonial

Rwanda as if nothing wrong had happened. Major General Paul Kagame, Vice President of Rwanda, in his address to the Conference on Genocide, made a pertinent remark on the role of the international community (in general) in the genocide, a comment that could also be applied to the role of Belgium. Right from the beginning, especially when the Arusha Peace talks started, there were many signs that preparations were being made by the Habyarimana regime to exterminate a section of the Rwandese people. Yet the international community kept quiet, and, in so doing, in a way condoned and abated crime in Rwanda.

Belgium, however, is to be commended for having cut off military assistance to Rwanda when the conflict flared up in 1990. Further, among the first few people to be killed after the plane crash on 6 April 1994, were ten Belgian U.N. peace keepers who had been guarding Agathe Uwilingiyimana.

Extremism in RPF/RPA

It would be a great omission not to briefly address the question of whether there was extremism in the RPF camp, which could also have contributed to the genocide in Rwanda. The bulk of RPF/A was made of people from one section of the Banyarwanda; the RPF/A was about 98 percent Batutsi. This certainly helped in concretizing Habyarimana's suspicion that his enemies were the Tutsi. There was also collaboration between RPF and Tutsi in Rwanda. One needs to note that the possibility of internally Tutsi-led uprising against the regime of Habyarimana was almost impossible. The RPF invasion, therefore, put the Tutsi in Rwanda at risk. The invasion in a way contributed to providing grounds and a target for extremism in Rwanda; one could call it extremism by implication.

Homelessness on the part of Rwandese, especially those that had been living in Uganda, was another possible source of extremism among the RPF. True, they had lived in the country for many years, and some of the RPA fighters had actually been born in Uganda. The leading figures of RPA had actually been key figures in Uganda's National Army, and some held high office in government.

However, they never were fully accepted in Ugandan society; they were still looked at as foreigners in spite of their contribution to National Liberation and development. This feeling of not being wanted in your host country nor in your own country made these young men and women a determined lot. This feeling created fearlessness and a determination that did not tolerate anything short of invading and "going back home" by force. The 1982 expulsions of Banyarwanda in Ankole and later on, the hostility and discrimination that Banyarwanda faced from among their colleagues in the Uganda National Army, gave them the determination to go home. In Uganda, Banyarwanda generally were, in spite of their status, still considered the underdogs in society.

Discrimination and disappointment may have given them not only an impervious will and determination to fight and go back to where they felt would at least be home, but the same "blind" determination could bring about intolerance and fanaticism among the RPF/A ranks. For example, the RPF/A were suspicious of anybody that had a different view from their conviction that a return could only be achieved through a military invasion. Those Banyarwanda, who, before the invasion were not actively involved in the preparation for the invasion were actually blacklisted as traitors of the RPF cause. A common saying to such people was, "Tusagusazisha"—meaning "we can make you old"—eliminate you, an expression also used by the Hutu extremists in Rwanda. Doctrinaire beliefs and intolerance breed extremism.

While circumstances leading to the death of Dr. Banyingana and Maj. General Fred Rwigyema—the leading commanders of RPF/A— have not fully been established, indicators point to the fact that there was disagreement about their route and method of invading Rwanda, a disagreement that led to their eventual death.

There may have been instances when ordinary RPF soldiers were also involved in extremist acts. The case of the murder of the Catholic Archbishop and ten other Bishops is a case in point. However, the difference with the Habyarimana regime is that such acts were not sanctioned by the Front; actually those that committed such crimes often met justice. So while we observe that because of their history, treatment and determination, the RPF/A were prone to extremism, their leadership on the other hand had a clear ideology that eventually led them to stopping the extremist acts of the Habyarimana regime. On the whole, the RPF/A can be said to have been disciplined, with a clear mission of liberating their country from the Habyarimana regime and the AKAZU. When the besieged 600 soldiers in the RPF were holed up in the Parliament building in Kigali when the coup took place on 6–7 April 1994 and shot their way out, they not only managed to save themselves but many other endangered residents of Kigali.[8]

Conclusion

It would be belaboring the point to say that the period 1990–1994

witnessed unprecedented killing in Rwanda. The work of these extremists was not work that started with the Habyarimana plane crash, but
began with the ideology of separating Rwanda on ethnic grounds as a
tool by the colonial masters. The post-colonial masters developed the
ideology further, until the 1990s when it consolidated into genocide.
All pointers that there would be a massacre in Rwanda were there;
however, ignorance of the history of Rwanda and the disinformation of
the extremist regime, helped by some members of the international
community, delayed or blocked any possible intervention to save lives
in Rwanda. Ethnicity, which the colonial masters had used to suit their
convenience, was also used by the post-colonial leaders, who politicized and later militarized an ethnic ideology. Extremism was a deliberate measure to suit one section of the Rwanda society. The massacres
were not a result of the spontaneous response by people who so loved
Habyarimana, and were pained by his death, and therefore acted to
eliminate his killers (as some circles have wanted the world believe).
The genocide was planned and implemented.

Notes

1. A study group, made up of lecturers in the Faculty of Arts Makerere University,
   Uganda, included Joan Kakwenzire and Dixon Kamukama, of the Department
   of History, the principle authors of this chapter. The others were Dr. Eustance
   Rutiba of the Department of Religious Studies, and Mwambutsya-Ndebesa of
   the Department of History, whose valuable contributions are acknowledged. This
   chapter, an examination of the causes of extremism in Rwanda within a historical context, is the product of a group effort by these four academicians. Those
   involved in the study were selected based on their differences in ethnic and
   social backgrounds, their previous studies on the problematic areas of Rwandan
   history, and their divergent views on African ethnic conflicts in general and the
   Rwanda genocide in particular. Dixon Kamukama, a historian and author of
   Rwanda Conflict: Its Roots and Regional Implications, has been involved in a
   variety of research on Rwanda. Mwambutsya-Ndebesa has been studying the
   social relations between the Bairu and Bahima of Ankole, who are closely related to the Bahutu and Batutsi of Rwanda respectively. Dr. Rubita has been
   involved in research on the church in Rwanda from colonial times to the present.
   Mrs Joan Kakwenzire, a historian and human rights activist, has been closely
   following the violations of human rights in Rwanda. She also contributed to the
   report on Genocide in Rwanda commissioned by the U.S Committee for Refugees. Though Joan Kakwenzire was originally contracted to undertake the study
   herself, she decided to make it a group effort, fearing she would not be objective
   in the overall analysis of the circumstances that led to the 1994 mass killings of
   kith and kin. The study draws heavily on secondary sources as well as the experience of the authors as interested parties in the conflict. Primary data was collected related to the separate areas of specialization of the four researchers. Lastly,
   the views were tested on a cross-section of participants at the *International Con-*

ference on Genocide, Impunity and Accountability held in Kigali 1–5 November 1995. Data and some interpretations from a variety of papers presented at this conference have been incorporated in this study. Interviews with some of the survivors of the genocide were also conducted at the conference.

2. Cf. Chalk 1990, chapter 5, and Chrétien 1995, 40–42 for more details on the newspaper *Kangura.*

3. Of course, this was an integral part of the history of Rwanda. Part of the blame must be attributed to the colonialists. They never made any effort to find a solution to the problem of ethnicity that had been amplified by the colonial regime. Political parties that were formed to usher the country to independence were all ethnically based and, therefore, could not think of a program that would counter ultranationalism.

4. An interview at the Genocide Conference.

5. This interview was conducted at that site of Genocide at Mugombwa. Agnes told the interviewer that she escaped death by being hidden by her maternal Hutu uncle Emmanuel, who vividly remembered exactly what happened; he was also interviewed at Mugombwa.

6. Human Rights Watch Arms Project provides an in depth description of France in the creation and consolidation of extremism in the country. The report notes that the French were not only involved in arming Rwanda (just as a business for a few French people), but that French government troops participated not only in training the extremists, but at times fought side by side with them.

   Immediately after the RPF launched its offensive...the number of French soldiers swelled to 680—four companies including paratroopers. Two of these companies were deployed on main roads north of the capital. The remainder were deployed in strategic positions in Kigali...the Arms Project witnessed first hand French military activities that at the least were tantamount to direct participation in the war...French soldiers provided artillery for Rwanda infantry troops..."

7. For a contrary interpretation, cf. Prunier (1995) 270–72 (Eds.).

8. Interview with an RPF soldier (KIKOFERO) who was at the CND building during the last battles for Kigali.

5

Hate Radio in Rwanda[1]

Frank Chalk

The Role of Radio

Radio is the premier means of reaching the public with news and information in countries where most of the population is illiterate and television sets are rare. But much of the world is not part of an electronic global village when it comes to radio news. Because of its crucial role, many governments rigorously control radio news through government-ownership of radio stations and regulations barring the broadcast of uncensored news by private stations. In these countries, false news is a staple part of the radio listener's diet. Rwanda, where hate radio flourished, was only one of the states in which the government used radio to mould the opinions of its rural citizens. Consider just a few examples. In Ethiopia,

> the vast majority of Ethiopians outside Addis Ababa have no ready access to the print media.... The Government controls radio, the most influential medium in reaching the rural population [85 percent of the population], as well as the sole television station, and ensures that TGE [the Transitional Government of Ethiopia] policies are reflected in their programming. (U.S. Congress 1995, 78–79, 83–84)

In Indonesia, a country with about 600 private radio broadcasting companies, as well as a government radio network, only the "National News" produced by the government can be broadcast. It is disseminated by private stations and forty-nine regional affiliates of the government station. Under Indonesian law, "the private radio stations may produce only 'light' news, such as human interest stories, and may not discuss politics" (U.S. Congress 1995, 598).

In strife-torn Somalia, the warlords prize radio transmitters almost as highly as heavy weapons. They established their own low power radio stations around the country and fought for control of the Mogadishu radio transmitter, the country's most powerful. Indicative of its importance to them, early in 1991, over 1,000 of General Mohammed Farah Aideed's militiamen were killed seizing the radio station from Mohammed Siad Barré's forces. Aideed still controlled the Mogadishu radio station in December 1992, when troops of the US-led United Nations Unified Task Force (UNITAF) landed in Somalia. He soon used it to excoriate the U.N. troops and incite violence against them (U.N. Department of Public Information 1994, 7, 13, 43; U.S. Congress, House 1993, 34).

U.N. forces retaliated on 12 June 1993, a week after the killing of twenty-four Pakistani soldiers serving with the U.N. Operation in Somalia (UNOSOM II) and the wounding of another fifty-four. They launched a series of coordinated air and ground attacks aimed at taking Radio Mogadishu out of Aideed's hands. A secondary goal of the attack was to put his transmitter at the disposal of the United Nations command. The U.N. troops captured the station, but in the attack they destroyed the transmitter by mistake. None of the remaining broadcast transmitters in Mogadishu had the power and the range to reach distant areas of Somalia. Aideed soon resumed broadcasting in the Mogadishu area, this time using a low power mobile transmitter. Thus, Somalia's airwaves were largely left in the hands of the rival warlords (U.N. Department of Public Information 1994, 7, 13, 43; U.S. Congress, Senate, and House 1995, 230). Developments in Somalia indicated that neither the United Nations nor the United States was equipped to utilize radio broadcasting appropriately in its operations.

Messages of Hate

In Rwanda, the encouragement of ethnic hatred on the radio, together with the creation and arming of militias, was one of the clearest early warning signs of an imminent genocide (U.S. Congress, Senate 1994, 46), The dissemination of hate propaganda, which included spreading ethnic hatred and inciting ethnocide and genocide, began in earnest in 1990 with newspaper and magazine articles aimed at convincing Hutu intellectuals and other literate members of the population (50 percent of those over fifteen; 64 percent of the males and 37 percent of the females) that their lives were menaced from inside and outside Rwanda by Tutsi infiltrators and Hutu supporters of democracy (Central Intelligence Agency 1994, 32; La Brosse 1995, 13). The leading disseminator of this message was the bimonthly magazine *Kangura*, founded in May 1990 by Hassan Ngeze, who, like President Juvénal Habyarimana, came from the northwestern prefecture of Gisenyi, a major center of anti-Tutsi and Hutu power sentiment (Prunier 1995, 13; Chrétien 1995, 38–44, 50). In 1991, *Kangura* was denounced by the International Commission of Jurists for its vicious incitement of racial hatred, while a liberal Belgian deputy attacked the publication's "Hitlerian" contents (La Brosse 1995, 39).

Despite the large number of Rwandese hate publications, the written press had only limited circulation. The newspapers rarely printed more than 3,000 copies of an issue and they circulated mainly in Kigali, where their high prices further limited their readership. With 400,000 to 500,000 AM/FM/short-wave radio receivers in homes and offices, and seven FM radio relay transmitters providing regular radio service to most of the country, it was radio that reached a broad public audience, especially the 90 percent of the population which lived in rural areas (Chrétien 1995, 57, 66; U.S. Congress, Senate, and House 1994, 204).

The messages of hate spread through the airwaves on 3 March 1992, when Radio Rwanda broadcast all day long false news reports that a leaflet issued by the Tutsi-based Parti Libéral had been discovered in Nairobi advocating the terrorist killing of twenty-two leading Hutu politicians, army officers, civil servants, priests, businessmen, and lawyers (Chrétien 1995, 57). The next day, following further incitements to "self-defence" by Radio Rwanda, *Interahamwe* ("Those who work together" in Kinyarwanda) militia brought in from Kigali began killing Tutsi and burning their huts in the Bugesera region of southeastern Rwanda. The killing led to the deaths of approximately 300 persons and lasted until 9 March.

When Western ambassadors lodged a stiff protest with the President of Rwanda, he fired Ferdinand Nahimana, the director of the Rwandese Information Office (*L'Office Rwandais d'Information*, known by the acronym ORINFOR). Nahimana, one of Rwanda's most distinguished historians. He was then rejected by the German government as counsellor to Rwanda's ambassador to Bonn and returned to his university post, where he developed the theory that Radio Rwanda had been infiltrated by agents of the Rwanda Patriotic Front, backed by evil foreign diplomats determined to undermine Hutu self-defence.[2] The Rwandese civil servants who were discovered to be responsible for the false news stories were let off by Prime Minister Sylvestre Nsanzimana with an administrative reprimand. The charges against over 400 persons implicated in the Bugesera massacres were dropped. In the meantime, the power of radio to mobilize the rural population against its Tutsi neighbors had been dramatically demonstrated (Chrétien 1995, 56–61; Prunier 1995, 19, 137).

In the summer of 1993, anti-Tutsi radio propaganda heated up with the start of radio transmissions by the privately owned *Radio-Télévision Libre des Mille Collines* (RTLM), aided by the staff and facilities of Radio Rwanda, the official government-owned station. RTLM was founded with the assistance of a wealthy businessman, Félicien Kabuga, whose daughter was married to a son of President Habyarimana, and by other members of the President's inner circle, the *AKAZU* ("little house" in Kinyarwanda). Prominent in this elite political group were several relatives of the President's wife, especially her brothers and cousins.[3] Conveniently for RTLM, its broadcasting studios were connected to the electric generators of the Presidential Palace, directly across the street, permitting it to continue operating in case of a power failure. RTLM was ostensibly founded to counter *Radio Muhabura* (Radio Beacon), the Rwanda Patriotic Front's (RPF) radio station, but no evidence has been found by Reporters sans frontières to suggest that the RPF station was guilty of spreading hate propaganda against the Hutu of Rwanda (La Brosse 1995, 34, 42–44). Indeed, with the benefit of hindsight, it seems likely that RTLM was founded to evade key clauses of the Arusha Peace Accords of 1993 which barred the Government of Rwanda, as well as the RPF, from incitements to violence, promoting discrimination based on ethnicity, and issuing propaganda inciting the people to hate (*République Rwandaise* 1993).

The preamble of RTLM's articles of incorporation represent it as aspiring to: become a model disseminator of democratic values; contribute to the positive evolution of a pluralist democracy; circulate diverse ideas; strengthen republican institutions; further the harmonious development of society; and educate the public through the fair and objective transmission of news. But the Hutu-extremist publication Kangura came closer to the truth when it celebrated the establishment of RTLM as a colleague in the struggle to unite the Hutu, "the majority people," and to awaken and defend them. Summarizing the actual agenda of RTLM in its report on human rights in Rwanda for 1994, the U.S. Department of State observed:

After President Habyarimana's death, Radio Mille Collines broadcast strident anti-Tutsi and anti-RPF propaganda, which ultimately had a lethal effect, calling on the Hutu majority to destroy the Tutsi minority. Experts cited Mille Collines as an important factor in the spread of genocide in the hours and days following Habyarimana's death. (U.S. Congress, Senate, and House 1995, 204)

Impact of Radio on the Genocide and Refugee Flows

By African standards, Rwandese enjoyed good access to RTLM and Radio Rwanda broadcasts. The BBC estimates that the median saturation of radios in sub-Saharan Africa in 1992 was about 13.5 per one-hundred persons, while radio ownership in Rwanda is 25 per one-hundred persons. The United States Information Agency (USIA) reports that RTLM's broadcasts of four hours per day in Kinyarwanda and French were clearly heard in the Kigali area, and Reporters sans frontières indicates that RTLM's programs were relayed to all parts of the country via a network of transmitters owned and operated by the government's Radio Rwanda.[4]

To the best of my knowledge, although they were monitored sporadically by the US Foreign Broadcast Information Service, the BBC, and the United Nations Assistance Mission for Rwanda (UNAMIR), no one has published complete transcripts of RTLM's and Radio Rwanda's broadcasts. However, selections from them have been quoted in testimony before US Congressional committees, in the reports of human rights groups, in the Western media generally and in Chrétien 1995. As the following excerpts from and about RTLM and Radio Rwanda broadcasts show, they played important roles as inciters and coordinators of the Rwandese genocide:[5]

End of 1993
RTLM named individual Tutsi and Hutu opposed to President Habyarimana as "enemies" or "traitors" who deserved death. In a typical broadcast attack, an RTLM announcer followed the song "Monique" by declaring: "Monique should be crucified in her front yard and eaten by dogs." The reference to Monique Mujawamariya, one of Rwanda's leading and most courageous human rights activists, would have been clear to all Rwandese listeners. (Alison DesForges 1995)

March 31, 1994
Radio Rwanda attributed to the RPF an ideology of "ethnic purification." It misleadingly described the Coalition pour la Défense de la République (CDR), a Hutu extremist party, as pacifist and realistic because it recognized the ethnic problem which had been eating away at Rwanda for centuries. It reported that the CDR had denounced the ideology of ethnic purification advocated by extremist RPF members and urged the RPF to renounce once and for all its ideology of power struggle based on vengeance and revenge.

April 7, 1994

RTLM called on Hutu to avenge the death of the Rwandese President. Within hours, it declared: "The graves are not yet quite full. Who is going to do the good work and help us fill them completely" (Prunier 1995, 224). *The Washington Post* quoted a radio broadcast warning Tutsi in Rwanda: "You cockroaches must know you are made of flesh! We won't let you kill! We will kill you!"

April 12, 1994

RTLM broadcast that "the International Committee of the Red Cross was saving the lives of Tutsi only."

April 19, 1994

Theodore Sindikubwabo, a Hutu extremist and "President" of the government of Rwanda which proclaimed itself after the death of Habyarimana, replaced Jean-Baptiste Habyarimana (not a relative of the former president), the human rights-oriented prefect of Butare, with Sylvain Nsabimana as civilian administrator, and Tarcisse Muvunyi, a military man sympathetic to slaughtering Hutu members of the political opposition and Tutsi. In a radio broadcast the same day, Sindikubwabo advocated the killing of "accomplices" in Butare. Units of the Presidential Guard then flew into Butare to begin ethnically and politically-based mass killing in that previously calm prefecture.

April 25, 1994

The Associated Press quoted U.N. spokesman in Kigali as saying, "Radio RTLM is calling on militias to step up the killing of civilians."

May 29, 1994

Radio Rwanda declared that the RPF was cheating people with smooth words while it was really a wolf which covered itself with a sheep's skin. It asserted that the RPF was killing Hutu despite RPF lies that it did no harm to them. It falsely claimed that the Tutsi *Inyenzi* (cockroaches) had butchered Hutu in Ruhengeri, Byumba, Kingungu, and Kigali.

June 23, 1994

According to the Reuters news service, Radio RTLM said the French were coming to fight on the side of the (Hutu extremist) interim government and were bringing new weapons.[6]

Many of the journalists who worked for RTLM came from the ranks of the Coalition pour la Défense de la République (CDR) and were even more extreme in their anti-Tutsi racism than their colleagues in the *Mouvement Révolutionnaire National pour le Développement* (*et la Démocratie*), the MRND(D). These true believers were also authentic radio innovators. They revolutionized Rwandese radio broadcasting by abandoning the tradition of stiff, formal presentations in favour of more relaxed Western-style "talk radio," punctuated by popular music, dirty jokes, and lots of street slang. As Gérard Prunier tells us, they slyly inserted culturally coded incitements into their patter, such as "soon 'one would have to reach for the top part of the house' (i.e., the place where traditionally weapons were hung)." Like Hassan Ngeze, the editor of *Kangura*, who prophesied that President Habyarimana would die in March 1994, an RTLM broadcast on Sunday, 3 April, reported by Prunier, hinted that the President was about to die and a blood bath would follow:

> On the 3rd, 4th, and 5th, heads will get heated up. On 6 April, there will be a respite, but 'little thing' might happen. Then on the 7th and the 8th and the other days in April, you will see something. (Prunier 1995, 222–23)

The important role of radio disinformation in the killing of neighbour by neighbour is emphasized by Bill Berkeley, who visited Rwanda twice in 1994. In an interview given to Berkeley, Pierre-Claver Rwangabo, a Hutu moderate, emphasized the role of radio broadcasts as an important source of mass participation in the genocide:

> I want to insist on the effect of propaganda.... Since the beginning of the war with the RPF, this propaganda always said that it was the Tutsi coming to attack the country. All they said all day was that it was the Tutsi coming to take power away from the Hutus. So when they got finished killing the opposition leaders after the crash, and the RPF came to protect the people from the massacres, the radio again said it was the Tutsi who are coming to take power. But they never said on the radio that the Hutu prime minister was killed. People listening to the radio thought it was the RPF who started the massacres.[7] (Berkeley 1995, A17)

A twenty-nine-year-old peasant, Alfred Kiruhura, who served with the Hutu death squads responsible for killing Tutsi, told Berkeley:

> I did not believe the Tutsi were coming to kill us...but when the government radio continued to broadcast that they were coming to take our land, were coming to kill the Hutu—when this was repeated over and over—I began to feel some kind of fear.

The lies broadcast by radio stations affiliated with the Rwandese government were "the match that started the fire," concludes Berkeley (Berkeley 1994, 18).

RPF troops drove the Provisional Government and the forces allied with the *AKAZU* out of Kigali in July 1994. RTLM went off the air on 3 July, but returned to the airwaves one week later. The makers of the genocide, resourceful as ever, introduced mobile FM transmitters and broadcast disinformation from Gisenyi, within the French-occupied *Opération Turquoise* zone on the border between Rwanda and Zaire. This time, their propaganda operation sent millions of Hutu who feared Tutsi reprisals fleeing toward refugee camps, where they could be regrouped and recruited as future fighters. More than two million Hutu sought refuge in Zaire, Tanzania, and Burundi, while roughly two million more abandoned their homes and fled to other parts of Rwanda. Human Rights Watch/Africa reports that the Hutu refugees

fled in panic about reports that the RPF was approaching their region, not because they had been attacked or seen others attacked by the incoming troops. They had been frightened by propaganda broadcast on the radio about supposed RPF atrocities. (U.S. Congress, Senate 1994, 52–53; U.S. Congress, Senate, and House 1995, 200)

On 14 and 15 July 1994, Reuters reported that the broadcasts of a mobile radio station operating in the vicinity of Gisenyi, on the Zaire border, were urging Rwandese Hutu to escape into Zaire. On 19 July, a French food relief organization, International Action Against Famine (AICF) declared that the radio

has prompted general hysteria among people who believe only in their leaders, who have made devils out of the Rwanda Patriotic Front. People are scared out of their wits. (U.S. Congress, Senate 1994, 78–79)

Western Responses

No Western country responded positively to proposals from human rights and humanitarian groups such as Human Rights Watch and the United States Committee for Refugees that it shut down or jam the broadcasts of RTLM and Radio Rwanda. Indeed, one of the first victims of the genocide was Faustin Rucogoza, a Hutu from the MDR *(Le mouvement démocratique républicain)* who as information minister had threatened to close down Radio Télévision Libre Mille Collines (Hilsum 1994, 14, 16). When Human Rights Watch/Africa protested the broadcasts to Bruno Delaye, Chief Counsellor on Africa to the French Presidency, he responded that "France was willing to stop the broadcasts but was unable to locate the transmitter." Human Rights Watch/Africa found:

[I]t wholly unbelievable that the French military, which had full control over the zone and had close relations with the FAR [Rwandese Armed Forces], was not in a position to locate this radio transmitter. (Human Rights Watch Arms Project 1995, 7)

The United States Committee for Refugees, exasperated, reported that

State Department officials on several occasions expressed to USCR that they were studying the possibility of jamming Radio Mille Collines and the government radio station in Rwanda—that they were aware of the insidious propaganda power of the broadcasts—but they ultimately said that various legal and technical possibilities precluded taking action.... Moreover, numerous military personnel and radio technicians have indicated to USCR that jamming radio stations—especially those with weak signals—is not technically difficult. U.S. officials on one occasion said they were prevented from jamming the broadcasts because they were unable to locate the frequency. USCR responded by informing the State Department that the broadcasts were airing on 94.1 FM. The Administration took no action. (U.S. Congress, Senate 1994, 66–67)

RTLM and Radio Rwanda wove rings around the U.N.'s military force, Western governments, and the foreign NGOs. Before the genocide was underway, there was no U.N. radio station to counter the incitement of violence against U.N. military personnel (Chrétien 1995, 269–73) or to set the record straight when RTLM and Radio Rwanda claimed the Belgians or the RPF had definitely shot down President Habaryimana's aeroplane. Once the genocide was underway, there were no broadcasts by UNAMIR, VOA, BBC, or Radio Deutschewelle to warn the extremist Hutu forces and those they deluded or intimidated into helping them that those who committed or abetted mass murder stood condemned in the eyes of the world and would be brought to justice. There were no broadcasts by third parties to the conflict urging Hutu villagers to defend their Tutsi friends and neighbors, to offer them refuge, or to combat the myth that the RPF was executing a genocide against Hutu Rwandese. And there were no serious attempts to deploy armed forces radio jamming specialists from any of the countries whose governments stood by and wrung their hands as hundreds of thousands of Tutsi and Hutu opponents of the regime were brutally killed.

The Jamming Issue

Major-General Roméo A. Dallaire, commander of the U.N. peace keepers in Kigali, has declared that "if he had been equipped with proper jamming devices, many lives might have been spared [in Rwanda]" (Broadbent 1995, B3). But, sadly, the danger posed by hate radio aroused little U.N. reaction beyond his Kigali headquarters until August, when the genocide had been accomplished and the massive flow of Hutu refugees had been underway for a month. Despite its attacks on diplomats in Kigali, many of the Western ambassadors—the American, the Canadian, and the French—took a benign view of RTLM and its broadcasts, opposing forceful measures to silence it. American Ambassador David P. Rawson claimed it was a good source of information and that its statements could be interpreted many ways. Canadian Ambassador Lucie Edwards, acknowledging that everybody listened to RTLM, found it difficult to take it seriously because "there were so many genuinely silly things being said on the station, so many obvious lies" (Adelman and Suhrke 1996, 20, endnotes 37, 45).

This was not the view of UNAMIR or its commander, who believed that the broadcasts undermined Rwandese respect for UNAMIR and his leadership. After monitoring Radio Rwanda and RTLM broadcasts inciting violence against UNAMIR troops, Dallaire had protested to the government of Rwanda and lodged several fruitless requests that it interdict the radio attacks. Then, on 7 April, Rwandan troops murdered Prime Minister Agathe Uwilingiyimana and 10 UNAMIR soldiers of the Belgian contingent guarding her. As the genocide proceeded, RTLM kept up its attacks on UNAMIR. On 18 April, UNAMIR monitored RTLM attacks on the U.N. force, "its Belgium crony and its General whose departure is the wish of everybody." On 29 April, RTLM accused Belgium of downing Habaryimana's airplane and demanded General Dallaire's resignation because he was allegedly siding with the RPF. Dallaire's informal requests for authority and special equipment to interdict such broadcasts were buried in the U.N.'s overwhelmed New York headquarters (Interview, U.N. Senior officials 1995).

It was the tidal wave of Hutu refugees flooding Zaire, not incitement to genocide or attacks on UNAMIR, that brought the hate broadcasts of RTLM officially to the attention of the U.N. Security Council. On 3 August, Secretary-General Boutros Boutros-Ghali reported to the Security Council that about 1.5 million Rwandese had fled to Zaire during a two-week period in July. He then went on to note that

> the swift RPF advance had the effect of causing large numbers of civilians to take flight from the areas of combat, but this displacement might well have been containable had not panic been caused by deliberately inflammatory broadcasts from radio stations controlled by elements of the former government. (U.N. Department of Public Information 1994, 17)

The next day, Kofi Annan, then still U.N. Under-Secretary for Peacekeeping Operations, forwarded to U.N. Special Representative Shahryar Khan, a United Kingdom request that the Secretary-General's Special Representative, the French and the Zairois find the ways and the means to stop the broadcasts. On 19 August, after two further weeks of RTLM broadcasts, UNAMIR headquarters in Kigali officially requested that the U.N. Department of Peace-keeping Operations ask Canada to provide it with a jamming capability. Nearly another week later, on 25 August, the Permanent Mission of Canada at the U.N. in New York sent a message to Canadian authorities in Ottawa asking them to look into providing such a capability. On 7 September, Canadian National Defence Headquarters refused that request on the grounds that UNAMIR was not an enforcement force and therefore had no mandate to engage in offensive operations such as jamming (Interview, Senior officials 1995).

Senior Defence and State Department officials in Washington were just as disinclined to take the radio broadcasts seriously as their U.N., Canadian, and French colleagues. Between the end of April and early June, American human rights and humanitarian aid specialists, including some at the Pentagon and the State Department, asked the Defence Department to mobilize an operation against RTLM. On the heels of their requests, in early June, Senator Edward Kennedy (Dem.-Mass.) appealed to the Clinton administration, encouraging it to launch a jamming operation. His intervention resulted in a National Security Council query to the Defence Department asking if jamming was feasible. In the absence of political will in the office of the Secretary of Defence and a clear order from the President to jam RTLM, risk averse Defence Department lawyers warned against violating the national sovereignty of states experiencing domestic conflicts and their citizens' right to free speech. The lawyers argued that under international law the US was bound to respect the sovereignty of the Rwandese government as long as it granted it diplomatic recognition and did not regard it as an enemy state. Respect for Rwandese sovereignty, in their view, also included non-interference with the First Amendment rights of Rwandese broadcasters. Defence Department officials also raised questions about who would reimburse their budget for the nearly $4 million that it estimated the operation would cost (Interview, Senior officials 1995).

Once the mammoth refugee flow hit Zaire, Washington joined the list of international players entreating France to put RTLM off the air. When the French issued their routine refusal, the Defence Department sparked meetings with the United States Information Agency, urging it to beam special broadcasts to the Hutu refugees in Zaire. Thus, in August 1994, long after Reporters sans frontières had established a temporary broadcasting unit transmitting accurate news reports to the refugees in Zaire, Defense Department officials were just starting talks with the United States Information Agency about reaching the refugees with specially designed VOA broadcasts (Interviews, Senior officials 1995; Burkhalter 1994, 51–52).

Conclusion

Not everyone at the State Department agrees that hate broadcasting played a key role in the genocide in Rwanda or the massive flight of refugees. Some officials contend that exaggerations of the effect of hate radio broadcasts hide the greater importance of underlying sociopolitical cleavages and that it was the political situation which largely accounted for the willingness of Hutu peasants to kill their Tutsi neighbors and for their readiness to flee when the RPF captured Kigali. These officials argue that if the U.N. had broadcast denials of a Tutsi conspiracy to annihilate Rwanda's Hutu, the broadcasts would have been integrated into Hutu conspiracy theories which claimed that the U.N. intended to deliver Rwanda into the hands of the RPF. Some American officials also argue that equal attention must be paid to the important role of newspapers and the "bush telegraph" in spreading hate propaganda. Yet even these critics admit that the broadcasts of Radio Mille Collines played a large part in coordinating the genocide (Interviews, Senior officials 1995).

State Department officials with expertise in psychological warfare agree that when a genocide is imminent or underway, efforts should be made to knock out the perpetrator's radio transmitters. Given the difficulties of rapidly jamming transmitters, they recommend sabotage, commando raids, or air attacks to accomplish this task. In their view, successful assaults on existing facilities would force perpetrators to fall back on low powered, shorter range FM transmitters, which, they argue, would be much easier to jam. A jamming force using the experts and the special technology of the former Western or Eastern blocs would actually find it easier to put FM jamming equipment quickly into position than to establish a high powered AM broadcasting system to counter the perpetrator's propaganda. Experts from the advanced industrial countries are far more skilled at jamming than perpetrators in countries like Rwanda and Somalia. It takes relatively little skill to operate one of the portable FM transmitters available from manufacturers in Canada and Germany, but a great deal of know-how to make a success of jamming them.[8]

In my view, freedom of speech arguments fail when radio broadcasts directly violate Article III (c) of the U.N. Genocide Convention, naming "direct and public incitement to commit genocide" as punishable under the Convention. As early as 1968, the Government of Canada took a major step towards implementing the Genocide Convention in its domestic legislation by outlawing hate propaganda advocating or promoting genocide against an identifiable group. American law echoes the Canadian precedent in this case. American Defence Department lawyers should have been aware that the Proxmire Act of 1987 provided for a fine of not more than $500,000 or imprisonment for not more than five years for individuals convicted of inciting others to commit genocide, and that, when passing the Proxmire Act, Congress clearly signified that the First Amendment does not protect those who advocate genocide "in circumstances under which there is substantial likelihood of imminently causing such conduct" (Interviews, Senior officials 1995; Chalk and Jonassohn 1990, 44–53). In the case of Rwanda, the imminence of genocide was not an issue; genocide was underway. It also should have been clear that incitements to hatred such as those occurring in Rwanda violated the terms of the 1966 U.N. International Covenant on Civil and Political Rights and the 1965 International Convention on the Elimination of All Forms of Racial Discrimination (Heintze and Frederick 1990, 91–97).

Senior U.S. government officials also expressed fears regarding the security of nations who cooperate with U.N. or NGO humanitarian broadcasters by lending them their facilities or permitting them to import their own transmission equipment. These American officials expressed concern that the humanitarian use of borrowed broadcasting facilities in the countries adjacent to a human rights crisis might increase international tensions and provoke armed attacks on the offending transmitters. The issue of armed attacks on U.N. and NGO transmitting facilities is a serious one. In the event that there were such attacks, the U.S. and the U.N. would indeed be challenged to respond. Since the U.N. has a clear mandate to defend its members against genocide and international aggression, it seems obvious to me that U.S. officials should place the burden of responsibility where it properly belongs—on the shoulders of the perpetrators of such offenses. Attacks on U.N. and NGO broadcasting equipment and personnel are likely to arouse public indignation against the attackers and to build support in the West for swift and powerful retaliatory measures that can only increase support for further aid to the victims of hate broadcasting. Moreover, the U.S. and the U.N. should have realized by now that the risks of supporting human rights broadcasting are far lower than the human and economic costs of passivity in the face of genocide and gross violations of human rights.

Since the genocide in Rwanda of April to July 1994, several pioneers of human rights broadcasting in Rwanda and Burundi have blazed new trails that should inspire emulation by governments and NGOs. They are:

- Philippe Dahinden, reporter for Swiss radio, who founded Radio Muraho ("Hello, How Are You?") which broadcast briefly around Rwanda with support from Reporters sans frontières and a group of Rwandese human rights activists in June 1994, while refusing any financial aid from the French government (Péronnet 1994, x).
- UNAMIR's own station, Radio Minuar, which finally made it to air in February 1995 (Agence France Presse 1995).
- Studio Ijambo (Crossroads Where Wise Conversation Takes Place in Kirundi), a radio station in Bujumbura which produces three to four hours of programming per week for broadcast on Burundi state radio and Radio Agatashya, a station in Eastern Zaire. Their broadcasts, intended to counteract hate radio and to promote peace and reconciliation in Burundi, are sponsored by Search for Common Ground, a Washington-based conflict resolution organization, using funds provided by the U.N., USAID, the National Endowment for Democracy, the Winston Foundation, and the Unitarian-Universalist Association (Search for Common Ground 1995).
- Montrealers Gérard Le Chêne of Informaction and Rose Ndeyahoze, who joined with TV5 Afrique, and a technical crew from Télévision sénégalaise to document in thirty segments the stories of courageous Hutu and Tutsi who helped each other amidst the horror of Rwanda's genocide. Their series was broadcast around the world by TV5 in May 1995 (InformAction 1995); and
- Radio Amwizero (Hope) of Burundi, funded with $500,000 by the European Commission at the instigation of Bernard Kouchner. It was licensed in February 1996 "to counteract the effects of 'hate media' and to work for peace..." at the same time that Radio Democracy, a hardline Hutu radio station which broadcasts from mobile transmitters in Zaire, came under attack by jammers broadcasting rock music over its frequency (Jennings 1996).

For too long, proponents of the extension of human rights and democratic development have neglected radio's potential as an influential medium. The architects of hate radio, using Western equipment and techniques, won the battle of the airwaves in Rwanda. Now is the time for the U.N., the democracies, and human rights NGOs to seize the initiative by assembling, funding, coordinating, and protecting the essential components of democratic radio in all the regions where genocide and gross violations of human rights are present or potentially imminent (Chalk 1995).

Notes

1. The author would like to acknowledge the help he received in researching this subject from a number of senior officers of the United States Department of

State, Department of Defense, and the United States Information Agency, as well as various Canadian military researchers and Brian Sawyer, a Canadian Broadcasting Corporation radio engineer. He is indebted to Edward Kissi and Patrick Reed for their conscientious and skilled assistance in research. He would also like to thank for their constructive comments on earlier drafts of this essay the members of the graduate student and faculty workshop of the Montreal Institute for Genocide and Human Rights Studies (MIGS): Karin Bjornson, Mervin Butovsky, Catherine Chatterlee, Natalie Fingerhut, Nicolas Gauvin, Kurt Jonassohn, Philip Katz, Edward Kissi, Krisha Starker, and Pat Reed. For any errors in this essay only the author is responsible.

2. Ferdinand Nahimana, one of eleven people alleged to be architects of Rwanda's 1994 genocide, was arrested in Yaounde, Cameroon in April 1996 and held for hearings to determine if he should be extradited for trial in Rwanda (Associated Press 1996, B1).

3. RTLM's director-in-chief was Gaspard Bahigi, formerly an officer of ORINFOR in charge of print media, later the director of the Rwanda national radio and a reporter for Agence France Presse based in Kigali (La Brosse 1995, 42; see also Chrétien 1995, 72).

4. Cf. United States Information Agency 1995, 9, 111–12; La Brosse 1995, 43–44. South Africans own the largest number of radios in Africa, per person, with thirty-three radios per one-hundred persons, while Somalis, with five to seven radios per one-hundred persons, are at the bottom of the list. Research indicates that the average radio has about five listeners, the size of a small African family (United States Information Agency 1995, 9, 111–12).

5. For a detailed account of broadcasts during the genocide itself, see the contributions by Faustin Kagame of unpublished transcripts of RTLM from April 1994, which he recorded and which are included in Linda Kirschke, Richard Carver, and Sandra Coliver, *Broadcasting Genocide: Censorship, Propaganda & State-Sponsored Violence in Rwanda 1990–1994*, London: Article 19, International Centre Against Censorship, October 1996. There are also extensive quotes throughout Chrétien 1995.

6. For the above and other quotes and comments, cf. Alison DesForges, Human Rights Watch/Africa and Jeff Drumtra, U.S. Committee for Refugees, Washington, D.C., U.S. Congress, Senate 1994, 50–51, 71–73, 77; Berkeley 1994, 18; Hilsum 1994, 14; African Rights 1994, 231–32; Prunier 1995, 240, 244; Chrétien 1995, 337–58 which includes translations of the songs; and especially Kirschke, *et al* 1996.

7. Pierre-Claver Rwangabo was assassinated by unknown assailants on 4 March 1995 (Berkeley 1995, A17).

8. Interviews, Ottawa, Senior Officials, 1995. In Somalia, it seems that jamming was tried by some of the clans, but they could not make it work (Interviews, Washington, Senior officials, 1995).

Part II

Preventive Diplomacy

6

The OAU: Conflict Prevention, Management and Resolution

Amare Tekle

Introduction

As in much of the rest of its activities, the record of the Organization of African Unity (OAU) in conflict resolution has been largely dismal. This is a reflection of the structural weaknesses of the organization. They, in turn, reflect, on the one hand, the nature of the post-colonial African state and, on the other, the organization's position and role in the international system during the Cold War.

In fact, the OAU was, by design, intended to be born stillborn because of the softness of the post-colonial African state. Originally, the OAU was created as a convenient cover for the bad governance and the political banalities of the vast majority of African governments as well as a disguise for their close links with extra-African powers. The principles on which it was based (e.g., nonintervention, noninterference) and subsequent decisions and resolutions (e.g., the sanctity of colonial boundaries), as well as the strong abhorrence and outright rejection of the military aspects of conflict management and resolution, were all rooted in the underlying premises on which the post-colonial African state was founded. These had serious implications for the mission it was expected to fulfill.

True, the OAU has, since its inception, been preoccupied with the management of African conflicts and the creation of appropriate organs for conflict management.[1] To this end, the Heads of State and Government had, in fact, created the Commission of Mediation, Conciliation, and Arbitration, which has been described as the *raison d'être* of the OAU itself and the "sole organ of the OAU *specifically and exclusively* [my italics] charged with conflict resolution" (Polhemus 1971, 113). However, it is a sad historical fact that the Commission was stillborn. Several attempts to give it new life were dismal failures. The Commission was seriously handicapped from the beginning because its jurisdiction was limited to interstate conflicts only (completely neglecting or ignoring intrastate disputes and conflicts) and because its sole mission was conflict *resolution* rather than conflict *prevention* (OAU, 1993: Part 1, 3). Further, the Assembly of Heads of State and Government (AHG), the supreme organ of the OAU, retained primary responsibility and ultimate authority for the resolution of conflicts and involved itself in many ways in conflict management, primarily as a catalyst for negotiations and private discussions, though it was the Council of Ministers which was the most active organ of conflict management during the first fourteen years of the OAU, meeting ten times in extraordinary sessions to consider African conflicts (Polhemus 1971, 81–82). Under the circumstances, the OAU routinely resorted to the creation of politically inspired *ad hoc* bodies by either the Assembly of Heads of State and Government or the Council of Ministers (Polhemus 1971, 311–12). For example, one such *ad hoc* body was created to study the Rwanda-Burundi conflict in 1968. *Ad hoc* bodies were favored largely because member states had shown a strong preference for political processes of conflict resolution rather than for judicial means of settlement [OAU, CM/1767 (LVIII); see also Polhemus 1971, 4 and 8]. While this *modus operandi* was useful in the initial years of enthusiasm following the creation of the OAU, it had become less and less useful afterwards, if only because it consumed a lot of time which neither the Heads of State and Government nor even their Foreign Ministers had.

Thus, it was not until the Chad crisis (1980) that the OAU had the first real opportunity to attempt a peacekeeping operation [OAU, CM/1767 (LVIII):25], although, prior to that, some African countries had participated in peacekeeping operations sponsored by the U.N. (Cervenka 1977, 101). Previous attempts by the OAU to deploy peacekeeping forces, as in the Congo (1965) [OAU, CM 1767 (LVIII):25] and Angola (1975) (Cervenka 1977, 103), had been fruitless.[2] The OAU involvement in Chad was unique because it was, on the one hand, its first operation and, on the other, it was a *military* involvement in conflict management.

Despite several failures,[3] the thirty-fifth ordinary session of the Council of Ministers, held in Freetown, Sierra Leone, from 18–28 June 1980, adopted a resolution which recommended one more attempt to find an

African solution to an African crisis. In particular, it decided to request African states *which were in a position to do so* to provide military contingents to a peacekeeping force *at their own expense and in accordance with conditions* to be determined by the Summit which was to follow the Council Session, provided that *logistic and operational costs would be met from voluntary contributions* [OAU, CM 1767 (LVIII):26–27]. As a precautionary measure, it was decided that the U.N. Security Council would be requested to provide assistance in the event of failure by the OAU to raise the necessary funds. (OAU, CM 1767 (LVIII):27) This was itself a recipe for ensuring failure, and although Nigeria, Senegal and Zaire volunteered troops, it was not possible to send such a peacekeeping force to Chad given the insurmountable logistical and financial costs.

One year later, the Nairobi summit mandated the then Current Chairman, President Daniel arap Moi of Kenya, to contact OAU member states *and other friendly countries* to raise money for such a fund. France volunteered to pay the transportation and logistical expenses of 600 Senegalese troops and the U.S. provided US $12 million for logistical help for the 700 Zairean and 2,000 Nigerian troops [OAU, CM 1767 (LVIII)]. This, however, was not enough. President Moi had to ask the U.N. Security Council for additional financial, material, and technical assistance. Declaring that "such an action would be unprecedented," the Security Council refused to make such a contribution unless the peacekeeping operation was under the direct political and military authority of the Security Council [OAU, CM 1767 (LVIII)]. This condition had a detrimental effect on the morale of the troops and, according to the OAU, jeopardized the whole operation.

Perhaps for this reason, there was a big debate concerning peacekeeping as opposed to peacemaking functions of the proposed OAU Mechanism for Conflict Prevention, Management, and Resolution. While there was almost total acceptance of the conflict resolution (peacemaking) role of the Mechanism,[4] there were misgivings about, and indeed strong objections to, its peacekeeping functions. The compromise that emerged from the lengthy discussions and consultations was that peacekeeping should be maintained as "a long-term measure" [OAU, CM 1767 (LVIII):40].

Changes in the OAU

The great events that shook the world in 1989–90 and challenged existing principles, norms, and values as well as state structures and, consequently, brought significant changes in both domestic and international politics have not been limited to Eastern Europe. Africa too had its shares of such historic events—some positive, some negative. Both negative and positive developments challenged the underlying legal premises and political assumptions on which the OAU had hitherto operated. The OAU was ripe for change. To their credit, most African leaders, and particularly Secretary General Salim Ahmed Salim, recognized the impact of these events and were ready to make the necessary positive arrangements to meet the new challenges.

The *Addis Ababa Declaration Of The Assembly of Heads of State and Government On The Political And Socio-Economic Situation In Africa And The Fundamental Changes Taking Place In The World*, adopted in July 1990, saw "in the light of the rapid changes taking place in the world and their impact on Africa" the need "to promote popular participation of our peoples in the process of government and development...to guarantee human rights and the observance of law...to recommit ourselves to the further democratization of our societies," and to make the OAU a viable instrument [OAU, AHG/Dec. 1 (XXVIII) 1990:1]

Two matters, the need for a conflict management mechanism and the revision of hopelessly outdated principles and resolutions on which many a catastrophic OAU decisions or action had been based, became plainly obvious. Of these, the principles of noninterference and nonintervention had become meaningless—indeed obstructionist—in view of the difficulties faced in solving African crises. According to the OAU, the 1990 Addis Ababa declaration was, therefore, "a path-breaking instrument to the extent that it was a manifestation of member states' broadening consensus on widening the definition of the noninterference principle" and that "it signaled acceptance by member states that the OAU could concern itself not only with inter-state conflicts *but with internal ones as well*" [OAU, CM/1710 (XVI) 1992:11].

Accordingly, the OAU Secretary General presented a proposal to create an OAU Mechanism for Conflict Prevention, Management, and Resolution to the Summit in Dakar, Senegal, in June 1992. By a Declaration made at its twenty-ninth ordinary session which met in Cairo between 28–30 June 1993, the Assembly of Heads of State and Government established the proposed Mechanism. The Declaration prescribed that the primary objective of the Mechanism would be "the anticipation and prevention of Conflicts...to undertake peace making and peace-building functions."[5]

This gave the OAU the essential opportunity to create a new institutional dynamism to prevent, manage, or resolve conflicts as speedily and effectively as possible. For once since its creation, it was being given a proactive role which required it to go beyond the adoption of platitudinous resolutions which merely appealed to the goodwill of conflicting parties to exercise restraint.

The "Central Organ," which was the main institution of the Mechanism, was to be composed of the state members of the Bureau of the Assembly of Heads of State and Government which is elected at every Summit, thus ensuring rotation. However, the states of the outgoing chairman and the incoming chairman, when known in advance, were also to be members, thus ensuring continuity and stability. The Central Organ was to be answerable to the Assembly.

Presumably, the Declaration also empowered the Secretary General to respond with speed and decisiveness either to prevent or, at any rate, to resolve any conflict situation that may arise in the continent [OAU, CM/1710 (VI) 1992:1].

Thus, the Secretary General was expected to:

- take initiatives in situations of emergency or actual conflicts; play the facilitating role of the neutral party in the management of change (through elections) within member states;
- research and monitor situations in advance with the objective of getting and analyzing information and thus establishing an *Early Warning System* to prevent conflicts;
- deploy appropriate measures in cases where conflicts have reached an advanced stage. [OAU, CM/1710 (VI) 1992:4]

In internal conflicts which, in the present political context, were seen to be the major preoccupation of the OAU, the fact that he was to be given a "free hand" to take initiatives on his own and "to engage in dialogue with the parties to such conflicts with a view to opening up direct dialogue between/amongst the parties" was regarded as a qualitative change in the role of the Secretary General [OAU, CM/1710 (VI) 1992].

Two precautionary notes must, however, be made. In the first place, in spite of the good will extended to the proposal, there were still lingering doubts about the OAU's role in conflict prevention. The debate during the Dakar Council of Ministers and Summit Sessions in June 1992, as well as the written responses made by member states to the OAU inquiries, revealed that while there was a near unanimity on the

OAU's potential role in peacemaking, there was a lack of consensus on its peacekeeping and prevention roles [OAU, CM/1747 (LVII) 1993: 9]. The ostensible reason given by those who urged the OAU to limit itself to a peacemaking role and to let the U.N. concentrate on peace-keeping, was "the high cost of such ventures" [OAU, CM/1747 (LVII) 1993:9]. In fact, it was as a "face-saving" device that a compromise was made to retain the OAU role in peacekeeping and prevention as "a long-term measure" [OAU, CM/1747 (LVII) 1993]. The real issue was the old concern of noninterference couched as "constitutional issues" [OAU, CM/1747 (LVII) 1993] evident from the clear determination of the sponsors of the Mechanism to convey to all concerned that the prin-ciples and norms on which the Mechanism itself was based were: non-interference in the internal affairs of state; respect of sovereignty and territorial integrity of each state; peaceful settlement of disputes by negotiation, mediation, conciliation, and arbitration, the inviolability of colonial borders and consent and cooperation of the parties to the conflict [OAU, CM/1747 (LVII) 1993:3].

Yet, there was, at the same time, an attempt to diminish the impact of even this commitment. First, the OAU seems to assert categorically that intervention may be more easily accepted only when there is a total breakdown of law and order (Somalia, Liberia) and where a spillover of human suffering is experienced by neighboring states. In such a situation, the OAU declares, "intervention may be justified on humanitarian grounds as well as on the need to restore law and order" [OAU, CM/1710 (XVI) Rev 1:12]. Secondly, it emphasizes that pre-emptive involvement "should also be permitted even in situations where tensions evolve to such a pitch that it becomes apparent that a conflict is in the making" and that "this would transform into real terms the OAU's expressed commitment to conflict prevention" [OAU, CM/1710 (XVI) Rev 1:12].

However, outdated principles have not been the only difficulties that faced the OAU in the fulfillment of its new mission. There were also "operationalization" difficulties, particularly related to manpower and finance. The Secretary General had, until recently, no executive power. From the beginning, the majority of the founding members wanted to avoid a strong and independently minded (not to mention charismatic) Secretary General. Until 1977, therefore, his title was *Administrative* Secretary General, insisted upon by the majority of the Founding Fa-thers. At the Libreville Summit (1977), when the "Administrative" was deleted from the title, he was also given competence to participate in the resolution of disputes—but only for one single time. It was only after the Cairo Summit (1993), which created the present mechanism, that the Secretary General was given an important role in the resolution of conflict. Equally, throughout its history, the OAU faced—and continues to face—critical financial problems which affect its conflict management operations.

Paragraph 23 of the Declaration that established the Mechanism had provided for the establishment of a *Special Fund* "for the purpose of providing financial resources to support *exclusively OAU operational activities* relating to conflict management and resolution (OAU, Central Organ/MEC/AMB. 3/REV. 1, 1994:5). An initial amount of US $1 million was to be made up of financial appropriations from the working capital budget of the OAU and to be supplemented by voluntary contributions from member states and other sources within Africa (OAU, Central Organ/MEC/AMB. 3/REV. 1, 1994:7). This initial budget was "to be replenished or added to" on an annual basis. On 7 December 1993, the Assembly decided that 5 percent of the OAU regular budget should be earmarked and transferred into the Peace Fund (OAU, CM/ 1805; OAU, Central Organ/MEC/AMB. 3/REV. 1, 1994:2). Since the Mechanism had to be an "essentially African affair," if it were to be credible and effective, it was emphasized that the African component of the funding must always be guaranteed [OAU, Central Organ/MEC/ AMB/RPT (1):26].

The OAU *Peace Fund* was launched by the Current Chairman of the OAU Council of Ministers, Foreign Minister Amr Mussa of Egypt, on 18 November 1993. Yet, by 1994, the African component consisted only of an Algerian contribution of US $10,000 and Ethiopian Birr 60,000 (about US $10,000) from the Ambassadors' Wives and other women in Addis Ababa [OAU, CM/1829 (LX) 1994:3]. On 19 July 1994, when the genocide in Rwanda was almost over, the Namibian government allocated US $250,000 for the Rwanda operation of the OAU [OAU, Central Organ/NEC/AMB/RPT (VI): 24]. Tunisia gave medication, tents, and blankets [OAU, Central Organ/NEC/AMB/RPT (VI): 22]. Ethiopia made "a symbolic contribution" of US $10,000 in July 199 [OAU, Central Organ/NEC/AMB/RPT (VI):15].

On the other hand, Italy had pledged 300,000,000 Lira (about US $200,000) while the US, China, and Indonesia had each pledged US $100,000, US $50,000, and US $15,000, respectively [OAU, CM/1829 (LX); OAU, Central Organ/NEC/AMB/RPT (VI): 3]. Yet, although the OAU was in dire need for money, an American offer of an additional

US $1.5 million to the OAU Peace Fund was to become a matter of intense debate in the meeting of the Central Organ of 1994 before it was accepted [OAU, Central Organ/MEC/AMB/RPT (VI): 7-15]. The fact is, African funding was not available; the OAU did not have enough money to finance military operations, specifically the Rwandese one as we shall see, though advances were made, and the OAU played an active and creative role in its more traditional involvement in preventive diplomacy and peacemaking.

The OAU Involvement in the Arusha Accords

The OAU had closely followed the Rwandese conflict since the outbreak of hostilities in October 1990. Encouraged by the adoption of the *Declaration On The Political And Socio-Economic Situation In Africa And The Fundamental Changes Taking Place In The World* by the Assembly of Heads of State and Government in 1990, the OAU had participated in the N'sele Cease-fire Agreement of 29 March, 1991 and the Gbadolite meeting of 16 September 1991 which amended the N'sele Agreement. Although the Secretary General had made himself available for consultations with both parties, the OAU had not been directly and materially involved in conflict resolution until after the cease-fire agreement signed in Arusha in July 1992 between the Government of Rwanda and the Rwandese Patriotic Front (RPF), where, after a number of amendments, the N'sele and Gbadolite agreements were signed.

Under Article III (1) of the agreement, it was accepted that "the verification and control of the cease-fire shall be conducted by the Neutral Military Observer Group (NMOG) under the supervision of the Secretary General of the OAU," while section (3) of the same article provided that "the Neutral Military Observer Group shall report any violation of the cease-fire to the Secretary General of the OAU and a Joint Political Military Commission" (JPMC). The creation of the latter was intended to ensure strict adherence by the two parties to the cease-fire and to monitor the implementation of the Peace Agreement [OAU, CM/1751 (LVII) 1993:1].

Accordingly, the Secretary General of the OAU appointed the OAU Assistant Secretary General for Political Affairs, Dr. M.T. Mapuranga, as his Special Representative to Rwanda. In addition, a resident Liaison/Political Officer and a commander of the NMOG were also appointed. The former was to monitor political developments in Rwanda, to follow the negotiation process, to liaise between the Rwandese Government and the Rwandese Patriotic Front, and to serve as a link between the NMOG and OAU headquarters. [OAU, CM/1751 (LVII) 1993:32].

The JPMC was created on 12 July 1992. Its first meeting, held from 26–28 July 1992 at the headquarters of the OAU, was convened by the Secretary General and attended by high-level representatives of the two sides as well as by observers from the OAU, Burundi, Tanzania, Uganda, Belgium, France, and the USA [OAU, CM/1751 (LVII) 1993:1].

The Secretary General then approached the countries (Nigeria, Senegal, and Zimbabwe) that had been identified as contributors to NMOG by the cease free agreement. Mali was also approached by the Secretary General after consultations with the Rwandese parties to the conflict and the Facilitator of the peace process, President Muniyi of Tanzania. Upon Mali's consent, the contingent of the NMOG was fully deployed in different operational zones in Rwanda by October 1992 [OAU, CM/1751 (LVII) 1993:4].

The Special Representative of the OAU Secretary General arrived in Rwanda on 31 July 1992 to "ensure an OAU presence on the eve of the cease-fire" [OAU, CM/1751 (LVII) 1993:4]. During this visit, the Special Representative discussed the cease-fire and the NMOG operation with the President of Rwanda, Juvenal Habyarimana, and other high-ranking Rwandese political and military officials. He visited various NMOG operational theaters in Northern Rwanda, discussed logistical and other needs of the NMOG with the representatives of Belgium, France, Germany, and the US, and briefed the representatives of Burundi, Tanzania, Uganda, and Zaire on both the conclusion of the cease-fire talks and the first meeting of the JPMC [OAU, CM/1751 (LVII) 1993:4].

This first visit to Rwanda was followed by several others with a view to consulting the warring parties on matters related "to the cease-fire, the deployment and operations of the NMOG, as well as political negotiations" [OAU, CM/1751 (LVII) 1993:4]. The Special Representative also managed to arrange for the release of political and RPF war prisoners held by the Rwandese Government and captured Rwandese Government soldiers held by the RPF [OAU, CM/1751 (LVII) 1993:5–6].

On the other hand, it was evident during these visits that the NMOG faced severe logistical and financial shortages. Under the circumstances, the Secretary General had to plead with the Heads of State of the OAU (with the exception of Liberia, Rwanda and Somalia) for financial contributions to support the NMOG [OAU, CM/1751 (LVII) 1993:6], but no favorable response was received. Thus, the OAU had, yet again, to depend on the assistance of foreign powers, notably Belgium, France, Germany, and the U.S. [OAU, CM/1751 (LVII) 1993:5]. Since the assistance given by these countries was not adequate to cover the NMOG operation, it was inevitable that the work and morale of the Group would be affected negatively.

In the meantime, the OAU observer delegation to the Peace Talks was led by the Secretary General himself. The first phase of the political negotiations following the Cease-fire Agreement of 12 July 1992 convened in Arusha, Tanzania during 10–18 August 1992. The meeting, chaired by Tanzanian Minister for Higher Education, Benjamin Mkapa, and attended by the Foreign Minister of Rwanda, Boniface Nuglinzira and the Chairman of the RPF, Colonel Alexis Kanyanengwe, produced the *Protocol on the Rule of Law*. This meeting was followed by three other sessions (17–18 September 1992; 5–30 October 1992; 23 November 1992–9 January 1993) devoted to the issue of power sharing within the framework of a broad-based transitional government and to the modalities for the formation of the: (a) Presidency; (b) Cabinet; (c) Transitional Assembly; and (d) Judiciary. The Protocol Agreement was signed on 9 January 1993.

The peace process was almost scuttled after the RPF launched a military offensive on 8 February following massacres of Tutsi civilians in January 1993 after the Protocol Agreement had been signed. The Secretary General held urgent consultations with the delegations of the Rwandese Government and the RPF in Dar-es-Salaam in an attempt to restore confidence in the peace process and to ensure the continuation of the cease-fire [OAU, CM/1751 (LVIII) 1993]. This was followed by a high-level meeting between the Government of Rwanda and the RPF from 5–7 March 1993 under the Chairmanship of the Tanzanian Prime Minister, John Malecela, and, as usual, full OAU participation. The two sides signed a joint communique which provided for the:

- commitment of the two parties to a negotiated settlement within the framework of the Arusha Peace Process;
- consolidation of the Cease-fire Agreement on the basis of the N'Sele Cease-fire Agreement;
- withdrawal of foreign troops and their replacement by a neutral force organized under the auspices of the OAU;
- acceptance of a new cease-fire, to be started on 9 March;
- acceptance of new cease-fire positions based on the RPF position on 8 February;

- taking of measures against officials who were directly or indirectly involved in the massacres;
- cessation of negative radio and newspaper campaigns against each other;
- commitment of the two parties to provide adequate security and protection to displaced persons;
- holding of a joint meeting on the buffer zone between the two parties under the auspices of the Neutral Military Observer Group (NMOG);
- working out modalities for the administration of displaced persons. [OAU, CM/1751 (LVIII) 1993:2]

All the provisions of the Dar-es-Salaam communique, except those which related to the withdrawal of foreign troops, taking action against officials involved in the January massacres, and the cessation of negative radio and newspaper campaigns by the Rwandese government, were implemented. The OAU then initiated several concrete steps to accelerate the implementation of the agreement.

Following the Dar-es-Salaam meeting, the OAU made arrangements with both the Rwandese Government and the RPF to obtain a list of representatives of the Rwandese refugee community. It submitted that list to the UNHCR with a view to sponsoring the participation of those representatives in the negotiations on Rwandese refugees to be held in Arusha soon thereafter [OAU, CM/1751 (LVIII) 1993:7–8].

However, very shortly after, alarming reports of the breakdown of peace and impending military confrontations forced the OAU Secretary General to meet with leaders of both groups at Kilimanjaro International Airport where he warned them on the folly and consequences of any contemplated military action and urged them to continue with the negotiations [OAU, CM/1751 (LVIII) 1993:8]. The Secretary General then sent his Special Representative to Rwanda in mid-April "to reiterate the position of the OAU with regard to the role of the NMOG and the peace process in general" [OAU, CM/1751 (LVIII) 1993:9] should hostilities resume. This was followed by a visit to Rwanda by an OAU military technical mission to assess developments *in situ* and to examine the possibility of relocating the NMOG headquarters to Byumbra, Northern Rwanda.

During the Dar-es-Salaam conference, the Secretary General was, as the supervisor of NMOG, requested by the two sides "to extend the mandate of the NMOG and to mobilize additional resources to enable it to fulfill its mission" [OAU, CM/1751 (LVIII) 1993:4]. In view of the severe shortage of resources besetting the OAU, the Secretary General determined that a battalion of five hundred (500) officers and men would be adequate to monitor the demilitarized zone [OAU, CM/1751 (LVIII) 1993].

The Secretary General then made a formal request to the United Nations, based on U.N. Resolution 812 (1993) (which the Secretary General and the African Group at the U.N. had helped formulate), asking that the U.N. Secretary General examine the possibility of a U.N. contribution to the OAU's effort in Rwanda [OAU, CM/1751 (LVIII) 1993]. However, based on his interpretation of Resolution 812, the U.N. Secretary General replied that such assistance could be considered by the U.N. only upon the signing of a peace agreement by the two parties [OAU, CM/1751 (LVIII) 1993:5]. In spite of the protracted exchange of views between the chief executives of the two organizations, no agreement could be reached on the interpretation of Resolution 812 [OAU, CM/1751 (LVIII) 1993]. The deployment of the International Neutral Force (INF) envisaged in the Arusha talks and resolution 812 was also delayed until the implementation of the Peace Agreement.

Meanwhile, the Secretariat of the OAU had prepared, in cooperation with the U.N.HCR, a "comprehensive document with appropriate recommendations on the action to be taken in the implementation of the Dar-es-Salaam Declaration on Rwandan refugees" and a *Plan of Action* to be presented at a donors' conference [OAU, CM/1751 (LVIII) 1993:7–8].

By 3 August 1993, the Protocol on the formation of a new army and various related issues was signed. Accordingly, a General Peace Agreement was signed at Arusha on 4 August 1993 to bring the state of war in Rwanda to an end. Within thirty-seven (37) days, transitional institutions were to be established—including a broad based Transitional Government of National Unity—for twenty two (22) months, that is until no later than 10 September 1994 [OAU, Central Organ/MEC/AMB/ RPT (1), 1993:13]. On the same day that the General Peace Agreement was signed, the OAU Secretary General sent a message to the U.N. Secretary General urging him to expedite the implementation of the accord, in particular, the establishment of a International Neutral Force of peacekeepers and monitors for Rwanda [OAU, Central Organ/MEC/ AMB/RPT (1) 1993:14].

From Arusha to 6 April 1994

The Secretary General also approached the governments of the Congo, Gabon, Nigeria, Senegal, Tunisia, and Zimbabwe for the secondment of new or additional military observers, as the case may be, to NMOG. Although the reaction of most of the governments was more or less favorable, deployment could not take place because of the lack of resources. In June 1993, only the fifty (50) original members of the force were available to fulfill the responsibilities of NMOG. By September, however, the Secretary General was able to report that a contingent of sixty (60) Tunisian officers and men had been deployed to complement Senegalese and Congolese forces in the NMOG contingent that by then consisted of one-hundred twenty-four (124); further, they were to be joined by an additional forty (40) officers and men from Egypt [OAU, Central Organ/MEC/AMB/RPT (1), 1993: 16–17].

He then informed the first ordinary session of the Central Organ of the OAU Mechanism For Conflict Prevention, Management and Resolution, which met in Addis Ababa on 13 September 1993, that:

- the mandate of NMOG, which was facing serious logistical problems, was almost completed since it was the Neutral International Force (NIF) which must take its place following the peace agreement which has already been signed;
- he had extended the mandate of NMOG only up to 31 October 1993 in the conviction that the NIF will have, by then, been deployed;
- the deployment of the NIF was imperative to ensure the successful implementation of the agreement;
- it was not possible to meet the 10 September deadline to form a transitional government because the deployment of the NIF had encountered difficulties;
- and that it too should make an urgent appeal to the U.N. Security Council. [OAU, Central Organ/MEC/AMB/RPT (1), 1993: 17–18]

The Secretary General further informed the Central Organ that the parties to the conflict had made their commitment to the *General Agreement* clear by deciding to send a joint delegation to the U.N. Security Council to urge it to deploy the NIF [OAU, Central Organ/MEC/AMB/RPT (1), 1993: 11]. The Central Organ sent messages to both the U.N. Secretary General and the Secretary Council "to speed up the deployment of the NIF...(and) to act and follow through a successful action initiated by the OAU and take over the financial burden of "NMOG II" [OAU, Central Organ/MEC/AMB 2 (1) Rev. 1: 12].

In spite of the creation of the United Nations Assistance Mission for Rwanda (UNAMIR) and the coordinated efforts of the OAU and the U.N. to implement the General Peace Agreement, the transitional institutions provided for in the Arusha Accords—in particular, a broad based

Transitional Government of National Unity—were not established, in part because of lack of agreement on representation (in both the Transitional Government and the Transitional National Assembly), not only among the different parties, but also within the different parties and factions within those parties represented in the government.

At the same time, the political and security situation in the country began to deteriorate steadily with the assassination of political leaders; the massacre of innocent civilians became widespread. The Central Organ of the OAU met in March 1994 and sent an appeal to the leaders of both the government of Rwanda and the RPF to join hands to arrest the deteriorating political and security situation and to institute the transitional institutions as early as possible to avert the political and security collapse of the country (OAU, Press Release, No. 39/93, March 24, 1994).

After a visit to Rwanda by the Tanzanian Foreign Minister Diria in March to mediate the dispute, President Muniyi of Tanzania convened a regional summit of the leaders of Burundi, Kenya, Rwanda, and Uganda in Dar-es-Salaam on 6 April 1994 to assess the situation in both Burundi and Rwanda and to attempt to resolve the crises in these countries. The OAU Secretary General was present at this meeting. The Summit issued a statement urging all Rwandese parties concerned to respect the letter and spirit of the General Peace Agreement and to establish, without any delay, the transitional institutions envisaged in the agreement [OAU, CM/1847 (LX): 2].

Unfortunately, both President Habyarimana of Rwanda and Ntaryamira of Burundi were killed in a plane crash on the same day on their way back from the summit. Rwanda was engulfed in total political turmoil. Once again, Rwandese government forces and the RPF resumed hostilities.

After 6 April 1994

After the death of both Presidents, the Central Organ of the OAU called for the immediate institution of "an independent and impartial investigation into the circumstances leading to the air crash," condemned the blood letting, called for the immediate end of massacres, wanton killings, and senseless violence in the country," reaffirmed the Arusha Peace Agreement as the only viable framework for the resolution of the Rwanda conflict, and appealed to the U.N. Security Council to ensure the continuous and effective functioning of UNAMIR (OAU, Press Release, No. 46/94, 14 April 1994).

The OAU Secretary General immediately established contact with both warring parties in the hope of bringing about an immediate end to the hostilities and the massacres. He entered into consultations with the current Chairman of the OAU, President Hosni Mubarak of Egypt, as well as with the leaders of the countries neighboring Rwanda and the representatives of the observer countries to the Arusha peace process. He also maintained regular contact with U.N. Secretary General Boutros Boutros-Ghali and appealed to both the Secretary General and the current President of the Security Council to maintain an increased and effective United Nations presence in Rwanda.

To his great surprise, on 21 April 1994 the Security Council decided, against the advice and strong objection of the African Group at the U.N., the Non-Aligned Movement, and most of the NGOs operating in Rwanda, and in spite of the escalating hostilities and increased massacres, to reduce the troop complement in U.N.AMIR from 2,500 to 270. The OAU Secretary General protested this action and called for a reconsideration of the resolution (OAU, CM/1847 (LX):5).

The U.N. determined to act on Rwanda only after a meeting in Pretoria (during the inauguration ceremony of South Africa's new President Mandela) between President Mwinyi of Tanzania, Vice-President Al Gore of the U.S. and U.N. Secretary General Boutros Boutros-Ghali. The OAU Secretary General also attended the meeting. The meeting produced a consensus that there was an urgent need for both assistance and for the provision of security for those whose lives were being threatened by the conflict [OAU, CM/1847 (LX):8].

Thus, on 16 May 1994, the U.N. Security Council passed Resolution 918 providing for an expansion of UNAMIR to 5,500 troops. UNAMIR's "humanitarian role would be to protect the civilian and displaced population" and the protection of humanitarian and relief supply convoys inside Rwanda [OAU, CM/1847 (LX)]. There is no need to repeat the description of the failure of these troops to be deployed in time to stop the genocide.

After the Genocide

The UNAMIR II mandate, which expired on 9 December 1994, was extended. In November, UNAMIR proposed to the Secretary General and the Security Council *The Rondoval Plan* which, inter alia,

• Proposes measures for national reconciliation and the creation of conditions for the return of displaced persons to their homes; this plan would involve regional efforts under the auspices of the OAU;

- Impresses upon donors the need to support the Rwandese government;
- Ensures respect for human rights through the presence of human rights monitors;
- Ensures the establishment of the International Tribunal to try those alleged to be responsible for the massacres and genocide in Rwanda;
- Supports the government through advice and other means, as well as by the possible establishment of a Lands Commission to get the country back to normalcy.

Earlier, Secretary General Salim Ahmed Salim sent a field mission to Tanzania and Burundi "to assess the refugee situation in the two countries as well as the impact of the presence of such large numbers of refugees on the socio-economic infrastructure of these countries" [OAU, CM/1847 (LX) Annex:1]. The OAU Humanitarian Mission to Tanzania and Burundi, as it was known, visited the two countries between 21 May and 1 June 1994 and held extensive discussions with high ranking officials of the two countries, representatives of the UNHCR and NGOs in both countries, visited selected refugee camps, and made *in situ* assessments. Its aim was "to find out how the OAU could be of assistance in the search for durable solutions to the problems" [OAU, CM/1847 (LX) Annex:2]. Nothing concrete came out of this endeavor. Nevertheless, on 15 July 1994, after his own intensive consultations with the leaders of the countries neighboring Rwanda, the Secretary General called for the convening of an International Humanitarian Conference on Rwanda. At the same time, however, he also took other steps to convene the Regional Conference on Refugees and Displaced Persons in the Great Lakes Region on the basis of an OAU resolution passed in Tunis in June 1994.

Upon the request of the new Rwandese government, the Secretary General sent an OAU representative to Kigali for an initial three month period to monitor developments closely and to provide the necessary information for OAU action regarding the reactivation of the peace process in Rwanda. The OAU representative worked very closely with the new government of Rwanda and U.N. agencies and NGOs. Accordingly, the Secretary General was able to report to the Sixty-First Ordinary Session of the Council of Ministers, which met in Addis Ababa, Ethiopia, from 23–27 January 1995, that, although certain sections of the General Peace Agreement had been overtaken by events, "the Rwandese Patriotic Front has attempted to constitute a government which, to a large extent, took cognizance of the framework of the Arusha Peace Agreement" [OAU, CM/1861 (LXI) 1995:2]. The Secretary General's report to the Council certified as broad based the new government formed by the RPF and other Rwandese political parties (but excluding ex-president Habyarimana's MRND) as well as the seventy (70) member Transitional National Assembly in which all the political parties, except the MRND and the CDR, were represented, accepting genocide as the reason for excluding the MRND [OAU, CM/1861 (LXI) 1995:2–3].

On the whole, the Secretary General was favorably—though in some instances critically—disposed toward the new government. He applauded the new government's position on reconciliation, castigated the military and political leaders of the former government for intransigence, informed the Council that it is "to the credit of the current government that there have been no systematic killing of people and armed robbery," blamed the remnants of the old government's army and militia in what was once the French Humanitarian Protection Zone and the refugee camps in Zaire and Tanzania as being the sources of insecurity "not just to the government but to the UNAMIR," and applauded the government for taking appropriate action against those of its own soldiers who had committed human rights violations [OAU, CM/1861 (LXI) 1995:3].

Thus, he requested the international community to assist, in concrete terms, the new government in its efforts to establish or reactivate the institutions of state and administrative structures "needed to meet the challenges of reconstruction, rehabilitation and reconciliation" [OAU, CM/1851 (LXI) 1995:10]. However, for good measure, he also requested "the African Human and People's Rights Commission to have a presence, however modest, in Rwanda *in order to support the efforts of the Government of Rwanda* and the U.N. human rights members in minimizing human rights violations" [OAU, CM/1861 (LXI):11]. This recommendation was perhaps made to allay the misgivings and apprehensions of the donor community, particularly the EU led by France, which had made the deployment of human rights monitors all over the country one of the conditions for assistance.

The issue of the presence in the refugee camps of about 30,000 soldiers and militia, led by some cabinet members of the former government of Rwanda who had formed a government-in exile, was viewed as a source of potential destabilization by the international community. Accordingly, the Secretary General reported that "any delay in resolving the problems could bring about renewed fighting" [OAU, CM/1861 (LXI):4] and consequently argued for the quick separation of the soldiers and militia from the refugee camps.

The international humanitarian conference, which the Secretary had called for in July of 1994, was eventually held in Bujumbura in February 1995, and adopted a *Plan of Action and Program of Assistance for Refugees, Returnees and Displaced Persons in the Great Lakes Region*. Its ultimate objective was to facilitate the repatriation and resettlement of the refugees and displaced persons [OAU, CM/1861 (LXI):6], particularly Rwandese.

Also, a meeting on Central African Refugees, convened at the OAU headquarters on 9 September 1994 by the OAU and the U.N. and jointly chaired by Secretary General Salim A. Salim and the head of UNHCR, Sadako Ogata, decided to create a *Joint Commission on Repatriation of Rwandese Refugees* composed of the OAU, the U.N., the Government of Rwanda, and representatives of the refugees. The Commission was inaugurated on December 1994 [OAU, CM/1861 (LXI):6–7].

Conclusions

The past thirty years of African history testify to the fact that African states have been anything but cohesive, except perhaps in the struggle against decolonization and Apartheid, although there were some exceptions even on these issues. Since the decade of independence, the politics of, and relations between, African states have been wracked by vast differences (ethnic, religious, ideological, and geopolitical) which have been the root causes of conflict and tension. It is obvious then that the OAU, whose major form of operation has been the search for consensus, would be very limited in its role in conflict resolution. It is also understandable that during the past three decades, the OAU attached more importance to those other functions which made consensual cooperation possible.

One direct consequence of the differences in, and between, its members, as well as the paucity of resources, is that the OAU does not—and possibly cannot—have the political, administrative and financial wherewithal to influence the behavior of its members. Yet, the OAU has not been as totally derelict as almost all authors who have studied conflict resolution in Africa assume it to have been. The OAU had, particularly in the early years, geared much effort to the resolution of conflicts and disputes by the actions of its highest bodies, i.e. the Assembly and the Council of Ministers. The annals of its meetings are eloquent testimony to the numerous *ad hoc* commissions, committees etc. that have lent their good offices to resolve disputes and conflicts between—if not within—states, although, it is true that these efforts have been frustrating and almost invariably fruitless.

On the other hand, it is not fair to reproach the OAU or to evaluate and scrutinize the activities of the organization in the abstract when it is the member states who decide on its structure, character, functions, and resources. The OAU's attitude to conflict resolution is, in fact, a reflection of the general characteristics of African international relations and the disdain that far too many African leaders have for international rules and principles as they have for their own domestic laws. Thus, although the OAU is now seemingly empowered institutionally to cope with intra- as well as interstate conflicts, it is not at all certain whether it will be able to assume a new relevance and if its central organ for conflict management and resolution will fare better than its predecessor, the Commission of Mediation, Conciliation, and Arbitration.

Notes

1. Cf. Organization of African Unity, *Charter*, May 1963, Addis Ababa, Article 3. Paragraph 4 in *Organization of African Unity, Basic Documents and Resolutions*, Addis Ababa, 1963.
2. Debate concerning the military aspects of conflict management in Africa started at about the same time as the creation of the OAU, Kwame Nkrumah referring to an African High Command during the Founding Conference of the OAU in May 1963 in conjunction with the proposal for a Continental Union Government. During the second ordinary session of the Council of Ministers in 1965, the Ghanian delegation proposed a peacekeeping force to deal with conflicts between African countries to police, protect and patrol disputed areas between African countries (cf. Wolfers, M., *Politics in the Organization of African Unity*, London: Methuen, 92–94). Though there was a consensus during the first meeting of the OAU Defence Commission on the need for a Pan-African force which would fill an institutional vacuum in the many crises besetting the continent, including the Algeria/Morocco conflict and the impending withdrawal of the United Nations Operations in the Congo (UNOC), the proposal to create an African defence Organization was rejected at the second meeting. Similar proposals were discussed to death at subsequent sessions of the Council of Ministers, for example following the invasion of Guinea by mercenaries in 1970 and at the Summit in Moravia, Liberia in 1979 [OAU, CM 1767 (LVIII) 21]. Even military operations which required only cease-fire operations, such as provided by the 1963 Bamako Cease-fire Commission, operated outside the framework of the OAU.
3. Nigeria had sent a peacekeeping force to Chad, with the support and approval of the OAU, on the basis of the Lagos Accord (Lagos II) reached in August 1979

agreed upon by the majority of the political groups in Chad, but Nigeria withdrew its forces when fighting broke out in mid-March 1980. The Secretary-General of the OAU then attempted to create a neutral African force composed of contingents from Benin, the Congo, and Guinea, again on the basis of the Lagos Accord, both to supervise a cease-fire and to chair a monitoring commission, but this initiative was abandoned when the only force that arrived, a Congolese force of 500, had to be evacuated as soon as it arrived because of renewed fighting in the Chadian capital, N'Djamena.

4. It was declared that the OAU "did not only have the right but also the obligation to get involved even before appealing to the international community" (Ibid, 31).

5. OAU, AHG/Dec. 3 (XXIX), 1993:28–30; see *Proposal for Strengthening The General Secretariat in the Field of Conflict Management,* Central Organ/Mec/ Amb 3, (11) Annex 2, 1.

7

The Arusha Peace Process

Bruce D. Jones

Introduction

While most accounts of the Arusha process in Rwanda date it from June of 1992 until the signing of the Arusha Peace Agreement in August 1993, we will refer to three phases of Arusha which ran from the outset of the civil war in 1990 until the RPF victory in July of 1994. These were:

1. A pre-negotiation phase, starting almost immediately after the outbreak of hostilities. While not formally conducted under the aegis of the Arusha process, the texts of agreements reached in this phase were incorporated into the final Arusha document, and in other important ways contextualize the formal Arusha process. This phase involved the regional and international efforts which led to the establishment of the Arusha political negotiations;

2. A formal negotiation phase, starting in June of 1992 and continuing, with interruptions, until the signing of the Peace Accord on 4 August 1993;

3. An implementation phase, during which the parties to the Arusha accord attempted to establish the transitional institutions called for in the agreement, and during which UNAMIR was deployed in Rwanda to help secure the transition process. This phase can also be taken to encompass the last-ditch efforts taken in April and May of 1994 to salvage the accords following the resumption of civil war and the commencement of the genocide following the 6 April 1994 assassination of President Habyarimana.

Each of these phases is considered in turn followed by an attempt to evaluate the Arusha process. Did the ultimate failure of Arusha result from the process itself or should that failure be attributed to external forces? With reference to these competing perspectives, was Arusha either a disastrous transition bargain or good preventive diplomacy sabotaged by the interference of outsiders? The central argument developed in this chapter is that the truth of the Arusha process lies somewhere between the perspective adhered to by some participants who argue that the agreement constituted excellent preventive diplomacy and was undermined by outsiders, and critical commentary which suggests that the Arusha process was foisted on Rwanda by outsiders and was inherently deeply flawed. Both perspectives miss key points. In evaluating conflict resolution efforts, such as Arusha, it is important to maintain a distinction between process and outcome. The argument developed here is that the Arusha *process* was sophisticated and well managed, but that the *outcome* was indeed flawed. The outcome reflected, in part, the inherent difficulties in achieving a stable transition bargain in the context of civil war.

Pre-Negotiation: Regional Peace Efforts

Efforts to bring the civil conflict in Rwanda to a peaceful resolution began within days of the RPF's invasion on 1 October. The Belgian government, as part of a compromise worked out between the Socialist and Christian Democrat parties around withdrawing Belgian troops from Rwanda, sent a peace mission to Kigali comprised of the Prime Minister, the Foreign Minister, and the Minister of Defence. This trio met with Habyarimana in Nairobi on 14 October 1990. Over the next three days, they held talks in Kenya, Uganda, and Tanzania. They also met with the OAU. This mission appears to have helped to stimulate a nascent regional process, which quickly became the focus of negotiations. A summit held three days later at Mwanza, Tanzania, formalized the involvement of Rwanda's neighbors in the peace process, laid the basis for further discussions, and shifted the locus of talks to the Organization for African Unity (*Mwanza Communique*, 17 October 1990). This regional peace process, in itself ineffective in containing fighting, can nevertheless be seen as forming a pre-negotiation phase to what eventually become the Arusha peace process.[1]

The regional process comprised two tracks. The first track was a series of official summit meetings between the heads of the members states of the *Communité Economique de Pays des Grands Lacs* (CEPGL); the members were Rwanda, Burundi, and Zaire. The second track consisted of broader meetings which brought the CEPGL members into contact with Ugandan, Tanzanian, OAU, and U.N. officials.

In two meetings held in late October in Gbadolite, Zaire, President Mobutu Sese Seko was appointed OAU Mediator for the peace process, despite the fact that Zaire had sent troops to Kigali to support Habyarimana earlier that month. The CEPGL countries, plus Uganda, also recommended the establishment of an African peacekeeping/monitoring force, the Neutral Military Observer Group (NMOG) under the observation of the OAU's Liberation Committee. Following the Gbadolite talks, a working meeting of the CEPGL was held in Goma on 20–22 November 1990, to which both Uganda and the RPF were invited. At that meeting, President Museveni of Uganda, in cooperation with President Mwinyi of Tanzania, was asked to organize a regional summit on the question of refugees (*Gbadolite Communique*, 20 November 1990).

The moves towards a refugee conference began with a meeting of regional foreign ministers in Kinshasa, Zaire, on 17–19 January 1991, at which the OAU and the U.N. High Commissioner for Refugees (UNHCR) were present. At this meeting, Habyarimana confirmed that Mwinyi would host the conference and a date for it was set. Then, immediately prior to the opening of the conference, Habyarimana attempted to gain the initiative by calling on all refugees to return, a grandstanding and futile gesture at that time given both the situation in Rwanda, his own past performance and the troubled history of refugee diplomacy in the region. Notwithstanding Habyarimana's grandstanding, the conference held in Dar-es-Salaam on 19 February was successful, insofar as it resulted in the *Dar-es-Salaam Declaration on Rwandese Refugees Problem*, which committed the Government of Rwanda to finding a "definitive and durable solution" to the refugee problem (*Dar es Salaam Declaration on the Rwandese Refugees Problem*, 19 February 1991, p.1, Art.5). This declaration became a pre-negotiation text for the Arusha process, and formed the core of the eventual Arusha protocol on refugees.

Another important development occurred at this time. At a preconference meeting between Mwinyi, Museveni, and Habyarimana, the Rwandese president was persuaded to sign the Zanzibar Communiqué, which restated a commitment, originally made in the Mwanza Communiqué, to finding a peaceful solution to the conflict through achieving a cease-fire agreement, through conducting a dialogue with the internal and external opposition, and through the regional conference on refugees (*Zanaibar Communique* 17 February 1991:1). The flurry of summitry had, to this point, done little to stop the fighting between the *Forces Armées Rwandaise* (FAR). and the RPF.[2] However, by the time of the Zanzibar Communiqué substance was added; the process moved from general principles towards negotiating a real cease fire.

The first of these was signed on 29 March 1991 in N'Sele, Zaire. The N'Sele Cease-fire Agreement Between the Government of the Republic of Rwanda and the Rwandese Patriotic Front was the first formal cease fire of the civil war. The N'Sele text established the terms of the cease fire, set part of the agenda for continuing talks, and formalized the creation and make-up of the Neutral Military Observer Group (NMOG), which was to police the cease fire and report to the OAU on violations. Originally, NMOG was to be composed of five officers from each of the CEPGL countries and five officers from each of Uganda and the RPF (*Cease-fire Agreement between the Government of the Republic of Rwanda and the Rwandese Patriotic Front*, 29 March 1991). Before NMOG had a chance to deploy, however, the FAR broke the cease fire by shelling RPF positions in north-eastern Rwanda. Fighting continued for some months with significant losses to government forces, though there was little movement on the ground since the RPF did not advance much further into Rwandese territory.

Having once failed to implement a cease fire, negotiating a second proved a more difficult task. Moves towards a second cease fire saw, for the first time, a significant role for nonregional actors, including the United States. The US lent its weight to the peace talks in a meeting organized by Deputy Assistant Secretary Hicks, at the Government of Rwanda's (GOR's). request, between the GOR and RPF representatives in Harare. The Hicks meeting did not produce anything concrete in the way of agreements, but kept the spirit of negotiations alive, and arguably laid the groundwork for a second round of cease-fire negotiations in Gbadolite.

The Gbadolite talks, held in September 1991, proved to be difficult to manage. The RPF refused to attend several sessions, despite the presence of their Ugandan backers. Nevertheless, there were two achievements: first, the difficulties with Rwandese government intransigence that NMOG first encountered while trying to deploy in May were addressed through creating a stronger structure which gave command of the force to a Nigerian officer (previously a Zairean had headed up the force), and replaced the Ugandan and CEPGL forces with twenty-five Nigerian and fifteen Zairois officers; second, the Gbadolite meeting reissued the N'Sele cease fire agreement in an amended form and reconfirmed the participants' commitment to peaceful resolution of the crisis (*The Gbadolite Cease* fire, 7 September 1991:1–2).

Even more significant than the content of the Gbadolite cease fire, the meeting proved to be both the apogee and the effective end of Mobutu's mediation role. According to both Rwandese and western sources, by this time all the parties recognized the incompetence of Mobuto in this role. Mobuto retained the formal title of "mediator," but from this point on had little to do with the peace process, with one late and disastrous exception described later in this chapter. The need to bypass Mobutu as mediator shifted the locus of the peace process, minimized the role played by the CEPGL, and increased the participation of nonregional states and actors. An intensification of American and French diplomatic activity following Gbadolite marked a significant change in direction for the peace process.

For several months, a series of French and American meetings with Rwandese participants ran in parallel, while each side kept each other informed of developments through working-level contacts. In France, the Quai d'Orsay's Director for Africa and the Maghreb, Mr. Paul Dijoud, called a 23–25 October 1991 meeting in Paris, but when Maj.-Gen. Paul Kagame, military head of the RPF, failed to show up, the meeting was canceled. A second attempt, on 14–15 January 1992, succeeded in bringing together Ambassador Pierre-Claver Kanyarushoki for the GOR and Mr. Bizimungu for the RPF. At the meeting, Dijoud told the RPF that there were two logics, the logic of peace and the logic of war: "Vous continuez à attaquer votre pays, votre pays se défend." He challenged the RPF to halt their attacks on Rwanda, and called on the GOR to listen more attentively to the RPF (*Front Patriotique Rwandais*, "compte rendu de la reunion du 14–15 janvier 1992 entre la delegation du gouvernement rwandais et celle dur f.p.r." 3).

In Washington, during the same period, a series of talks and initiatives were taken by the Africa Bureau of the State Department. The first of these was a working level contact made between RPF representatives in Washington and the State Department's desk officer for Rwanda, Carol Fuller. The continuation of these talks eventually led to the involvement of the Assistant Secretary of State for Africa, Herman Cohen. Cohen convened an inter-agency meeting to discuss the situation in Rwanda. This interagency forum would continue to meet for the next two years to coordinate American efforts in Rwanda.[3] Having received the support of other relevant agencies to deepen American involvement in the process, and with the formation of a real coalition government in Rwanda in April 1992,[4] Cohen traveled to Kampala on 8 May 1992 and met with Museveni. At the meeting, Cohen not only offered U.S. technical assistance for the negotiations, but also cajoled Museveni into buying into the negotiation process. Cohen argued that Uganda could not only ease the internal pressure caused by the Rwandese refugees by helping the RPF negotiate power-sharing in Rwanda, but he could also thereby deal a blow to Habyarimana with whom Museveni had long-running tensions. Cohen then followed this visit with a two day stop in Kigali where he also offered us technical support for negotiations.[5]

Independently of each other, the American and French efforts advanced the course of negotiations but made no formal breakthrough concerning peace negotiations. However, on his return from Rwanda, Cohen was asked by director Dijoud to attend a meeting at the Quai d'Orsay with Ssemogerere, the Ugandan Foreign Minister. Cohen took the opportunity of talking with Ssemogerere and taking a harder line; citing Ugandan military support for the RPF, Cohen threatened to cut America's foreign assistance to Uganda if Uganda did not pressure the RPF to participate in political negotiations towards a peace settlement. The most critical meeting prior to the Arusha talks was one hosted at the Quai d'Orsay by Dijoud at which Cohen was again present. At this session, on June 6–8 1992, the RPF and the GOR finally agreed to hold comprehensive political negotiations under Tanzanian mediation and to meet in July to launch that process.[6]

Negotiations: The Arusha Process as Preventive Diplomacy

Informed by a cogent theoretical analysis, the formal Arusha peace process was an extraordinary story of a sophisticated conflict resolution process which went disastrously wrong. The process was also co-operative, perhaps to a surprising extent. In Tanzania, the end result was celebrated among participants as the framework for a "new order" providing a comprehensive agreement that went beyond the traditional *settlement* of conflict, for the agreement made real inroads into *resolving* some of the underlying tensions which had sparked the civil war. Yet, nine months after its signing, extremist forces in Kigali implemented their own bloody version of the new order. Did the Arusha agreements contain inherent flaws which helped escalate this violence? Or was any potential peace agreement bound to be attacked by forces over which the parties to the agreement had virtually no control?

The negotiation phase of the Arusha talks lasted thirteen months, the two sides[7] reaching agreement and then deadlock and then agreement again on a series of agenda items. As characterized by a French participant at Arusha, the agenda for discussion was set and the process facilitated by Tanzania.[8] The agenda covered the issue of a cease fire, the principles of law, power sharing, the integration of armies, and the repatriation of refugees. A cease fire agreement, as an amended version of a twice amended cease fire which originated in N'sele, was quickly reached. In the other areas, key issues stalled negotiations and, at various points, threatened the peace process. A partial account of this process and these issues follows.

The agreement to meet in Arusha came on 8 June 1992, and the two sides met there for the first time on 12 July 1992. On 14 July they announced a cease fire scheduled to come into effect on 31 July and a start to peace negotiations by 10 August with a deadline of 10 October. Fighting in northern Rwanda on 29 July seemed to threaten that timetable, but the cease fire did in fact come into effect as planned and held until the 10 October deadline. Both sides also agreed to yet another restructuring of NMOG which removed from the force any officers from neighboring countries and replaced them with officers from Senegal, Zimbabwe, Nigeria, and Mali.

Very significantly, this first round of Arusha talks also called for the creation of a joint political military commission to be established in Addis Ababa at OAU headquarters.[9] The JPMC, as it became known, was composed of five representatives of the Rwandese government and five representatives of the RPF, and had parallel observers from states observing the Arusha talks as well as those who had contributed to NMOG, as it was restructured by the Arusha cease fire of 12 July 1992. Its mandate was to "ensure the follow-up of the implementation of the cease-fire agreement" and to "ensure the follow-up of the implementation of the peace agreement to be signed at the conclusion of the political negotiations."[10] As characterized by members of two Western observer teams, the JPMC served as a place to meet but not negotiate, a place where complaints could be aired, where the neutral military observer group could lodge complaints or accusations of violations, and in general where problems could be addressed without interfering with the process of negotiations.[11] The JPMC became effectively a second channel through which the thorny issues of the Arusha process could be hammered out. Talks in November 1992 at Kigali, in northern Rwanda, under the chairmanship of the Nigerian commander of NMOG, produced an agreement on the deployment of NMOG forces along a neutral zone.[12]

This first phase of the Arusha talks led quickly to the second, which on 17 August 1992 announced an agreement on a protocol on the rule of law (signed on the 18th). The quick agreement on this protocol appears to have been made possible by an internal agreement among the delegates to leave some of the tricky issues—such as the composition of a transitional government—out of the protocol at this stage, and focus discussion on broad principles. The outstanding items were deferred to the end of the process.[13]

Arusha III ran from 7–18 September, and saw Foreign Minister Ngulinzira of Rwanda table a series of conciliatory proposals. Agreements on power sharing, unification, and political cooperation were initialed but not signed, and the two sides returned to their respective bases for consultation. It quickly emerged that Ngulinzira had acted without Habyarimana's support. However, subsequent negotiations inside Kigali, between Habyarimana and the opposition parties, produced an agreement on instructions for the delegates, who returned to Arusha for a fourth round of talks on 6 October. By 12 October, the delegates reached agreement on the issues of the nature of presidential power under a broad-based transitional government (BBTG). It was agreed that the BBTG would last for no more than twenty-two months and would be followed by free elections to determine the government of the country. The system of authority was to be parliamentary in large measure rather than presidential; the RPF insisted that power reside in a council of ministers (effectively a cabinet) rather than with the president and presidential advisors. The powers of the president were diminished to those of a ceremonial head of state who did not even have the power to name his own government. His authority, such as it was, was secondary to that of the prime minister. The protocol to this effect was signed and issued on 31 October 1992.

This protocol also created a transitional national assembly (TNA) to replace the *Conseil National de Development* (CND), which from the moment of the signing of the accord was prohibited from passing new laws. Between the BBTG and the national assembly, a fairly typical parliamentary relationship was instituted wherein the president of the republic could dissolve the assembly, but the assembly could in turn censure the BBTG. The TNA was also given the unusual power of electing the president and vice-president of the supreme court; it was, thus, a powerful institution. However, the protocol did not resolve the fundamental issue of seats in the TNA, nor the distribution of cabinet posts in the BBTG (Reyntjens, 1994).

Arusha V commenced on 25 November 1992, with the agenda focused on the difficult topic of the precise composition of the transitional institutions on which agreement had been reached on the framework.[14] These discussions, which required three months of background negotiations to conclude, formed the first of the major sticking points in the Arusha process, and would come back to bedevil the implementation phase. Two issues were at the heart of discussions. First, the RPF objected to a government proposal which included the *coalition pour le défense de la republique* (CDR). in the government. Apart from denouncing the extremist nature of the CDR, the RPF (accurately). argued that it was a political organization but not a political party, and as such ineligible for membership in the transitional institutions. However, the government delegation insisted on the inclusion of the CDR and were backed in this demand by the French. According to one of its members, the French delegation argued that it was better to have the CDR in the government, where they could be controlled, than on the outside where they could wreak havoc. Equally, the Tanzanians argued that it was better to have the extremists "on the inside of the tent, pissing out, than on the outside of the tent, pissing in."[15]

In the end, however, the RPF prevailed; the CDR was, at this stage, excluded from the transitional institutions. Further, a protocol signed on 22 December contained the following agreement about seats in the transitional government: MDR—four portfolios including Prime Minister and Foreign Minister; RPF five portfolios including the Vice-Prime Minister and the Minister for Interior; MRND—five portfolios including Defence, Public Works, and the Presidency; PSD—three, including Finance; PL—three, including Justice; and the PDC one portfolio. Seats in the assembly were divided among the major parties: the MRND, RPF, MDR, PSD, and PL each had eleven seats; the PDC had four; and a number of small parties obtained one seat each. As Reyntjens has noted, the composition of the parliament meant that agreement from at least four parties was required to reach a majority. From a government perspective, it was clear that the RPF would have an easier time in mustering opposition votes than would the MRND (see Reyntjens, 1994).

The distribution of seats among parties in the transitional institutions, if put in place, would have marginalized the Habyarimana regime in the "new order." Key members of the Habyarimana power structure, both within and surrounding the MRND, would have been excluded from any substantial role in the Arusha institutions. Critically, without the CDR in the transitional institutions to bolster their numbers, the MRND itself would have had little chance of mustering adequate votes in either the BBTG or the TNA. First, their own share of seats or votes was to be matched by those of the RPF. Second, as the civil war dragged on and the process of multipartyism continued, the opposition parties in Kigali, being "moderate" virtually by definition through their opposition to the dominance of the MRND, were seen as natural allies of the RPF. Third, the power of the presidency was so reduced as to turn the post into a symbolic one. Thus, members of the Habyarimana regime reacted to the negotiated provisions of Arusha, not as a transition bargain producing real power-sharing arrangements, but as political victories by the RPF which denied them a meaningful share in power.

The perceived marginalization of the regime was furthered when the parties reconvened in Arusha on 5 January to tackle the question of the distribution of seats in the TNA. The agreement reached on 10 January allocated seats among the parties as follows: MRND (11), RPF (11), MDR, PL, and PSD (11 each). The leftover seats were distributed among small parties and "political groups"—a compromise reference to the CDR attached to this compromise, however, was a caveat that political groups which wished to be included in the TNA must sign a "code of ethics" committing them to the maintenance of new, peaceful institutions—which the CDR promptly refused to do.

At a symbolic level, the question of the exclusion of the CDR came to be seen by the observer delegations in Arusha, and to a certain extent in the capital itself, as a test of the RPF willingness to cooperate with the regime within power-sharing arrangements. Though in real terms the power equation was far more complex, involving as it did tacit and shifting alliances with various and competing wings of the opposition parties, the CDR became a symbolic flash point for the agreements.[16]

The question of whether or not to include extremist organizations such as the CDR in negotiations in the first place, is one which has bedeviled conflict resolution. The experience of the United Nations in bringing the Khmer Rouge into discussions with difficult consequences provides a counter case to the experience in South Africa, where all political elements were included in negotiations, with apparent success. That the French were supportive of the inclusion of the CDR could easily be dismissed as evidence of French complicity with the Habyarimana regime.[17] But this was also the position of a more clearly neutral negotiating team, the Americans. According to the State Department's desk officer for Rwanda at the time of the negotiations, an inter-agency meeting on conflict resolution in Rwanda agreed as early as March 1992 to take the approach of bringing the extremists into the government. Again, tent analogies were used: an American official commented that their analysis was that "if you don't bring them [the CDR] into the tent, they're going to burn the tent down" (confidential interview, state department, Washington, June 1993). The eventual exclusion of the CDR from power, as one central part of a broader marginalization of the regime, was interpreted by most western governments as a turning point away from constructive negotiations over an effective transition bargain in favor of a victor's deal which reflected RPF views much more than it did a true compromise.

Within days of the signing of the agreement on distribution of seats within the TNA, the CDR and MRND in Kigali were involved in demonstrations against the peace talks, especially in Ruhengiri and Gisenyi. The demonstrations were precursors to violence: between 22 and 31 January, over three-hundred Tutsi civilians in the north were murdered. This civil violence, in turn, led to a renewal of the civil war: on the 8 February 1993 the RPF launched a major offensive, claiming it was occasioned by the recent massacres. However, more was at issue than the recent killings; after all, periodic killings of civilians on a similar scale had been conducted in Rwanda almost from the onset of the invasion. Perhaps a more realistic explanation can be found in tactical thinking about the next agenda item for the Arusha discussions: integration of the armed forces. Negotiating strength on this issue would turn out to be a precise function of fighting strength on the ground. In this interpretation, the RPF launched the offensive at this point to prove their fighting strength and thus put them on firm ground for these most important negotiations.

The offensive certainly did confirm their strength. Within two weeks of fighting the RPF had doubled the amount of territory under its control (*African Research Bulletin,* 1–28 February 1993, 10902). The impact on the balance of strength was so significant that Rwanda had to ask France to send reinforcements to bolster the army, which France did in two waves, on 9 February (150 troops) and 20 February (250 troops). The latter deployment was justified by France as being necessary since the RPF advance threatened Kigali. Tanzanian and French intelligence sources concluded at the time that the RPF could overrun the FAR were it not for the presence of the French troops in Kigali. This conclusion would form the backdrop to the subsequent round of negotiations.[18] This perception evidently was shared by Habyarimana, for he personally called for a return to the Arusha process on 23 February. The next round would prove decisive.

That final round of negotiations dealt with two sets of issues: refugees and security, the latter including the composition of a neutral military force, the integration of the armed forces into a single national army, and the composition of the army command structure. The refugee issue was settled quickly, as the framework for agreement had already been laid by the Dar-es-Salaam Declaration on the Rwandese refugee problem. That declaration was for all intents and purposes simply reformulated in the framework of Arusha to form the protocol on the Repatriation of Rwandese refugees and resettlement of displaced persons; agreement was announced on 10 June 1993. The security issues were more complex.

The issue of the authority for a neutral military force was fairly easily dealt with through effective American third-party mediation and request to the OAU to ascertain whether they could assume such a responsibility. The division had been over whether the force should be under the authority of the OAU (which the RPF favored) or the U.N. The real limitations of the OAU to carry out such a task determined the outcome. The issue was settled by the OAU's announcement at the JPMC that it could not meet the requirements specified by the two sides. On 6 April 1993 the GOR and RPF agreed to ask the U.N. to compose a "neutral international force" to oversee the final agreement.

The far more difficult negotiation in this phase concerned the critical issue of integrating the two armies into one national army, and the percentage split of army command positions. These issues took months of negotiations. On two occasions, they threatened to collapse the entire process. The government of Rwanda started off negotiating on this issue by suggesting a 15 percent share of armed command for the RPF to reflect the percentage of Tutsi in Rwanda. The RPF rejected this outright, both because the figure was too low and because the rationale used for arriving at it contradicted their platform of fighting for democracy for all Rwandese. The RPF counter offer was 50–50, which the government delegation also rejected outright. However, the RPF stuck to their position, and in an unusual breach from their "honest-broker" role, the Tanzanians supported the RPF position. Negotiations took the number to 25 percent, then 30 percent, then 35 percent, then 40 percent, and finally reached 50 percent.

The even stickier issue of how far down the command chain this split should go caused more problems. An eventual agreement was brokered wherein the command level was to be split 50–50, and the forces were to be drawn 60 percent from government and 40 percent from the RPF. At senior levels, the RPF would be given the head of the gendarmerie and the government was to retain control of the head of the armed forces. Both armies would be integrated into a 13,000 strong army supplemented by a 6,000 strong gendarmerie. The announcement of this agreement on 24 June seemed to presage an imminent signing of the peace package.

This putative agreement was taken back to Kigali on 24 June by the government's negotiating team. It was rejected by Habyarimana. An American participant observed at the time that the division of the army as it stood would never be accepted by hard-line factions in the army, and threatened to collapse the talks.[19] Differences emerged as to what constituted a command level position. When the issue returned to Arusha, the RPF not only stood their ground, they upped the ante in anger over the government's reneging on the agreement, and called for a 60–40 split weighted in their favor. After heavy intercession by the Tanzanian, French, and American teams, the two sides agreed again on the original deal, with the clarification that "command level" extended all the way to field command positions. This represented a significant new victory for the RPF in terms of their capacity to control the merged security forces.

The Arusha Accords were now complete and were signed on 4 August 1993.

The Implementation Phase

For nine months after signing that agreement, elements of the Rwandese political system, the United Nations, and the participants in the Arusha process struggled to implement its provisions: the establishment of the transitional institutions, principally the BBTG the *mise en place* of a "neutral international force" to secure the transitional government; and the integration of armed forces and demobilization of redundant troops by both sides. As the forces of peace struggled to implement this first phase, extremist forces methodically and efficiently undermined their efforts.

The Arusha peace agreement called for the establishment of the BBTG within thirty-seven days of the signing of the accord, and the deployment of a U.N. force within the same time period, both of which goals were quickly shown to be hopelessly unrealistic. Immediately after the signing of Arusha, France began to win agreement in the Security Council for a U.N. force, but was unable to succeed before the 5 October when Security Council Resolution 872 established the United Nations Assistance Mission in Rwanda (UNAMIR). UNAMIR was established under Chapter VI authority, with a mission to enhance security in Kigali and assist in providing security for the transitional government. The mission was to be led by a Canadian, Brig.-Gen. Romeo Dallaire.

General Dallaire and an advance party of twenty-one troops eventually arrived in Kigali on the 21 October 1993, the same day that the Tutsi-dominated army of Burundi assassinated the newly elected president, Melchior Ndadaye, a Hutu, and commenced the killing of tens of thousands of Burundi Hutu. The assassination and killings were rich material for the extremists in Rwanda, who used the events to lend credence to their claims that the Tutsi of the RPF were returning to Rwanda to reestablish their historic dominance over the Hutu. The contrast could not have been more stark between the violence in Burundi and the late token arrival of the neutral international security force.

Indeed, many observers, including members of the Tanzanian negotiating team, agreed that the assassination of Ndadaye was the turning point for the peace process in Rwanda. The voices of radical ethnic hatred gained credence as events in Burundi seemed to unfold according to the extremist's doomsday scenario for Rwanda.[20] Those who counted on the U.N. to provide security for the transition could only be disappointed by the partial U.N. presence. For many observers, the momentum of fear and opposition took sway over the momentum for security and peace.[21]

Despite events in Burundi, efforts to establish the transitional institutions in Kigali began with the appointment of the MDR's Faustin Twagiramungu to the Prime Ministership, as agreed in the final days of Arusha. Almost simultaneously, the opposition parties in Kigali began to splinter. Twagiramungu's party itself divided into factions, and intense squabbles broke out among the *parti liberal* (Pl) and the *parti socialist democratique* (psd). Attempts to convene the BBTG on 8 January 1994 failed, because of a deadlock within the MDR and PL by 10 February, the deadlock within the PL was so intense that the other opposition parties, and the MRND, agreed to go ahead and establish the BBTG without PL participation. Before this could occur, Felicien Gatabazi, the leader of the PSD, was assassinated in Kigali, an event which was immediately followed by the killing of Martin Bucyana of the CDR. On 23 February, all opposition parties boycotted an MRND attempt to hold up the installation ceremonies for the BBTG.

UNAMIR, its resources already stretched by the general deterioration of security in Kigali, was able to restore some sense of security following these killings, but not before a sense of chaos and impending catastrophe had already pervaded the Rwandese political system. Michel Moussali, a UNHCR special envoy, argued on 23 February that Rwanda would experience "a bloodbath of unparalleled proportions" if efforts were not made to salvage the peace process.

The bloodbath was already in preparation. As revealed in a confidential, but by now widely circulated UNAMIR communication to U.N. headquarters in New York,[22] the assassination of Gatabazi was part of a plan: to disrupt the establishment of the BBTG, compile lists of Tutsi in Rwanda for the purpose of their extermination, undermine UNAMIR by killing Belgian peacekeepers, thereby precipitating their departure, and resume the war against the RPF.

The plan was generated and controlled by the extremist elements in Rwanda. It had been developed prior to the signing of the Arusha Accords, but their effective loss of power in the Arusha process spurred them on. These military elements of the one-party state, who would lose their authority in a democratic regime, were located in the Presidential Guard, the CDR, and extremist elements of the MRND, all of whose senior ranks were held by members of the *AKAZU*. They were at the heart of the planning to undermine the peace process. These three elements together financed and coordinated the training of extremist militia groups, the *interahamwe* and the *impuzamugambi*. They also directed the spread of propaganda based on ethnic fear, transmitted through many media but most notoriously the *Radio-télévision Libre des mille collines*, or RTLM. Focused on building the institutions of peaceful transition, international and peaceful forces in Rwanda underestimated the potency and deadly seriousness of both the propaganda and the planning.

Even after the assassination of Gatabazi, frantic attempts were made to salvage the Arusha deal. A special representative of the U.N. Secretary General met with the RPF on 1 March to try to find ways to put the peace process back on track. Tanzania, the Arusha facilitator, also kept up its efforts to persuade the two sides to implement the agreement. Ultimately, Tanzania persuaded Habyarimana to attend a summit in Arusha on the crisis in Burundi, with the intention of pressuring him to reaffirm his commitment to the BBTG. Habyarimana attended the meeting and did issue a statement reaffirming the Arusha agreement: it was on his flight back from this conference, on 6 April 1994, that the plane carrying both him and President Ntariyamana of Burundi was shot down, killing both men.

As events spiraled out of control in Kigali, Tanzanian authorities tried desperately to renew the Arusha process and thereby restore order in Rwanda. On 7 April 1994, Tanzania ordered gasoline shipments to Rwanda to be held at the border in order to place pressure on what remained of the government to negotiate with UNAMIR and the RPF. On 19 April, President Ali Hassan Mwinyi called for a return to Arusha for 23 April. On 22 April, the RPF agreed to attend and to talk, not to the putative government, but to the Rwandese army. On the 23rd, an RPF delegation turned up in Arusha ready to announce a unilateral cease fire; no government delegation presented itself at Arusha.

As it turned out, Zaire's Mobuto Sese Seko had, disastrously, chosen this moment to reassert his authority as formal mediator of the Arusha process. He had called the government of Rwanda to parallel talks in Zaire on 23 April. The effective government had gone to Zaire, and had itself supposedly been ready to announce a unilateral cease fire. The Tanzanian government allowed diplomacy to win out over outrage when it regretted Mobutu's interference, saying simply that "two unilaterally decided cease fires do not add up to one that is effective" (Tanzanian Ministry of Foreign Affairs, Official Statement, 25 April 1994). While it is not clear that the two cease fires would have been mutually acceptable or could have returned order to Rwanda, it is certainly evidence that Mobutu's interference denied the Arusha process any possible last chance.

23 April 1994 thus marks the effective end of the Arusha process. Tanzania would in fact thrice more attempt to launch new peace initiatives for Rwanda, each time without success. Having disastrously missed a possible opportunity to achieve a cease fire in late April, the Arusha process was effectively consigned to futile final efforts. The jaws of genocide closed around the peace process in Rwanda.

Analysis of the Arusha Process

Two competing accounts of the Arusha process warrant critical analysis. The first, which we can term the diplomatic perspective,[23] suggests that Arusha was almost perfect preventive diplomacy. Western negotiators and diplomats argued that the Arusha Peace Agreement was the best peace agreement in Africa since Lancaster House, and moreover was the best agreement which could possibly have been reached. From this perspective, the collapse of the accords should be attributed exclusively to manipulation by Hutu extremists who were outside of the control of the Arusha process.

The second perspective, which has been forcibly presented by René Lemarchand (1994), a noted scholar of the region, takes issue with the diplomatic perspective:

> [T]he transition bargain in Rwanda emerges in retrospect as a recipe for disaster: not only were the negotiations conducted under tremendous *external pressures,* but, partly for this reason, the concessions made to the FPR were seen by Hutu hard-liners as a sell-out *imposed by outsiders.* For the Tutsi "rebels" to end up claiming as many cabinet posts in the transitional government as the ruling MRND (including Interior and Communal Development), as well as half of the field-grade officers and above, was immediately viewed by extremists in the so-called *"mouvance presidentielle"* as a surrender to blackmail. Many indeed wondered whether the Arusha accords would have been signed in the absence of *repeated nudging* from the OAU, Tanzania, France, the United States, and Belgium (my italics).

Lemarchand's argument has two important premises: namely that the deal was negotiated between moderates; and that it was rejected by extremists once its contents became known. Thus, Lemarchand criticizes not only the content of the Arusha deal but also the process by which it was reached. By dealing with each of the points in this analysis, and their premises, we can help weigh the merits of this competing account of Arusha.

The extent of pressure (external *and* internal). on the Habyarimana regime was certainly considerable. Western pressure for democratic reforms had pushed Habyarimana to accept, in principle, multiparty democracy in 1989; falling world coffee prices had sharpened economic decline in the country; the war with the RPF had exposed Rwanda to western human rights monitors who were working with Rwandese groups to expose extra-judicial executions, disappearances, and other violations by the regime; and Habyarimana was certainly pushed into negotiations by his western allies (Belgium and France) and pulled into them by his regional counterparts.

That being said, the external pressure on the regime *within* the Arusha process cannot be seen as being overwhelming because of the presence of supportive regimes like France and Zaire in the talks. Rather, the pressure came from the nature of the process. Arusha was fundamentally about power-sharing, and the power to share was all held by the regime. Thus, the nature of the process itself was such that every conceivable resolution of an issue involved some limitation on the regime's power. What's more, at some points the external delegations, or observers, actually tried to limit the concessions made in Arusha. The most important example of this was the American delegation's attempt to convince the Arusha participants that the deal on the armed forces had moved past what was acceptable in Kigali. I will return to this last point.

Lemarchand was not wrong to say that the process involved major concessions to the RPF: that was precisely the essence of the process. What is inaccurate, however, is to argue that these concessions were somehow deals made between moderates and the RPF without the full comprehension of Habyarimana or the hard-liners, or that they were only reached because of pressure from outsiders. For while the Government of Rwanda delegation to Arusha was led by opposition party moderates, two other delegation members fulfilled other functions. Colonel Bagosora, a known extremist (who had earned the nickname "the Colonel of Death" for his role in directing killings against Tutsi) was present for the entire Arusha process, and provided a direct link between the process and the Hutu extremist groups in Kigali. Ambassador Kanyarushoki was seen by western delegates to Arusha as the eyes and ears of Habyarimana, and he too was present for the entire Arusha process. The political communities these two represented—Habyarimana and his closest supporters, and the Hutu extremists (groups which certainly overlapped but may not have been identical)—were fully aware of the course of Arusha as it was negotiated. This can be seen in the fact that on at least three occasions the Arusha process was suspended in order to refer agreements reached to Kigali, where they were rejected by Habyarimana in response to the reactions from these two communities. The argument is not that Bagasora and Kanyarushoki were able to contain the negotiating process, but simply that they fed information about the process directly to Habyarimana and the hard-liners throughout the course of negotiations. These constituencies had input into the course of negotiations as revealed in a comment made by Foreign Minister Ngulinzira, who remarked to one western observer that it was more difficult to negotiate with his own team than with the RPF.

How is it then that the Arusha process appeared to most western observers to go too far with respect to the integration of armed forces, the distribution of command posts, and arguably on the exclusion of the CDR from the transitional institutions of the BBTG? If the external pressures were not excessive, if Arusha was not entirely controlled by moderates, why were these agreements reached by August 1993?

The critical explanatory variable, which is missing from both the "preventive diplomacy" and the Lemarchand account, was the strength of the RPF—their superior position both on the ground and in the negotiating room. Although the two sides appeared to be in a military stalemate when the Arusha process had begun, the February offensive had proven decisively that the RPF had a significant military advantage on the ground, and were poised to continue winning military victories should the negotiations break down. This, then, created a second form of strength, namely a superior bargaining position.

Further, the RPF offensive in February increased the displaced population to almost a million people. Aside from the huge financial burden this displaced population placed on the government, these internal refugees came largely from Ruhengiri and Bambi, two of Rwanda's "breadbasket" regions. This intensified the economic pressures on the Habyarimana regime. Militarily dominant, and free from the government's position of having to try to run a country at war in full-scale economic collapse, the RPF was in a position effectively to dictate the terms of 'agreement' at this stage in the negotiations. Ultimately it was not "repeated nudging" from the observers and facilitators that produced the positions taken on the contentious elements of the deal; rather, it was RPF bargaining strength and intransigence in some parts, as well as intransigence on the part of the CDR and elements of the government delegation in others. The contentious positions on the CDR and the military split were taken *precisely contrary* to the nudges, and occasionally concerted pressure, of the observers. For this reason, the final version of the Arusha agreement reads like a victor's deal, rather than a general settlement between relatively equal sides which was the perspective of the third-parties.

Thus, both the preventive diplomacy argument and the Lemarchand critique each capture an aspect of truth, but conflate a critical distinction between *content* and *process*. As a preventive diplomacy *process*, the Arusha process was excellent in a number of respects: the right mix of relevant regional players, committed international players, and neutral elements around the table; the innovative and effective use of the

JPMC to negotiate military elements while having peace negotiations continue; the representation in the government delegation to Arusha of the major power groupings in Kigali itself; actually addressing *and resolving* in the agreement itself, in many dimensions, fundamental causes of conflict (i.e., the question of refugees) as opposed to merely settling the fighting; adumbrating and making provision for a neutral international force to secure the transition. However, the final *result* did indeed prove to be a failure, in part, at least, because it pushed well beyond what was acceptable in Kigali with respect to distribution of command posts and the exclusion of hard-liners from the final transitional arrangements.

This still leaves open the question of whether the alternative would have been better—including the "spoilers"[24] or extremists (the CDR) within the transitional government, and giving more power to Habyarimana and his faction. In any case, the "exemplary preventive diplomacy" analysis, while correct in terms of process, must be rejected in terms of the content of the final deal. On the one hand, the Arusha accords violated traditional key tenets of conflict resolution in the context of protracted social conflicts by effectively excluding the CDR from power, and thus marginalizing even the MRND, diverging from the tenet that forces which comprise the problem must be made part of the solution. On the other hand, the steps which were taken to enact the alternative—namely, remove extremist forces from power and tackle them militarily—were far from sufficient; the Accords called only for a "neutral international force" to perform the far from neutral task of tackling violent opposition to the peace deal, though it did request that the Neutral Force be charged with protecting civilians, a charge which the U.N. did not take up.[25]

Second, the Arusha Accords failed to balance properly the security concerns of the combatants. The twin victories won by the RPF over the CDR and the structure of the integrated forces created a situation in which a powerful political force in Kigali was deprived, not only of their absolute military control over the security forces in Rwanda, even though the FAR continued to appoint the head of the integrated armed forces and the MRND appointed the Minister of Defence, but also of the political control over those forces. On the other hand, the only way to achieve the latter would have required the RPF to concede power to the CDR. It could be argued that the fault was that agreement had the form of a victor's deal but not enough of the content. It fell between the two stools, and almost a million Tutsi civilians, as well as the peace process itself, were the victims.

Thus, while the Arusha process was effective in raising key issues and allowing the parties to the conflict an opportunity to negotiate alternatives, the final outcome was indeed deeply flawed, and ended up, despite the apparent intentions of those involved, contributing to the dynamic which resulted in the massive bloodshed of the spring and summer of 1994.

This argument relies on an unprovable counterfactual argument, namely that there were alternatives, that different decisions at different stages could have produced a more viable, sustainable outcome. In theoretical terms, the counterfactual is easily constructed. On the one hand, a more balanced power-sharing arrangement between the regime and its opponents, one which did not trump the MRND at every turn, could have produced an incentive structure for members of the regime to participate in securing the establishment and survival of the transitional institutions. More sensitive handling of the issue of army command may have produced less of a feeling of insecurity among those in Kigali who would lose absolute control of a military base and any effective political base to contain the damage of such a loss. This was the agreement sought by the Tanzanian facilitator, by the American delegation, and by the French.

The second step in this counterfactual position is to argue that, having been given a more substantive role in transitional institutions, those who did in fact execute the genocide would not have done so. This is unprovable though the argument for the position was made by the Tanzanians and the Americans. They argued that it would simply have been more difficult to plan, coordinate, and launch a genocide—or any form of violent opposition—from within the government than from without. Faced with the imminent loss of power, those who controlled the genocide had little to lose by destroying the transitional institutions; with a substantive role in those institutions, the argument goes, at least some of those potentially involved in violent opposition would see their interests in securing a position in the "new order" and limiting their resort to the use of violence.

Further, the argument goes, the potential for fracture and dissent among the old guard would be higher in conditions where members of that old guard had a greater stake in the new Rwandese state. Thus, while it is clear that a core group of extremists among the Habyarimana inner circle were developing a genocidal plan from the very outset of negotiations, their capacity to attract wider sympathy to that plan might have been scuttled by offering members of the regime a choice. President Mwinyi of Tanzania used allegorical terms to extol this position:

when chasing a cat in a house, he instructed his facilitation team, make sure to leave a window open; or else, be prepared to be scratched.[26] By denying the regime a substantive enough role in the "new order," the power-sharing protocols of Arusha failed to leave a window sufficiently wide open and, instead, backed the regime into a corner. Instead of offering members of the regime a choice between sufficient power and violent opposition, the far more stark choice was offered of effective loss of power or violent opposition.

Providing greater control of the military and a more substantive political role for the Habyarimana regime would have involved, for the RPF, a substantial risk as well as the morally and psychologically difficult step of cooperating with those whose rhetoric called for their own elimination. As Stedman (1991) has pointed out, finding a negotiated settlement in a civil war necessarily involves the psychological stress of "working with the enemy." On the other hand, Stedman has since argued that there are enemies with whom one is engaged in violent conflict and there are "enemies" with whom one is engaged in death to the finish. This is the other side of the counterfactual. Would the small core of extremists determined to destroy the Arusha Accords and any cooperation with their sworn foes have been even more effective if their allies had been given a greater role, or would they have been neutralized in executing their monstrous plans?

Conclusion

Conflict resolution theory would suggest two options in dealing with those who lose out in political transformation, the first of which is to give them a stake in the new arrangements in order to minimize their destructiveness (i.e., keeping minority whites in the political system in South Africa). The successful transition in South Africa, and earlier successes in Rhodesia/Zimbabwe, prove that peace agreements which forge transition bargains of this nature can succeed. Alternatively, a peace settlement may accept the exclusion of certain powerful groups but find ways to ensure that they are unable to undermine the transition bargain (i.e., pushing and pulling the military *junta* out of power in Haiti). The international peace efforts for Rwanda took neither option. Had the Arusha process given the Habyarimana regime a more meaningful stake in power, perhaps the neutral peacekeeping mandate of UNAMIR would have been successful in securing the transition process. As it was, Arusha resulted in a decidedly non-neutral transition bargain, with clear winners and losers.[27] Were a robust peacekeeping force available to control those losers—who, it should be recalled, were in a position of considerable power, including control of the army and various militias—it might have been the right decision to exclude those hard-liners from the "new order" for Rwanda.

From most western and diplomatic perspectives, in the context of the possible, the second-best choice—to buy the hard-liners off by giving them a greater stake in the transitional institutions, and thus some security also—should have been adopted in the Arusha Accords. From other perspectives, especially the RPF, this was not only morally unpalatable, but was inherently unworkable. For most western and diplomatic observers, the first would certainly have been preferable to taking the large physical and moral risk of marginalizing powerful forces without taking adequate precautions against their inevitable reaction. For many others, the failure rests with those who had the resources and the means to deploy effective military forces to hold the extremists at bay and protect civilians but who did not fulfill what had been expected of them in the Arusha Accords.

Notes

1. The timeline contained herein was developed, except where otherwise noted, through reference to documents obtained from western embassies in Dar-es-Salaam in December 1993 and January 1994; discussions with American, French, Canadian, Rwandese, and Tanzanian officials in Dar-es-Salaam, Ottawa, London, Washington, New York, and Bergen; and from the texts of the accords themselves. American sources may appear to be prominent: this is largely because of all the interviews conducted, only Americans were willing to go on record and even allow their names to be used.
2. After the FAR and its allies stopped the October invasion in its tracks, the RPF launched another offensive in November. Heavy clashes followed. In January 1991, the RPF briefly held Ruhengiri, the power base of Habyarimana and his cohorts.
3. Interview 14 December 1994 with Carol Fuller, Former. Rwanda Desk Officer, Africa Bureau, Department of State, Washington, DC.
4. This was distinct from the MRND dominated pseudo-coalition created in December 1991. True moderates now occupied important positions in the government, and the new government adopted a policy of seeking a peace agreement with the RPF.
5. This account draws principally on interviews conducted with present and former members of the State Department, including Carol Fuller, Charles Snyder and former Assistant Secretary of State for Africa, Herman Cohen, Washington, June 30, 1995, as well as with Quai d'Orsay officials involved in the pre-Arusha talks, and compares notes with Howard Adelman and Astri Suhrke, who held similar interviews.
6. Second track diplomacy may have contributed to the success of the talks in

Paris. The second track consisted of a number of initiatives at unofficial levels: contacts between members of the RPF's diaspora network and Rwandese government officials in embassies overseas; efforts by NGOs, specifically by a former Ugandan official working for Christian Aid in London, who facilitated the meeting between the RPF and the GOR in Bujumbura (disclosed in a talk given by a Christian Aid representative at an Open Forum on Rwanda convened by International Alert, London, 27 January 1995); a Rwandan church-based initiative; and Vatican efforts to support church initiatives (confidential interview, Rome, April 1995). These moves may generally have been atmospheric and supportive of the first track diplomacy. But one process seems to have had a direct effect. In May of 1992, after meetings between the Rwandese church leaders and the RPF in Bujumbura, under the aegis of the Papal Nuncio in Burundi, the new foreign minister of Rwanda, Ngulinzira, met with the Papal Nuncio in Rwanda which led to a trip pf Ngulinzira to the Vatican. This facilitated the meeting between Ngulinzira and the RPF in Kinihara, Rwanda on 23 May 1992, at which both agreed to attend Dijoud's Paris meeting.

7. The RPF delegation, according to all observers at the talks that I interviewed, was by far the most disciplined and effective of the two negotiating parties. Led by Dr. Theogene Rudasingwa, General Secretary of the RPF and the eyes and ears of Paul Kagame, it included Pasteur Bizimungu, who would later become President of the Republic, and Patrick Mazimhaka, Vice Chairman of the RPF. The GOR delegation was both divided and undisciplined and included members from at least three parties; beside the government it included the opposition MDR (Dr. Ngulinzira, the new Foreign Minister of Rwanda in the coalition government and Mr. Landoald, Minister of Labour and Social Affairs) and the PL. Colonel Bagasora, the extremist from CDR, and Ambassador Kanyarushoki to Tanzania, with a direct line to Habyarimana, were also delegates.

8. In addition to the two formal delegations at Arusha, the Government of Rwanda (GOR) and the Rwandese Patriotic front (RPF), three regional/functional categories of observer delegates were present at the talks: (1) African—in addition to the facilitation team from Tanzania, it included delegations from Zaire (its delegates were largely absent except for the initial meetings), Uganda, Burundi, and Senegal (Abdou Diouf was chair of the OAU when the Arusha process began, and the Senegalese delegate, Ambassador Papa Louis Fall, was respected by both sides); (2) inter-governmental organizations—the OAU and the U.N.; and (3) Western—delegations from the US, Belgium (Ambassador Conte Michel d'Aviola to Tanzania in the first phases), France, and Germany (Ambassador Hans Peter Repnik to Tanzania who was more a witness than a participant). Britain, Canada, the Netherlands, and the EU decided not to participate but followed the negotiations closely from their embassies in the region.

9. Because the observer teams to the Arusha negotiations and the JPMC overlapped, the JPMC often met in Arusha instead of Addis.

10. *The N'Sele Ceasefire Agreement between the Government of the Rwandese Republic and the Rwandese Patriotic Front, as Amended at Gbadolite, 16 September 1991,* and at *Arusha 12 July 1992,* Article IV, p.7 (hereafter referred to as the Arusha Ceasefire). The Arusha Ceasefire had restructured the NMOG (from that point on referred to as NMOG II), so that it was composed of ten officers from each of Nigeria, Senegal, Zimbabwe, and an African country to be named later, and five officers each from the GOR and RPF.

11. Interview with officials of the Quai d'Orsay; with Lt. Col. Marley, Political-Military Advisor, Africa Bureau, State Department, Washington, 13 December 1994. Col. Marley was a military representative of the US observer team at Arusha.

12. JPMC/RWD/OAU/1 (I) Rev.2, "Rules of Procedure for the Joint Political-Military Commission (JPMC)"; JPMC/RWD/OAU/2 (I), "Terms of Reference of the Neutral Military Observer Group."
13. Interview. Also, Interview, Lt. Col. Marley.
14. It should be noted that although the Arusha talks formally adjourned between these periods, discussions, and negotiations continued in Kigali, Kampala, Addis Ababa, and Dar-es-Salaam throughout these intervals, both under the aegis of the JPMC and in informal meetings at various embassies in the region.
15. Confidential interview. The editors of this volume were given the same interpretation of the French and Tanzanian positions in their interviews. Further, the Americans supported the French and Tanzanians.
16. For instance, Canadian and Dutch observers in Dar-es-Salaam reacted to the RPF's unwillingness to include the CDR as evidence of their insincerity in participating in real power sharing; members of the Tanzanian facilitation team also saw in this position a too-rigid stance. Interviews, Dar-es-Salaam, December 1993; Bergen 1995.
17. Other chapters tackle the question of France's role in Rwanda in some depth. It is worth stating here, however, that, within the Quai d'Orsay, their analysis suggested that the Habyarimana regime would be unable to hold out against the RPF, and thus that a negotiated settlement would be an acceptable second best for France's interests (Interviews with Quai d'Orsay officials). Thus, France's delegation to Arusha was not one which simply fought for the GOR positions, but, according to American, Tanzanian and other third-party participants, was cooperative and constructive.
18. Confidential document supplied by western embassy, Dar-es-Salaam, December 1993.
19. Lt. Col. Marley confirmed this perception.
20. It is important to note that the account of the killings in Burundi which were current in the Great Lakes region in 1993 were of 100,000 Hutu having been killed by the Tutsi army. The fact is that the killings were rather of the order of 35,000–50,000. More importantly, they were roughly evenly split between Hutu and Tutsi (according to USAID and *Médecins sans Frontières*). This was not information which made its way into Rwanda or Tanzania at the time. Interviews with Sarah Poole, Rwanda-Burundi Information Officer, USAID Disaster Assistance Response Team, Washington, July 1994; and with Samantha Bolton, Public Information Officer, Médecins sans Frontières, New York, December 1995.
21. This account, which was first given to me in Tanzania in December 1993 and has been repeated since by American, Belgian, Canadian, Tanzanian, Vatican, and French officials, suggests that as late as October 1993 the forces which were moving to genocide had not yet won the day. The logic of the position suggests that the core extremists were able to use events in Burundi to sell their vision to a broader constituency which might, were it not for the killings in Bujumbura, still have been won over by the transitional government.
22. This refers to the 11 January message of Force Commander Romeo Dallaire to the U.N. headquarters in New York on the contents of very high level information he received about the detailed plans of the extremists (cf. Adelman and Suhrke, 1996).
23. The diplomatic perspective is important to understanding the positions of "inside-outsiders" in the negotiating process and to conflict resolution more generally. A shared analysis had been developed based on a common negotiating history among Tanzanian, American, and French officials who were instrumental in setting up the process. They considered the conflict in Rwanda to be part of a

protracted social conflict which would be resolved, not by high-level summitry, but over a period of time in which the belligerents would have an opportunity to examine their sense of insecurity vis-a-vis one another and forge agreements which would meet the security needs of both sides. Whether or not the diplomats rooted their convictions in theoretical studies, the theoretical foundations of this position can be found in Edward Azar, *Protracted Social Conflict*, and in the writings of John Burton. At least one key diplomat expressed familiarity with this literature. The diplomats' position was certainly based on the historical experience of conflict resolution processes in other parts of Africa, such as that of Ami Mpungwe, former Director of the Africa and Middle East Department in the Foreign Ministry and Tanzania's principal facilitator of the Arusha talks, who left the Namibia negotiations in February 1992 to take the lead in the build up to Arusha, Charles Snyder and John Byerly, members of Cohen's conflict resolution team who had been involved with Namibia and Angola.

24. Professor Steve Stedman, now at Stanford University, coined the phrase "spoilers" for those who try to sabotage a peace agreement after it has been signed. Stedman argues that conciliation with respect to "spoilers" is ineffective. The report written by the editors also argued that the spoilers had to be neutralized by "defanging" them—removing them from military power—if they were not to be made part of the transitional power structure. This still leaves open the question of whether the latter option would have worked. The fact is, the Arusha Agreement neither defanged the extremists nor included them in the transitional power structure.

25. It is arguable that the RPF believed that the neutral international force would indeed prove an effective block on any violent opposition to the peace deal. If so, this among other failures of communication between the U.N. and the OAU/Tanzanians about the transition from mediation to implementation becomes a crucial weakness in the overall response. However, simple reference to Mozambique, Namibia, and Angola—conflicts with which the RPF command was certainly familiar—would have been enough to sew substantial doubts that a U.N. peacekeeping presence could—or should—be relied upon to provide resistance to violent opposition and effectively protect a civilian population. The U.N. only agreed to *assist* the local gendarmie in its protective functions.

26. This allegory was relayed to me by a senior member of the Tanzanian negotiating team.

27. The Arusha failure resulted from a series of negotiating "victories" by the RPF which so structured the final outcome of Arusha as to make it unacceptable to powerful forces in Kigali. Critically, these decisions were not, as has been argued, foisted on Rwanda by outsiders; rather they were taken precisely in opposition to both neutral and partisan third-party advice and pressure. The determining variable, missed by both the diplomatic and the critical perspectives, was the superior strength of the RPF, both on the battlefield and in the negotiating rooms. In defiance of advice and pressure from regional and international actors, the RPF used their bargaining strength to marginalize the Habyarimana regime within the negotiated power structures and erode major elements of their power base. In both the political and military spheres, the RPF insisted on arrangements which deprived hard-liners surrounding Habyarimana.

8

French Policy in Rwanda

Agnès Callamard

Introduction[1]

In the aftermath of the April 1994 genocide in Rwanda, a large portion of the French media and most NGOs vigorously denounced French policy in Rwanda, going as far as accusing the government, in particular, the President, of complicity in the genocide.[2] Much was then written on the personal connections between French President François Mitterand and his Rwandese counterpart, Juvénal Habyarimana, and between the two sons of the Presidents, on the business deals between Paris and the Rwandese capital, Kigali, the secret sale of arms by Paris to the Rwandese military involved in the genocide, and on hashish deals and even gorillas.

In response, the French government insisted that it had supported Arusha and contributed to the peace process in Rwanda. François Mitterand was said to have been shocked: "I am convinced that we have helped this country, like others, to take the road to democracy" (*Le Nouvel Observateur* 1994, 40). Similarly, Edouard Balladur said the accusations were scandalous: "France supported the regular/legal government of Rwanda. It was revealed afterwards that this government was not as regular as it claimed."[3] These claims of innocence, however, did not persuade many observers.

The question remained: after the genocide how should these accusations, claims of innocence or, more generally, French policy towards Rwanda from 1990 to 1994 be assessed? The main arguments of this chapter are twofold. First, the most striking features of French policies in Rwanda were that they responded to and reflected the usual framework of Franco-African relationships: France gave military and diplo-

157

matic support to a dictatorial regime, trained government armed forces as part of a cooperation agreement, and intervened to protect a regime against what was then considered to be external aggression. Official policy was cemented by patrimonial relationships between leaders and possibly by secret business, military, or other deals between the two countries. These are all common features of French relations with Francophone Africa and consistent with the framework that determined French policy towards the region in the post-independence period.

The second argument of this chapter is that these common features proved especially catastrophic because of three main factors: The first one is that the diplomatic logic (or "soft track" as it is also called) never predominated for very long, if at all[4]; the military logic was applied in the first days of October 1990, never lost its significance, and became increasingly prominent as the peace process weakened. The second factor is the depoliticization of Rwandan affairs; there is little evidence of a politically based, politically controlled, and politically motivated management of Rwandan affairs and of a thorough synchronization between military actions and diplomatic steps.[5] The third factor is that the conflict in Rwanda was perceived and analyzed through *corrective lenses* which fed and cemented the military logic and the preeminence of military actors.

The Peace Process and the French Diplomatic Role

Background to French Diplomatic Efforts:
The 1990 Military Intervention

The first Technical Military Assistance Agreement (TMAA) between Rwanda and France was signed on 18 July 1975 under Valery Giscard d'Estaing's presidency as part of France's attempt to extend its zone of influence beyond its former empire.[6] This agreement was not a defense agreement: it sought to provide financial assistance, as well as actual training for the Rwandese gendarmerie, and supplies of military equipment for both the gendarmerie and the army. In fact, like many TMAAs signed between France and African countries, this one stipulated that French soldiers could not be associated with the preparation and execution of war operations or the maintenance of domestic peace (cf. Gattegno, *Le Monde*, 1994; Verschave 1994). French military assistance to Rwanda remained modest for several years, averaging 4 million francs per year (*Le Monde,* 22 June 1994). In January 1985, there were twenty French military advisors in Rwanda (Chipman 1995, 24), while the number of Rwandese officers trained in France increased slightly from twenty-three in 1982 to thirty-three in 1988.[7] According to *Le Monde,* the 1975 TMAA was officially (and a posteriori) revised on 26 August 1991 when an agreement between Ambassador Martre and Rwandese Defense Minister Ngulinzira incorporated the Rwandese Armed Forces (in addition to the gendarmerie) as beneficiaries of the military agreement (Gattegno 1994).

Evidently, the October 1990 RPF invasion drastically transformed the nature and extent of the military relationship between France and Rwanda. Francois Mitterand's decision to launch Operation Noroît,[8] officially to protect the French expatriates present in Rwanda in case of unrest, was taken almost immediately.[9] The force consisted of 150 soldiers drawn from the French force stationed in the Central African Republic (Human Rights Watch Arms Project, 1994), a number that increased to 350 in November, at the same time as Belgian soldiers were leaving the country. Following the RPF's renewed offensive on 8 February 1993, France sent 300 additional troops to Kigali,[10] bringing the total contingent to about 700 troops.[11] France also supplied the government with important military equipment[12] as well as military advisers.[13]

The presidential decisions to send French troops, equipment, and advisers in 1990,[14] and reinforce them in February 1993, were taken outside the scope of the TMMA (recall that it was not a defense agreement) and without parliamentary consent. These were two facts which raised little surprise or concern at the time, given French past practices. As Chipman noted, "for French military intervention to take place it is not necessary that there exist a formal defense agreement.... In fact, France has intervened more often in countries not having defense agreements (Mauritania, Chad, and Zaire), than in those (Gabon and CAR) with whom she has been, from a juridical point of view, more closely allied (Chipman 1995, 28). Cohen also emphasizes that the military interventions were undertaken without prior authorization of the French parliament, and without encountering significant opposition (cf. Cohen and Clarke 1990, 205–06, 212).

From the perspective of Franco-African relations, the French intervention satisfied two main, albeit minimalist, criteria[15] that have guided French interventions on the continent[16]: it took place at the urging of the Rwandese president[17] and in response to an "external" aggression.

The latter condition had just been reiterated at the La Baule summit meeting where Mitterand had stated that French troops would continue to help countries facing external threats; the RPF invasion was launched from Uganda. Operation Noroît also appears to have been guided by one additional consideration—the RPF was considered by French military and political leaders as a threat to *francophonie* and *la françafrique*. This certainly played a role in the presidential decision. From this perspective, the intervention was probably conceived first and foremost as an easy way to reinforce France's "guardian angel" image vis-à-vis African leaders, and to support "a good guy," President Habyarimana who, after all, was trying his best.

Two aspects of this assessment proved to be wrong: Habyarimana did not try his best, and the intervention was not easy given the limited capacity of the Rwandese army. The Rwandese armed forces were so few (about 3,000 soldiers, according to most sources, although the figure of 6,000 has also been advanced) and, according to French military officials (confidential interview, Ministry of Cooperation, May 1995), also badly prepared and badly equipped; only 2,000 of the troops knew how to fight. One month after the beginning of the war, it became clear that the RPF would not easily be defeated. By the end of 1990, the weakness of the Rwandese army had been the object of French military intelligence reports which suggested that the RPF was actually capable of defeating the FAR in conventional warfare.[18] The RPF offensive on 8 February 1993 further confirmed these French assessments as French military intelligence reported that the RPF had only stopped short of Kigali because of the presence of French troops there, an assessment shared by Tanzanian intelligence.[19] In light of this assessment, and established policy of not providing open-ended military support for a long period of time, it appears that by the end of 1990, the French government faced two options. They were not mutually exclusive and both were eventually embraced: supporting the peace process, and strengthening the Rwanda armed forces.

French Diplomatic Efforts—October 1990 to August 1993

Most accounts attribute the turning point of French policies in Rwanda—the "shift" from the military to the diplomatic track—either to the end of 1992 or to the beginning of 1993 when "cohabitation" commenced.[20] In fact, the "soft" track was already in action in March 1991 (at the time of the cease-fire agreement brokered at N'Sele, Zaire) and was followed up in subsequent years, but never seemed to prevail over the military logic. Contrary to most beliefs, moreover, the main diplomatic issue at the end of the period of negotiating the Arusha Accords was not so much French military withdrawal—that issue was settled quite early[21]—as it was about the nature of the international peacekeeping operation to replace the French soldiers—whether it would be under OAU or U.N. authority, France lobbying hard for the latter.

France was an important diplomatic actor in the pre-Arusha and Arusha phases when France initiated a number of bilateral meetings and participated in multilateral conferences. The reorientation towards military disengagement and the peace process began in the early months of 1991, perhaps at the end of 1990,[22] at a time when a socialist government was still in power in France. By 1991, the French government was pushing for a peace settlement between the Rwandese government and the RPF,[23] and was prepared to withdraw its troops from Rwanda. The Quai d'Orsay was present at the N'Sele talks and encouraged the Government of Rwanda (GOR) to sign the cease-fire agreement of 29 March 1991, an agreement which, among other things, called for the withdrawal of all foreign troops (article ii). The N'Sele agreement was followed in the fall of 1991 by negotiations, led by the Elysée Africa Bureau, to bring the Government of Rwanda and the RPF together; in the spring and summer of 1992, the Quai d'Orsay held a series of informal talks between the two parties.[24] These efforts culminated in the Paris meeting of June 1992 between the RPF and GOR delegations; the agenda included fusion of the two armies, establishment of a broad-based transitional government, and political guarantees.

All these diplomatic activities were probably instrumental in bringing the government of Rwanda to the negotiation table at Arusha in July 1992. The Quai d'Orsay was present as an observer,[25] lending support to the Rwandese government and ensuring that the negotiations did not fundamentally jeopardize the interests of the Habyarimana regime. This role was especially reflected in the French backing of the government's (unsuccessful) requests for a 1:2 ratio for the new integrated army and for the inclusion of the Coalition for the Defense of the Republic (CDR) within the broad-based government (Adelman and Suhrke 1996). Some six months later, on 28 February, following the RPF offensive in February 1993, Marcel Debarge, Cooperation Minister, went to Kigali to reaffirm French support for Habyarimana and convince him to implement the Arusha agreement.[26]

French diplomatic strategy during these two years was based primarily on an appreciation of the military capacity of the two parties and its own reluctance to sustain a long-term war. The implication was that France was walking on a fine, not to say self-destructive, line. On one hand, France could not afford the repeated breaking of cease fires and the prospect of a long peacemaking process. On the other, it had to secure Habyarimana's agreement (and reinforce his position at the bargaining table), and thus be perceived by the GOR as fulfilling its commitments. Hence Mitterand made promises not to withdraw French troops without the government's agreement,[27] and not before the Rwandan armed forces were strengthened. In the same logic, the second major component of France's soft-track approach[28] was to obtain a U.N. peacekeeping force[29] that would enhance the survival chances of its protegé.[30] According to the N'Sele agreement, French troops would remain until a neutral military force could be deployed.[31] Reiterated in article 72[32] of the Arusha Accords, this clause represented France's biggest bargaining chip at Arusha, and it was on this point that French diplomatic efforts were concentrated.

French lobbying for a United Nations military presence—with the dual function of monitoring the Rwandan/Ugandan border and acting as an interpositional force between the RPF and the Rwandese army— took place within the Security Council of the United Nations. In the fall of 1992, the French representative began asking for an interpositional U.N. force, a request rejected until March 1993 by the UK and the US which wanted the OAU to take the lead. On 9 March 1993 the French delegation presented the Security Council members with a draft resolution which supported the Secretary General's initiative to send a goodwill mission to Rwanda and requested that the Secretary-General make recommendations for the possible establishment of a United Nations monitoring force to act, together with OAU forces,[33] as a buffer (Adelman and Suhrke, 1996). Resolution 812/93 was eventually passed on March 12, after intense French lobbying in the Security Council. The French efforts succeeded: following consultations between the OAU and the U.N., it was decided at the beginning of June 1993 following a formal request from the government of Rwanda[34] that the United Nations would provide the neutral international force. Further, the French referred to the protection of civilians as one of the functions of the international force.[35] The formal resolution (872/1993) was passed on 5 October 1993.

This interpretation of French diplomatic efforts gives credit to the claims advanced by the French government immediately after the April

1994 genocide. The government did support the Arusha process and was instrumental in getting Habyarimana to the negotiation table. This being said, the extent of the synchronization between diplomatic and military action[36] is questionable. The French diplomatic strategy, it will be recalled, was preceded by a military intervention and predicated upon a military balance of power in the field. It would remain driven by military policy and military evolution on the ground.

French Diplomacy: The Actors

Analysts of French policy in Rwanda attributed a catalytic role to the Quai d'Orsay and to "the cohabitation" in terms of supporting the diplomatic track and the peace process at Arusha.[37] The coming into power of a new majority, with Juppé as Minister of Foreign Affairs and Balladur as Prime Minister, certainly reinforced the power of the Quai vis-à-vis the Elysée. A possible blow to the old way came from the growing power of a new brand of French technocrats, whose influence had grown with the arrival of Balladur as Prime Minister.

> [Balladur] has little of his peer's sentimental attachment to Africa.. He is a Treasury man: his aim seems to be to prise Africa policy out of the Elysée's tight grasp and give the foreign minister a reasonable purchase on it. Mr. Balladur's team is quietly trying to snuff out the old palace-to-palace networks.[38]

Cohabitation also allowed more emphasis to be given to the multilateral and diplomatic tracks, and probably reinforced the notion that France had to open a dialogue with the RPF, but it is highly unlikely that cohabitation constituted a significant turning point in French African policy.[39] It is doubtful if Habyarimana would have signed the peace accords, which gave heavy concessions to the RPF, without pressure and guarantees from the Elysée through François Mitterand's personal emissaries, and possibly from representatives of the Military Mission of Cooperation, specifically Général Huchon.[40] The Elysée defined the policy, took care of personal and bilateral diplomacy, while the Quai pursued the soft-track side and was responsible for multilateral negotiations.

That being said, François Mitterand's role remains unclear. He did authorize the 1990 intervention—all French military interventions are presidential prerogatives. The reason for this decision can be partly located in the personal and patrimonial ties that existed at the time, but this was not unusual as personal contacts between French and African leaders have been at the core of French-African relationships since de

Gaulle. The "mitterandisation" of French policy in Rwanda, which numerous accounts claimed after the genocide,[41] has probably been exaggerated. During the three to four years that preceded the genocide, Mitterand had to deal with the Kuwait-Iraq war, Somalia, Serbia, "cohabitation," the making of the European Union, and his own illnesses, to cite just a few items. The relative importance of Rwanda must be assessed in this context. Existing evidence available to the writer suggests that if the President of the Republic erred seriously in Rwanda, these were errors of omission rather than commission.

The same may be said of the ministers of foreign affairs, defense or cooperation from 1990 to 1993: Rwanda was not the main issue on their agenda, and the diplomatic strategy even less so. To return to the Arusha process, there was only one French representative there, the chargé d'affaires in Tanzania. The Quai did not send additional observers and, according to persons present at Arusha from July 1992 to August 1993, the French representative received few communications and only vague instructions from Paris. However, French military officers (presumably based in Kigali) came to Arusha to consult with the French representative on a number of occasions. In itself it is hardly surprising that military actors worked alongside diplomats in negotiations of this kind. On the other hand, the general political detachment from Rwandan affairs would have enabled the military—more specifically the special military unit in the Ministry of Cooperation—to take a leading role, which seems to have been the case.

The relationship between Paris and Kigali reinforces the point. According to a French official, the embassy received little direction and instructions from Paris (Interview, Paris, May 1995). The picture emerging from Kigali is one of a vacuum, of a missing political link between the French diplomats posted to Rwanda and officials based in Paris. This state of affairs is not surprising because the few officials in Paris who followed and supported the soft-track approach in Paris were few and relatively powerless. According to an official in the Ministry of Cooperation, during the three years that preceded the genocide, there were only two French officials who supported the peace process and opposed the perspective offered by General Huchon, then in charge of the Mission Militaire de Cooperation. The two were "somebody in Tanzania [probably the chargé d'affaires] and someone, here in Paris, at the Ministry of Cooperation" (Interview, Paris, May 1995).

Other ministries also had Arusha proponents, but their views did not prevail. Hence, at the *Délégation aux affaires stratégiques* (DAS) of the Minister of Defense, created in 1992 by Pierre Joxe,[42] proposals for military disengagement are said to have been launched but quickly repressed. Similarly, while the hiring of new experts within the CAP (*Centre d'analyse et de Prévision*) in the Ministry of Foreign Affairs meant more support for the disengagement approach.

> The Quai decided that we were on the wrong track at the end of 1992. Researchers at the CAP and diplomats argued that we needed to talk to the RPF, and that the military thesis was wrong. (Interview, Paris)

Their advice did not seem to have had much impact. In sum, Rwanda was not of great concern at the highest level of the French government—the level of Mitterand, Juppé, and Balladur—nor, for that matter, in the Elysée or Ministry of Foreign Affairs generally. The political vacuum has had three main implications and/or characteristics. It first meant that the diplomatic and political use of Franco-Rwandese relationships in general and French military intervention in particular have been more important than their management, a characteristic of both the pre-genocide and the post-genocide periods. Second, it has implied that the tasks of analyzing the future of Rwanda, and by extension the path and management of French involvement, has been left to a limited set of actors; depoliticization entailed that the management of French policy has been, above all, the product of these actors' respective power both among themselves and in relationship to higher levels of decision-making. Thirdly, depoliticization signified that the Rwandan crisis and situation have been analyzed, read and advanced through self-absorbed, narcissistic lenses. One consequence, as noted, was the ascendancy of what I have referred to as the military logic (to be discussed in detail in the next section). The overall picture is one of the poverty of institutional mechanisms and of the actors.[43]

The Hegemonic View: The Military Logic

> General Kagame: *"You armed and trained the Presidential Guards; you have accepted that the Presidential Guards armed and trained, in front of you, the Hutu extremists. You have not required the President of Rwanda to abandon ethnic identity cards; vous portez donc une lourde part de responsabilité dans le génocide en cours."*
> (*Le Figaro*, 25 June 1994)

> *"Africa is the only continent that remains within
> the reach of French influence. It is the only place
> where she can still, with 300 men, change the
> course of history."*
> (Louis de Guirangaud, Foreign Minister in 1979,
> quoted in Chaigneau 1989, 340)

The French Military

The exact role of French troops in Rwanda from 1990 to 1993 is unclear and controversial. Officially, "French military troops were in Rwanda to protect French citizens and other foreigners. They have never been given a mission against the RPF."[44] As opposed to this official position, journalists and eye witnesses argued that French soldiers did much more than just protect French expatriates, and in fact went as far as engaging in combat. For instance, a Nigerian colonel of the international military observer group (NMOG) is said to have accused French troops of bombarding the RPF position in Ruhengiri (AFP and Reuters, 15 February 1993), an accusation disputed by French officials.[45] Similar types of accusations have been made by several French journalists[46] as well as Human Rights Watch. Equally seriously, the Belgian lawyer, Eric Gillet, present in Rwanda in August 1991, reported that French army officers were responsible for questioning seventeen or eighteen RPF prisoners (see for instance Exuperry 1994). French soldiers manned checkpoints north of Kigali, demanding identification cards from civilians.[47]

In retrospect, focusing on France's rules and practice of engagement does not capture the dynamic of the French-Rwandese relationship. This is not to underestimate its importance: French intervention changed the course of history in that it stalled the RPF invasion[48] and later temporarily prevented the Front from taking Kigali.[49] However, the most important and dramatic consequence of French intervention does not reside in the possible involvement of French soldiers in combat, but in their functions in "internal security" matters.[50]

One issue that attracted particular attention was the nomination in February 1992 of Lieutenant-Colonel Chollet to head the *Détachement d'Assistance Militaire et d'Instruction* (DAMI) in Rwanda. Chollet took on the role of advisor to both the President Habyarimana and to the Chief Commander of the Rwandese Armed Forces.[51] When Chollet was eventually recalled, Lieutenant-Colonel Maurin, assistant to the military attaché, took over these functions. As Chipman noticed in his analysis of French military policy in Africa, "it is very hard to distinguish between honest and impartial technical advice given to a minister or armed services officer and interference in the internal affairs of another state" (Chipman 1995, 25).

In fact, the arrival of four French specialists in June 1992 to constitute a "judicial inquiry section" to fight terrorism (i.e., to engage in counter-insurgency) helped produce the report of the Rwandese gendarmie, "Terrorism in Rwanda since 1990," which blamed all acts of terror on the RPF without once mentioning widely reported massacres of civilians by Hutu (cf. *Republique Rwandaise* 1993). More significant is the charge that the French military actually trained the *interahamwe*.[52]

In the Rwanda case, there are two ways of looking at the French military presence. On one hand, Rwanda was at war and the government forces were ill-prepared. French military advice was thus of primary importance and could be justified from a strictly military perspective (i.e., war against "foreign" aggression). The same may be said about French contributions to the strengthening of Rwanda's military capacity.[53] On the other hand, the war efforts of the Habyarimana regime were clearly accompanied by action against the perceived "internal enemy," including massacres, targeted killings, arrests, and other forms of human rights violations. From this perspective, the appointment of French advisers within the highest ranks of Rwandese military and political authority, the presence of French soldiers manning checkpoints, and France's contribution to the rapid expansion of the armed forces and Presidential Guard are sufficient in and by themselves to raise very serious concerns regarding French military ethics in particular and French policy more generally.

Information Gathering

More needs to be said about the inadequacy of French intelligence, for the French problem was rooted in a mindblindness, a mental incapacity to see. At the outset, French military officers in Kigali or at the Military Mission of Cooperation in Paris did not believe in Arusha: "Arusha, it's Munich," one official said in the course of an interview. Nor did they trust the RPF: "It was not in the logic of the RPF to follow and obey the agreement" (interview, Paris, May 1995). The assessment of civilian French officials and journalists on the position of the French military was that the "Hutu track" predominated and that the military establishment did not support Arusha. In fact, according to a European diplomat in Kigali quoted by Human Rights Watch, "Cussac [in charge of the DAMI] is a man in favor of a military solution."

Given these views, it is not exaggerated to refer to the concerns of the French military establishment vis-à-vis the RPF and its military gains as "obsessional." All the energy of intelligence gathering, (dis)information activities, and analysis centered on the "Ugandan Tutsi," including their continuous strategy of "Talk and Fight," their incursions within the Rwandan territory, massacres of civilians, and later their covert activities within the Demilitarized Zone. In the months following the genocide, journalists were often approached by French military officials who handed over documents, pictures, and leaked information on the RPF, most of which could not be independently confirmed.[54]

However, French soldiers and/or their superiors were also aware of other disturbing facts, including strategies of intimidation, murder, and political manipulation at the highest level of the Rwandese government designed to stall the implementation of the transitional government agreed to at Arusha, and the repeated massacres and murders committed by extremist Hutu during this period. In July 1991, a French intelligence assessment, which eventually found its way to other chancelleries, had identified three critical circles of power in relation to the peace process: the President's in-laws and associates (the *AKAZU*), an outer circle of relatively more moderate members of the military and the cabinet, and an amorphous grouping of younger officers and intellectuals willing to entertain change. The assessment went on to estimate that since the principle objective of the first circle was to retain power, any form of imposed negotiation would provoke their resistance. In addition, various officials and journalists have stressed the existence of a number of French intelligence reports dealing with massacres taking place in the country, the role of the Rwandese President's wife, Agathe Habyarimana, Radio Mille Collines, and the like.[55]

French gendarmes in Rwanda and their superiors also had some knowledge of human rights violations committed in Rwanda. According to a Rwandese human rights activist, "I worked quite well together with the French gendarmes. Whenever I had proof that a Rwandese gendarme was torturing persons placed under his responsibility, and reported the facts and name to the French gendarmes, they were always successful in having the Rwandese gendarme transferred, usually to places close to the front-line in the newly 'liberated territories' that were unpopulated and where he could not harm anybody" (interview, July 1985).

The testimony of the human rights activist underlines two important points. First, French gendarmes had some degree of knowledge and understanding of the evolution of the regime. By extension, it is simply not believable that their colleagues in the French armed forces, who spent months training Rwandese armed forces, did not have any knowledge of some of their trainees' deadly activities at a time when these activities were already reported by a large number of local and international human rights organizations and were known by expatriates in Rwanda. Second, French gendarmes were sympathetic enough to the pleas of the human rights activist and to the accusations brought against their trainees to act rapidly on the information.[56] Consequently, their actions underline the extent of their power and influence on the Rwandese gendarmerie, an influence they did not use to its full potential.

If the French military establishment did not appear sufficiently concerned with the exactions committed by the Habyarimana regime, neither did French diplomats. The absence of French diplomatic interventions against human rights violations committed by the Rwandese regime has been widely reported in the media. But their failure to even report these violations is as shocking.

More than two years after the genocide, on this issue, not one good or positive statement has been made about the role of Ambassador Georges Martre, who was in Rwanda until March 1993. Interviews conducted in Paris among French officials support the point. His successor, Jean-Philippe Marlaud, has been judged in a somewhat more positive light.

In contrast to other ambassadors in Kigali (especially the Belgian), the French never seemed to have taken seriously the multiple accusations and evidence of human rights violations and massacres committed by members of the Rwandese government or with its consent. The lack of reaction was made especially clear in January 1993, when Ambassador Martre refused to give credit to the investigation and chilling discoveries of the FIDH, describing them as "rumors."[57] To make matters worse, the French ambassador multiplied personal contacts with the Rwandese President, and was the only foreign official present at the wedding of the President's son.[58] One day before his departure from Rwanda, and the arrival of his successor, a human rights activist met with Martre in his office.

I spoke to him about Habyarimana, about the violations committed by the regime. His reply was astonishing. He told me, "I had dinner yesterday night with President Habyarimana; he is a nice man. I even drank champagne with him. I know him, he is a charming person." (Interview, Montreal, July 1995)

According to officials in the Ministry of Foreign Affairs and the Ministry of Cooperation, Ambassador Martre never reported on the rise of the extremists, Hutu power, and the continuous violence during his tour in Rwanda from 1990 until 1993 (interview, Paris, May 1995).

Mr. Marlaud, French ambassador from March 1993 to April 1994, has received more praise, both from French officials and non-French expatriates in Rwanda at the time.[59] Unlike Mr. Martre, the new ambassador was said to have belonged to the "new" diplomatic school: he believed in opening up the political process and in the "third" political force in Rwanda, the one that was eventually decimated in April 1994 (interview, Paris, March 1995). However, his first contacts with local human rights activists did not begin very well. Shortly after his arrival, one such activist spent several hours in his office, describing the human rights situation to him; Marlaud replied that he had not come to Rwanda to contradict his predecessor (interview, July 1995).

There is little information on which to assess Mr. Marlaud's record in Rwanda, but he seemed to have had a more balanced view of the Rwandese situation than did Mr. Martre and a number of both French and non-French officials concluded that he was "better" than his predecessor. There is also an interesting statement he made to the representatives of the United Nations Reconnaissance Mission in August 1993, which was preparing the U.N. peacekeeping mission.

He [Mr. Marlaud] was worried that the vacuum created by the non-presence of the NIF [Neutral International Force] on September 10 might be very tempting for the extremists who opposed the Arusha Accords and were waiting for the first opportunity to conclude that it was "dead." He stated that it was imperative that some means be found to reassure the Rwandese people on 10 September. Even a simple gesture might allay the fears of the population and discourage the extremists from taking action. As far as France was concerned, it would respect the Arusha Accords and leave Kigali whatever the size of the NIF, 10 or 10,000 men. He suggested that the NIF should wait a week or two to settle solidly in Kigali before letting the RPF enter the capital. Pending the arrival of the NIF, the Ambassador expressed the hope that the Security Council would agree to the deployment of an element of avant-garde to avoid the psychological negative impact of the simultaneous departure of the French troops and arrival of the RPF battalion. (*Report of the Reconnaissance Mission, Political Aspects*, New York, DPKO, pp. 6–7)

In retrospect, one might be tempted to evaluate the ambassador's statement regarding the "extremists" as a clear early warning message. At least in August 1993, one French official knew of the existence of extremists and the possibility they might take deadly action. Given the intentions of the "extremists," he clearly perceived the French military presence in Kigali as ensuring some form of stability as well as helping to allay fears and negative psychological reactions. His statement is also striking in being based solely on a military logic and military evaluation of the forces present.

To summarize the extent and nature of French information gathering: the ambassador (at least the first one) did not play his role; military officials were obsessed with the RPF—the French secret services seemed mainly to collect information on Uganda and the RPF. The early warning process with regard to "Hutu power" barely functioned. The question of sharing of information was less relevant since all intelligence sources were under the same roof (the French embassy), and the ministries in Paris relied on identical sources for their analysis.[60] However, during the three years that preceded the genocide, signals contrary to the ones sent by the embassy and the military were also available to the Ministry of Foreign Affairs, the Ministry of Defense, Cooperation and the Elysée. A large number of reports from international human rights organizations and, much fewer from the media, as well as the dissenting voices within the various ministries, all argued that the military thesis was wrong.

Despite these messages, Paris was no more concerned about the state of human rights violations in Rwanda than were its representatives in Kigali, and disregarded opinions contrary to the ones provided by the French military or the French ambassador, at least up to March 1993. The chilling human rights report from the FIDH received little attention and was rapidly buried at the Elysée, the Quai, the Ministries of Defense and Cooperation (Interview, Paris, May 1995; see also Verschave 1994, 75). This dismissal of information has three origins: individual, institutional, and "ideological."

Rwanda through Corrective Lenses

Well in evidence in Herodotus and Thucydides, the idea that peoples have an aggregate moral character and political temperament is one of the foundations of Western statecraft. For better or for worse, whether they are treated as explicit working hypothesis or remain unspoken assumptions, whether they are triggered off by journalistic images or learned from scholarly accounts, such general notions are almost always a starting point for the analysis of societies other than our own. The impressions formed on first contact, the initial discoveries of the others, generally have a long life. They act as the durable lenses through which distant realities are perceived.[61]

It is not surprising, given the narrow spectrum of sources and the predispositional perspectives on Rwanda, that one view predominated. Further, the balance of power within and among French officials in this case favored the military side, especially represented by Général Huchon, rather than the human rights organizations or the "dissenting" voices.

General Huchon has been described as talented and shrewd, one who knew how to convince a minister. He held considerable power, not only within his own Ministry of Cooperation, but also at the Quai d'Orsay and of course at the Elysée where he used to work. According to an official from his ministry, General Huchon wielded a strong influence even during the cohabitation period. There were dissenting voices, but they were never powerful or numerous enough to prevail over General Huchon's analysis.[62]

This state of affairs also reflected institutional problems. There is a gap between the powers of the president and the instruments available to him[63] as well as an outdated division of prerogatives and responsibilities between the Ministry of Foreign Affairs and the Ministry of Cooperation, with the latter dealing exclusively with what has been termed "les pays du champ,"[64] that is French-speaking African countries. One of the major consequences is that the management of French-speaking African affairs escapes the responsibility of the Ministry of Foreign Affairs, contributing to ministerial turf wars and lack of coordination.[65] The mismanagement of the Rwanda crisis is also linked to institutional barriers within each ministerial department. For instance, General Huchon's power—in part a reflection of his personality, in part the result of his position first at the Elysée and then as the Head of the Mission Militaire de Cooperation[66]—as well as the influence of French diplomats posted to Kigali, were reinforced by weaknesses of information-gathering and decisionmaking elsewhere.[67]

Ultimately, however, the key to an understanding of the French political establishment's dismissal of early warning signs from the rest of the international community and its blind support for the analysis constructed within its ranks and from the military, stems from a mixture of ideology and culture. The Rwandan crisis was read and analyzed through corrective lenses, which tells us more about France than it does about Rwanda.

One such lens is that of "democracy." Here, the images of the 1789 revolution and French democratic principles based on universal suffrage have been superimposed on the Rwandese reality. To support Habyarimana, that is the Hutu, made democratic sense: the Hutu, too, had a (1959) social revolution, constituted the majority, and Habyarimana, like one of the leaders of the French revolution, would eventually emerge as the strong man of the democratization process.

In comparison, the RPF was drawn from a social and ethnic minority, and was hungry for power, revenge, and ethnic killings (in the French view). They were, in other words, the "black Khmers."[68] The implication of this reading was that military support was necessary to ensure that the democratic process would not be short-circuited by the ambitions of a minority.

The second lens is the old Franco-Britain rivalry: the century-long, losing battle of the French language against English, and the even longer antagonism between France and Great Britain which found a specific African meaning in the Fashoda incident in 1898. Hence the multiple references[69] after the genocide to the "Fashoda syndrome" as a way of explaining French policies[70] and sharp critiques of this "geo-political infantilism" (Verschave 1994, 62). Statements of this sort were not exceptional in the months preceding the Rwandese carnage and indicated growing criticism, at times, rage, against the French political scene.[71]

French Intentions and Responsibilities

Three interpretations may be offered to explain France's intentions and responsibilities in Rwanda. They are not mutually exclusive, especially when applied to different actors at different times. The first interpretation concerns the failure of both the political and the military establishment to draw the line between what might have been a limited response by the Rwandan armed forces to the October 1990 invasion, and what rapidly became fascist and genocidal strategies. Analyses of the pregenocide period in Rwanda underlined the constant linkage between the war and internal strife, and the blurring of the boundary between military measures and actions against civilian populations. In Rwanda, the government came to implement and justify the latter with reference to the former. It may be that perceptions and activities of French officials in Kigali underwent a similar process and permeated the communication between Paris and Kigali. Or, as Lemarchand (1994) observed, by turning a blind eye and deaf ear to the multiple signs of human rights violations and a coming genocide emerging from the Habyarimana regime,[72] while "substantially strengthening the military capabilities of the regime against its internal and external foes," French officials "created major disincentives for the Habyarimana clique to make concessions to the opposition" (Lemarchand 1994, 603).

> France helped give the Habyarimana regime a degree of credibility that proved totally illusory, and thus created false expectations about its commitment to democracy...[N]o amount of retrospective guilt can diminish its place in history as the principal villain in the Rwandan apocalypse. (Lemarchand 1994, 603)

A second possible interpretation is that French policy sought to contain extremism. Unlike the rest of the international community, French representatives, especially the military, did not isolate the extremists or treat them as outcasts. France appeared to have been the only country that had regular contacts with the CDR, for instance. The general tenor of French policy—defined above all by assisting the military and not holding the government accountable for its human rights violations—may be interpreted as efforts to manage the extremists by going some way to accommodate them, consistent with France's practices elsewhere, according to some observers.

French governments do not make a fetish of consistency. In the 1980s some terrorists were punished, some were tolerated. Illegal aliens with no connection to violence were rounded up while deals were cut with real terrorists. The pattern was repeated with Iranian, Syrian, and Palestinian groups. The purpose was not to eliminate the sources of terrorism, only to reach an understanding with its organizers.

The third and more "diabolic" version is that some French military officials contributed to the development of the extremists' strategies, if not in their chilling details, at least in the overall objective of destroying the peace process. The possibility has been suggested by the noted scholar Jean-François Bayart:

> Some French military officials seem to have suggested, both to the Habyarimana regime and to his entourage, that the Arusha accord was neither good nor ineluctable. Even if they did not want this atrocious genocide, one may ask whether they had not put the seed of the idea, among the extremists of the regime, that this accord had to be sabotaged at all costs. (Bayart 1994)

What others have called incompetence here becomes intentional. In this perspective, the poor reporting on the evolving extremist fringe, along with France's involvement in Rwanda's internal war, appear to be the result of acceptance of "Hutu power" ideology in French decision-making circles. French officials themselves acknowledged that Hutu extremist ideology had found support in the French bureaucracy.

Shortly after the genocide was launched, one French official is reported to have said: "We got rid of the most extremists [officials] of our past policy, in fact, [they were] totally pro-Hutu."[73]

The statement raises several questions. If the existence of French, pro-Hutu extremists was known within the political establishment, why had they had not been moved aside a long time ago? Whatever the reason, the political responsibility for inaction in this respect is enormous. Second, the political establishment could not have chosen a worse time to wake up from four years of consenting amnesia. If some French actors were totally pro-Hutu, they were the only ones who could have had some influence upon the Rwandese extremists during the first phase of the genocide and could perhaps have limited the killings.[74]

Conclusion: France and the April 1994 Genocide— Return to a Political Logic

On 8 April 1994, two days after the plane crash that killed Habyarimana, and without any warning to the United Nations, 190 French soldiers landed and secured the Kigali airport. The following day, 400 additional troops arrived and proceeded to evacuate French expatriates in the midst of horrendous massacres and chaos. After evacuating some 1,361 persons, the last French troops withdrew on 14 April. Among those evacuated were some 450 French nationals, but also 178 Rwandese officials or their families, including the widow and close associates of the assassinated President.[75] No other Rwandese nationals, not even the local Tutsi personnel of the French embassy, or some well-known opponents to the Habyarimana regime targeted by the militia, were brought to safety.[76] Els de Temmerman, a Belgian journalist who covered the evacuation, testified as follows:

> I arrived in Kigali on April 10th, with a plane sent by World Food Program.... There were 50 journalists following the French and Belgian troops. I was in a French convoy. At some point, we witnessed the murder of 6 persons in front of us. The journalists begged the soldiers to intervene; we were crying. "It is not our mandate," one of the soldiers replied. I was so revolted and disgusted.... People were laughing in front of the mountains of corpses. (Els de Temmerman, oral presentation, Conference on " the Media and Rwanda," Montreal, May 1995. My translation.)

On 8 April 1994, the French political establishment had finally decided that enough was enough and that France's military adventures in Rwanda had to end. The rescue operation was short and restricted: with the last expatriate evacuated, the French troops withdrew. The decision to limit French involvement in 1994 to a rescue operation was not a military but a political decision taken by the political establishment and it might have made political, albeit not moral, sense. Huchon and some of the most extremist, pro-Hutu, agents of France's previous policy were against a limited military intervention, and lobbied hard for a larger mandate that would prolong the presence of French troops as well as protect civilians.

> On April 8, in the course of an emergency meeting, the military officials claimed that a massacre of 100,000 Tutsis would occur and decided that French troops should withdraw. General Huchon was furious, "[T]hey don't care about 100,000 Rwandese deaths." (interviews, Paris, May 1995)

The French decision to launch a intervention sharply limited in time and mandate was triggered by the realization that assigning other objectives would necessarily involve a military confrontation with the RPF, something that had been ruled out from the first days of French involvement in Rwanda. This implication became explicit on 12 April— if not earlier—when the RPF warned the Belgian and French national forces to leave Kigali. In addition, an RPF representative had made it clear in the course of an 8 April meeting with the New Zealand President of the Security Council that it would not accept any strengthening of U.N. forces that would impede the advance of RPF troops.

In April 1994, the pendulum of French relations with Rwanda for some four years had returned to the logic of the political establishment. But the consequences of the political logic were no less "diabolic" than the military one that preceded it. The results were captured in the images of the women, men, and children who climbed the gates of the French embassy, and of those who served the French government, but were left to fend for themselves in the face of the genocide, while those who, for years had sown the seeds of ethnic hatred and helped build a vast machinery of death, were lifted to safety in French planes.

Notes

1. Much of the information on which this chapter is based was collected in interviews in Paris during the first half of 1995. Translations from French books, articles and newspapers are my own.
2. Cf. Krop 1994; in a more subtle fashion, see Verschave 1994. On 15 May 1994 on French television, Dr. Jean-Hervé Bradol from *Medeçins Sans Frontieres* virulently attacked French policy in Africa.

3. Ibid. See also the interview with Michel Roussin, Minister of Cooperation in *Le Monde*, 16 July 1994.
4. Editors: from the perspective of the negotiations at Arusha, as analyzed in the previous chapter by Jones, negotiation strategy was the predominant element in French policy *at those negotiations* (Cf. Lemarchand 1994, 602 for a discussion of the diplomatic or "soft track").
5. To borrow from Cohen's (Paris 1994, p. 139) reading of what constitutes good crisis management.
6. Cf. Chipman 1989, 134 and Chipman 1995. Burundi and Zaire also signed the TMAA with France.
7. Cf. Chipman 1989, 132. For example, this compared with 269 from the Ivory Coast, 197 from Gabon, 40 from Zaire.
8. The 1990 intervention has not been the object of much analysis or research. Anton Andereggen, in his 1994 work on France's relationship with Sub-Sahara Africa, does not even mention it. Cohen (1994, 123) makes only one brief reference to the 1993 intervention in Rwanda.
9. Prunier 1995, 100. On 2 October, President Habyarimana also called Jean-Christophe Mitterand, then at the Africa Unit of the Elysée, to reiterate his request for assistance. Habyarimana made a similar (and successful) plea with the Belgian king.
10. Braeckman 1994, 257. According to Colette Braeckman, this new troop movement consisted of the first regiment of marine infantry, originally based in Bayonne.
11. Africa Watch 1993, 26. It should be noted that figures of French troops present in Rwanda from 1990 to 1993 slightly vary from source to source. In a later report, the *Arms Project* of Human Rights Watch estimated that there were at least 680 troops as of March 1993. (Cf. Human Rights Watch Arms Project 1994, 23.) The figure most often cited by researchers and journalists is around 700, although it remains quite unclear as to when exactly the troops were either sent to Kigali or brought back to their bases. According to Braeckman (1994, 260), at some point there were more than 1000 men in Rwanda, while in a confidential interview, an official from the Ministry of Cooperation in Paris stated that there was only one company in 1991, and that at the peak of French presence in Rwanda, there were 500 soldiers (Field notes, Paris, May 1995.)
12. According to *Le Monde* (22 September 1994), military equipment aid grew from a 4 million franc value in 1990 to 14 million in 1992. If reports of clandestine assistance are added, the total actually grew to 20 million francs. Human Rights Watch Arms uncovered a $6 million bank guarantee from a French nationalized bank, *le crédit lyonnais*, for a Rwanda arms supply deal from Egypt (6:2, January 1994). Following the genocide and despite the arms embargo, five shipments of arms took place in Goma, Zaire from May to June 1994 (7:4, 1995).
13. There were 150 according to Gattengo (1994).
14. According to Prunier's account (1995), the decision to launch Operation Noroît and the objectives of the intervention were not the subject of intense discussions in Paris. Prunier was present when Mitterand had the 3–4 minute discussion with Habyarimana. This reinforces the interpretation that Rwanda did not preoccupy Mitterand but was a matter of routine African policy. Jean-Christophe Ferney, however, reports that during his travels, François Mitterand kept himself constantly informed of the Rwandese military situation (Cf. Ferney, 1993).
15. As stated previously, it does not appear that the initial decision to launch the operation had been the subject of much discussion. The criteria, however, have certainly played a major role in defining the nature and extent of the support later provided to the Rwandese regime by the French troops.

16. The 1979 French operation resulting in the overthrow of Emperor Bokassa in the Central African Republic owed very little to these criteria. Yet, even when these two conditions are met, French response is not automatic. While France rendered assistance to Mba in Gabon in 1964, to Mobutu in Zaire (against the forces of the *Front de Libération Nationale*) in 1977–78, to Eyadema in Togo in 1986, to Tchad in 1983–84, and discretely to Cameroon in 1981, France did not intervene for Tsiranama in Madagascar in 1973, Diori in Niger in 1974, or Dacko of the Central African Republic in 1981 (Cf. Chipman 1989, 135).

17. After the Baule summit announcing France's democratization "vision" for Africa, Habyarimana was said to have asked for French support and a guarantee of military assistance in case of aggression.

18. See the previous chapter by Jones and his manuscript, "Intervention Without Borders: Humanitarian Interventions in Rwanda, 1990–1994," unpublished at the time this chapter was written.

19. Ibid. Bruce Jones conducted extensive research among diplomatic circles in Tanzania. However, he does not cite the name of the French military services to which he was referring. It could have been the DGSE or the DRM (*Direction du Renseignement Militaire*). The DGSE was most likely since the DRM was only created in April 1992 (under General Jean Heinrich) in order to gather intelligence in an open manner through the "traditional" work of military attachés in embassies and intelligence officers in uniform. As of July 1994, the DGSE was providing information collected in Burundi, Uganda, Zaire, and in those parts of Rwanda under the control of the RPF, while the DRM was concentrating on the zone in which French troops were pursuing Operation Turquoise (Cf. *Intelligence Newsletter*, No.245, 26 July 1994).

20. Cohabitation refers to the political situation in France when the Presidency is controlled by one party and parliament is controlled by the opposition. Thus, the President and the Prime Minister come from opposing parties.

21. According to an informant from the Ministry of Cooperation, the French decision to disengage was already evident in 1990: "We did not want to remain alone.... There were great powers behind the RPF. Uganda could send 30,000 to 40,000 soldiers..."

22. Interview, Paris, March 1995. French withdrawal may have already been discussed in November 1990, when a French delegation led by the Minister of Cooperation, Mr. Pelletier, and the Elysée African advisor, Jean-Christophe Mitterand, met with various European and African leaders, including leaders from Burundi, Rwanda, and Uganda, to discuss the situation in Rwanda.

23. This shift may have been facilitated by the replacement of Jean-Christophe Mitterand by Bruno Delaye as the Elysée African advisor in 1991, although opinions on this issue differ sharply. Most journalists, researchers, and French officials have analyzed the arrival of Bruno Delaye as an important turning point in French policies in Rwanda. Others (a minority) were skeptical: they did not perceive Bruno Delaye as having imposed a new orientation to French policies.

24. Increased French diplomatic activities were probably stimulated, and even triggered, by similar American efforts. For details of the initiatives and the meetings, see the previous chapter by Jones.

25. Jean-Christophe Béliard, *chargé d'affaires* in Tanzania, represented the Quai d'Orsay during the Arusha process.

26. (Cf. Prunier 1995, 29). Debarge also asked Habyarimana and the opposition to "*faire un front commun,*" which, in Prunier's opinion, could be interpreted as a call for interethnic struggle, given that the opposition and the regime were both Hutu.

27. Mitterand's letter to Habyarimana has been mostly interpreted as another proof of France's unconditional support to what became a genocidal government. The interpretation given here is more benign. Mitterand's promise was necessary to bring Habyarimana to accept participation in the peace talks and eventually concessions to the RPF.

28. French military assistance may have been a necessary component in its diplomatic strategy. First, it added crucial leverage to the otherwise very weak position of the Rwandese government. Second, it allowed French diplomats to bring pressure on Habyarimana to negotiate. Third, the Western diplomatic community (though not the human rights NGOs) not only regarded the French presence in Rwanda as an evil necessity, but as a security blanket for their own expatriates in Rwanda (Interview, Ottawa, April 1995). In February of 1991, the Canadian Foreign Minister, Joe Clarke, wrote a letter to Roland Dumas, then his French equivalent, thanking him for the role French parachutists played in evacuating Canadian citizens from Ruhengiri. Finally, the French military presence was intended to serve as a push factor on the RPF, provided the RPF believed in French political will to back the military.

29. The theoretical alternative was an OAU force (see chapter 6); Belgium in October of 1990 had requested that France and Germany provide logistical support for just such a force.

30. France's stated reason for pushing for a U.N. force was that the OAU lacked the means and experience of peacekeeping operations. OAU lacked experience *in managing peacekeeping operations.* (An exception could be Liberia, although it was not an OAU operation but a regional one.) The OAU did lack the financial and technical means to sustain peacekeeping activities, and would have required extensive logistical assistance and military equipment from United Nations member states. But three other factors probably also explained France's insistence on U.N. troops. First, at the time of the RPF invasion in October 1990, the Ugandan president was the Secretary General of the OAU, which meant, within French strategic parameters, that the OAU could not be trusted. Second, a U.N.-led peacekeeping operation necessarily involved the Security Council in which France is a permanent member, hence allowing France greater control over the mandate and activities of a U.N. deployed peacekeeping force. According to members of the Security Council, France tried to increase its influence in Africa, using the United Nations as a cover. Thirdly, as long as the peacekeeping operation remained a U.N. operation, there remained the slight possibility that some French troops would be integrated within the peacekeeping forces.

31. When Dallaire's reconnaissance mission went to Africa in August to draw up the details of the Neutral International Force (NIF) that would become UNAMIR, the RPF representative insisted that the RPF battalion would not be deployed in Kigali as long as French troops were in the capital. Article 72 of the Arusha Accords also provided that foreign troops would only be required to be withdrawn after the deployment of the NIF or the expansion of NMOG under the control of the U.N. Kagame suggested that the U.N. provide the logistics to enable the OAU to deploy an Egyptian battalion and meet the 10 September deadline. This would enable the French troops to depart. But the French ambassador insisted that such a battalion would be insufficient to counterbalance the presence of an RPF battalion (Cf. U.N. *Report of the Reconnaissance Mission,* September, 1993).

32. The article states that the withdrawal of foreign troops shall take place after the deployment of the Neutral International Force (NIF) or the expanded NMOG under the command and control of the United Nations.

33. Three out of nine operative paragraphs of the resolution passed in the Security Council in March of 1993 called for or welcomed U.N. cooperation with the OAU (Cf. Security Council Informal Discussions, 9 March 1993).
34. Letter from the permanent representative of Rwanda to the United Nations, addressed to the President of the Security Council, 14 June, 1993.
35. Following the passing of the resolution, Hervé Ladsous (Assistant to the French Permanent Representative) explicitly referred to the possibility of a U.N. contribution to the protection of civilians. Further, in the course of the Security Council discussion of 9 March 1992, the French representative, though indicating clearly that this was not what France desired, offered to consider providing French peacekeepers if both sides in Rwanda made such a request.
36. According to Cohen (1994, 139) such a thorough synchronization is the primary requirement for good crisis management.
37. Roussin, interviewed in *Le Monde*, 16 July 1994, stated that: "The Rwandan file is essentially handled by the Quai d'Orsay and the Defense Ministry. The Minister of Foreign Affairs is responsible for French policy. Increasingly, the Quai d'Orsay handles African affairs."
38. *The Economist*, 23 July 1994. As part of his dealing with Africa, Balladur pushed through a painful, but long overdue, 50 percent devaluation of the CFA franc.
39. Interview, Paris, May 1965. The idea that cohabitation led to a transformation or shift in French policies is undermined also by the fact that during the first period of cohabitation (1986–88), there was little dissent over African policy when Chirac was Prime Minister. In fact, Cohen and Clarke (1990) argue that it was characterized by harmony.
40. Respondents interviewed for this chapter in early 1995 indicated, for instance, that Bruno Delaye met with various regional leaders (including Habyarimana and Museveni) on numerous occasions, and that General Huchon conducted several missions in Rwanda in 1992 and 1993 where he met with Habyarimana. The principle French actors of this military track were General Huchon, in charge of the Mission Militaire de Cooperation and previously (at the time of the 1990 invasion) at the Elysée Palace as the Assistant to the Commander-In-Chief (General Lanxade); Colonel Cussac, French military attaché and head of the French Military Assistance Mission in Rwanda, and his assistant, Lieutenant-colonel Maurin.
41. Cf. Whiteman (1983, 334) and Golan (1981, 3–12). She quotes the then Liberian Foreign Minister, Cecil Dennis. Those who explain the secret of the French role in Africa in terms of personal diplomacy at the highest level seem to be exaggerating. Mitterand only visited Rwanda twice, in May and October of 1982 (Cf. Andreggen, 1994). The two presidents met at various Franco-African summits and in Paris in 1993.
42. M Pierre Joxe had meant to provide the Defense Ministry with a tool to reflect upon international, strategic, and defense issues (Cf. Cohen 1994, 98).
43. Cf. Bourmaud 1994. "Elites, be they intellectual or leaders, have deserted the African continent for a long time already.... The French parliament did not make Africa an exception to its passivity."
44. Colonel Cussac, French military Attaché, Head of the French Military Assistance, French Mission to Rwanda, quoted in Human Rights Watch Arms Project 1994, 23.
45. Confidential interview, Ministry of Foreign Affairs. According to this source, at one of the JPMC meetings, this same Nigerian colonel testified, under questioning from France, that French troops were not fighting.
46. Interviews with French journalists, May 1995; see also Girard, 1995.

47. Human Rights Watch, various journalists, and French, Canadian, and American individuals present in Rwanda at the time that I interviewed in 1995, told stories about unnerving encounters with French soldiers along the road to Kigali (Cf. Braeckman 1994, 258).
48. As one respondent hinted, without such an intervention France, Rwanda, and the world community might have also have avoided a genocide.
49. AFP, 11 October 1991, transcribed in Guichaoua (1995, op cit 712). According to the AFP release, the questioning was correctly handled, and the prisoners did not refuse to respond.
50. The 1991 creation of a "self-defense" program, which included the distribution of arms to civilians and their training, also underlines the amalgamation of the military and civil spheres in Rwanda.
51. Among other sources, this information is reported by *Liberation*, 18 May 1994; *L'Humanité*, 30 June 1994, Reyntjens (1994, 176); Krop (1994, 75–76); Verschave (1994, 40). It should be noticed that Braeckman dates Chollet's nomination as of 1 January 1992 (Cf. Braeckman 1994, 259).
52. (Cf. *Le Flambeau*, 17 December 1993.) "About 8000 *interahamwe* sufficiently trained and equipped by the French army await the signal to begin the assassinations among the city of Kigali and its surroundings" (quoted in African Rights 1994, 54–55) More direct testimony came from Janvier Afrika, a former militia member. "French militaries taught us how to capture our victims and tie them up...the French taught the interahamwe to throw knives and assemble rifles. The French trained us...for a total of 4 months between February 1991 and January 1992" (Cf. Gattegno, *Le Monde* 1994), who alleged French soldiers were present when the Presidential Guard perpetrated a large number of massacres in April 1994. Jean Carbonar, a member of the International Enquiry Commission that went to Rwanda in January 1993, claimed that French trainers were present in the Bigogwe military camp where hundreds of civilians were brought, tortured and killed (Cf. *Le Nouvel Observateur*, 4 August 1994). However, the testimony from K. Gasana, former Minister of Defense under Habyarimana, who fled to Switzerland in July of 1993, claimed that French training of the militia began only at the end of 1993 and stopped in December (Cf. Gasana 1995, 690).
53. All informants for this article, including persons who were present in Rwanda during this period and some who were relatively sympathetic to France's actions, found the presence of the French soldiers highly disturbing. Feelings ranged from "they really exaggerated," to "this was disgusting, revolting, total colonialism, they were arrogant, etc." In March 1993, the Rwandese Association for Human Rights complained openly of the French soldiers' ethnic discrimination at roadblocks, and considered, along with the other opposition parties, that "the French soldiers (*militaires*) constitute an additional force of oppression" (cited Braeckman 1994, 258).
54. Nevertheless, the allegations of the French military should not be rejected outright. Human rights violations committed by RPF troops have been reported by other sources, including local and international human rights organization. RPF border crossings between Uganda and Rwanda, and the role of the Ugandan army (NRA) in blocking UNOMUR patrols have been acknowledged by the United Nations as cited in various cables sent from UNAMIR in Kigali to U.N. Headquarters in New York.
55. Most significantly, this former DGSE high-ranked official states: "[S]ince independence, Western military apparatus never stopped to support African leaders on the basis that a nation could not exist without an army.... This policy has

resulted [in Rwanda] in the increasing integration of French military *cooperants* within the governmental forces…and in the repression that they organized." Clause Silberzahn also implied that his intelligence service had foreseen the RPF victory over the Rwandese armed forces (Silberzahn 1995, 203).

56. According to the activist, the French gendarmes were totally obsessed with human rights violations allegedly committed by the RPF. Interview, July 1995.

57. At the invitation of local human rights groups, from 7 to 21 January 1993, eleven experts from eight different countries, as part of the International Commission of Investigation on Human Rights Violations in Rwanda sponsored by international human rights organizations, investigated allegations of human rights violations by the Rwandan government and the RPF. The Human Rights and Watch organizations provided the most accurate record of Rwanda's deteriorating human rights situation. Just after the Commission arrived in Kigali, the government's crackdown on opponents and a slaughter of members of the Tutsi minority followed Habyarimana's protocol on power-sharing on 9 January 1993. The accuracy of the information and analysis was confirmed by a separate U.N. Human Rights commission investigation in March of 1993 (Cf. Adelman 1997; Braeckman 1994, 261; Brauman 1994, 52).

58. Interview, Paris, May 1995; Ottawa, March 1995. This fact especially struck the expatriate population in Kigali as totally unwarranted and unethical.

59. Interviews, Paris, Ottawa, 1995. It should be noticed, however, that General Kagame refused to meet with him and former Ambassador to Kampala, Yannick Gerard, in June 1995, considering him to be a supporter of Habyarimana.

60. This point was reiterated by all officials interviewed, be they from the Ministries of Foreign Affairs, Cooperation, or Defense.

61. Cf. Zolberg 1973, 728. While written some twenty years ago, Zolberg's perceptive analysis is as relevant as ever.

62. Interviews, Paris, May 1995. According to a French official at the Ministry of Cooperation, during the three years that preceded the genocide, there were only two French officials who presented a perspective different from Huchon's. They were "somebody in Tanzania (likely the chargé d'affaires) and someone here in Paris at the Ministry of Cooperation."

63. The gap between means and ends is discussed in Bayart (1984, 103); Cohen and Clarke (1990, 213) use a ship metaphor—the gap between the captain's power and the navigational instruments—to make the same point.

64. One possible and nonliteral translation is "countries in the backyard."

65. A number of books and articles have denounced the institutional disfunctioning that characterizes the running of African affairs. In addition to Cohen and Clarke (1990) and Bayart (1994), Reyntjens (1994, 179) and Verschave (1994, 58) comment on the problem. Others have highlighted the predominance of parallel networks in defining African policies. See, for instance, Kalfleche 1988, 56; Péan 1983; Glaser and Smith; the newsletter *Billets d'Afrique et d'ailleurs*, published by the association Survie, Paris, which focuses on the mismanagement of French Official Development Assistance.

66. However, as one informant pointed out, it is all too easy for the political establishment to go after one (politically appointed) individual and make him a scapegoat of this establishment's incompetence.

67. Reyntjens (1994) with respect to the monopoly and poor quality of information in Central Africa attributes the failure of intelligence to secrecy (Cf. Cohen and Clarke 1990, 213; and, more generally, Verschave 1994).

68. This reference was still used to describe the Rwandese government during my interviews in Paris in 1995.

69. Almost every single book or articles cited in the core of this paper include reference to the Fashoda syndrome.

70. This interpretation is legitimate both in Africa and elsewhere, as long as it entails respect for human and minority rights, none of which were in effect in Rwanda. It also holds to some degree for other French-speaking Western states, such as Canada and Belgium, but they do not seem to be nearly as obsessed as France. There might be two reasons for this difference: first, the Rwandan crisis came at a time when both Canada and Belgium had begun to disengage from Africa, and their interest in Rwanda was even more limited and narrow than that of France; second, it is also possible that both countries, with a history based on the existence of so-called linguistic minorities, had a different understanding of the meaning of democracy, i.e., one that is based on the rights of minorities.

71. In a similar fashion, Rwanda fed the collective fantasies and constructed visions of "self" in both Canada and Belgium. Colette Braeckman argues that Rwanda constituted a mirror image for the Belgians: "They projected themselves on Rwanda, they have read Rwanda's history according to their own history, their own social conflicts" (Braeckman 1994, 247). A similar "self-reflecting" process was noticeable in Canada. Canadian perceptions of the RPF, Habyarimana, and the role of Uganda divided neatly along language lines, with French-speaking Canadians opposing the Anglophones (interviews, Ottawa March 1995; see the next chapter by Adelman). However, what distinguished both Canada and Belgium from France is that the self-reflective lenses proved insufficient to define or bind the policies of the state. This was not the case in France, perhaps because "France is the only country that wants to express its foreign policy in universal, logical terms," as Romano (1986, 35–41) has suggested in a different context.

72. Interviews, Canada and France, March 1995. Two sources interviewed for this article reported that some French soldiers, upon realizing that Rwandese soldiers were involved in extra-judicial killings, communicated the information to their superiors. No follow-up was given to their warning except for them being requested to "shut-up."

73. The French version is: "On a mis sur la touche les plus extremistes de notre politique passée, en effet totalement pro-hutu." These words reverberated throughout the French media (cf. Verschave 1994, 40).

74. What might have occurred, however, is that the military conditions imposed by these so-called "totally pro-Hutu" elements were totally unacceptable from the perspective of the political establishment, and therefore precluded their participation and contribution to the conflict management process. The journalist, Steven Smith, also questioned the nature of the French intervention in Rwanda, comparing it with the one that took place in Burundi in October 1993, which, in his opinion, contributed to limiting the massacres and counter-massacres (Smith 1995, 452).

75. Cf. Guichaoua 1995, 697–701. Guichaoua lists all 178 persons evacuated, a large number of whom were children.

76. The testimony of the former employee of the French cultural center is especially heart gripping. It has been quoted in a large number of articles and books (Cf. Krop 1994, 91–99). Despite the pressing requests from André Guichaoua and the apostolic nuncio, no action was taken to insure the protection of François-Xavier Nsanzuwera, the public prosecutor in Kigali (Guichaoua 1995, 707).

9

Canadian Policy in Rwanda

Howard Adelman

Canadian foreign policy might seem irrelevant with respect to Rwanda since Canada is not an important player on the world stage in general—and in Africa in particular—compared to the U.S. and France. Further, in relationship to the "realist" policies of the United States and the cynical policies of France, Canadian policy may seem totally naive. But if middle players who have a commitment to foreign aid and multilateralism, as is the case with Canada, the Nordics, the Netherlands, and the like, then considering Canadian policy in Rwanda is a valuable exercise, particularly since, with respect to Rwanda, Canada was the most influential middle power in Rwanda, and Canadian policy makers have been at or near the forefront of multilateralist activity ever since the U.N. was created.

But Canadian policy has not only been based on aid and multilateralism. In fact, as this chapter tries to demonstrate, as Canadian aid diminished and as Canada stood four square behind the structural adjustment policies of the IMF applied to Rwanda since 1989 when structural adjustment became a central priority, Canada became more active diplomatically and morally, becoming a prime mover in disclosing the human rights abuses of the Habyarimana regime. What is less well-known is how Canadian foreign policy is a projection of domestic binational policy at home while projecting itself abroad as a leader in international peacekeeping. If Americans drew the lesson from Somalia that they should avoid peacekeeping, Canadians became even more committed.

But commitment does not entail that Canadian policy was any more intelligent or informed. And though Canadians took the lessons of Rwanda very seriously, that seriousness translated into exhibitionist rather than in-depth policy, and more recently has followed the precedent of the NGOs in the civil society in pursuing single issue international policy, with some dramatic success on the issue of banning land mines, but at the cost of a coherent global international foreign policy.

This case study not only describes the role of an important middle player in Rwanda, but demonstrates that the "good guys" in the international arena may have added their own proportion of errors to those of the realists and cynics.

Canadian Involvement in Rwanda[1]

Since the 1960s, Canada has had a close association with Rwanda through the involvement of individual Canadians and at the government level. Since 1990, two Canadian priests, Father Cardinal[2] in 1992 and Father Simard on 17 October 1994, were victims of the violence in Rwanda. As well, seven Rwandese nationals who held Canadian citizenship were slaughtered in the genocide.[3]

Canada was not only intimately linked to victims of the genocide, but to alleged perpetrators as well. Léon Mugesera, who had been a close colleague of President Habyarimana of Rwanda,[4] was admitted to Canada as a refugee, though he has since been ordered to be deported by the Canadian government[5]; Mugesera was accused of abetting crimes against humanity and by some of being the intellectual architect of the genocide against the Tutsi.

Behind the personal stories, there is also a story of the Canadian government involvement with Rwanda. Following the genocide in Rwanda, Prime Time News on 29 November 1994 on the CBC English Canadian network and, much more pointedly, Le Point on French-Canadian television on 23 January 1995, accused the government of ignoring the alarm signals of the impending genocide. Le Point actually charged Canada with complicity in the genocide.[6] The Prime Time News special item was the kinder of the two. First, it claimed that Canada was but one member of the international community accused of "wilful blindness that led to the kind of horror that the world thought that it would never see again." The thesis of the show was unequivocal: "the United Nations ignored clear and repeated warnings of a state-sponsored plan for genocide in Rwanda" (transcript, CBC Prime Time News, Toronto: CBC Corporation, 29 November 1994:9). Le Point was much stronger. That show asserted that Canada was guilty of abetting the genocide through both its actions and inactions:

"By her inaction Canada was an accomplice to the genocide."

"In Rwanda, for more than thirty years, some Canadians witnessed and experienced all stages of the crisis which led to the systematic genocide of an ethnic group. One of them was even in the direct service of the state. It would be false to conclude that some Canadians were accomplices to the massacre. But they saw all the preparations over the course of years.

"The Canadian foreign minister and CIDA who had their own representatives on location, who kept the witnesses who had been privy to this historic drama from testifying. (St-Pierre, 1995:19)

The charge of complicity in genocide is based on claims that there was plenty of information about the impending genocide; Canadian blindness, ineptitude, and overt miscalculations abetted the mass murderers. In this chapter we will depict the Canadian attitude to Rwanda by the Canadian International Development Agency (CIDA) at the time of the invasion of Rwanda by the RPF on 1 October 1990, the subsequent shift in focus of policy by what was then called the Department of External Affairs, subsequently renamed the Department of Foreign Affairs and International Trade (DFAIT) the role and different perspective developed by the quasi-governmental agency, the International Commission for Human Rights and Democratic Development (ICHRDD), and then the role of the Canadian military in leading the peacekeeping mission to Rwanda following the signing of the Arusha Accords on 4 August 1993 until the end of the genocide in July of 1994.[7]

This chapter approaches the Canadian role in a traditional chronological fashion and attempts to describe various perspectives on Rwanda by Canadian officials in order to understand and explain Canadian actions in the context of policies and practices that emerged in a global context. The chapter attempts to make clear what was known, who knew it, what the basis of that knowledge was, to whom that knowledge was transmitted, and how that knowledge or lack of knowledge translated into Canadian policy. Whatever else one might want to say about Canadian misjudgment and error, I trust it will become clear that the accusation of wilful "blindness" or of being "complice du génocide" is unwarranted.

Background

Rwanda, even though a small country, occupies an important position in Canadian government foreign policy concerns. The reasons are historic. For thirty years, Canada was involved in the development of Rwanda. Just after Rwanda gained independence, the Rwandese government asked the Dominicans in Rome to assist them in setting up a university in Rwanda. The Dominican fathers solicited one of their Dominican brothers, Père Lévesque, who was then Dean of Social Sciences at Laval University in Québec city, to undertake the task.[8] He did. Since Lévesque's involvement in the creation of the National University of Rwanda in Butare in 1962, Canadians, led by Lévesque, have been intimately involved in the training of the elites of Rwanda. Many Rwandese came to Canada for training. An extensive network among Rwandese and Canadians developed, with many Canadians taking Rwandese wives. When President Habyarimana had to cut short his visit to Canada and return to Rwanda via Paris and Brussels to deal with the October 1990 invasion, he missed being personally present when l'Université du Québec awarded him an honorary doctorate for his contribution to the development of the National University of Rwanda.

In 1982, Canada initiated a number of bilateral projects beyond the previous aid provided to the National University of Rwanda. As the Canadian overseas development budget expanded and Africa became the most important focus of that development aid,[9] Rwanda was considered the jewel in the crown of countries receiving Canadian aid. During the 1980s, Rwanda was perceived by Canadian CIDA officials as incredibly stable with virtually no corruption; a very small portion of its gross national product was expended on its relatively small military force of 5,000 personnel.[10] Rwanda was, in turn, rewarded for its perceived commitment to the rule of law and for delivering results in its partnership with Canada in aid projects, by becoming the highest recipient of aid per capita of any other country.[11]

Rwandese exiles accused Canadian policy makers in particular and the international community in general of closing their eyes to the persecution of Tutsi in Rwanda under the guise of regional and ethnic balance.[12] And by the end of the eighties, the Canadian government perception of Rwanda began to alter. With the crash of coffee prices in 1988, Rwanda's main staple export crop, exacerbated by the influx in 1988 of 75,000 refugees fleeing the slaughter of Hutu by Tutsi in Burundi, Rwanda underwent drastic changes. Canadians began to note the creeping corruption of political and business elites in Rwanda following the pattern of other recipient countries in Africa such as Zaire and Uganda. For example, trading companies were allegedly owned by relatives of elites who benefited from their connections.[13] Canada by the late eighties endorsed[14] the structural adjustment programs of the World Bank to satisfy World Bank demands that the Rwandese government deal with the country's economic crisis brought on by the collapse of coffee prices.[15]

The shifts in the economic approach were paralleled by shifts in the attitude to internal politics in Rwanda. The Canadian development experts involved and committed to Rwanda had no sense of popular unrest even in the late eighties. For them, the anti-Rwandese propaganda efforts were considered to be the product of Tutsis who had been forced out of Rwanda over twenty years ago. Their vitriolic attacks were perceived as lacking any credibility. According to these veteran Rwandan development hands, President Habyarimana, though his image was beginning to tarnish slightly when this century celebrated its ninetieth birthday, remained the knight of purity for the vast majority of Rwandans, a man dedicated to the well-being of his people who could do little wrong in the eyes of those he ruled.[16]

The old refugees who had fled with the overturn of the monarchy just after Rwanda gained its independence from Belgium thirty years earlier, remained a problem. But as these Canadian experts perceived the situation, Rwanda was the most densely populated country in Africa (with a population growth rate of 3.9 percent per year and a population density of 290 inhabitants per square kilometer). According to the CIDA experts, there was no place to which the refugees could return in a country where 90 percent of the population lived on agricultural land, and arable land was in short supply because of both the hilly terrain and stretches of swampy lands. The economy was undiversified, with manufacturing almost exclusively devoted to satisfying domestic needs.

The new push towards democratization was initiated by the foreign policy mandarins rather than the experts on economic development. For the experienced Canadian Rwandan development experts, Rwanda, at the grass roots, was more democratic than its western counterparts. There was widespread consultation and involvement of the people in initiating and executing development projects. However, Canada had also developed a policy of linking aid to the process of democratization, a process based on multiparty democracy and the protection of human rights. Political adjustments were pushed on Rwanda at the same time as Canada required Rwanda to adopt a structural adjustment approach to its economy.

When the internal economic and political crisis came to a head in 1990 in Rwanda, Habyarimana committed his country to complying with the structural adjustment program imposed by the World Bank with its traditional mix of reducing public sector spending, reform of the public enterprise sector, liberalizing the economy, and relying on market forces and the private sector to return to viable external and domestic economic positions. Habyarimana also introduced his new constitution in June of 1990. The military were required to remain outside of politics. Multiparty democracy was initiated. President Habyarimana also agreed to solve the situation of the refugees with the promise that at least some of the refugees would be given an opportunity to return.

While many saw this as a new beginning for Rwanda, some veteran development officers in CIDA with long experience in and with Rwanda saw this as the beginning of a slide down the slippery slope to disaster when these initiatives were followed by the October 1990 invasion of Rwanda by the experienced and highly trained Tutsi military forces which had helped Museveni gain power in Uganda (cf. Otunnu, Chapter 2).

Canadian Policy—1990–92

In the 1990s, Canadian policy towards Rwanda diverged from its almost exclusive focus on development aid to include three new areas of concentration—preventive diplomacy, human rights, and, in 1993, peacekeeping.[17] Canada has never had an embassy in Rwanda. When President Habyarimana's plane was shot down on April 6, 1994, and the systematic slaughter of Tutsi mushroomed from small targeted killings to widespread wholesale mass murder, the Canadian government presence in Rwanda still only consisted of three Canadian International Development Aid (CIDA) officials. Canadian diplomatic contacts were run from the Canadian embassy in Kinshasa, Zaire, until Canada closed that embassy in May of 1993 as a result of budgetary cutbacks.

Operating from the Canadian embassy in Kenya, Lucie Edwards also served as the ambassador to Rwanda. She was succeeded by Bernard Dussault in the spring of 1994 who was named Canadian Ambassador for Central Africa operating out of a base in the Pearson building in Ottawa.

Canadian involvement in Rwanda became a matter of diplomatic concern in 1990 even before the invasion of the rebels from Uganda. Like many western countries, because of the economic downturn and the rise of dissent, as well as the increasing number of reported incidences of human rights abuses, Canada was afraid that the country, which had previously shown such promise in economic development, was very quickly going downhill.

To illustrate the relative prominence of Rwanda in Canadian foreign policy and not just aid concerns, Brian Mulroney, the Canadian Prime Minister during the beginning of the 1990s until he retired from politics in 1993, wrote President Habyarimana three times after he spoke personally to him at the Francophone Summit in October of 1991. Habyarimana had buttonholed Mulroney at the summit to complain about the Ugandan role in the invasion and to ask Mulroney for more aid. Mulroney, in turn, suggested that Habyarimana had helped bring the problems on himself and his country by refusing to repatriate the refugees from Uganda and Tanzania and for increasing the amount of funds devoted to defense from a very low ratio in 1970 of 2.5 percent of government expenditures to what Mulroney would point out in a subsequent letter in 1992 amounted to over 25 percent of the government budget.[18] Brian Mulroney also accused Habyarimana in his correspondence, in diplomatic language of course, of dragging his feet in the peace negotiations.

The significance of Mulroney's remonstrations of Habyarimana can be indicated by the fact that it was only the second time during his term of office that Mulroney had written a critical letter to an African leader. More significantly, Mulroney had a propensity to say yes to African requests for assistance.[19] There was a second significance to the Mulroney letters. They ran contrary to the interpretations and concerns of Francophone officials at CIDA who had a long involvement with Rwanda.

The invasion of Rwanda by the RPF forces from Uganda on the first of October of 1990 moved Rwanda to the top of the list of African countries of major concern to Canada. Canadians feared regional instability. Human rights concerns by then were a cornerstone of Canadian policy. Canada strongly supported a negotiated settlement in the pursuit of both reconciliation between the rebel forces as well as strengthening human rights in Rwanda. The latter concern predated the invasion. Thus, for example, the Canadian ambassador, using Canadian clout as a large donor to Rwanda (the Canadian ambassador spoke directly with the director of prisoners), became one of the significant moving forces to enable the ICRC to gain access to political prisoners, access which had been cut off from October of 1987 to June of 1990.

In 1991 Canada adopted a two-prong approach to the developing Rwandan crisis. One of the prongs was diplomatic. It was directed at the Rwanda government itself, the RPF invaders and other neighboring governments concerned with Rwanda—primarily Uganda perceived as the prime supporter of the RPF invaders, with secondary efforts targeting Zaire and Tanzania. There was also a small effort directed at perceived British support of the RPF, but there is no evidence that diplomatic pressure was expended on French support for the government.[20]

The second prong of Canadian foreign policy was directed at the civil society and strengthening both the protection of human rights and democratic processes and institutions within Rwanda. By 1993, Canada would add a defense and a humanitarian aid component to its efforts to influence the developing crisis in Rwanda.

The diplomatic prong directed at Zaire was dropped when diplomats met the Foreign Minister of Zaire to entreat his cooperation, but the Foreign Minister was subsequently pushed out of his post by President Mobutu. Canada continued to put pressure on Uganda. A Canadian diplomatic representative in Ottawa met Alex Kanyarengwe, the Hutu president of the RPF. Diplomatic efforts directed towards Tanzania through the Canadian embassy in Dar es Salaam increased gradually as Tanzania coordinated the peace efforts leading to and following the signing of peace accords in Arusha on 4 August 1993. Canada was a strong supporter and believer in the positive role Tanzania played in moving the peace process forward (cf. Jones, chapter 6).

The Canadian government initiatives on the human rights area and in support of democratic institutions was not merely based on diplomatic exchanges. On 6 December 1991, the External Affairs Minister wrote Ed Broadbent, a former leader of the small opposition federal New Democratic Party, whom Brian Mulroney had appointed in a rare non-patronage gesture following Broadbent's retirement as leader of that party, to head a new independent but government financed International Centre for Human Rights and Democratic Development (ICHRDD) based in Montreal. This letter followed the Francophone summit in October of that year and expressed the government concern with the increasing number of human rights violations in Rwanda as well as the government's support of the opening towards democracy in Rwanda that had begun in 1990. In that letter, the Minister suggested that Broadbent visit Rwanda and consider initiating some program in that country.

At the same time, on the fifteenth of December, the Minister of External Affairs also wrote her equivalent in Uganda expressing the Canadian concern with the armed incursions into Rwanda being launched from Ugandan soil which Canada felt would destabilize the region. Canada urged Uganda to play a positive and supporting role in the negotiations beginning in Arusha, negotiations which Canada supported. Canada, unlike the Americans, never sent an observer to Arusha; the reasons were economic rather than political.

Canadian government officials were divided on their interpretation of the Ugandan role. Some were convinced that Museveni was embarrassed by the desertion of military units from the Ugandan army made up of Tutsi to constitute the invading army of the Rwandese Patriotic Front (RPF), especially since Museveni had just become head of the OAU. Others believed that Museveni was a strong backer of the invasion in spite of his constant denials. After all, they noted, Museveni was half Tutsi on his mother's side,[21] and his Minister of Defense, his Chief of Staff, and the head of the Ugandan intelligence were all Tutsi. Museveni owed his military success and the capture of the Presidency to the support of the Tutsi. At the same time, he could use his presidency of the OAU to discourage criticism of any role Uganda played in supporting the rebellion. In turn, supporting the RPF invasion would help resolve rising tribal problems and resentments within Uganda at the prominent role of Tutsis in the Ugandan government (cf. Otunnu, chapter 2). Canadian officials who believed Uganda actively backed the invasion saw Museveni as one of the brightest and most intellectually astute of African leaders who was too smart not to know that some of his leading supporters and ministers were about to desert with whole units of the Ugandan army to invade Rwanda.

Those who believed that Museveni secretly supported the invasion won the day given the fact that the Canadian foreign minister wrote her counterpart in Uganda diplomatically raising the issue and suggesting that Uganda should play a far more positive role in the peace efforts with respect to Rwanda. This was followed by another letter from the Canadian External Affairs Minister on the eleventh of February in 1992, this time to her counterpart in Britain, followed by a personal visit, encouraging Britain to dissuade the Ugandans from permitting incursions into Rwanda from Ugandan territory. Canada was aware that Britain had a military attaché in Uganda, but the British denied any knowledge or reports of Ugandan support for the RPF invasion, a denial the Canadians suspected of being disingenuous.

At the same time, the External Affairs Minister wrote the President of Nigeria, who then occupied the Presidency of the OAU, asking that the OAU take the lead in reactivating the peace negotiations not only between the RPF and the Rwandan government, but between Rwanda and

Uganda. This was followed by the Canadian Prime Minister's letter to Habyarimana on 4 March 1992 discussed above, where Mulroney linked future development aid to Rwanda to decreased expenses in the military area. In June, the Prime Minister also wrote Museveni reiterating Canadian concerns with destabilization in that part of Africa and urging a Ugandan-Rwandese-RPF dialogue and movement towards a peaceful solution to the conflict. It is clear that Canadian policy makers saw the Ugandan government as a central player and possibly instigator in the conflict in Rwanda. Though the Prime Minister did not convey this interpretation in his third letter to Habyarimana in September of 1992, he did indicate that he had written Museveni urging that the parties search for a durable solution to both the conflict and the problem of the refugees.

At the same time as Mulroney was writing Museveni, the Minister of External Affairs again wrote Broadbent urging that the International Centre for Human Rights and Democratic Development take an active interest in Rwanda. Broadbent followed up with his visit to Rwanda in November of 1992. As a result of that visit, Broadbent came away with a very different portrait of Habyarimana than that of the CIDA experts on Rwanda and the Rwandese experts in External Affairs. Whereas Canadian diplomats, much like the Americans, viewed Habyarimana as not nearly as sharp as Museveni nor as a man of vision or ideas, they did respect him as trying his best to accommodate various competing forces and pressures with no great egomaniacal stake in the results, though they did not glorify his leadership as some officials in CIDA seemed to have done. In contrast to this image of a rather accommodating figure (or a noble leader on the road to democracy), Broadbent, along with virtually all the human rights activists dealing with Rwanda, came away with an impression of Habyarimana as a man who was clever, devious, and double dealing, appearing outwardly as accommodating, helpful, and open while behind the scenes he looked the other way if he did not actually organize the murder of those who reported human rights abuses. His ostensible cooperation with the human rights organizations was just a cover to gather intelligence on those who were critical of the government. It was an image directly contrary to the diplomats' and development specialists' perspective.

The Development of Canadian Policy During 1993

When the rights organizations took credit for initiating the initiative into the inquiry into human rights abuses in Rwanda without crediting the government for stimulating the inquiry, and when the rights organizations seemed to ignore the interstate components of the conflict with a singular concentration on the rights issues, and since the two groups had such diametrically opposed views of Habyarimana,[22] the diplomats and the rights groups began to follow two very divergent paths. When the international human rights commission set up at the initiative of Broadbent returned from Rwanda and gave a press conference in January in Brussels accusing Habyarimana of being directly responsible for a genocide in Rwanda,[23] diplomats in Canadian missions were very annoyed and considered the rights report partisan, nonobjective, and hysterical. They questioned not only the claim that the murders were centrally and systematically directed, but even the objectivity of the members. They considered that the report lacked substantive proof of the charges made.

Thus, the human rights initiative was viewed as setting back rather than advancing Canadian foreign policy objectives in Rwanda, for the report was considered counterproductive in advancing and reinforcing human rights in Rwanda at the same time as it seemed to undermine Canadian diplomatic initiatives.

The Canadian government became further annoyed when the human rights organization claimed that, as a result of their report on human rights abuses in Rwanda, Canadian aid to Rwanda had been canceled. Though the cut of aid by about one-third immediately followed the release of the results of the Human Rights Commission to Rwanda, in fact, the aid cut-off resulted from budget cuts and a decision to focus aid on specific countries. Zaire was cut off as well as Rwanda. Aid officials did indicate that the decision to cut off aid in certain countries was influenced by reports of human rights abuses, but the report sponsored by the Centre for Human Rights and Democratic Development came too late to influence the decision. Nevertheless, the ambassador indicated to Rwanda that a prime reason for the cut in aid was the failure to do anything about human rights abuses (correspondence, October, 1995).

During the 1992 diplomatic initiatives, there is no evidence that Canada made any diplomatic representations to France about its military support and the arms supplies to the Rwandan government, even though the Canadian government was fully aware of the French role. The absence of any evidence of representations to France, which had troops on the ground aiding the Rwandan government, while diplomatic representations were made to Britain simply because Britain had a military attaché in Kampala, indicates that Canadian foreign policy was based on holding the Ugandan government and the invasion as a much more serious cause of destabilization in the region than the French support for the Rwandan government. As one diplomat said: what should Canadian policy be if a Palestinian refugee force suddenly launched a full scale invasion of Israel supported by Jordan (interview, Ottawa, May 1995)? The Canadian government, like the Americans, regarded the Ugandan government and the RPF as more democratically inclined than the President of Rwanda. Nevertheless, Canada, along with the US, regarded the interstate support for the rebels as a more serious destabilizing force than the actions of the government in repressing dissent.

In 1993, Canada initiated another front in its efforts to try to avert a disaster in Rwanda. Following a U.N. goodwill mission during the first two weeks of March led by Macaire Pedanou, during which a cease-fire was signed on 9 March which required foreign troops to be withdrawn and an international joint U.N./OAU interpositional force be established, the mission went onto Arusha in Tanzania to observe the opening of the peace talks which had been started on 16 March between the Rwandan government and the RPF. However, the Arusha talks quickly became deadlocked, and France requested that the Secretary General deploy U.N. military observers in an attempt to avert the renewal of hostilities. A Canadian general, Major General Maurice Baril, who was in charge of the Planning Division as well as serving as Military Adviser to Kofi Annan, then Under-Secretary General who ran the Department of Peace-keeping Operations (DPKO) of the U.N. and subsequently became Secretary-General of the United Nations, led a technical mission to both Rwanda and Uganda in the first week of April. The mission recommended that 100 U.N. military observers (UNMOs) be placed on the Ugandan side. As well, preparations should be made to send a larger force to supervise the cease-fire, disarm the combatants, organize and train a merged military/police force and provide election observers if a peace agreement were signed.

The United Nations approached Canada asking that personnel be sent as part of the mission. Canada's initial response was negative because Canada questioned the absence of any high profile leadership to the mission. At the same time, Canada agreed to consider a request to provide such leadership if asked. A formal request of precisely that type followed. Canada asked General Romeo Dallaire to accompany Major General Baril on the technical mission. As a result of that mission, the Secretary General on 20 May 1993 requested authorization for a United Nations Military Observer force for Uganda and Rwanda (UNOMUR). In the interim, the OAU sent a Neutral Military Observer Group (NMOG) to Rwanda.

On 22 June 1993, the Security Council passed resolution 846 establishing a military observer mission to visit Rwanda. The resolution was a compromise between those who wanted the U.N. to play a larger role and be deployed within Rwanda, and countries such as the United States which were not only wary of a larger role for UNOMUR, but were wary about whether the combatants were yet ready for peace. On 21 July, Major General Romeo Dallaire was chosen to command the mission. Shortly thereafter, on 4 August, President Juvénal Habyarimana and Alexis Kanyarengwe, President of the RPF, signed the Arusha Accords. Another technical mission led by Dallaire this time determined that a larger force should be sent with a broader mandate. Resolution 872 was passed by the Security Council authorizing UNAMIR, with NMOG and UNOMUR falling under its responsibilities.

On 5 October, the Security Council established UNAMIR under the command of Dallaire. In the same period, the Associate Deputy Minister for African Affairs and the Middle East met Herman Cohen, his US equivalent, to discuss Rwanda and Zaire. The Canadian diplomat came away convinced that he and Cohen shared the same views of the situation.

Parallel to this diplomatic effort, a large scale humanitarian effort was underway within the country. At the beginning of 1993, there were 300,000 internally displaced within the country. By February of 1993, that number had increased to 800,000 as a direct consequence of the latest RPF offensive in the war. By the end of the year, the number of internally displaced, in spite of peace negotiations, cease fires and signing a peace agreement, had reached a million. Almost one in seven of Rwandan citizens had been displaced. Canada was a financial contributor to that humanitarian effort in which agencies, such as UNICEF, assumed a major responsibility for latrine construction, the clean water supply, and supplementary feeding for pregnant women and undernourished children. In the war zone itself, the ICRC, as a widely perceived neutral and independent body, was very active. In the south, other U.N. agencies and Red Cross/Red Crescent societies took the lead.

It must be recalled that events in Burundi made Rwanda look optimistic in comparison. Further, with the massacres of the Hutu in Burundi in October and the flight of 300,000 refugees, the reprisals against Tutsis in Rwanda that followed seemed like spontaneous tit for tat actions, even though it was widely believed by Canadian diplomats that the reprisals, particularly in Kigali, were initiated by the *Interahamwe*, the militias that were then being expanded and armed by the government in Rwanda at the same time as the peace accords were supposed to be bringing peace.

In spite of the increasing numbers of internally displaced, the success of the diplomatic effort in Arusha and the deployment of UNAMIR made Canadian government officials cautiously optimistic. By the end of the year that optimism began to unravel as Habyarimana stalled on implementing the peace accord. However, the background noise, to which they did not attend, was even more ominous. Rumors were rampant that targeted lists of victims were being drawn up. In September of 1994, Radio Mille Collines filled the air waves with hate propaganda directed at the Tutsi (cf. Chalk, chapter 5). General Dallaire, in investigating two massacres in November and December, found clear evidence of an organized effort behind the killings. For example, in one case of slaughters that occurred in five different areas during the night in a single precinct, the local precinct government was able to announce those massacres at 7:00 A.M.

January to 6 April 1994

In the beginning of 1994, several hundred Burundi-Hutu refugees left their camps south of Kibungo (near the Burundi border in the south) and traveled north by bus to Gabiro in the northeast where the army was training the militia. The army was also training militia in the southwest. There was also a January report of a plane landing in the middle of the night full of weapons for the *Interahamwe*. Most significantly, on 11 January 1994, General Dallaire sent an intelligence report to U.N. headquarters in New York that a very high level informant had information on secret arms caches, a plot to restart the war by provoking the RPF, instigating the Belgian peacekeepers (the most effective and best-equipped unit in UNAMIR) to withdraw by killing some of the soldiers, killing moderate Hutu and, most significantly, to kill all the Tutsis in Kigali. In fact, a calculation had been done, based on previous slaughters, that they could murder 1,000 people every twenty minutes.[24]

These and other signs, along with President Habyarimana's stalling, stimulated the international community to increase the pressures on the President. Contrary to the interpretations that the international community ignored such signs, the evidence is that they paid attention to them, but interpreted them as signs to spur the peace process forward at a faster pace, but failed to read them as indicators that they should also act to do something about the increasing signs of organized and centrally directed violence. The arming of the militias was interpreted as a preparation for renewed fighting against the RPF rather than as a preparation for a war of a very different kind, a war against the defenseless Tutsi civilians (and Hutu moderates) by the extremists in the military and their trained militias (cf. Kakwenzire and Kamukama, chapter 4).

April 6 to August 1994

As Lucie Edwards wrote, Canadian diplomats were taken totally off-guard by the genocide itself as well as its scope and size. They suspected conspiracy and anticipated massacre, but not of the dimensions that took place. Caught unprepared, Canada's initial reaction and first concern was the safety of Canadians. Within several days, all those willing to go were evacuated.

Canada's efforts now concentrated on peacekeeping and then emergency assistance. The Canadian contribution to UNAMIR II, Operation Lance, included a radio heavy brigade-sized headquarters and signal squadron to provide force level communication and headquarters support along with a force signal officer and experienced planning staff along with a lawyer and MPs. In addition, to ensure self-sufficiency, half of a regimental support squadron was also deployed. The unit also had a troop-size engineer surge capability, a security platoon and an air support detachment which reopened and supported the operation of Kigali airport. The unit was intended to provide signal support to meet operational tasks. An advance party of forty personnel left Canada on 15 July on a commercial aircraft. Twelve days later, 160 soldiers were deployed on an airbus for Entebbe. They arrived in Kigali on 28 July followed by a second aircraft with ninety-five soldiers on August 16. The airlift of equipment began on 26 July and was completed on 2 September. In the end, total troop strength stood at a complement of about 450 officers and enlisted soldiers. However, by the time they were deployed, the genocide was over.

Conclusion

Canada was a strong supporter of the Habyarimana regime in the period prior to 1990. However, after 1990, Canada used the gamut of diplomatic tools at its disposal to move the rival parties in the conflict towards peace. Canada was the one aid country to practice human rights conditionality, even though budget constraints and a realignment of priorities made it convenient for Canada to do so. Canada, through ICHRDD, was a leading participant in the International Commission on Human Rights which was the first to indicate that a genocide was underway in which the central government was directly implicated. Canada not only provided the Force Commander for UNAMIR, but General Dallaire was the source of some of the best early information flowing back to New York indicating that a centrally organized conspiracy to commit genocide was underway. When New York failed to respond to those warnings or to provide UNAMIR with the tools it needed, and when the coup took place and the genocide was underway, the peacekeeping troops managed to save some lives not only by guarding the stadium and hospital where refugees had fled, but, contrary to instructions from U.N. headquarters, small groups of lightly armed soldiers actively rescued frightened civilians and escorted them past armed barriers to bring them back to the stadium where they were safe. Further, Canada was the only country to reinforce its small contingent of peacekeepers when the Belgians and others decided to withdraw. When the Americans landed at Kigali airport in July on their way to Goma, they did so because Canadian military communication experts and Ghanian peacekeepers held the airport.

What is clear is that Canada remained committed to helpful mediation and multilateralism,[25] to financial support for the U.N. in spite of criticisms and the need for reform, and remained committed to the principles and practices of peacekeeping. What is also clear is that Canadian policy within this overall umbrella of middle-power brokerage politics was also fragmented among units of the government and shifted dramatically over a few short years. While CIDA old-hands continued to find virtue in the merits of the Habyarimana government, the Ministry of External Affairs pushed strongly for human rights conditionality through quiet diplomacy, but were critical if not hostile to the open remonstrations that ICHRDD leveled at the Habyarimana regime. However, Canadian peacekeepers through its unauthorized intelligence activities demonstrated that these concerns were more than warranted, but nevertheless followed official channels in warning U.N. headquarters in New York.

One can speculate what might have happened if Canadian policymakers had been able to build a policy that was more rather than less than the sum of its parts, and if Canadians had been able to take a greater initiative and to assume a more direct responsibility for Rwanda. But Canadian efforts had exhibited internal inconsistencies over the years. It had failed to exert any pressure on France. It had failed to ensure that a more coherent and effective multilateral strategy was in place.

This, however, is the wisdom of hindsight. What effect have the failures had on Canadian foreign policy with respect to the Great Lakes region of Africa since the horrific 1994 genocide? Have we learned from the studies of that failure?[26] Canada, unlike the United States, took the international report[27] on the genocide as a landmark study and is convinced that "she heard the message that political will is crucial, and responded with conviction" (*The Joint Evaluation of Emergency Assistance to Rwanda: A Review of Follow-up and Impact Fifteen Months After Publication,* hereinafter referred to as the JEFF Report, 1997:33). In the Canadian view, the lessons learned required the Canadian government to continue to be involved in the Great Lakes region and to act on the findings of the Evaluation, to develop a rapid response capability to deal with similar situations, and to support peace-building in the region, steps consistent with the overall direction of Canadian policy.

Canada did conduct numerous seminars in Ottawa to discuss the lessons of the report. Canada convened a donor meeting in Geneva in November 1996 to deal with refugee reintegration in the region and chaired a follow-up meeting in December in Kigali which gathered pledges for reintegration and reconstruction. Further, on the humanitarian front, Canada is in the process of developing a Disaster Assistance Response Team (DART) as a rapid response capability in humanitarian disaster. In addition to enhanced humanitarian aid initiatives, Canada has also taken steps on the peacekeeping front, acting to improve coordination between NGOs and Canadian peacekeepers, enhancing the roster of Canadians available as human rights monitors, taken initiatives to involve NGOs more directly into the peace-building policy process,[28] and established a peace-building fund of CAN $10 million. Canada has targeted significant funds for humanitarian assistance, social reconstruction, support for human rights, democracy and good governance, including improvements in the justice system, for the Great Lakes region of Africa.

However, although there has been a great deal of effort to ensure much greater coordination in Canadian policy in the region involving not only various different sectors of government, but the NGO and academic communities as well, the aborted Canadian government initiative to lead a humanitarian peacekeeping rescue mission on behalf of the refugees in Zaire in November and terminated at the end of 1996 (cf. Gnamo, chapter 16) does not indicate that Canadians learned the lesson on early warning (cf. discussion in the Preface).

Canada has not been able to develop any coherence in international multilateral policy with respect to peacekeeping as the aborted peacekeeping mission indicated.[29] That initiative was very late in the day and a response to a crisis already well underway which ignored much earlier warnings of the need for action to disarm the militias and to deal with what Paul Kagame referred to as the continuing genocide in Zaire against the Banyarwanda. Further, the initiative ignored the recommendations about deferring to some degree to the initiatives of regional actors, ignoring the determinations of the local African states that the militias and ex-FAR militant components controlling the refugee camps needed to be disarmed, and instead came up with a feeble but very well-intentioned initiative that patched together the eagerness of the French to become involved under multilateral auspices and the total reluctance of the America defense and foreign policy establishment to do anything at all, perhaps because they covertly supported the militant actions of the rebels supported by Rwanda and Uganda.

Canada seems to continue to believe that good will and intentions constitute political will, even when the political will lacks a critical and well-thought out strategic analysis based on quality information.[30] The intervention in Zaire was a response to some superficial lessons learned from the Rwanda genocide and was more a response to media coverage than to a detailed analysis of the Zaire crisis.[31]

Notes

1. The understanding of Canadian policy development was acquired through interviews with Canadian officials and restricted access to Canadian government documents (quotes of direct citations were not allowed) as part of the preparation of the report co-authored with Astri Suhrke, *Early Warning and Conflict Management in Rwanda*, Copenhagen: DANIDA, 1996.
2. Canadian officials at the time accepted the interpretation that Cardinal's murder had been committed by four criminals.
3. The most prominent was the wife of Landoald Ndasingwa, a member of the opposition *Parti libéral* established in 1991 and leader of its moderate faction; he became Minister of Labor and Social Affairs in the transitional government installed on July 1992, one of the rare Tutsi in that cabinet. On April 7, the day on which the genocide started, she, along with her husband, two children, and mother-in-law, were murdered.

4. In Gisenyi préfecture, Mugesera was Vice-President of the *Mouvement Révolutionaire National pour le Développement* (MRND—National Revolutionary Movement for Development which added the phrase et *de la démocratie* to its name in 1991), the ruling party President Habyarimana created in 1975, two years after his military coup and the ouster the previous Kayibanda government. Mugesera was considered to be the intellectual architect of an ideology which equated any opposition to the government as equivalent to siding with the enemy and, hence, being a traitor and worthy of death. More significantly, he was the ideologue and contributing architect of the genocide against the Tutsi, as well as its most vocal advocate and propagandist. In a widely reported speech in 1992, and rebroadcast subsequently on Radio-Télévision Libre des Mille Collines (RTLM), he already advocated the arrest and *extermination* of Tutsi.

5. The Canadian government announced its intention of expelling Mugesera on 12 July 1996 on the grounds that he had incited genocide. Mugesera lost his initial appeal of the decision.

6. The effect of these shows was to make Canadian policymakers very sensitive about publicity on the Canadian role in Rwanda; at the same time, government officials were very concerned to set the record straight. Thus, the investigation of the Canadian role may have been more difficult because of the sensitivities and defensiveness of many of those interviewed, but also easier as it also seemed to induce many to be more forthcoming than they might otherwise have been.

7. The Canadian government itself commissioned one retrospective study on early warning and conflict management in Rwanda (cf. LaRose-Edwards, 1994). It also prepared a departmental think piece on prospective future policy for Rwanda (cf. Soroka, Gary and Christopher Cooter, "Central Africa: Turning a Tide," Ottawa: Political and Security Policy Staff Commentary, Department of External Affairs and International Trade, December, 1994.

8. The fundamental principles of the National University of Rwanda as articulated by Pere Georges-Henri Lévesque was "de travailler à la préservation et au développementde votre culture nationale. Chaque homme reçoit de sa naissance, et de son éducation, de sa famille, de son groupe ethnique une culture particulière déterminée à laquelle il doit rester fidèle puisqu'elle fait corps avec sa personalité" (transcript, "Le Role du Canada au Rwanda Depuis 30 Ans," Le Pointe, January 23, 1995, pp. 4–5.) Note that the social mission of the university was not professional development of a set of skills, nor a commitment to resolving the social problems of a society, but the development and preservation of a unique cultural heritage. This was the foundation stone of the National University of Rwanda (cf. Adelman, 1973), which distinguishes between the Sanctuary of Truth dedicated to perpetuating values, the Sanctuary of Method, a university dedicated to the development of professionals in culture and science as well as those fields such as medicine and law more narrowly defined as professions, and the university as a social service station, the contemporary dominant model of the university committed primarily to serving society rather than producing independent professionals or ensuring the continuation and preservation of a set of values.

9. In the tension between using aid strictly for humanitarian goals and linking aid with the promotion of trade, until the 1990s Canada managed to maintain, and sometimes increase its aid directed at countries most in need. The Latin American debt crisis, India's testing of a nuclear device which utilized Canadian nuclear technology, and the 1984–85 famine in sub-saharan Africa meant that an increasing proportion of such aid went to Africa [cf. David R. Morrison, "The Choice of Bilateral Aid recipients," in Pratt (1994) 123–55]. Rwanda had become a core country for receiving aid by 1981.

10. Eight years later this was not considered to be a virtue, particularly in France (see Callamard's chapter). The small army in which only 2,000 of the 5,000 in the force were considered well trained to fight, was characterized by French intelligence as a sign of the government's incapability to sustain itself.

11. (Cf. Carlson, 1995: 7). As Margaret Carley Carlson said at the twenty-fifth anniversary celebrations of Rwandan independence, Canada participated in over 150 development aid projects to Rwanda and had contributed $150 million (transcript, "La Role du Canada au Rwanda Depuis 30 Ans," Le Point, January 23, 1995, p. 7).

12. "The great politic of regional ethnic equality, officially, while a very nice idea, is a euphemism to say that governmental resources have been divvied up between different groups of the population, but everyone in Rwanda knew that it was in place to prevent the Tutsi civil servants from acceding to positions of leadership; no Tutsis in the army, but the politic called ethnic and regional and ethnic, everyone knew, but of which no one spoke... continued to go to his government, everyone knew that it was a racist and regional government, but had a certain complicity towards silence on the part of the international community" (transcript, "La Role du Canada au Rwanda depuis 30 ans," Le Point, January 23, 1995, p. 7).

13. In fact, the World Bank Report (1991) suggested the decline in the economy was due to more structural causes and dated back to the early 1980s. "After 1980, Rwanda's economic growth slowed and became more erratic. Compared to an average yearly GDP growth of 6.5 percent over 1973–80, 1980–87 growth averaged only 3.1 percent, including a decline of 0.3 percent in 1987 [when coffee prices began to decline, but the explanation the World Bank gave for the 1987 decline was that quality declined due primarily to a producer price policy that did not discriminate for quality]. Real GDP stagnated in 1988 and declined by 5.7 percent in 1989, mostly reflecting weather conditions and world-market prices for coffee." According to the World Bank, during the 1980s, "imports continued to expand at a time when export earnings were declining." Further, there was a loss of export competitiveness when, "between 1980 and October 1990 the real effective exchange rate of Rwanda appreciated by about 30 percent, mainly as a result of depreciation of the dollar." A sharp decline in tax income on coffee exports accompanied by increased government expenditures beginning in 1981, led to persistent budgetary deficits, which during 1987–89 rose to 8 percent of GDP. The domestic debt quadrupled between 1981 and 1988 and net reserves fell from five months of imports in 1987 to two months in 1989. There was, however, one positive sign—reduction in the inflation rate from the average of 10.6 percent between 1977–82 to 2 percent per year during the 1983–89 period (468–69). However, during the 1990s, the annual reports became successively more ominous. In 1993, the President of the World Bank, Lewis Preston, wrote a letter to Habyarimana that was circulated among the entire diplomatic corps which insisted that Habyarimana immediately take steps to reduce military expenditures and get on with peace. As the 1993 report had indicated, "The fiscal situation continued to deteriorate in 1992. Current expenditures exceeded by 23 percent the target set in June 1992. The overspending was caused by military expenditures, which reached about 8 percent of GDP, compared to 2 percent in 1989, and by the government continuing subsidizing coffee producers"(427). Rwanda's primary deficit had risen to 8.2 percent of GDP financed by the central bank and accumulated domestic arrears. Foreign reserves had been depleted, and Rwanda was effectively broke by 1993, thus very susceptible to international pressures.

14. Canada began to support structural adjustment programs in the mid-1980s. In the CIDA document *Sharing Our Future* issued in 1987 (CIDA, *Sharing Our future: Canada's International development Assistance*, Ottawa: Supply and services, 1987), structural adjustment was one of six priorities set out for Canadian aid policy. "By 1989, support for the IMF/World Bank structural adjustment policies had become a central preoccupation of the Canadian International Development Agency (CIDA)" (Burdette, 1994: 211).

15. Structural adjustment programs (SAPs) are economic reforms involving changes in pricing and trade policies, reductions in the size of government, and its involvement in and regulation of production, in order to integrate those countries more fully into the international market economy. Countries (usually third world) are required to make these economic changes in order to receive funds from the IMF and the World Bank.

16. Cf. Callamard's account of the France's official attitude in this volume, which was almost identical. Canadian Rwandese policy was dominated by French Canadians who shared many of the views of the French, except perhaps the predominance of the "Fashoda syndrome" (cf. Prunier's chapter).

17. This was in keeping with a general shift in Canadian foreign policy underway in the nineties. Cf. the White Paper outlining and consolidating these changes, and articulating the principles of current Canadian foreign policy: "The promotion of global peace as the key to protecting our security remains a central element of our foreign policy" [*Canada in the World*, Ottawa: Department of Foreign Affairs and International Trade (DFAIT), February 1995]. Note that security no longer means just protecting one's own country against military attack from an enemy, but has come to take on a global meaning in two senses: first, the security of the whole globe is a precondition for the security of one's own country; secondly, the threats include not only outbreaks of civil and inter-state war elsewhere in the globe, but the population explosion, poverty, human rights violations, good governance, refugee flows, threats of the spread of disease and environmental issues. As part of this conceptual shift, the Department of Foreign Affairs created the Bureau of Global Issues and Culture with five divisions: Environment; Human Rights and Justice; Peace building and Democratic Development; Population; Social and Economic Development. The Canadian Foreign Affairs Minister, Andrè Ouellet, in his address to the conference, *Conflict Prevention: African Perspective*, for the International Francophone Meeting, Ottawa, September, 1995 conveyed this perspective when he said that "problems that transcend national boundaries are erasing the dividing line between domestic and foreign policy" *(Proceedings*, Ottawa: Government of Canada, 47). This revised view of security was first put forth in Canada, to the best of my knowledge, by my colleague, Professor David Dewitt, Director, Centre for International and Security Studies, York University, Toronto, who in fact changed the name of his Centre from "Strategic" to "Security" Studies to take into account this conceptional shift (cf. *Idem*, "Confidence and Security Building Measures in the Third World: Is there a Role?" *International Journal*, XLII:3, summer 1987, 509–35). With the fall of the Berlin Wall and the end of the Cold War, in a process of general recycling still underway, many other scholars adopted the same conception (cf. Jessica Matthews, "Redefining Security," *Foreign Affairs*, 68:2, 1989, 168–71; Ken Booth, "Security and Emancipation," *Review of International Studies*, 1991, 313–26; Barry Buzan, *People, States and Fear: An Agenda for International Security Studies in the Post-Cold War Era*, Boulder: Lynne Rienner, 1991; Helga Haftendorn, "The Security Puzzle: Theory-Building and Discipline-Building in International Security," *International Studies*

Quarterly, 35, 1991, 3–17; Michael Intrilgator, "Defining Global Security," *Disarmament*, 14, 1991, 59–72; Patrick Morgan, "Forum: 'What is Security and Security Studies?' Revisited," *Arms Control*, 13:3, December, 1991; Edward Kolodziej, "Renaissance in Security Studies? Caveat Lector!" *International Studies Quarterly*, 36, 1992, 421–38), and was a central theme of a recent collection of scholarly articles—Michael Klare and Daniel Thomas, eds., *World Security: Challenges for a New Century*, New York: St. Martin's Press, 1994. This shift is summarized very well in Simon Dalby's paper, "Contesting an Essential Concept: Dilemmas in Contemporary Security Discourse," a paper presented at the conference, *Strategies in Conflict: Critical Approaches to Security Studies*, Centre for International and Security Studies, York University, May 1994.

18. Again, this is a complete contrast with the view in France which deplored the poor state of the armed forces in Rwanda. Again cf. Callamard's chapter.

19. I personally recall being present at a dinner Mulroney had for Mandela after he had been released from prison when Mulroney used the occasion to announce a contribution of $5,000,000 to the ANC. When Mandela rose to thank Mulroney, with a twinkle in his eye that would make any Irishman envious, Mandela expressed his gratitude to Canada, but with diplomatic chutzpah added, "Of course, that will be in American dollars" (the Canadian dollar was then worth just under 80 American cents). As the rest of the dinner guests laughed, Mulroney with his wide grin nodded his assent.

20. The only record of formal communications with France that we learned about was a letter from the Canadian Foreign Minister (then called the Minister of External Affairs), Joe Clarke, to his French counterpart thanking him for landing French parachutists in Rwanda and protecting the lives of Canadian expatriates (cf. Callamard).

21. Alison des Forges (correspondence November 1995), one of the foremost experts on Rwanda, has pooh-poohed this factor as totally irrelevant in explaining Museveni's actions.

22. A detailed examination of the role of the rights organizations is undertaken in a separate paper.

23. The genocide description was partially retracted in their published report in March, but not the attribution to the government of a prime role in organized slaughter.

24. The unofficial intelligence units with the Belgian peace-keepers were given monies for informants by Belgium and sent detailed information on the plans back to the Belgian Foreign Ministry. We have no evidence that Dallaire sent equivalent information to Ottawa, though prior to 6 April, Dallaire had alerted key officers in the Department of Defense to prepare to send him more troops.

25. "Canadian policy makers have consistently been at or near the forefront of multilateralist activity for the past fifty years. Based on recent policies Canadian support for multilateralism remains as strong as ever" (Tom Keating, "The Future of Canadian Multilateralism," Maureen Appel Molot and Herald von Riekoff, eds., *Canada Among Nations 1994: A Part of The Peace*, Ottawa: Carleton University Press, 1994, 74). Multilateralism is defined as the coordination of behavior among three or more states on the basis of generalized principles of conduct (cf. Robert O. Keohane, "Multilateralism: An Agenda for Research," *International Journal*, XLV: 4, Autumn 1990, 731–64). John Ruggie, "Multilateralism: the anatomy of an institution," *International Organization*, 46:3, Summer, 1993, 574. See also Robert Cox, "Multilateralism and world order," *Review of International Studies*, 18:2, April 1992. For a survey of Canada's economic multilateralism from a gramscian viewpoint, cf. David Black and Clair

Turenne Sjolander, "Multilateralism Re-constituted and the Discourse of Canadian Foreign Policy," *Studies in Political Economics*, 49, Spring 1996, 7–36. Most importantly, see Tom Keating's full book on the issue, *Canada and world order: the multilateralist tradition in Canadian foreign policy*, Toronto: McLelland and Stewart, 1993. For an account that challenges the theory of the preeminence of multilateralism in Canadian foreign policy, cf. Claire Cutler and Mark Zacher, "Introduction" in *idem*, eds., *Canadian Foreign Policy and International Economic Regimes*, Vancouver: UBC Press, 1992.

26. There is also the view that we learn from trial and error and not primarily academic scholarship (cf. "Taking Stock: A Survey of Canadian Thinking and Activities on Peace building," Ottawa: Parliamentary Paper, March 1995).

27. The reference is to the report of the Joint Evaluation of Emergency Assistance to Rwanda of which I was the co-author of study II and of parts of the Synthesis Report that dealt with Early Warning and Conflict Management.

28. As an example and initial step, the Peacebuilding and Human Development Division of the Global Issues Bureau at what is now called the Department of Foreign Affairs and International Trade (AGP-DFAIT) has entered into a partnership with the Canadian Peacebuilding Coordinating Committee in Ottawa along with the International Development Research Centre (IDRC) and the Norman Paterson School of International Affairs at Carleton University in Ottawa to compile a database on the peacebuilding activities, programming, policy directions and advocacy work among Canadian NGOs and research communities.

29. It also raises questions about the effectiveness of some aspects related to peace and governance of what has been billed as the largest U.N. undertaking in history, the coordinated action across the entire U.N. system—the United Nations System-wide Special Initiative on Africa to enhance the capacity of African institutions. But that is not the subject of this chapter.

30. The Canadian government adopted a very different, and, I believe, very misconceived notion of early warning. That view is superbly summarized (and advocated) in an excellent paper by Jean Guilmette (an expert on Africa, a long time civil servant with CIDA in Canada and now with the International Development and Research Centre in Ottawa), first circulated to me privately for comment, and then presented at the International Francophone Meeting: *Conflict Prevention: African Perspective*, Ottawa, 19–22 September 1995. For Guilmette, and now Canadian policy implementers, early warning entails a critical third factor in addition to the first, information collection, and the second, analysis. In what he calls this third link, "the information is developed and once again translated into ordinary language. *Common wisdom must be produced to provide policy makers with a basis for action that will be viewed as legitimate by citizens*" (his emphasis). (*Proceedings*, Ottawa, Government of Canada, 1995, 93–94.) Early warning comes to mean a public relations exercise. The third stage is *not* the conversion of the analysis into strategic options. (For an articulation of that view of early warning, cf. two of my own articles—"The Concept of Early Warning: The Practice of International Organizations," in *Early Warning and Conflict Prevention: Limitations and Opportunities*, eds. Alfred van Staden and Klaas van Walgraven, The Hague: Clingendael,, 1997; and "Early Warning and Prevention: The Case of Rwanda," chapter 3 in *Evolving International Concepts and Regimes*, ed. Frances Nicholson, Cambridge: Cambridge University Press, 1997). The process of translating the analysis into a strategic action plan is relegated to early warning experts, compressed into the second stage and reduced to a single conclusion about what to do. From the Foreign Affairs Department's

own study of the Rwanda genocide (cf. Paul Larose-Edwards, 1995) and mistakenly from our own study of the international response to the genocide in Rwanda, the conclusion has been drawn, as Kenneth Bush put it so succinctly, that "the fundamental and essential ingredient is political will" (cf. *Idem*, Draft, "Fitting the Pieces Together: Canadian Contributions to the Challenge of Rebuilding War-torn Societies," Ottawa: IDRC, July, 1995, 22). In this conception of early warning, the focus is on "the *visibility* of information as a means of provoking political will" (cf. "Lessons Learned: Canadian NGOs Review the Impact of United Nations' Peacekeeping Interventions on Humanitarian Aid in Regions of Civil and Ethnic Conflict," Ottawa: Canadian Council for International Cooperation, 1993; Bush, op. cit., 22; and Kenneth Bush, "When Two Anarchies Meet: International Intervention in Somalia," in Robert Miller, ed., *Missions for Peace: Canadian Experience and Future Roles*, forthcoming). If Americans drew the lesson from Somalia that they should avoid such involvements, Canadians drew the lesson that the problem was a lack of political will (Bush, ibid, 30). This misconceived conjunction of early warning and public relations in order to garner political will, and the total failure to undertake a detailed analysis of the Zaire crisis and develop and weigh strategic alternatives is behind the failure of the November Zaire initiative. Unfortunately, this conjunction of lack of political will and public relations is a one hundred and eighty degree shift from the earlier assessment by the Canadian Foreign Minister that the lack of political will was to be traced to the absence of a well thought-out strategy and the mechanisms to implement it. Cf. the remarks made by the Canadian Foreign Affairs Minister, Andrè Ouellet, in his address to the conference, *Conflict Prevention: African Perspective*, for the International Francophone Meeting, Ottawa, September, 1995 when he said that, "The power to act is useless without the will to act. Rwanda and now Burundi afford proof that the weakness of preventive diplomacy lies not in a lack of ways to identify conflict situations, but in the international community's inability to decide how best to prevent and contain conflicts" (*Proceedings*, Ottawa: Government of Canada, 48).

31. The brilliant international diplomat, Mohamed Sahnoun was both prescient and wise when he criticized institutions when they "take the facts on the ground only partially into account and are sometimes motivated by pressure from the media. The result is that these recipes may well prove sterile if not harmful" (*Proceedings—Conflict Prevention: African Perspective*, for the International Francophone Meeting, Ottawa, September, 1995, 57). He also endorsed "decentralization and empowerment," not exactly the policy followed in the Zaire initiative which ignored the decision of the regional African states at their summit on 5 November 1996 in Nairobi stating that the first priority had to be the disarming of the ex-FAR and interahamwe militias in the refugee camps.

10

Rwanda: U.S. Policy and Television Coverage

Steven Livingston and Todd Eachus

Editor's Note

Other chapters have referred and will refer to the "Somalia Syndrome" and PDD-25 (see the next chapter as an example). The effect of the American involvement and debacle in the latter part of the peacekeeping operation in Somalia had made Americans very wary of any involvement in peacekeeping. When the coup took place in Rwanda on 6 April 1994 and during the genocide that immediately followed, the Executive Office had already drafted Presidential Decision Directive 25 (see section on policy considerations, below) which severely restricted U.S. involvement in peacekeeping operations, including U.S. authorization and financing for such operations. PDD 25 was issued in May of 1994. Thus, the question is not why Americans did not support a more proactive operation in Rwanda, on which this examination will provide some further analysis, but why Americans became involved once more in the peacekeeping operation related to the humanitarian assistance towards refugees in Zaire. This chapter focuses on the formation of public opinion through television coverage and the impact of that TV coverage and public opinion on American policy. Since there was virtually no coverage of Rwanda until 6 April 1994, this paper concentrates on the TV coverage during the genocide in Rwanda.

Introduction

The scale of the Rwandese tragedy in the spring and summer of 1994 was almost beyond belief. ABC News' veteran correspondent, Jim Wooten, claimed that "it is not like anything I've ever seen in 30 years as a reporter. It is, I think, the standard against which all further tragedies will be measured" (ABC News 1994). Yet, despite the ghastly scale of suffering in Rwanda, American television news paid relatively modest attention to the story during its first three bloody months. It was only later, after the crisis of violence had been transformed into a crisis of refugees and disease, did television news remain focused on the story. We will argue that this had rather profound policy consequences, at least in the case of the response of the United States. Rwanda was the first test case for a new, very cautious U.S. posture toward humanitarian crises. The episodic coverage given to Rwanda by television news in the initial months of violence gave encouragement to the Clinton administration's limited policy response.

American television news coverage of Rwanda came in three phases. The first phase came prior to 6 April 1994, the day President Juvenal Habyarimana of Rwanda and President Cyprien Ntaryamira of Burundi were killed in a mysterious plane crash. During this first phase almost nothing at all was heard of Rwanda on American network television.

The second phase came in the weeks immediately following the crash, and in the midst of the massive killing. In this period we see a substantial increase in news attention, as one would expect in the systematic murder of tens of thousands of people. But as data presented below indicate, coverage was still relatively modest, at least when one considers the scale of the killing occurring at the time.

Most of the coverage was found in a third phase, beginning roughly in July. It was devoted to refugees in—or in a route to—camps in neighboring Tanzania and Zaire.

While we will use this general structure to describe news coverage of events in and around Rwanda, at the same time it must be said that, with the exception of the April plane crash, no clear point of demarcation signifies the transition between phases. Stories regarding massacres did not suddenly give way to stories solely about refugees. The two blended and twisted together until some point in August when world attention was largely focused on a sea of humanity in a disease-ridden camp called Goma, Zaire.

Methods

The primary research methodology used in conducting this study was quantitative media content analysis. Using an archival computer database, we obtained all broadcast transcripts of ABC World News (n=92) and CNN (N=423) programming relating to Rwanda for a five-month period, April through August 1994. We also used computer-assisted searches on several other occasions to provide specific points of information. After obtaining the transcripts, we coded all ABC World News coverage and a sample of CNN coverage of Rwanda for the time period under consideration.[1]

Data were also obtained for NBC Nightly News and CBS Evening News. This included Rwanda story frequencies (how often they appeared on the network news shows), story length measured in minutes, Rwanda story segments' placement within the news program, who the reporting correspondent was, and the origin of the story (i.e., whether it originated in Rwanda, Zaire, Washington, New York, or elsewhere).

Our study was also informed by the field work by one of the authors who was in Nairobi, Kenya during the initial weeks of the massacres in Rwanda. The purpose of his stay there was to interview and observe Western correspondents in Nairobi, the base of nearly all Western press operations for the northern half of Africa, including Rwanda. For more than three weeks he interviewed correspondents, attended news conferences, spoke with diplomats, and attended editorial meetings concerning strategies for covering the emerging situation in Rwanda.

In the analysis to follow, we offer mostly aggregate quantitative data concerning American television coverage of events in and around Rwanda during the spring and summer of 1994. In turn, using insights gained from field experience and the research literature, we suggest why each phase of coverage looked as it did.

Phase One

The first phase is an open-ended period leading up to the April plane crash that killed the presidents of Burundi and Rwanda. In particular, this phase includes the period following a military offensive in Rwanda by the Rwandan Patriotic Front in October 1990 from their sanctuaries in Uganda. It is perhaps the most important of the three phases, indicated by what was not reported, rather than what was. The lack of coverage in this phase, we argue, contributed to the sometimes superficial coverage found in the subsequent news of the Rwandan tragedy.

On 10 September 1993, approximately seven months prior to one of the worst periods of bloodshed in human history, CNN's Gary Strieker reported that the signing of the Arusha Accords on August 4 had ushered in a new sense of optimism in Rwanda. A U.N. representative in

Rwanda was quoted as saying "there is an enormous amount of positive, optimistic hope for the future through this mission." According to this, the only American television news story in 1993 to focus on political developments in Rwanda, things were looking up for the tiny Central African nation.[2] Whether CNN should be faulted for missing the emerging crisis in Rwanda is not the point. More important was the total lack of attention—except for this one report—regarding the events there by all American television media prior to the bloodshed of 1994. There was, of course, nothing new in this. Records dating back to the spring of 1991 indicated that none of the broadcast networks reported on the political situation in Rwanda.

Yet, according to Human Rights Watch, between October 1990 and April 1994 human rights abuses by both the RPF and Rwandan military were commonplace. Even more astonishing, when over 50,000 persons were killed in neighboring Burundi in 1993, the horrific events there were given no broadcast media attention whatsoever. The year before, Human Rights Watch had even tried drawing greater attention to Burundi and Rwanda by issuing a report that spelled out quite clearly that "the developments in Burundi, tragic in themselves, also complicate the situation in Rwanda." The report received no press coverage (MacGuire 1994, 42). And when in the first week of April 1994 regional leaders gathered in Dar es Salaam to work out an accommodation that might finally bring an end to the violence, no broadcast networks carried news of the meeting, though, as we already mentioned, CNN did.

Such inattention to Rwanda was not out of the ordinary for American news coverage of Africa. With the exception of South Africa, sub-Sahara Africa has been consistently ignored by the networks. In 1986, only 1 percent of the broadcast time of the three broadcast networks was devoted to black Africa (Corry 1986, C17). This lack of media attention to Rwanda was the result of several factors.

Television News

Part of the problem may have rested with a redefinition of news resulting from the dramatic changes wrought by CNN. Broadcast networks, under pressure from CNN's twenty-four-hour format, began making international video available to their affiliates, something they had not done before for fear of undermining the exclusivity of their own national evening newscasts. As it turned out, that fear may have been well founded. "It turned network news into water, like a utility," as one news executive was quoted by the *New York Times*. "CNN created news on demand. That hurt the networks. It also hurt CNN. I think CNN's ratings problem is tied into a jadedness about world events" (Carter 1993, A20).

At the beginning of 1994, CNN's ratings had dropped by about 25 percent, giving it an average prime-time audience of about 500,000 households. By May its average daily audience had fallen to about 250,000 households, the lowest level since 1982 when CNN was disparagingly referred to as "Chicken Noodle News."[3] It was a stunning predicament. In a period marked by the continuing crisis in Bosnia and the systematic slaughter of tens of thousands of persons in Rwanda, CNN could not get Americans to watch the news.

This came at a time when the television news business was not good to begin with, particularly for NBC and CBS. Of the broadcast networks, NBC and CBS paid the least attention to Rwanda (see figure 10.1). This is not surprising, for both networks were in a shambles at the time, particularly NBC.

Michael G. Gartner, President of NBC's News Division since 1988, had resigned in 1993 in the midst of several trying controversies, all relating to questions of news judgment and budget restraints. At the time he had taken over the news division it was losing more than $100 million a year. General Electric, the corporate owners of NBC since 1986, wanted Gartner to make the news division profitable, which he did with staff reductions, elimination of bureaus, and through greater reliance on outside video and information sources.

The year Gartner left, NBC News showed a profit of $20 million. But according to Don Browne, executive vice president of NBC News, the cost cutting took "an emotional and spiritual toll" on the division. In the judgment of some, it also led to poorer quality news.

Besides the general malaise of the news business, the task of getting the news in Africa suffered perhaps the most. A relatively small corps of Africa-based journalists was laden with covering an extraordinarily complex array of issues over a vast range of territory. During the initial stages of the crisis in Rwanda in 1993, the Africa-based press corps was responsible for covering, to mention but a few cases, the ongoing civil war in the Sudan, rising political conflict in Kenya, the emergence of an unstable democracy in Ethiopia, continued political and civil strife in Zaire, and, of course, Somalia. *The Washington Post, New York Times,* and *Christian Science Monitor* each had one-person bureaus in Nairobi.

The Associated Press and Reuters had larger staffs, but still not enough to cover the region adequately. *The Los Angeles Times* bureau consisted of a room with a desk and a secretary who arrived for a few hours most days, but no correspondent. One flew in from time to time to do a story and then left.

Television news resources in Africa were stretched even thinner. With so few resources, the amount of news devoted to even major stories was not great. In 1993, ABC, CBS, and NBC carried a combined total of 66 stories concerning Somalia. (As a point of comparison, on the twenty-four-hour cable news channel, CNN, there were 1,597 stories.)[4] In South Africa in 1993, the year white minority rule ended and Nelson Mandela became president, the three broadcast networks presented a total of twenty-five stories.

As mentioned earlier, the three broadcast networks completely missed the bloodshed in Burundi where an estimated 50,000 were killed following the overthrow and assassination of President Melchior Ndadaye in October 1993. CNN mentioned Burundi on four occasions, three of them on talk shows. The fourth news item was a report by correspondent Gary Streiker on October 29 from along the Rwandan-Burundi river border. He had stumbled across bodies floating downriver out of Burundi, victims of the fighting there.

Inadequate staffing in 1993 of American news bureaus in Africa made covering even the more obvious political crises difficult. Working alone, CNN's Streiker was responsible for covering much of the northern half of Africa, from coast to coast. During a thirty-day stay in Nairobi in overlapping portions of May and June 1994, one of the authors of the present study found Streiker in Nairobi, where his home was located, for a total of one afternoon. In a telephone interview that afternoon Streiker explained that as the only CNN correspondent in that part of Africa he was "constantly living out of a backpack" (interview, Kenya 1994).

Besides CNN, the other English-language television news bureaus in Nairobi belonged to Reuters, formerly known as Visnews, and a BBC bureau. The latter served BBC World Television (currently unavailable in the United States) and the British domestic market. Reuters Television, as with its print counterpart, is in the business of selling news, in this case video news, to other news organization. The Reuters bureau in Nairobi was headed by the highly respected Mohamed Amin, best known for the video footage he shot of the catastrophic Ethiopian famine in 1984. The video was credited with mobilizing the massive famine relief effort that year.

The lack of permanent bureau staffing by American networks in Nairobi meant that when a story broke, such as Ethiopia in 1984, Somalia in 1992, or Rwanda in 1994, the networks sent in "parachute journalists," generalist reporters and sometimes even anchors, who were usually unfamiliar with the history and culture of the area. As Mohamed Amin noted of the parachute journalists who finally came to document the Ethiopian famine, "These guys didn't know where anything was. They were lost" (interview, Kenya 1994). Sometimes they were quite literally lost. In a 1985 interview with the *New York Times*, he told a story that keenly captured the problem with parachute journalists: "They (the newly arrived correspondents during the Ethiopian famine) had to ask questions and take our word for it. One correspondent I know wanted to go to Zaire and couldn't remember the name: he told the airport worker he wanted to go to that Z country." They sent him off to Zambia instead of Zaire" (Kaplan 1985, C26).

Ancient Hatreds

But one can lose one's way in the complex affairs of Africa in more serious ways. This was evident in the coverage of Rwanda during the first several weeks following the plane crash. Not having covered Rwanda for years, network correspondents and producers seemed to believe nothing of importance had happened there prior to their arrival and that as with other regions and other "ethnic conflicts," the violence in Rwanda was the result of the "resurgence of ancient ethnic hatreds" mysteriously and inextricably exploding to the surface.

Yet as one critic remarked, "the massacre in Rwanda was not 'sudden' at all, but the culmination of years of trouble, which the press for the most part did not cover" (MacGuire 1994, 40). Not understanding Rwanda and its complex politics, both domestic and international, television news relied on vague references to ethnic violence to explain events they otherwise did not understand.

Understanding the role and ambitions of France in Africa, for example, was important for understanding events in Rwanda. Just two years after Habyarimana had seized power in a 1973 coup d'état, France signed a military agreement with his regime. Since 1959, many of the leaders of the Tutsi-dominated Rwandan Patriotic Front (RPF) had come to speak English, rather than the French more commonly found among the Hutu elite in Rwanda. Furthermore, members of the RPF had served in the British-trained Uganda Army before joining the rebels. This led to some in the European press to speculate that in actuality, the bloodshed in Rwanda was something of a proxy war between the British and French. Though denied by both governments, the *New York Times* noted that "it remains a fact that the civil war is being fought between English-speaking and French-speaking officers" (Simons 1994, A6).

In response to the RPF invasion of Rwanda in 1990, the Habyarimana government militarized. With French assistance, the Rwandan army expanded from 5,000 to more than 30,000 in the span of three years. French soldiers also provided intelligence and ran government checkpoints in the countryside. As one aid worker put it, "There, in the middle of Africa, French military would ask you for your passport" (Simons 1994).

All this was explained by French Prime Minister Edouard Balladur in the spring of 1994. "France sees itself as a world power," said Balladur. "This is its ambition and its honor and I wish for it to preserve this ambition. And its main field of action is Africa, where it has an important role to play because of long-standing tradition—especially in French-speaking Africa" (Simons 1994).

Among those accused of orchestrating the attacks by the military and militias in April 1994 were Rwandan Army officers who had studied with French officers at St. Cyr and the Defense University, France's top military academies. To understand Rwanda in the spring of 1994 required something much more than vague references to tribalism and ancient ethnic conflicts. It require an understanding of political ambitions, both in Rwanda and elsewhere.

Phase Two

In the early months of 1994 prior to the plane crash on April 6, CNN carried one story about Rwanda (concerning the mountain gorillas), while the broadcast networks failed to mention it at all. That pattern soon changed.

Figure 10.1 shows the broadcast networks coverage from April through August. Four distinct episodes of coverage are evident, particularly in the coverage provided by ABC and CBS. As can be seen, of the broadcast networks ABC World News devoted the most attention to Rwanda, especially during the later stages of the story. In fact, by July and August ABC was devoting twice as much air time to Rwanda as were the other two broadcast networks.

Figure 10.2 shows a similar pattern with CNN's coverage of Rwanda, though the period from the end of May through the first week of July is

FIGURE 10.1
Television Coverage in Minutes (Networks)

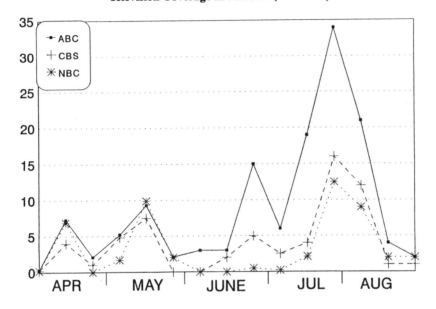

FIGURE 10.2
Television Coverage in Minutes (Cable News Network)

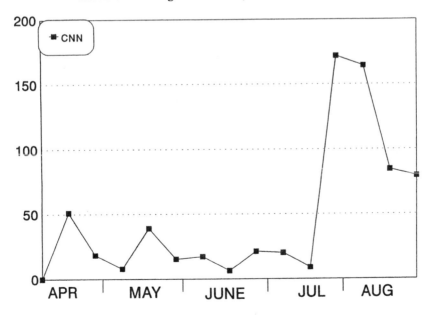

relatively flat, and almost nonexistent in mid-June. This is in part explained by the emergence of several other news stories. As figure 10.2 indicates, Haiti's continuing unrest and the expanding exodus of refugees to the United States became a growing focus of attention for CNN and the broadcast networks, actually eclipsing coverage of Rwanda by a significant degree.

Beginning with the second week of June, the big story for American television news, bigger than Haiti or Rwanda, and certainly bigger than Bosnia, was the seemingly never-ending saga of O.J. Simpson, the American football player and television personality who was accused of murdering his wife and her friend.

The initial April peak in coverage shown in figure 10.1 concerns, of course, the plane crash that killed presidents Habyarimana and Ntaryamira, the first of the massacres, and the evacuation of Westerners. The first network reports of the plane crash came on April 7, with ABC devoting twenty seconds and CBS and NBC each devoting fifteen seconds to the story. On April 8, CBS made no mention of Rwanda, while ABC and NBC noted the outbreak of fighting and the beginning evacuation of Americans.

By 11 April, the bloodshed had begun to make an impression on the networks, with a story breaking the two-minute mark for the first time on ABC. That network's anchor, Peter Jennings, called it the "terrifying civil war in Rwanda," while NBC referred to the "unspeakable atrocities" and CBS to "ethnic violence." This established a pattern in at least the initial television coverage of Rwanda. For the lack of a better explanation, the violence was attributed to "tribal" or "ethnic" slaughter.

Critics of television coverage of Rwanda must be careful, however, not to overstate the degree to which the news relied on this explanation. While it is certainly true that references such as "tribal violence" were common, there were more sophisticated analyses also offered, though late in the development of the story.

ABC News, for example, aired a story on 7 May, fully one month after the onset of the violence, that went beyond the more superficial explanations of the violence. ABC correspondent Ron Allen reported that events in Rwanda suggested something more than spontaneous tribal violence. "As investigators try to make sense of the killing," reported Allen, "there is more evidence Rwanda's massacres may be a premeditated political act, not a spontaneous eruption of ethnic hatred. Those responsible, human rights investigators say, are Hutu extremists with Rwanda's government trying to grab more power." The report includes an interview with a human rights investigator who says the killings were "intended to wipe out opposition from whatever quarter it came from, political or ethnic groups, once and for all. It really was intended as a final solution."

Hutu extremists feared that Habyarimana was moving toward a reconciliation and power-sharing agreement with the Tutsi minority. In response, they shot his plane down and activated a well-planned "final solution," all the while claiming the bloodshed was the result of spontaneous rage at the killing of Habyarimana by Tutsi rebels.[5] As one person interviewed in Allen's account said, "I think this thing was very carefully planned, was very well-planned, well in advance. There was absolutely nothing spontaneous about it."

FIGURE 10.3
Network Coverage by Topic (Coverage in Minutes)

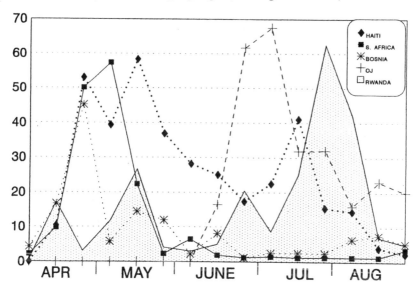

Aggregate coverage of ABC, CBS and NBC Nightly Newscasts

The May peak in coverage of Rwanda seen in figure 10.1 is largely explained by the presence of television crews who were sent to cover the South African election. Once in Africa, they were reassigned to cover Rwanda (see also figure 10.3). Nelson Mandela was declared winner of the election on May 3 and was sworn in as president on May 10. Mark Foley, ABC News' assignment manager in London, explained the coverage by noting that, "Rwanda was a hugely important story for us. We initially pulled one crew from the South Africa story to cover Rwanda" (interview, 1995). Additional crews followed.

The precipitous drop in the two stories parallel one another, as seen in figure 10.2, and reflected the withdrawal of the additional network resources sent for the South African election and Mandela's inauguration. The May coverage of Rwanda was, at least in part, an artifact of the South Africa story, reflecting as it did the temporary availability of additional crews in Africa there to cover the South Africa election. In the larger scheme of Africa news coverage, this makes sense.

As we have mentioned already, death and destruction in black Africa, even on the scale seen in Rwanda in May, does not necessarily translate into news coverage. In 1993, the murder of upwards of 50,000 persons in Burundi did not result in a single broadcast network story. Likewise, wars in the Sudan, Liberia, and Angola (particularly since the end of the Cold War) have killed thousands, but were rarely if ever covered by the American networks (Livingston 1996; Livingston and Eachus 1995, 413–30).

By May, as the RPF was met with greater battlefield success and took control of more and more territory, and the Hutu population began to flee in fear of Tutsi retribution, Rwanda became a story about refugees, rather than a story about massacres. As we have seen in figures 10.1 and 10.2, most of the coverage came in the July-August time frame. More than anything else, Rwanda-related stories were mostly about the refugees, and not the killing itself.

This was particularly true of CNN coverage. Figure 10.4 shows the percentage distribution of stories according to the location of the action or events in the news segment. CNN devoted much of its coverage to the refugee story, something in the area of 70 percent. As a point of comparison, ABC devoted about 50 percent of its overall Rwanda coverage to the refugees, as seen in figure 10.4.

This is the same story told by figures 10.5 and 10.6, which show the frequencies of datelines from Rwandan versus those from Zaire between April and August for CNN and broadcast network coverage.[6] As

FIGURE 10.4
Characteristics of Coverage
Location (in Percents)

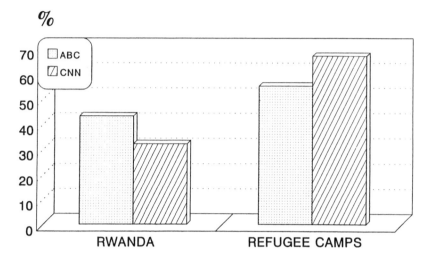

ABC N=92, CNN N=298

can be clearly seen, for American television news, the story of the crisis in Rwanda was not the massacres as much as it was the exodus of Hutu refugees who feared Tutsi reprisals.

Phase Three

Most news attention to Rwanda came in July and August and was devoted to Goma, Zaire, where 1.2, million mostly Hutu refugees were ravaged by dehydration, cholera, and dysentery. Given the scale of the suffering, the intense coverage made sense.[7]

The reasons for this pattern of coverage, we believe, are rather straightforward. Once the scale of the violence became clear, news organizations, including television, made the determination to cover the

FIGURE 10.5
Datelines (Cable News Network)

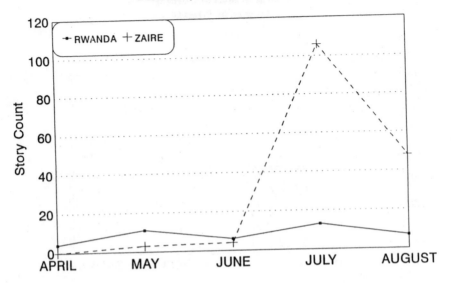

FIGURE 10.6
Datelines (Networks)

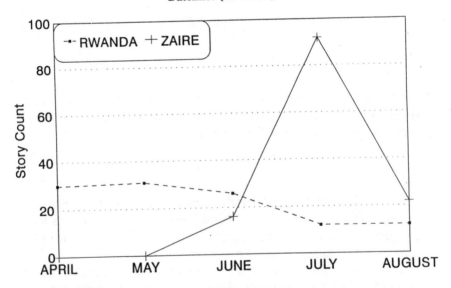

story. This was assisted by the additional crews in Africa covering the South Africa election.

The problem, however, was access. As with Somalia the year before, the news crews' own security was at risk in Rwanda. In recent years, we have seen the creation of a new kind of war correspondent, as Senator Daniel Patrick Moynihan has noted: One who covers massacres rather than battles. Those who carry out the massacre of civilians have no qualms about killing journalists, as data from the Committee for the Protection of Journalists can attest. Covering Rwanda in the midst of the killing spree was not an easy or safe proposition.

One of the authors of the present study had the opportunity to spend several days with Reid G. Miller, Nairobi bureau chief for the Associated Press, and Mohamed Amin, Nairobi bureau chief for Reuters Television, among other media professionals in Nairobi, as they desperately tried to find ways to get their correspondents into Rwanda. At one point, Terry Leonard of the Associated Press had gotten as far as the airport in Kigali, only to find he could go no further. Covering the violence of Rwanda during those initial weeks was a risky, uncertain undertaking.

A popular alternative was Lake Victoria. As the killing progressed, bodies were being dumped into rivers. By the end of May, officials in bordering Uganda had estimated that as many as 10,000 bodies had washed down the Kagera River.[8] Bodies lined the shore of Lake Victoria, offering a horrific display. As Donatella Lorch of the New York Times put it, the bodies were "shocking the world with the magnitude of the slaughter." In a sense, the slaughter was thus brought to the correspondents feet as they visited the safer shores of Lake Victoria, rather than venture to the source of the carnage in the killing fields of Rwanda.[9]

As a news story, going from watching the dead to watching those in the process of dying was a minor transition. They were both spectacles, easy to film and full of pathos. Refugees in the camps in Zaire were the dead-in-waiting. The networks, still not burdened by the subtleties of the conflict, chose the spectacle of Goma, with its familiar (read Western) actors. CBS, for example, sent in its physician correspondent to report to the viewers about how the fight against disease in the camp was going. It all made for great television.

Figures 10.7 and 10.8 show the relative prevalence of two Rwanda news frames. As one can see, both ABC and CNN began focusing most of their attention on the scourge of disease in the camps. Again, we see that most of the story concerning Rwanda was about Hutu refugees fleeing in fear from the RPF, rather than the killing of Tutsi by Hutu military and militia groups. For American television news, this was the story of choice.

Policy Considerations

What about the possible effects such coverage might have on policy responses? Much of what might be said on this point is speculative, but this much can be suggested: In the case of the policy response of the United States, the coverage of the massacre had only a minimal effect.

During its first two years in office the Clinton administration had vacillated on the use of military forces in humanitarian crises. During the 1992 campaign and during the first several months of his administration, Bill Clinton spoke of "assertive multilateralism" and the need to come to the assistance of people in need. But following the American experience in Somalia, the Clinton administration reversed course and instituted strict guidelines for future U.S. intervention in similar crises. Under the provisions of Presidential Decision Directive (PDD) 25, issued in May 1994, approval of the use of U.S. forces for humanitarian undertakings became highly unlikely. Among the conditions to be met before the United States involved itself in U.N. peacekeeping operations was a clear statement of American interests in the operation, the approval of Congress, the availability of funds for the operation, a specifically fixed date of withdrawal of U.S. forces, and an agreed upon command and control structure (Minear and Weiss 1995). Larry Minear and Thomas G. Weiss have suggested that, "since new and urgent needs will rarely, if ever, satisfy these political conditions, the effect of Washington's policy is to place severe limits on humanitarian initiatives" (Minear and Weiss 1995, 36).

As a result of PDD 25, the Clinton administration effectively isolated itself—and in some measure other nations as well—from involvement in Rwanda during the period of the massacres. Douglas Jehl of the New York Times summarized the situation this way: "Seeing Rwanda as a first test of its restrictive new guidelines on peacekeeping [PDD 25], the Administration has not only ruled out sending American troops but has stood in the way of an aggressive United Nations plan to dispatch an African force of 5,500" (Jehl 1994, A8). The administration was intent on doing as little as possible.

The 1948 Genocide Convention obligates signers to investigate and punish those who are responsible for the systematic killing of members of specific racial or ethnic groups. Wary of the obligations that ensued

FIGURE 10.7
Characteristics of Coverage (News Frames)

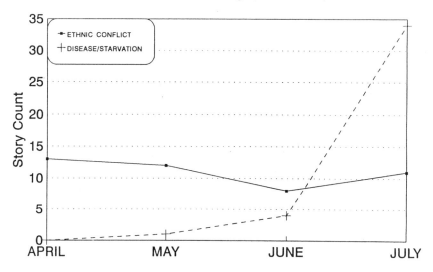

Source: ABC Nightly News

FIGURE 10.8
Characteristics of Coverage (News Frames)

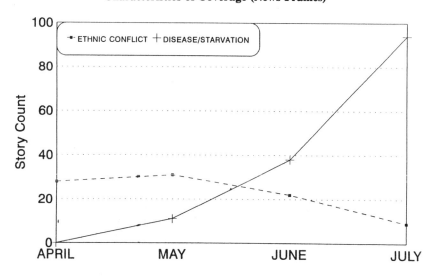

Source: Cable Network News

as a result of the use of the term, the State Department and the National Security Council drafted guidance instructing spokesmen to say instead that "acts of genocide may have occurred" in Rwanda, rather than bluntly stating that the Hutu slaughter of Tutsi and other political opponents constituted genocide. Quite simply, as Jehl noted, the administration was attempting to avoid the moral pressure to stop the mass killing in Rwanda by pretending it was something else.

But this is where television coverage served as a potential threat to the administration's desired policy ends. As Jehl pointed out, though perhaps overstating the case in the process, "a gruesome feature of international news coverage since early April" was coverage of the massacres. As a result, he said, those upset with the passive nature of the international response, particularly that of the United States, began to protest the lack of U.S. involvement in Rwanda.

Our argument has been that in actuality, television coverage during the massacres was rather episodic and often misleading, encouraging the mistaken belief that the slaughter in Rwanda was simply an example of "ancient tribal hatreds," rather than a planned, politically inspired genocide. There are fewer rational responses to irrational behavior, such as a presumably spontaneous massacre. But had American news organizations been more forceful, had they, for instance, stayed with the Rwanda story beyond the May piggy-backing on the South Africa coverage (see figure 10.3), the Clinton administration would have probably experienced greater difficulty pursuing its dogged policy of doing nothing.

Conclusions

Much has been made in recent years of the so called CNN effect, the rather ill-defined constellation of policy consequences said to result from the injection of stark media images into the political and policy process. We have argued that the Clinton administration made a conscious effort to distance itself, and the policy process, from the effects of media images. Further, we have argued that they were successful in doing so, in some measure, because the media themselves did not fully cover Rwanda's bloodshed during the early months of 1994. What the media did cover, and cover in great detail, was the plight of the refugees, which was certainly understandable and worthwhile. But if there was a policy response borne of television coverage, as with the coverage itself, the policy was too late.

There were two Rwanda stories in 1994, and they should not be confused. One was that of the massacres. That story is seen in the flat graph lines of figures 10.7 and 10.8. The second story was Goma and other refugee camps. That is seen in the rising line of the same graphs. If there was a "CNN effect," it came in response to this second story. The administration was quite ready to employ Pentagon resources in a "feeding and watering" operation, as it was commonly referred to at the Pentagon. What it was not willing to do, and would not allow television pictures to force it to do, was stop the slaughter early on. As a result, both the United States government and the networks offered too little too late to stop the killing.

Notes

1. While we were able to review all of the major television coverage transcripts concerning Rwanda, it is important to point out that we were not able to review what was perhaps the most important component of television news: the visual image. The costs associated with obtaining video archived material was prohibitive. We were therefore limited to an analysis of variables other than the visual image.

2. In total, there were two television news programs directly concerning Rwanda in 1993 (several CNN reports concerning neighboring Burundi also mentioned Rwanda). As a point of comparison, *The New York Times* carried several articles regarding the Arusha Peace Accords and U.N. actions. See "U.N. Approves Troops for Rwanda," *The New York Times*, 6 October, 1993, A17; "Accord Ends 3-year Civil War in Rwanda," *The New York Times*, 5 August, 1993, A12; Donatella Lorch, "Refugees Trying to Flee a War Settle for Limbo," *The New York Times*, 8 July, 1993, A4; Steven A. Holmes, "Africa, From the Cold War to Cold Shoulders," *The New York Times*, 7 March, 1993, 4; "Rwanda's Aristocratic Guerillas," *The New York Times Magazine*, 17 January, 1993, 10.

3. This began to change in mid-June, helped by O.J. Simpson. In July, CNN posted a ratings gain. When asked why CNN was devoting so much time to the O.J. Simpson arraignment and trial, CNN correspondent Ralph Begleiter said quite simply that it was because ratings were about five times what they would otherwise be.

4. It is important to always keep in mind that these numbers reflect not only the fact that CNN is a twenty-four-hour news network, but also that programming includes talk shows and other formats. There were not, in short 1,500 reports from Somalia in 1993. Rather, there were 1,500 news items of various types regarding Somalia.

5. Cf. ch. 4 for a discussion of various theories explaining the shooting down of the plane and Prunier 1995 ch. 8.

6. most instances, location and dateline are the same.

7. The first Rwandese refugee stories, however, came from Tanzania during the first week of May. On 3 May, ABC and NBC reported on the large number of refugees at the Tanzanian border, which ABC put at 300,000.

8. Lorch, Donatella. "Bodies From Rwanda Cast a Pall on Lakeside Villagers in Uganda," The *New York Times*, 28 May 1994, A1. Only a small and relatively

innocuous portion of the available video ever made its way to American television. One author spent an afternoon sitting with Reuters editors as they reviewed hour after hour of horrific video pictures of bodies being pulled from Lake Victoria. Bodies sometimes came apart as they were lifted from the water. Only the more circumspect—within the bounds of what was possible—of video was sent back to New York or London.

9. It is important to note that in no way are we suggesting that the journalists covering the slaughter in Rwanda were anything less than professional, and in many cases exceedingly brave in providing the coverage they did. We only wish to point out that covering the actual violence proved difficult and that substitutes were used.

Part III

Peacekeeping

11

U.N. Peacekeeping in Rwanda

Turid Laegreid

Introduction

One of the most important aspects of U.N. involvement in Rwanda related to the peacekeeping operations of UNAMIR I and II. This chapter will discuss the formation and functions of the two missions.

The Arusha Process and the Establishment of UNAMIR

The Arusha Peace Agreement of 4 August 1993—designed to end three years of civil war in Rwanda—envisaged a major role for the United Nations in implementing the Accords. A twenty-two-month transitional period was to begin with the formation of a transitional government and a multiparty National Assembly, leading to national elections to be held by the end of 1995. To help monitor the process and maintain security in the transition period, the Security Council authorized on 5 October 1993 a U.N. Assistance Mission in Rwanda (UNAMIR). A U.N. observation force established in June 1993 to monitor the border between Rwanda and Uganda (UNOMUR) was folded into UNAMIR, although it remained an autonomous body that kept its original mandate.

UNAMIR's mandate, as outlined in Security Council Resolution 872, was to contribute to the security of the city of Kigali and monitor a weapons-secure area to be established by the Rwandese parties in and around the city. The force was to monitor the observance of the cease-fire agreement, including the establishment of cantonment and assembly zones, and the demarcation of the new demilitarized zone (DMZ), and to monitor the security situation during the final period of the tran-

sitional government's mandate before the elections. UNAMIR also was
to assist with mine clearance. The Mission was authorized to investigate alleged noncompliance with the provisions of the Arusha Peace
Agreement and investigate complaints regarding the activities of the
gendarmerie and police. Finally, it was to help coordinate relief assistance and monitor the process of repatriation of Rwandese refugees
and displaced persons.

The initial perception of many U.N. personnel involved was that the
Arusha Agreement would proceed smoothly and that UNAMIR would
be a "success story." However, there were some differences when assessing what size would be appropriate for the new force. The final
result was due more to political and economical considerations than
military ones, which was unexceptional in U.N. peacekeeping. The Force
Commander, General Romeo Dallaire, had initially considered 4.500
as a maximum option, and 2,600 as a minimum. The U.N. Reconnaissance Mission to Rwanda in August, which he headed, presented two
lower options in its report, thus already reflecting a compromise. The
minimum option was now 1,935 troops, while the Mission's recommended option was 2,538 troops. The latter, described by the Mission
as a "reasonable, responsible, credible and decisive option," was finally adopted (Report, U.N. Reconnaissance Mission to Rwanda 1993).

The Reconnaissance Mission's report also underlined the need for
mobility to enable the force to react in a timely fashion and with sufficient strength to diffuse potentially dangerous situations. The nature of
the terrain in Rwanda, the lack of local resources and the fragile road
network called for several armored personnel carriers (APCs) and helicopters. In U.N. peacekeeping operations, however, APCs and helicopters have traditionally been contingent-owned equipment (i.e., to be
provided by nations contributing troops and to be subsequently reim-
bursed by the U.N.). If contributing nations fail to provide the requested
material, the U.N. has no logistical reserves upon which to depend. In
the Rwanda case, only the Belgian contingent arrived with APCs. The
U.N. Department of Peacekeeping Operations (DPKO) succeeded in
borrowing eight additional APCs from the U.N. operation in
Mozambique, but they were Russian vehicles with manuals written only
in Russian. In any case, there were no spare parts, access to the engines
were locked, and the Bangladeshi contingent in UNAMIR that was
supposed to man the APCs lacked basic knowledge and experience in
operating them. Almost all of them quickly broke down. When it was
clear that no contributing country would provide the helicopter unit

authorized by the Security Council, private contractors were hired. However, when the war broke out in April 1994, the contractors were unavailable.

In virtually all peacekeeping operations, lack of trained personnel, equipment, and finances have been continuous problems. Troop contributing nations fail to provide equipment as pledged, or troops arrive with totally inadequate equipment and training. Such "best-case scenario" thinking gives the operation few possibilities for flexible adaptation, and makes it extremely vulnerable to changing conditions. The Rwanda operation was in this matter not a unique case, but the limitations would have devastating consequences when the crisis erupted in early April.

UNAMIR was to be deployed in four phases, beginning with the departure of foreign forces and the establishment of a secure area in Kigali. Preparations for the disengagement, demobilization, and integration of the armed forces and gendarmerie were to be completed during phase II, due to begin with the installment of the transitional government. In this phase, the force would be deployed at the maximum strength of 2,538, including 331 observers. In phase III, the force would gradually be reduced to a strength of 1,240, which would conclude the disengagement and demobilization process. In phase IV a further reduction would take place. In this final phase, the force would be monitoring the general security situation in the country leading up to the national elections to be held between October and December 1995.

By the end of phase I, the Rwandese parties to the peace agreement had made little progress towards its implementation. Formation of the transitional political institutions was held up as the splitting of political parties caused havoc with the formulas for representation in the National Assembly and the transitional government. Therefore, while UNAMIR could not keep to its scheduled tasks, deployment proceeded—indeed, was slightly speeded up. The second battalion was deployed in the DMZ in January 1993. By the end of March, the force had been brought to its maximum strength.[1]

During the first months of 1994, UNAMIR expressed concern over the deteriorating security situation in Rwanda. Political violence in February included the assassination of the two political leaders, Fèlicien Gatabazi and Martin Bucyana. There was evidence of importation of arms and reports that weapons were distributed to civilians. In January a high-ranking official in the Interahamwe militia informed UNAMIR that he had been ordered to plan for the extermination of the Tutsi minority community; plans were also being made for a plot against the Belgian peacekeepers. The alleged plot included an attempt to provoke a fire-exchange with the UN, with the aim of killing Belgian soldiers in the hope that this would make the contingent withdraw.[2] Although he had no confirmation of this information, Force Commander Dallaire requested U.N./DPKO for permission to conduct a cordon and search in areas of Kigali identified by the informant as hiding weapons caches. The request was rejected on the grounds that this would be an offensive operation and not in accordance with the mission's Chapter VI mandate.

According to key DPKO officials in New York, the reluctance to take offensive action was due to lack of additional information confirming the alleged plot, which made it difficult to rule out the possibility of its being a trap. It was also believed that offensive operations would meet with opposition from U.N. members that would be concerned that this might create a precedent for stretching mandates. With the memory of the Somalia experience fresh, the DPKO did not want to propose any changes in the mandate that would not be accepted by members of the Security Council. The information in the cable, moreover, was only one of many indications that Rwanda's Hutu extremists were obstructing the peace process. Since some of the information that had reached New York indicated that the President himself was involved in these incidents, offensive action of the kind proposed by the Force Commander might provoke protests from the government of Rwanda.[3] Moreover, UNAMIR's mandate specifically limited the force to carry out its security functions in co-operation with the local police and gendarmerie.

The Force Commander, who from January onwards became increasingly aware that the situation was deteriorating, repeatedly sent requests to U.N./New York for all the equipment originally authorized by the Security Council. He also asked for an additional infantry company, which DPKO tried to acquire from Canada in vain. The Belgian Foreign Minister, Willy Claes, reportedly also asked the U.N. to give UNAMIR a more flexible mandate to permit an active search for weapons.

In New York, Secretary-General Boutros Boutros-Ghali repeatedly underlined that the success of the mission depended on the cooperation of the Rwandese parties and their willingness to implement the Arusha Agreement. Evidence that the political process had stalled and was being undermined caused concern in the Security Council when the members discussed the renewal of UNAMIR's mandate in January, and again in the first week of April 1994 (Res. 909/1994). The decision to authorize a U.N. continued presence was disputed, and several members wanted to withdraw the force, or withdraw their contribution to it. Supporters of the force, on the other hand, emphasized that the one basic premise for the operation—the cease fire—was holding.

The Crisis of 6 April

President Habyarimana, his Chief of Staff and President Ntaryamira of Burundi were all killed as their aircraft was shot down when approaching Kigali Airport on 6 April 1994. There is strong evidence that the Rwandese government forces were responsible for both the assault on the president and the killings which starting immediately afterwards.[4] The first roadblocks were set up in Kigali even before the news of the plane crash had been announced, and UNAMIR observers who went to investigate were denied access to the site of the crash of the Presidential Guard.

The first to be killed were prominent opposition politicians, both moderate Hutu and Tutsi. Among the first victims early on 7 April, were Prime Minister Agathe Unwilingiyamana and ten Belgian peacekeepers who were guarding her but taken by the Presidential Guard and killed in an army compound. The second objective was to eliminate dissent. Critical journalists, human rights activists, lawyers, and civil servants were targeted during the first phase of the slaughter.[5] The killings reignited the civil war. The RPF battalion stationed in Kigali to protect the RPF political leaders immediately broke out to avoid entrapment, and engaged the government forces. Some RPF units from the DMZ in the north advanced rapidly towards Kigali, reaching the outskirts of the capital on the morning of 10 April, but did not enter the city until the 13 April.

Giving the UNAMIR Force Commander only 40 minutes prior notice, French troops landed at Kigali Airport by 9 April in order to evacuate their nationals.[6] They controlled the airport and used vehicles of Rwanda's Presidential Guard to collect expatriates. The evacuation operation was conducted effectively and rapidly, with the last French troops leaving on 14 April. The Belgians started a similar operation out of Nairobi on 10 April and took control over the airport after the French left. Also three Italian C-130 aircraft left for Nairobi to help in the evacuation of foreign nationals from Rwanda. The U.S. sent about 300 troops to Bujumbura in neighboring Burundi for the same purpose, but did not enter Rwanda, as U.S. civilians were escorted to the border by UNAMIR, and were airlifted from there. Most expatriates were evacuated by 14 April, but individuals continued coming to UNAMIR assembly areas during the next week to be escorted out of the country. When the crisis broke, UNAMIR had been responsible for evacuating U.N. personnel, and, on 8 April, the Force Commander began negotiating with the RPF on the freedom of movement for UNAMIR to escort convoys through RPF sectors for purposes of evacuation.

Several mortar shells exploded at the Kigali airport on 13 April, but the evacuation did not otherwise meet with armed resistance. Nevertheless, both the Rwandese "interim government" and the RPF urged non-UNAMIR troops to leave as soon as possible. The RPF, which was most skeptical towards the presence of French and Belgian national troops, told both on 12 April to leave within twenty-four hours. The demand was later modified to 12 hours after the evacuation of expatriates was completed.

There was some initial discomfort with the non-U.N. evacuation operations in the U.N./DPKO and among some members of the Security Council. One concern was that command and control problems might arise similar to the Somali operation in 1993.[7] On the other hand, the members recognized the benefits of having the French and later Belgian (national) units secure the airport, and that UNAMIR itself could play only a limited role in the evacuation.

The radical deterioration of the situation after 6 April put UNAMIR in an impossible situation. Its mandate was closely tied to the peace agreement, and the success of the operation required that the Rwandan parties work to implement the Accords. Both premises vanished in early April. Though Dallaire's version of the Rules of Engagement seemed to be quite broad (see chapter 12), the Rules of Engagement as understood by U.N. New York headquarters permitted use of force only in self-defense, which in itself became difficult due to the degree of hostilities, and because the force was more lightly equipped than originally planned. The other critical factor was the decision by the Belgian government, formally announced on 14 April, to withdraw its battalion from UNAMIR. The withdrawal began on 19 April and was completed the next day.

The problem of varying standards for troops is a generic one in peacekeeping operations. Under normal circumstances it causes frustration and decreases the operational capacity of the force; in unstable and hostile situations it becomes a matter of life and death. UNAMIR had struggled with such problems since its deployment. The Belgian contingent was by far the best equipped and best trained unit. The equally more professional Ghanaian battalion was deployed in the DMZ but, lacking vehicles to move and caught in heavy fighting around Buyumbura, the contingent did not reach Kigali until April 13.

The Force Commander's main concerns during the first weeks were to protect the force and U.N. personnel, assist in evacuating U.N. personnel and expatriates, protect civilians at assembly points, secure the airport and—as instructed by the revised mission terms formulated in New York—try to establish a new cease-fire agreement between the two warring parties (see chapter 13).

The cease-fire talks, however, led nowhere. Fighting between the RPF and government forces in Kigali continued unabated until 18 April when RPF forces took control of the northern part of the city, surrounding the gendarmerie camp at Kacyiru (northeast of Kigali) and the quarters of the Presidential Guard. The fighting then slowed, although still continued at a low level at different places in the city.

During this period, UNAMIR became increasingly involved in self-protection tasks as well as trying to protect or extract the many thousands of people under U.N. protection. Initially, the Rwanda government forces (RGF) did not allow movement of U.N. troops and UNMOs in Kigali, while the RPF was not generally hostile to U.N. forces. By April 18 the situation had improved somewhat. Neither the RGF nor the RPF were reported hostile to UNAMIR, while the militia showed little or no regard for the U.N. flag or the Red Cross, and stopped convoys and attacked even Rwandese U.N. guards.

The Force Commander had redeployed UNAMIR units from DMZ to Kigali so as better to protect his own force and civilians. Once the Belgian UNAMIR contingent had left, the Ghanaian unit was assigned the critical task of securing the airport. UNAMIR HQ was regrouped to Hotel Meridien, initially protected by the French and Belgian troops sent in to evacuate foreigners. The Tunisian company was regrouped to Hotel Meridien and assigned to protect the nearby Faisal Hospital (which also served UNAMIR personnel). The Amahoro Stadium was selected as an assembly point for the evacuation of expatriates, and on 16 April declared a "U.N. installation"; it was guarded by the Bangaldeshi battalion and soon Rwandese also sought shelter there.

The number of refugees increased daily, and within a week, some 14,000 civilians had gathered under U.N. protection. There was an acute shortage of accommodation, food, and water for the refugees during the first week, with some improvement only by the end of the second week. The stadium was under indirect, but intense fire most of the time. Both the hospital and the stadium were hit by mortars—resulting in the death of one U.N. soldier and around forty civilian casualties—but there was no direct attack on either. Additional Rules of Engagement regarding all U.N. installations, defined as a "compound containing U.N. personnel or equipment and vital grounds defended by U.N. troops," were issued on 17 April. Without being specifically outlined in the new RoE, the adjustments opened the possibility of the defense of civilians. However, UNAMIR's capability of stopping a direct attack was severely limited, as the Force Commander acknowledged.

The security of the airfield was a constant worry to the Force Commander. He considered it his "lifeline," the only way to ensure that supplies could get in, but also the only exit if withdrawal were necessary. Dallaire spent considerable time trying to persuade both parties to accept the airport and surrounding area as a neutral zone. Both refused, however, and the airport was constantly in danger of indirect fire.

Having very limited resources, Dallaire clearly was directing an extremely vulnerable force. When the Belgians announced that their battalion would be withdrawn, and no additional resources were provided for him, his concern about the safety of the force became accentuated. The force had no possibility of protecting itself. "We had no defense structures, no sand bags, no timber for the troops to dig in," as he later recalled (interview 1995). He also lacked trucks and protective vehicles (only one APC was functioning), and communication was difficult during the first week since few UNAMIR channels were operational. The Force Commander nevertheless staked out a proactive course, and within the first few days of the crisis asked for additional troops and equipment as well as a change in RoEs to actively protect civilians. This was turned down by U.N. Headquarters.

U.N./New York initially had difficulty assessing the situation on the ground, both with regard to the security of U.N. personnel and the scale of the killing of civilians. The decision-making process was further complicated by the memory of the U.N. debacle in Somalia, which had given negative connotations to both the terms "humanitarian intervention" and "peace enforcement." The main lessons drawn from that experience, both in the Secretariat and the Security Council, was that if the basic principles of traditional peacekeeping are abandoned, escalation and war will follow.

The Secretariat

In retrospect, DPKO officials stress that although their task was to draw up plans and offer options based on their independent analysis of the situation, the political restraints communicated by the Security Council was that no "Somali type" operation (i.e., under chapter VII) would be authorized. This severely restrained the range of options for the DPKO which was charged with formulating plans. The fact that UNAMIR was gradually dismantled by unilateral national decisions was also of great concern. The withdrawal of the Belgian unit deprived UNAMIR of its strongest and best equipped unit. Soon after the Belgian withdrawal was announced, the Government of Bangladesh announced it might follow suit.[8] With a cease-fire seemingly remote, there was severe doubt in the Secretariat whether keeping the force on the ground without reinforcements was a viable option.

In the period from when killings started on 6 April, to 21 April when the Security Council decided to reduce UNAMIR's force to a "political" presence, the crisis response in New York went through several phases. The death of the ten Belgian peacekeepers created an initial, deep concern for the safety of military and civilian U.N. personnel. This is reflected in the Secretary-General's letter to the Security Council of 9 April, where he suggested that the evacuation of civilian U.N. staff and foreign nationals "might become unavoidable." If UNAMIR were to effect such an evacuation, this would require two to three additional battalions and a changed mandate and RoEs, he concluded. In the informal consultations in the Security Council on 8 April France suggested that a change in the mandate of UNAMIR to assist the evacuation of nationals would be necessary. At that very time, France was preparing its own evacuation operation, although without informing the U.N.

The option of withdrawing the force was held open. On 9 April, Boutros-Ghali (who happened to be in Geneva) told the then Under-Secretary-General Kofi Annan that if the Force Commander and SRSG together with DPKO judged the situation to be sufficiently dangerous, UNAMIR should be withdrawn, and adding, that in this case he would inform, rather than seek prior instructions from, the Security Council. When briefing the Security Council later the same day, Annan passed on the message that withdrawal of the force could not be ruled out, depending on factors such as loss in UNAMIR credibility due to the French and Belgian unilateral operations, or if there was increased hostility towards UNAMIR.[9]

From 11 April and onwards, the focus shifted to discussions about the future of UNAMIR. There was grave doubt in the DPKO that the force could function satisfactorily without being strengthened both in terms of size and mandate. DPKO officials also concluded that this was not a very likely outcome.

The message that UNAMIR had to be strengthened if it were to have any impact on the ground was communicated to the Security Council on several occasions. When the Security Council on 11 April discussed a possible evacuation of the force, Kofi Annan argued in his briefing that UNAMIR's mandate might have to change, otherwise, if the force was to carry on, additional resources might have to be allocated. Briefing the Security Council on 13 April, Assistant Secretary-General Iqbal Riza raised the question of protecting civilian nationals in the long term. He also conveyed the opinion of the Force Commander, that if the Belgian contingent of UNAMIR left, the security of the rest of the force could not be guaranteed; nor could the airport remain secure. Furthermore he maintained that protection of civilians would require more resources, and that the Council should consider whether peacekeeping operations should include this task (consultations, Security Council 1994). Also the Secretary-General's letter of 13 April stressed that, with the withdrawal of the Belgian contingent, UNAMIR would be unable to carry out its mandate, and stated that "in these circumstances, I have asked my Special Representative and the Force Commander to prepare plans for the withdrawal of UNAMIR, should this prove necessary" (Leitenberg 1994, vol. 23 no. 6). His representative stressed to the Security Council , however, that this did not constitute a recommendation to withdraw.

The signals from the Security Council were clear. The Council would not accept another "Somali operation" to resolve the crisis and, on 13 April, asked the Secretariat for feasible options that were between a Somali-type enforcement action and a total withdrawal. When the Secretariat gave options to the Security Council for the first time on 14 April, these reflected the instructions of charting "mid-way" courses. One was to keep a reduced mission in place (the present UNAMIR without the Belgian contingent), with the parties being given about three weeks to reach an agreement to return to the Arusha Accords. A few days before the deadline expired, the parties would be given a warning, while the troops would prepare for withdrawal. The other option was to reduce the U.N. presence to a very small level, a total of 200, on the assumption that there would be no quick resumption of the peace process. Both options, however, were based on the unlikely premise of a cease fire, a condition which was criticized by several Security Council members as being unrealistic. But the Security Council could still not agree on any action. The only consensus on 14 April was on what not to do: neither total withdrawal nor any enforcement or expansion of the force.

There was no attempt to draw a distinction between the fighting between the RPF and the interim government, and the massacres carried out by individuals or lightly armed militias against unarmed civilians.[10] The Secretariat's focus on the cease-fire as a condition for ending the massacres might, therefore, have led it to exclude the concept of "humanitarian intervention," that is, a peace enforcement operation focusing on protection or more explicit law-and-order tasks.

On 19 April, during the final drafting of the Secretary-General's report to the Security Council, the Secretary-General's Task Force suggested a sharp reduction of UNAMIR (although keeping a presence in a neighboring country). An important factor that contributed to this recommendation was that another main troop contributing country, Bangladesh, had signaled to DPKO its desire to withdraw. The DPKO representative argued that the force was unable to function, and there was no prospect for a cease fire. The Task Force decided to present the option of sharp withdrawal as a strong recommendation to the Security Council. The recommendation by the Task Force was, however, not fully followed by the Secretary-General, who in his report the following day (S/1994/470) did not exclude the possibility of massive enforcement.

In his report to the Security Council of 20 April 1994, the Secretary-General underlined that the UNAMIR personnel "cannot be left at risk indefinitely when there is no possibility for their performing the tasks for which they were dispatched" (Rwanda U.N. Doc. S/1994/470 1994). UNAMIR military personnel on that date numbered 1515, down from 2165, and there were 190 military observers, down from 321. The Secretary-General outlined three alternatives for the Security Council. Assuming there was no realistic prospect for a cease fire in the immediate future, fighting and massacres could only be averted by an immediate and massive reinforcement of UNAMIR and a change in its mandate to an enforcement operation. This would require several thousand additional troops and might require UNAMIR being given enforcement powers under Chapter VII of the U.N. Charter. Option II was to keep a small U.N. detachment in Kigali to act as an intermediary between the parties in an attempt to make them agree on a cease fire. This effort could be maintained for a period of up to two weeks or longer. Under this option, the military personnel would number about 270. However, a full relief effort would be impossible without a cease-fire under this arrangement. Finally, the Secretary-General noted that UNAMIR could be completely withdrawn, although he did not favor this alternative, as the cost of a withdrawal in human lives could be very severe.

The Secretary-General's report reflected the indecisiveness in the Secretariat during the first, crucial weeks of the crisis. While claiming that UNAMIR required an expanded mandate and reinforcements in order to function, no contingency planning was made, and a firm recommendation for an offensive operation was never forwarded. Nevertheless, by not excluding an enforcement operation in this round, the Secretary-General could legitimately call for forceful action as soon as two weeks later. For two weeks after 6 April, the Security Council held almost daily consultations on the Rwandan crisis. During the first week there was little consistency in the discussions, and Council members complained about lack of information and clear options from the Secretariat. But the Security Council, when presented with options on 14 April, was unable to decide how to react, only agreeing that extreme options of a Somali-type operation and a complete withdrawal were unacceptable.

After the first few days, the U.S. delegation argued consistently against a continuing presence.[11] The main reason was the U.S. failure in Somalia, which became an important turning point in the Clinton administration's policy on peacekeeping. The Rwanda crisis erupted during the last phase of the drafting of a new doctrine (PDD 25) that strictly limited U.S. support for U.N. peacekeeping. The main message from Washington was that "the U.N. must learn when to say no," and that "hard questions" had to be asked before a new peacekeeping force would be authorized. Belgium's campaign to withdraw the force was also important. The Belgians were afraid of giving the impression of leaving an impossible mission behind in great danger, and wanted all of UNAMIR to withdraw. The phone call from the Belgian Foreign Minster, Willy Claes, to U.S. Secretary of State Warren Christopher, is regarded by many American officials as being decisive for the U.S. final recommendation to withdraw.[12] On the other hand, Belgians were possibly pushing on an open door.

The United Kingdom repeatedly warned against leaving a vulnerable force in unstable conditions, but ended up voting for a reduction of the force. France did not play a prominent role in the discussions. Nigeria, representing the NAM (Non-Aligned Members) caucus, initially criticized the focus on the safety of expatriates, and wanted more protection for Rwandese civilians. On 13 April, Nigeria circulated a draft resolution to extend UNAMIR's mandate, but withdrew it when it became clear that it would not receive support in the Security Council. The OAU supported the Nigerian initiative, urging the Security Council to "take urgent actions to help protect the lives and property of civilians in Rwanda and to consider expanding the size and mandate of UNAMIR in Rwanda" (New York/OAU/AG/1/94 1994). New Zealand, which held the presidency in the Security Council at the time, preferred a more activist role for UNAMIR, but did not forward specific proposals for an extended mandate. Under the circumstances, and to counter the push for full withdrawal, the New Zealand delegation actually preferred a "non-decision" [i.e., to give the Force Commander more time to work with the existing force and continue the tasks he was conducting (interview 1995)].

On 21 April, the Security Council decided in its resolution 912 (1994) to reduce UNAMIR to the number recommended by the Secretary-General in his option II. Simultaneously, the mandate of UNAMIR was adjusted: the force was to act as an intermediary between the parties in an attempt to obtain a cease-fire, assist in the resumption of humanitarian relief operations to the extent feasible, and monitor developments in Rwanda, including the safety and security of civilians who sought refuge with UNAMIR.

The decision to withdraw the main bulk of the peacekeeping force was met with criticism from several quarters, including the Organization of African Unity, which denounced the withdrawal as "a sign of indifference or lack of sufficient concern" for Africans (Leitenberg 1994).

The Secretary-General Seizes the Initiative

On 29 April, Boutros-Ghali appealed to the Security Council to take more forceful action to stop the massacres (S/1994/518). The initiative marked a shift of focus and direction in the Secretary-General's attitude toward the Rwandan crisis. The massacres and the need to protect civilians in Rwanda now became his main priority, although he did not use the term "genocide" until late May. The Secretary-General had by now numerous reports on the immense scale of the humanitarian catas-

trophe and referred to estimates of 200,000 killed in the previous three
weeks (U.N. Department of Public Information 1995). The
Undersecretary-General for Humanitarian Affairs, Peter Hansen, had
recently paid a visit to Rwanda, and had launched a DHA "flash appeal" on behalf of U.N. agencies for immediate emergency operations.
UNAMIR was reporting on the ongoing violence and massacres of civilians in Kigali and beyond.

By raising doubts about the viability of the revised mandate given to
UNAMIR by the Security Council 21 April, the Secretary-General implicitly criticized the Security Council for not making appropriate decisions. Now calling for "forceful action," even though that would
require a "commitment of human and material resources on a scale
which Member States had so far proved reluctant to contemplate," the
Secretary-General argued that the scale of human suffering and its implications for the stability of neighboring countries left the Security
Council with no other alternative (S/1994/518).

The Expansion of UNAMIR

With no Western state willing to commit troops to an expanded
UNAMIR, the U.N.'s only alternative was to create a strengthened force
comprised of African contingents with Western financial and logistic
support. A few African countries indicated that they might have some
lightly armed infantry, but requested more details about the mandate,
operational plans, the size of the force and the logistics available. Soon,
this became a "chicken-egg situation" since the U.S. said there was no
point in the Council discussing a possible mandate until it knew roughly
what resources would be available.

Informal discussions in the Security Council on 6 May resulted in a
request for indicative contingency planning with regard to the delivery
of humanitarian assistance as well as support to the displaced persons
in Rwanda. At the urging of the U.K. representative, the Security Council
requested options in the form of a "non-paper" from the Secretary-
General in order to pre-empt a forceful directive such as the one made
by Boutros-Ghali on 29 April (Security Council 1994). There was no
agreement on an operational concept, especially regarding the question
of a cease fire and co-operation of the parties. The proposal from France
was to focus on humanitarian assistance, with the concept of "humanitarian corridors," as tried out in Iraq, with the political aspect left aside.
The U.K., advocating its own peacekeeping doctrine firmly based on

consent, opposed this perspective, claiming that co-operation was essential unless it was to be a full-scale chapter VII-type operation with helicopter gun ships.

The Force Commander's operational concept was a highly mobile force with deterrent capacity, preferably with a chapter VII mandate. The Secretary-General's proposal, presented in the non-paper of 9 May, was built on the Force Commander's recommendation. Although authorized under a chapter VI mandate, Rules of Engagement would be strong, including an extended interpretation of self-defense or "mission defense."[13] For the protection of civilians, the Secretary-General included the possibility of establishing safety zones.

The U.S. had reservations about the proposal which they read as establishing a large peace enforcement mission to restore order and pacify the population, and called for a small force restricted to monitoring "protective zones" on the borders. The U.S. finally agreed to the Secretary-General's concept, but insisted that only the first phase could be implemented without a functioning cease fire. The U.S. conditionality, which dominated the whole process of establishing the expanded operation, was a direct consequence of the new Presidential Decision Directive (PDD 25) on peace operations that had been released the same month. The expansion of UNAMIR was seen as an occasion to apply the new doctrine for the first time. The result was to delay the process further, and the U.S. insistence of phased deployment was criticized by several Security Council members, as well as by Boutros-Ghali and General Dallaire.[14]

The first phase would include about 150 unarmed observers and a battalion from Ghana of 800 men to secure the airport. Authorization for the deployment of the bulk of the force was, at U.S. insistence, made dependent on a further report regarding the co-operation of the parties, the duration of the mandate and the availability of troops.

In a resolution on 17 May, the Security Council adjusted the mandate for UNAMIR and increased its strength to 5,500 troops. Following most of the recommendations of the Secretary-General, UNAMIR would support and provide safe conditions for displaced persons and other groups in Rwanda and would help with the provision of assistance by humanitarian organizations (S/Res/918/1994). UNAMIR would also monitor border crossing points. Authorized under chapter VI of the U.N. Charter, the operation's rules of engagement did not include enforcement action, but permitted a proactive role to protect civilians. The Security Council solved this apparent inconsistency by introducing an expanded definition of "self-defense" in Res.918: the force could be "required to take action in self-defense against those who threatened protected sites and populations and the means of delivery and distribution of humanitarian relief." Until then, similar protection mandates in U.N. operations—notably the "no fly zone" and "safe havens in Bosnia, and the humanitarian zone in Northern Iraq—had been based on chapter VII.

Failure to Activate the U.N. Stand-by Roster

The U.N.'s stand-by roster for peacekeeping, a recently established and at the time highly applauded mechanism for quickly providing troops for peacekeeping missions, was tried in the process of expanding UNAMIR. Although thirty-four countries had committed troops and logistics to the stand-by roster, the only function it had in reality was to get a quicker no from member states. Also, the African countries which had criticized the downsizing of UNAMIR were quick to pledge troops in response to requests from OAU's Secretary-General, but of the nine African countries that by early May had volunteered units, all but one had inadequate equipment (Karhilo, 1995). DPKO officials spent the following months in endless negotiations trying to provide logistics and equipment from Western countries. The combination of excessive lists of demands from the African troop contributing countries and lack of response from the Western countries made the deployment of UNAMIR a slow and difficult task.[15] As of mid-June, UNAMIR had only reached a strength of 354 troops and 124 military observers (i.e., less than 10 percent of the authorized force).

The delays in setting up the expanded UNAMIR force pointed to the long-standing problem of recruiting troops for peacekeeping operations. Normally it takes up to 6 months to set up a peacekeeping force. The stand-by rooster was an improvement by giving the Secretariat a clearer overview of troops and equipment potentially available. Yet stand-by arrangements do not guarantee that member states actually will commit troops.[16]

From Failed Protection to Failed Peace-building?

When the expanded UNAMIR finally was brought up to full strength in August-October, the conditions in Rwanda were totally changed. The resolutions of 17 May (918) and 8 June 1994 (925) authorized UNAMIR to protect civilians and internally displaced persons threatened by genocide, but by mid-July, the RPF controlled practically all Rwandan territory, and both the civil war and the genocide had effectively ended.

The new situation required a different role for U.N. military assistance. While retaining its formal mandate, UNAMIR's functions in practice became closely tied to repatriation of refugees and internally displaced persons (IDPs), and in assisting the Government in reconstructing basic infrastructure and providing general security.[17]

The first task was to receive control from the French forces in the "safe humanitarian zone" in the southwest. There was widespread fear that the French withdrawal would be completed before deployment of the new UNAMIR troops, and that this would create further refugee flows into Zaire. UNAMIR began deploying troops in the zone on 10 August, and on 21 August the full transfer took place. A large refugee outflow was averted, and, in co-operation with UNAMIR, the Rwandese Government gradually established its authority in the area.

UNAMIR's civil police component of ninety observers was originally planned to monitor the local gendarmerie and the police force. However, no police force was left when the civil war ended. The government therefore requested UNAMIR to start a training program for future local police and a gendarmerie. UNAMIR immediately started new training programs and by mid-November had helped train about 100 gendarmes. The strength of the police component was increased to 120, but attempts to get more French-speaking staff proved unsuccessful, and by April 1995 only fifty-eight police observers were deployed (U.N. Doc. S/1995/297 1995).

The refugee camps in Zaire and the IDP camps in the southwest of the country posed serious and immediate security threats for the new government of Rwanda. Militants and the old leadership in the camps were trying to prevent IDPs from returning home, and used the camps as bases for raids. Launching Operation Hope and Operation Retour in December 1994, concerted efforts were made by the humanitarian organizations, UNAMIR and the government to empty the camps. UNAMIR and RPA were to jointly provide security for the returning refugees. The establishment of Open Relief Centers (ORCs), where accommodation, food and protection would be provided, represented an attempt to create safe corridors for returning IDPs and refugees. By January 1995, about half of the remaining 350,000 IDPs had returned home, though a large concentration remained at the Kibeho camp and other smaller ones.

On 18 April, a new offensive was initiated by the government to close the remaining camps. The operation was supposed to take place without force, and with UNAMIR providing safe escort for the IDPs in co-operation with the RPA. However, the closure of the Kibeho camp led to the killing of a very large number of persons, mostly by RPA soldiers. While an Independent International Commission generally exonerated the Rwandese authorities, international condemnation was swift and, to the Rwandese government, stood in stark contrast to the world's lack of commitment during the genocide (U.N. Doc. S/1995/411 1995).

The Kibeho incident further complicated relations between the U.N. and the Rwanda government. Throughout the autumn of 1994, the relationship between UNAMIR and the government had been reported to be "cordial and co-operative" and the Secretary-General expressed confidence regarding the government's efforts in reconciliation and rehabilitation. The discipline of the Rwandan Patriotic Army was recognized, although incidents of intimidation were reported. In March and April 1995, however, reports of mistrust and deliberate attacks on the U.N. force caused concern in UNAMIR as well as in New York. RPA frequently restricted the movement of UNAMIR personnel, and denied it access to certain areas (UN Doc. S/1995/297 1995). Armed robberies, allegedly by uniformed individuals, increased. State-run radio stations began accusing UNAMIR of aiding criminals and having sex with Rwandan women (Reuter News report 1995).

When the Secretary-General in June 1995 outlined the future of UNAMIR (S/1995/457), he stressed the changing nature of the mission. He argued that the force should be transformed into a confidence-building instrument, rather than focusing on traditional peacekeeping tasks. Paradoxically, this initiative came when the relationship between the government and the international community was at its lowest ebb. The Security Council decided on 9 June to reduce the force to 2,330 within three months, and 1,800 within four months (S/Res.997/1995). The new mandate reduced the security and protective functions of UNAMIR, leaving almost exclusively humanitarian functions like logistics support for relief and rehabilitation.

The downsizing was a response to the Rwandese government's discomfort with the force. Kigali asserted that the U.N. force was neither needed, nor wanted, and told the press that the force was "costly, useless and undisciplined" (International Herald Tribune 1995). Several factors contributed to the distrust and lack of cooperation. First, the

Rwandese government was far more in need of development assistance and frustrated over what it regarded as a niggardly international response. More important, the U.N.'s withdrawal of the peacekeeping force, and failure to react when a genocide was unfolding, was not forgotten. There was also a sense that the main security threat—cross-border insurgencies by former government forces—could be countered most efficiently without a U.N. military presence. UNAMIR, in effect, was seen as an international "control mechanism." There were also indications that the government was increasingly interested in bilateral military support, like military advisors and training experts, which required the departure of UNAMIR. Finally, UNAMIR arguably had become a mission without a credible rationale since its humanitarian functions could be better provided by humanitarian agencies that did not antagonize the population to the same extent.

Conclusions

The Rwanda crisis sheds light on the doctrinal shortcomings of international peace operations. The U.N. Secretary-General's concept of peace, introduced in his *An Agenda for Peace, 1992,* would have been applicable in this case. But the concept needs to be further developed. Attempts to define an alternative between the black and white options of peacekeeping, which is mainly a diplomatic tool, and massive enforcement action against an international aggressor as described in Chapter VII of the U.N. Charter, were set back by the experiments in Somalia. The result was a conceptual vacuum. Peace enforcement can mean a range of actions between these two extremes. The escalation of the Rwandan conflict in early April required a decisive intervention of this intermediate kind Somali-type operation, not a peacekeeping force with a few more weapons and "robust" RoE.

The Rwanda crisis also highlighted the need for a rapid and more predictable reaction capacity. The U.N. decision-making structures and laborious system for mobilizing personnel have repeatedly proved inadequate. The gradually expanding stand-by roster is an improvement but not the appropriate answer in crises like that in Rwanda, as was demonstrated in May and June 1994 when an attempt was made to activate the roster.

Based on the experience of spending months requesting troops while a massive genocide was developing, the Secretary-General has called for a "U.N. rapid reaction force for peacekeeping" to be activated on a short notice (U.N. Doc. A/50/60 1995). He has deliberately not recommended a specific model, rather giving an open invitation to member states or interested groups to take initiatives within a wide framework. By mid-1995, some responses were circulating. A Dutch proposal to set up an independent U.N. brigade, individually recruited, and under the direct command of the U.N. was one proposal. The financial costs of establishing a new military structure, combined with poor, or nonexisting, military command and control systems in the U.N., make this proposal a point of departure for discussion, but it is not an answer in the short-term. More realistic is the Danish proposal for a multinational "U.N. Stand-By Force High Readiness Brigade," where national stand-by units would be integrated in a larger multinational brigade. The strength of this proposal is that the different units would have coordinated training programs and some joint maneuvers prior to deployment. Nevertheless, national contributions are subject to the political will of member states in each new situation.

Arguably, Western reluctance to get involved militarily in African conflicts must also be met by an effort to enhance the regional capacity for conflict management on the continent. Although the OAU has improved its capacity by establishing a "Mechanism for Conflict Prevention, Management and Resolution," this cannot deal with larger emergencies. Problems related to lack of resources, training and experience must be addressed by both Western nations and the U.N. In partnership with African actors, there is a need for funding, assets and training programs.

Notes

1. The major part of the force, consisting of two infantry battalions, and two companies, was deployed in the Kigali sector. Their main task was to establish and monitor the Kigali Weapon Secure Area (KWSA), located within a 10 km radius of the Kigali city center. A Belgian infantry battalion was deployed in the southern sector, city center and airport. A Bangladeshi infantry battalion was deployed to the northern part of the KWSA. In addition, a Tunisian company was deployed at the CND building complex where the Rwandese Patriotic Front (RPF) and its battalion were quartered. A Ghanaian company was transferred from the DMZ to provide security for UNAMIR in the weapons secure area. A Ghanaian infantry battalion, thirty-two military observers (UNMOs) and a Force Engineer Company operated within the Demilitarized Zone. Two UNMO teams were deployed in the RPF sector and the Rwandese government sector, respectively. Thirty-two UNMOs were responsible for the monitoring of the southern part of the country. UNOMUR continued to monitor the Uganda-Rwanda border according to its mandate of June 1993.
2. Referred to in a cable from UNAMIR Force Commander to UN/DPKO, 11 January 1994.

3. UNAMIR lacked a political analytic capacity in political affairs, that is, specialized staff (civilian or military) to monitor and analyze the situation.
4. Cf. Prunier 1995, ch. 7 for a discussion of the various theories.
5. The account of the killings is based on African Rights (1994) and Karhilo (1995).
6. The unit consisted of four C-130 aircraft carrying around 280 soldiers and a medical team. The following day the French troops reached battalion strength.
7. As was said at the Secretary-General's Task Force meeting on 12 April: "The deployment of the non-U.N. Belgian unit for the evacuation exercise, collocated in Kigali with a Belgian unit serving under U.N. command in UNAMIR, recalled the U.N./U.S. difficulties in Somalia."
8. Around 15 April, the Permanent Representative of Bangladesh to the U.N. started communicating to DPKO that his Government "under pressure from some governments" was on the brink of announcing withdrawal from UNAMIR. In an internal DPKO letter, concern was expressed about this development. Other observers claim that the undersized Bangladeshi battalion by then was at the point of deserting.
9. Referred to in notes of the meeting of the Secretary-General's Task Force on United Nations Operations, 12 April 1994.
10. This has been pointed out by several critics, including Oxfam 1995.
11. According to an official in the U.S. delegation to the U.N., this position was "to the discomfort of working level people in the delegation" (interview May 1995). On 12 April, the U.S. representative expressed "major doubts about the viability of UNAMIR in the present circumstances; it certainly could not carry out its mandate, and may even be a destabilizing factor." On 13 April the delegation "suggested leaving a small skeletal operation." On 15 April the U.S. position was that in the current circumstances, there was no role that could be performed by a U.N. peacekeeping force; the U.S. opposition to keeping UNAMIR in place was firm (see Adelman and Suhrke 1996).
12. LaRose-Edwards (1995) comments that the claim of the impact of Belgian lobbying "seems a bit of an overstatement."
13. For a discussion on traditional principles of use of force in peacekeeping, see for example Hägglund 1990.
14. An official in the American U.N. delegation later noted that this insistence on conditionality was damaging to the process, and that it contributed to a similar reluctance among potential troop contributors to get involved (Barnett 1995).
15. Also member states which had agreed to provide equipment contributed to delays in deployment. The delivery of 50 APCs from the U.S. was delayed for weeks, the first APC arriving in Rwanda on 30 July. Pentagon officials said this was "normal" delivery time, but there is no doubt that a political decision could have speeded up the process (see Adelman and Suhrke, op.cit.).
16. For a discussion on the short-comings in stand-by arrangements, see Leurdik 1995.
17. With a normal deployment time of up to 6 months for a peacekeeping mission, the mismatch between the mandate given at one stage of a conflict and the changed realities on the ground when the force is deployed is a quite common, but it is seldom as striking as in the case of the expanded UNAMIR force.

12

Dilemmas of Protection:
The Log of the Kigali Battalion

Astri Suhrke

Introduction

The shooting down of President Habyarimana's plane over the Rwandan capital Kigali on 6 April 1994 set off multiple crises. There was the genocide itself—the systematic hunting down and killing of several hundred thousand persons—and a smaller civil war which unfolded alongside it. The events produced something akin to a crisis as well in the U.N. peacekeeping mission in Rwanda. Deployed half a year earlier to help implement the peace agreement, UNAMIR was suddenly in the midst of a situation that was totally different than that for which it had been prepared and equipped. In the annals of U.N. peacekeeping gone awry, the UNAMIR mission was soon to become a classic.

As a general failure of U.N. peacekeeping, the Rwanda case has been well documented. From the perspective of the forces on the ground, however, much has remained unexplored and unknown. What did the transformed situation mean to the U.N. contingent in operational, policy, and moral terms? At the outset of the crisis, ten Belgian blue berets stationed in Kigali were killed by Rwandan soldiers. Rumors of evacuation of the peacekeepers followed. Systematic "cleansing" and killings took place all around them. This chapter tries to present the consequent dilemmas of protection as they appeared to the Belgian battalion in Kigali (KIBAT), which by virtue of its location and strength in UNAMIR as a whole took the brunt of the question of how to respond.

The account is based largely on the battalion logbook which became available recently and constitutes a uniquely valuable source. Because of the historical importance of the events of April 1994, and the enduring controversies which surround them, the Belgian unit most closely involved subsequently sought to present the record as it appeared in their sources. The 2nd Commando battalion, which formed the Kigali Battalion, systematically undertook to reconstruct events from 6 until 19 April 1994, when its last men were withdrawn. After three months of research based on the battalion logbook, records of the Belgian paratrooper unit which flew in to help with the evacuation of expatriates, other notes and numerous interviews, the narrative was completed in September 1995. It is a detailed—at times minute-by-minute—account of the first crucial days as the Belgian unit experienced them. The account, entitled KIBAT: Chronique 06avr-19avr 1994, is written in the format of a military log and was eventually published by the battalion commander, Col. J. Dewez. While presumably reflecting institutional biases, it remains a valuable primary source for an analysis of the peacekeepers' dilemmas during the first days of crisis in Kigali.[1]

At times, the dilemma appeared to be one of saving themselves versus saving others. At other times, the choice was between protecting expatriates or Rwandans. At critical points the choice was made for them. During the few days after 6 April when the battalion remained in Kigali, its resources were tied up by orders to help evacuate expatriates. About the same time, the Belgian government gave priority to saving the Belgian peacekeepers by unilaterally deciding to withdraw the battalion (announced on 12 April). In the U.N., the Security Council readily followed the Belgian example by voting on 21 April to withdraw all but a token number of the entire force. The decision effectively terminated any significant international presence in Rwanda during the next several months, permitting the organizers of the genocide to proceed unhindered.

What happened during the first few days and nights after 6 April has remained of extraordinary concern and controversy, both in Rwanda and outside. Apart from the international tribunal proceedings against those guilty of genocide, the most intense attention abroad was probably sustained in Belgium. The head of the Kigali sector of UNAMIR, the Belgian Colonel Luc Marchal, was charged and subjected to possible court-martial in Brussels in 1996 for failing to protect his men. A legal process was initially initiated by the families of the ten Belgian commandos who were killed, but the court-martial process pre-empted the possibility of a civil trial; it ended in acquittal. Col. Marchal was widely viewed as a scapegoat for more deep-seated anger and bewilderment—anger against the seeming messiness of U.N. peacekeeping operations, and bewilderment in such situations about what constitutes moral and political responsibility and where it resides. In an effort to sort out these issues, a Belgian parliamentary commission of inquiry was established; by the end of 1997, the commission had assembled a prodigious amount of testimony.[2]

General Deployment

The Chronique opens by emphasizing that KIBAT was instructed to operate in a defensive mode. The battalion deployed in Rwanda had previously served in the U.N. force in Somalia. As they prepared for the Rwanda mission, the men were continuously told that this was not like Somalia; this was peacekeeping—not peaceenforcement. Force was to be used only in self-defense, or when specifically authorized by higher levels.

In the kit given each soldier was a one-page summary of the Rules of Engagement (RoE), condensed into six points from the complicated and detailed original rules issued (in English) by the U.N. Department of Peacekeeping Operations (DPKO),[3] purportedly from the complicated and detailed original rules issued (in English). The six points, however, were clear. Force was to be used only in self-defense, or when specifically authorized by higher echelons. If incidents arose, the soldiers were instructed to demonstrate nonaggressive and cooperative behavior: Try first to defuse the situation verbally, the rules proclaimed, then enlist the help of the Rwandan gendarmerie, UNAMIR's designated local partner. If that does not work, do not use force unless authorized. Before firing a single shot from a non-automatic weapon, obtain authorization from the battalion commander. Use of heavier weapons required higher authority: semiautomatic weapons (Mi.5) had to be authorized by the UNAMIR Sector Commander for Kigali, and the use of automatic weapons (Mag) had to be cleared at the very top, by the Force Commander himself. Machine-guns were, in any case, in short supply and the special fittings necessary to mount them on vehicles were unavailable.

While not mentioned in the Chronique, an incident in March of 1994—only a month before the genocide—served more than anything else to bring home the central message that force was not to be used without authorization.[4] At that time, a battalion unit had reacted to a nasty crowd situation by shooting without obtaining prior authorization. Although no one was hurt, the unit involved was sternly reprimanded and sent home early.

When deployed in Kigali, KIBAT was not at the full strength of 800 men originally envisaged; the Belgian army could spare only 450 men at the time. Bangladeshi soldiers made up the rest of the U.N. force in the Kigali sector. The Bangladeshi battalion was not only below strength, but poorly equipped and inexperienced. Named the Rutongo Battalion (RUTBAT) after its place of deployment just outside Kigali, the Bangladeshi contingent included a logistics unit and was assigned UNAMIR's armored vehicles. The eight APCs were mostly immobile; they were Russian APCs taken from Mozambique with no keys to access the engines and no spare parts making maintenance virtually impossible. The Bangladeshis had few other vehicles. As a result, regular patrolling and protection activities fell mainly to the Belgians.

KIBAT became the backbone of the U.N. force in Kigali and, to that extent, of UNAMIR as a whole. The other main unit was a Ghanaian battalion deployed in the demilitarized zone in the North. The total force level authorized by the U.N. was 2,548, including unarmed military observers.

The small, hybrid U.N. force in Kigali was, like the town itself, spread out. The Belgians were scattered in small, isolated cantonments—a fact which was to assume considerable significance during the first week of crisis. KIBAT's small helicopter detachment, consisting of nine persons to look after two machines, was installed in a private house. Six of the eleven members of the medical unit were in another private house, a considerable distance from the remaining five members of the unit who were on another hill. The logistical base was put in the warehouse of a large state-owned coffee trading company, RWANDEX. One of the platoons assigned to the airfield was cantoned at the technical school run by Franciscan monks in the center of town (ATS Don Bosco); the other platoon was near the airport. The staff and most of the rest of KIBAT were divided in groups of fifteen to thirty-six in various private houses. The largest unit of 90 men was put up at the Technical School (ETO). Code-named Beverly Hills, this particular cantonment was later to become infamous during the killings. UNAMIR's HQ was in the modest Amahoro hotel, near the large stadium by the same name which was to become another landmark in the history of April 1994.

The scatter effect was accentuated by the geography of Kigali, a rural-looking capital laid out on numerous hills connected by a maze of roads which connected at strategically placed round-abouts. The traffic circles were central coordinates on the city map and ideal points for controlling movement. UNAMIR's Sector Command for Kigali had numbered them on their maps from N1 to N15.

The main reason for KIBAT's dispersion was lack of central accommodation and the need for quick deployment. As long as UNAMIR was engaged in classic peacekeeping, the decentralized cantonment was hardly more than a nuisance, and perhaps a blessing in disguise by making the blue berets more visible. With a mandate that excluded actions to deter or retaliate, as the Security Council had formulated the authorizing resolution on 5 October 1993, UNAMIR had to rely on the power of presence. When the situation changed radically with renewed civil war and widespread killings of civilians, the cantonment pattern had different implications.

6 April

The night of 6 April started with the usual coca-cola patrols (Goffin, 1995). Accompanied by Rwandan gendarmes, the Belgians were demonstrating U.N. presence by making patrols in Kigali and stopping at roadside cafes to make contact with the locals. On the night of 6 April, they were interrupted by the explosion of the downed jet at 8:30 p.m. While the source of the explosion initially was unknown, UNAMIR was soon informed that the president's plane had gone down and realized that an entirely new scenario was unfolding that night in Kigali. Four Belgian soldiers on their way to the airport to meet a Belgian transport-plane (C-130), which regularly carried supplies for UNAMIR from Nairobi, were the first to notice.

At one airport gate, the Belgian blue berets were stopped by a group of visibly nervous gendarmes. The Presidential Guard—the elite battalion of the Rwandan armed forces (FAR)—had blocked the access at the other gate and opened fire when the two jeeps with the Belgians approached. The Belgians were stopped, their arms confiscated, and they were held at the roadside with a group of civilian Rwandans who were also stopped. The civilian Rwandans were hostile as well. One of the Belgians, who was of Rwandan origin and spoke kinyarwanda, overheard them trying to set the soldiers up against the Belgians. Other Belgians who later tried to enter the airport area were aggressively stopped by government soldiers, but all were unharmed.

Although it was not so clear to any individuals at the time, a pattern emerges from the Chronique soon after 6 April. In the next few days, Belgian soldiers who went into the city to escort expatriates to safe areas or, more rarely, Rwandans, or who were leaving small and exposed cantonment areas for larger assembly points, were stopped at roadblocks run by the Rwandan army and occasionally the gendarmerie. Hostile crowds also gathered at the roadblocks, armed with machetes, stones, and grenades, and when a stone was hurled it could look dangerously like a grenade. The crowds, the Belgians noted, were easily controlled by the FAR—surging forward when the Rwandan soldiers permitted, and moving back when ordered. The outcome varied. KIBAT detachments were sometimes turned back, and sometimes pushed their way through by a combination of bravado and diplomacy. They never shot their way through. As a matter of policy, escorts were normally requested from the gendarmerie, or even friendly elements in FAR, in order to pass roadblocks, especially on out-of-town missions to evacuate expatriates. Escorts were sometimes provided, but mostly not.

The gendarmiere had been designated as UNAMIR's local partner because it supposedly constituted a neutral, national force, unlike the competing forces of the government (FAR) and the rebels (RPA). When the crisis struck, however, the gendarmerie tended to melt away or appeared at roadblocks. At one o'clock in the morning of 7 April, Col. Marchal ordered patrols to resume in order to show a U.N. presence in the city, but insisted on the usual participation by the gendarmerie. The gendarmerie was reluctant, perhaps not so much from a determination to oppose the U.N., but more likely from an unwillingness to take risks in a new situation. As long as UNAMIR followed the rules of joint patrol to the letter, the gendarmes could frustrate activity by the force simply by not responding.

On 7 April at the ETO cantonment (Beverly Hills), Lt. Lemaire is ready to resume patrols but can only get two of the six gendarmes he needs. At the airport, Capt. Vandriessche cannot get anyone from the gendarme post to join patrols, but finally locates one unenthusiastic fellow who consents to go 500 meters towards the city from the airport, but no further. Other patrols do not fare much better. Five days later the pattern is much the same. On 12 April, a unit ordered to evacuate 80 expatriates from the Rwamagana area outside Kigali can find only one single gendarme for escort—he is from Rwamagana and wants a ride home. Along the way, the convoy is stopped by the local gendarmes, but—as an indication of the decentralized nature of the opposition—the Belgians contact the local gendarmerie commander and the roadblock opens.

The source of the hostility towards the Belgian soldiers soon became apparent. At six o'clock in the morning of 7 April, KIBAT commander Dewez reported by radio to all stations that rumors had been planted that the Belgians had shot down the plane and killed the president. In reality, the attack was probably organized by Hutu extremists as a first step to seizing power and eliminating the Tutsi minority as well as the political opposition, whether Hutu or Tutsi.[5] Targeting the latter directly involved UNAMIR as it had from the beginning been assigned to protect opposition members of the present and designated future coalition government. Of these, the mission to protect the Prime Minister, Agathe Uwilingiyimana—generally known among expatriates as Mme Agathe—turned out to be unique because of the obstacles involved as well as the consequences.

Protecting the Prime Minister

In a courageous defiance of the extremists, the Prime Minister announced soon after the shooting down of the plane that she would give a radio address at 5:50 in the morning of 7 April to demonstrate that her government was still in control. The commander of UNAMIR's Kigali Sector, Col. Marchal, ordered an escort. Two KIBAT units were sent to the Radio Rwanda building, and a platoon headed by Lt. Lotin was to escort Mme Agathe from her residence to the radio station a brief distance away. Both buildings were located in the small, so-called presidential quarter of the city which also housed the U.N. compound, the U.S. embassy and up-scale residences. Just before 4 am in the morning of the 7 April, the KIBAT units reported back to headquarters:

> The "presidential quarter" is hermetically sealed off by roadblocks reinforced by armored cars. The gendarmes who accompany the Belgian platoons cannot get them through. The staff officer on duty says he will try to contact liaison officers at FAR to lift the roadblock. In the meantime, the Belgians seek another passage in the maze of roads and find a roadblock on the southern side that seems more penetrable. They argue their way through, and the four jeeps race down Avenue of Paul VI towards Agathe's house. Here they come under fire but get through. Inside the gate of Agathe's house they join the 3 Ghanaian U.N. soldiers (BUYBAT) who had been assigned to guard the Prime Minister. Outside the gates, an armored car of the Presidential Guard is aiming at the U.N. vehicles; the sound of gun fire and exploding grenades are heard from the neighborhood.

> Agathe decides not to proceed with the radio address and asks for more U.N. protection. She waits in vain for two hours, then flees on her own through a bamboo fence in a desperate effort to reach safety at the U.N. compound nearby. She is caught and killed. Having advised the Prime Minister not to leave, the Belgians remain at her house. Ten minutes later a Rwandan army major approaches, asks them to turn over their weapons, and escorts them away. It is about 8:30 a.m.

By late afternoon, the ten Belgians were all dead. The arrest and subsequent killings of the Belgians were a defining event for UNAMIR and, more generally, for the international response towards the swiftly developing genocide. The Belgian government responded by withdrawing KIBAT. This in turn triggered the U.N. decision to abandon the mission, leaving the coup makers to carry out the genocide during the next two and a half months virtually unhindered by the international community. The question whether there were alternative courses of action has naturally been raised. Given the restraints of the situation, could the events on 7 April and the momentous consequences have been avoided?

While the exact developments on the ground remain controversial, there seems to be consensus on the key points described in the Chronique.

> Told by the Rwandan army major to surrender their arms, and hearing hostile murmurs from Rwandan soldiers ("if you don't, you will be killed"), Lt. Lotin radios for instructions. While lightly armed, they have a capacity to resist: each of his men has an automatic rifle (FNC), half of them also have revolvers, and there are two semi-automatics (Minimi) in the vehicles. (Goffin, 45) Battalion commander Col. Dewez tells them not to give up their arms, but the Sector commander, Col. Marchal, intervenes: "It is up to you to decide, you are on the spot."[7] A few minutes later, Lotin radios back. The situation is getting worse; three of his men have been disarmed and are on the ground. At that point Dewez says, "it is best to do what they ask."

Lotin and his men give up their arms and, along with the Ghanaians, are taken away in a minibus. The next and the last that is heard from the Belgians is Lotin's voice on a cellular phone: "We have been disarmed and taken to I don't know where. Mon colonel, je crois qu'on va se faire lyncher." The call is logged in at 9:06 in the morning on 7 April. It takes the Sector Command only a couple of minutes to decide that the men must be at the Rwandan army's Camp Kigali. The Motorola phone belongs to a Togolese U.N. military observer at the camp. What to do now?

Col. Marchal informs the Force Headquarters (9:08) and then tries to contact the Chief of Staff of FAR by telephone. Not getting through, he tries to contact the military observer with the Motorola. There is no answer. At 9:45, he is still trying to make contact by telephone, pointedly affirming that the Rules of Engagement remain unchanged. At 10:30 he announces on the battalion-wide radio band that Lotin apparently has been killed. The efforts on the telephone intensify; part of the problem is that UNAMIR has mainly worked with the gendarmerie and does not have close liaison with the army. There is a scramble for telephone numbers. The liaison officer of the gendarmerie is asked to help, but by 1 p.m., the Sector Command has still not succeeded in establishing telephonic contact with FAR. Later in the afternoon, the U.N. military observer and the Ghanaians taken from Agathe's house are released from Camp Kigali and inform the force that the Belgians have been killed at the camp.

Alternatives to the telephone were hardly considered before being shelved. At the very moment when the Belgian soldiers were being slaughtered by the Rwandan Presidential Guard, the U.N. Force Commander, General Romeo Dallaire, was on his way to a meeting of the Crisis Committee called by the Rwandan coup-leaders.[8] The meeting was held at the École Superieure Militaire, located 200 meters from Camp Kigali. In the car with him were a Rwandan and a Belgian officer. All were unarmed. As Dallaire later recalls events, when passing Camp Kigali he saw bodies on the ground inside the compound; they appeared to be Europeans. Making inquiries, he was told that they were not Belgians, and that he could not enter to investigate due to chaotic conditions in the compound where the soldiers were rebelling. Dallaire proceeded to the meeting at the Crisis Committee, which was headed by the well-known Hutu extremist, Col. Bagosora. Dallaire again asked for permission to go to Camp Kigali, but was rebuffed. It was too dangerous because of the chaos in the camp, Bagosora said.

In the evening, Dallaire went to the morgue to identify the bodies. They were in such a state that it took some time to sort out how many there were—ten? eleven? As recorded in a later TV-interview, Dallaire at this point in the recollection covers his face, visibly upset.

In the slow-moving drama that morning (the last Belgian was not killed until the afternoon) a rescue mission clearly could have arrived in time. The decision not to send one was taken, in effect, by default. In the detailed records of the Chronique for that day, there is no mention of a discussion to launch a rescue mission, either at the Sector Commander level or in the communications with the Force HQ. UNAMIR continued to operate in the diplomatic mode, a mode that was determined—according to Dallaire—by the balance of forces. A counterattack would have been "suicidal," he later said in a Belgian TV interview. With a weak and dispersed force, he was extremely vulnerable to retaliation. "Had Marchal at that moment asked me [to counterattack], I would have said no," Dallaire concluded, adding; "It would not have succeeded" (Les oubliés de Kigali).

Dallaire sent a similar assessment to U.N. headquarters in New York the next day. In a cable dated April 8, he outlined the grim situation in Kigali. KIBAT is "separated into confined camps which are isolated by fighting, firing and roadblocks, and the battalion's elements are focused on self defense. In addition, these elements are separated from their logistical support, i.e., water and food sources (except emergency rations), and no resupply of power, washing water, gasoline, sanitation, and most importantly, given the threat of the present situation, their supporting field hospital.... This is a defensive survival exercise for UNAMIR."[9]

It was also clear that Rwandan forces were determined to prevent UNAMIR from carrying out its monitoring and protection role during the very first phase of the crisis. They used force to block U.N. efforts to protect the Prime Minister and other political personalities in the presidential quarter. They aggressively cordoned off the airport and the adjacent site of the plane crash. When the KIBAT helicopter unit tried to make reconnaissance flights over the city early on the morning of 7 April, Presidential Guard soldiers fired at them; the mission was aborted. But it is also striking that during the entire rest of the Chronique, only one other incident is recorded in which Rwandans fire directly at the Belgian blue berets. That incident also occurred on 7 April and involved a gendarme and municipal police. The gendarme fired at two Belgian soldiers who had set up a machine-gun in front of their cantonment (one of the medical units, code named Vitamine). The Belgians fired back and the gendarme took off. Nobody was hurt.

One explanation is that Rwandan forces did not need to use force to make the Belgians comply. The U.N. force quietly absorbed the deliberate killing of ten of its members; abandoned rather than used force when its monitoring and escort functions were frustrated; and was soon ordered to prepare withdrawing from Rwanda altogether. Quite possibly, and perhaps likely, the killings of the Belgians were a deliberate provocation to that end. As earlier intelligence information picked up by UNAMIR had indicated and later events seemed to confirm, those who planned the coup and the genocide evidently wanted to get the U.N. out of Rwanda so as to achieve their objectives without foreign witnesses and interference (Adelman and Suhrke, 1996).

In a telling entry on 8 April, the Chronique notes that the KIBAT Commander calls FAR for escorts to collect the bodies of the ten soldiers. The army is ready to cooperate. In the early afternoon they leave the morgue. Accompanied by two light armored cars and a Rwandan army captain, the convoy of the dead—protected by their killers—moved swiftly through all roadblocks.

Protecting Expatriates

As part of the survival exercise, small and isolated UNAMIR units were regrouped in a few assembly areas soon after the crisis struck. Regrouping was designed to reduce their vulnerability to direct attack from Rwandan units or mobs, and from indirect fire from the war which FAR and RPA units fought in a moving front-line through the town. The supply situation was serious as well. Some cantonments had only one to two days of drinking water, and most units had only two to three days of fuel. A Tunisian company on guard duty had not eaten for two days when it staggered into the Amahoro stadium. However, as a result of the regrouping exercise, UNAMIR spent much of its scarce resources reassembling for self-protection.

As for protecting others, first priority was given to U.N. civilian personnel and expatriates. In particular, the decision taken by the French and Belgian governments soon after 6 April to send in a military force to evacuate their nationals effectively set the agenda for UNAMIR as well. The French force landed in Kigali in the early morning of the 9 April, and the advance party of the Belgian "Operation Silver Back" arrived the following night. A division of labor was agreed upon: the Belgian paratroopers would guard the airport, the French would secure the access areas, and UNAMIR would provide escort to the evacuees. During the next few days, most of the remaining energy of UNAMIR was used to escort expatriates for evacuation.

Numerous individual requests for expatriate protection are littered throughout the Chronique in this period: the Italians call on the morning of 9 April—there is a hostile crowd at the gate; the Americans want protection at the American Club, and so on. Also embassies ask for protection, although the Belgian ambassador (Johan Swinnen) not only refrained from "nationalizing" the Belgian battalion, but apparently refused offers by Col. Marchal for U.N. protection and was among the last to order evacuation of nationals.[10] Some embassies evacuated overland, covering the short distance to the border in convoys on their own. Still, during the crucial first days when the genocide gathered momentum, KIBAT was heavily preoccupied with expatriate evacuation.

It is not clear who decided on the division of labor among the military units during the evacuation, or why UNAMIR soldiers were involved in the operation at all. The U.N. Secretariat and the Security Council had on 7–8 April explored the idea of giving UNAMIR the responsibility for evacuation and considered strengthening the force for that purpose (Adelman and Suhrke, 1996). The initiative was overtaken by the French decision to launch a national evacuation force, followed by similar moves by other governments who had sizable expatriate communities in Rwanda (Belgium and Italy).

UNAMIR did have a general mandate to "contribute to the security of Kigali," but nothing in its mandate suggested that the force had a particular responsibility to protect expatriates, including businessmen, missionaries and embassy personnel of various countries. However, the force defined its mission to include "protection during evacuation of UNAMIR, U.N. personnel, diplomatic personnel and expatriates"(Chronique, 1), and contingency plans for this purpose had been prepared at UNAMIR headquarters (Dewez, written communication 5 December 1997).

Protecting Rwandans

While events seemed chaotic during the first few days of the crisis, a few things were clear to the U.N. soldiers at the outset. The Chronique records distress calls received from Rwandans from early 7 April and onwards, as well as reports from Belgian soldiers of systematic cleansing and killings in the various cantonment areas. General Dallaire used the terms "a very well planned, programmed, deliberate and conducted campaign of terror" when describing the violence in a report to U.N. Headquarters on 8 April (outgoing code cable, 8 April 1994). Belgian soldiers later described the scenes around them: "There were two kinds of cries: the shouts of those doing the killing and mutilation, and the cries of those being mutilated" (Reuters, Brussels, 13 April 1994).

It was also clear that UNAMIR had various mandates to protect Rwandan civilians. Protection of key personalities in the Rwandan political process was integral to the task of implementing the Arusha peace accords and was undertaken from the beginning of the mission. The Force Commander interpreted the general mandate issued by the Security Council to include other specific protection functions. As drafted by Dallaire in the Rules of Engagement, this included use of force to defend "persons under [U.N.] protection against direct attack" (#11(a)); and the use of armed force against armed persons "when other lives are in mortal danger" (#13-k) (i.e., other than self defense). Most importantly, a compelling but highly unusual clause stated that, with or without the support of local authorities, "UNAMIR will take the necessary action to prevent any crime against humanity" (# 17).[11]

UNAMIR did protect Rwandan civilians during the violence in April. Some were political VIPs belonging to the opposition parties who previously had been under U.N. guard. Others sought safety in the de facto "sanctuaries" established and partly guarded by the blue berets at various places in Kigali—at the Amahoro stadium, the King Faisal Hospital, and the Hotel Mille Collines. These sanctuaries saved perhaps 15–20,000 lives. But it is also clear that the U.N. force had little capacity, and mostly assigned lowest priority, to protect ordinary Rwandan civilians.

On the evening of 7 April, the Kigali Sector Commander, Col. Marchal, announced the policy regarding the protection of Rwandans: all Rwandan refugees who had sought safety at the UNAMIR cantonments throughout town had to be out by next morning at 0600 hours. In the despair and chaos that followed, different responses emerged.

At the Franciscan school, the fathers protested and KIBAT battalion commander, Col. Dewez effectively countermands Marchal's order: "The fathers are masters in their own house," he tells the Belgian unit stationed at the school. From the medical post "Vitamine," however, some thirty Rwandans leave during the night, hoping to take cover of the darkness. From the post "Pegasus," some twenty refugees leave with the Belgian blue berets, and all reach safety at the Meridian Hotel. At the technical school ETO ("Beverly Hills"), refugees have arrived in the school compound throughout the day and night, mostly ordinary Rwandan civilians but also priests and expatriates. The officer in charge, Lt. Lemaire, calls the sector headquarters: Is he to protect only the clergy who have gathered there or also the ordinary Rwandan refugees? The operations officers on the band, Capt. Choffray, interprets the rules in his own way: "Protect all."

At times, the competing demands for protection involved horrible dilemmas, as the Belgian soldiers at the ETO acutely came to realize. The government technical school had soon become the largest single U.N. sanctuary outside the stadium. Already by 8 April, around 2,000 refugees had gathered for protection. About 150 were European. Many of the Rwandans were badly wounded by machete cuts. There was hardly any food or water, and sanitary conditions were appalling. Yet, there was no attack on the cantonment, and new refugees were allowed in. Lt. Lemaire even went personally out to look for a Rwandan priest and a child reported to be in danger. By 9 April, however, the precariously balanced situation was upset by the order to regroup.

Just before midday on 9 April, Col. Dewez tells all KIBAT stations that UNAMIR may be evacuated. "Pack your bags and get ready to evacuate in the early afternoon." Marchal says that the Security Council will decide on the evacuation issue in two hours. Lt. Lemaire asks who will give protection to the Rwandan refugees in his compound when his unit leaves. Nobody answers. The next morning, Lemaire is ordered to provide escort to the airport for the 150 expatriates in the compound, but he objects. Taking out men for escort duty will jeopardize the security of the Rwandans under his protection. "We have 2000 refugees here". A hostile crowd is gathering outside the compound. In the afternoon he contacts the Medicins Sans Frontières. Can they do anything for the refugees? The answer is negative.

Lemaire achieved some short-term victories. His objections to provide escort for expatriates were sustained. Instead, French soldiers came to ETO to collect the evacuees. The French troops were initially prepared to take only the French and the Italians among the expatriates gathered at the ETO. Lemaire objected again—they should take all the Europeans and the Rwandan clergy. The French grudgingly agreed; it meant a second trip.

The next day Lemaire is again told to take a jeep, three trucks and a platoon to pick up expatriates from Gitarama and Kabgay. The Rwandan Army will provide security to the convoy. Lemaire again questions the order: diversion of a platoon will reduce security and endanger the 2,000 refugees who are crammed into the compound. His battalion commander is categorical: the Gitarama mission has priority. The mission is later canceled for other reasons.

The unit at "Beverly Hills" was the last one to be regrouped. Early in the morning on 11 April Col. Dewez told Lemaire to stand by for evacuation to the Meridian hotel. Shortly after noon, Lemaire requested permission to go—there were no expatriates left in the compound, and the southern route used by the French evacuation troops to reach the airport was still open. Dewez asked the Sector Commander: Could Lemaire move out, and—the log pointedly noted—leave 2,000 refugees at "Beverly Hills"? Marchal approved. At 13:45 Lemaire and his men departed, leaving behind them two broken-down vehicles and desperate refugees facing a hostile crowd. As the Rwandans left the compound to seek safety elsewhere, most were attacked and killed.

The story of the ETO is partly an account of the limits of personal heroism. There was a certain risk associated with protecting Rwandans, as the events at Agathe's house showed. Small units of Belgian U.N.

soldiers were likewise harassed when trying to protect other Rwandan VIPs or bring out Rwandan refugees. For instance, a convoy heading for the airport had hidden Rwandans among the expatriates, but was stopped by Rwandan soldiers. The incident led Col. Marchal to issue a new rule: UNAMIR was no longer to take Rwandan refugees in the evacuation convoys as it might endanger the transport (Chronique, 44).

But the record also shows the considerable power exerted by a few Belgian soldiers and a U.N. flag. It is thus equally a record of possibilities unexplored and potentials unused. Apart from the Amahoro Stadium, which was shelled, and took several indirect hits, none of the cantonments were attacked directly. What happened at ETO was only the clearest and most dramatic illustration of a general rule: the Rwandans were safe as long as they were gathered under U.N. protection, and as long as the blue berets were there, showing the flag. It was when the U.N. forces left the site, that the killings started.

Protection of opposition VIPs involved different trade-offs. The pattern of the protection mission for Mme Agathe was not repeated, however. In other missions, only the Rwandans were targeted and killed; occasionally UNAMIR succeeded in bringing some to safety.

The pattern played itself out in and near the house of Félicien Ngango, the leader of the opposition party PSD. Since late March he had been given U.N. guards. When the plane was downed, orders went out to strengthen the protection of VIPs. The new situation placed heavy demands on KIBAT. Six groups had been set aside for escort service; the attempt to get Agathe to Radio Rwanda tied up half of them the first night.

On the evening of 6 April, three men from Lt. Lemaire's unit were on duty at Ngango's house. Ngango himself was away, but his wife and family were home. The house was in the Kimihurura area where many ministers and political personalities of the opposition lived. Reports of systematic "cleansing" in the area by the Presidential Guard and gendarmes started coming in to UNAMIR's Kigali Sector Command early in the morning of 7 April. The source was the unit of Lt. Lotin, code named "Viking," which was cantoned in a house on the same street as the Ngango household. At 6:30 a.m. Col Marchal ordered a firm response: KIBAT must urgently deploy a complete platoon in the "Viking" cantonment.

> Battalion commander Dewez interprets this as an order to "intervene in the quarter," and sets about finding men. Almost half the "Viking" group of 25 are at Agathe's houses, but the airfield group of 50 at the Franciscan Order's Technical

School is only five blocks away. Together they form a group and set out, but are stopped at the roadblocks by Rwandan soldiers and the gendarmes. The Belgians turn back. The Sector Command discusses calling in the Bangladeshi who have some APCs. But the Bangladeshi have reacted to the crisis by first looking after their own safety; they have regrouped inside the gates at the Amahoro stadium and will not open the gates, let alone come out.

It is still a few minutes past 6:30 in the morning when efforts to mobilize a larger force are overtaken by events at the Ngango house. About 20 Rwandan soldiers are at the house and tell the three Belgians on guard duty to get out. The Rwandans are excited and threatening, the Belgians report. Concerned about the security of his men, Lt. Lemaire asks Dewez if he can evacuate them to the "Viking" post just up the street He gets permission, but is told to bring the Ngango family out as well.

Four men from "Viking" set out towards the Ngango house only 30 meters down the street, a fifth is in the garden with a heavy machine gun to cover them. Half-way down the street the group is stopped by a roadblock. The Rwandan soldiers will permit the Belgians to collect their comrades at the Ngango house, but the Rwandans must stay. Two men from the "Viking" unit are let through. Returning, the blue berets are stopped and their vehicle searched. Back at the Ngango house, the soldiers close in on their victims. The entire family is killed.

The pattern continued during the day of the 7th, the KIBAT log shows. At 11:38 in the morning of 7 April, the Sector Commander informed the net that systematic search and cleansing continues in the Kimihurura district where the Lotin-group is cantoned, but that the soldiers attack only Rwandans. Expatriates and U.N. personnel apparently had nothing to fear.

Some Rwandan political leaders were saved. The most famous rescue operation involved Faustin Twagiramungu, Prime Minister-designate under the Arusha Accords and considered a key person in efforts to save the peace agreement. Jumping over the wall of his house, he was rescued by one of UNAMIR's few armored vehicles, and later evacuated to Nairobi and Belgium (Africa Rights 1995, 194).

Mandate, Force, and Options

Members of the Kigali Battalion were later to say that they did not have the mandate to protect either themselves or civilians. When stepping off the plane as they returned to Belgium, some angrily threw their berets on the tarmac and tore the U.N. insignia from their uniforms.

It is beyond dispute that the force was established in a diplomatic mode and remained so despite the radically changed situation. It also seems clear that this did not so much reflect limitations of the mandate, but of force capabilities. With RoEs which permitted necessary action to prevent crimes against humanity, but no capacity to force even a roadblock, the unit had limited options. Nevertheless, within these constraints there were choices to be made between protecting expatriates and Rwandans, and in the risks taken to protect others as against protecting self. The logbook of the Kigali battalion records these excruciating dilemmas of protection.

In some cases, the dilemmas were false. As the ETO experience shows, a few Belgian soldiers did provide significant protection to some two thousand Rwandan refugees with little evident risk to themselves. Expatriates were escorted to the airport by the French forces flown in for the evacuation operation; there was little justification for tying up scarce U.N. resources for that purpose. Had this "power of presence" been more fully recognized, and had policy as a result been changed to extend greater protection to those most at risk, quite possibly more lives could have been saved even within the resource restraints of the situation.

Yet, given the restraints of the situation, even under the best of circumstances the most UNAMIR could hope for was to buy time. Without reinforcements of men, material, or supply—including drinking water and food at places like ETO—protection of civilians could last for only a short while and buy time for a political or military solution. The only genuine way of easing the dilemmas of protection, therefore, required introducing a larger and differently constituted force. At the time, General Dallaire claimed that with a force of some 5,000 men, he could effectively have staved off the genocide. His claim was subsequently endorsed by an international panel of military experts assembled by the Carnegie Commission on Preventing Deadly Conflict to examine the lessons of peacekeeping in Rwanda. Assessing various scenarios in the conflict situation, the panel agreed that a better equipped and more unified force of some 5,000 men, had they been introduced during the critical, early phase of the crisis, "could have significantly altered the outcome" (Scott, 1996).

Notes

1. The KIBAT Chronique is chronologically organized according to events and the movements of the various battalion units. Here, references to the Chronique mostly make use of these coordinates rather than page numbers.
2. The Commission d'enquête parlementaire concernant les événements du Rwanda was originally established under the President of the Belgian Senate. Reports of

the proceedings (Compte rendu analytique) were published regularly as documents of the Belgian Senate. In 1997, it was published in two volumes.

3. The RoE had been drafted by General Dallaire and their formal status by April 1994 was still that of a draft.

4. I am indebted to Allison des Forges for this information (17 September 1997).

5. For an authoritative analysis of the various interpretations, see Reyntjens (1995). Reyntjens accepts the version which makes Hutu-extremist responsible.

6. Agathe first tried to scale the wall of her neighbor's garden, the DCM at the U.S. Embassy, but it was too high. The U.S. residence might not have been safe at any rate. FAR soldiers later entered the house and, not finding whoever they were looking for, shot up the refrigerator.

7. Col. Marchal denies saying this; Col. Dewez says that the radio operator maintains that it was said, and it was, therefore, entered into the record. Letters from Dewez to author, 5 December 1997, and from Marchal, 12 December 1997.

8. This account is based on interviews with General Dallaire and a documentary covering the events of April 6–7, Les oublies de Kigali, produced for the Belgian French-language television corporation (RTBF) by Frederic François, who used among other sources a two-hour taped, background interview with General Dallaire.

9. "An update on the current situation in Rwanda and military aspects of the mission," 8 April 1994. Outgoing code cable. This is a joint cable with separate sections from the SRSG Booh-Booh and Dallaire, addressed to Annan/Goulding, U.N., New York.

10. The record as presented to the Belgian commission of inquiry is unclear on this point. Ambassador Swinnen says Col. Marchal offered the embassy UNAMIR protection, but Swinnen refused because he feared that in the prevailing animosity against the Belgian soldiers this would attract hostility. Swinnen later accepted protection when informed that he was on a death list. (For further elaboration on the death list, cf. Prunier 1995, 222, n. 22.) Marchal disputes the offer of protection. Senat de Belgique, 1–86, COM-3, Compte rendu analytique des auditions, 20 June 1997.

11. The first RoE draft is dated October 1993 and appears as "Force Commander Directive No:01." Apart from minor editing changes, it is identical with a later version which appears as "Operational Directive No.02: Rules of Engagement(Interim)," 19 November 1993, also issued by the Force Commander. The role of UN/DPKO in the drafting process is unclear.

13

In Search of a New Cease-Fire (April–July 1994)

Jacques Castonguay

Introduction

A lot has been said and written about the cease-fire signed on 29 March 1991, at N'sele, in Zaïre, but not much concerning the negotiations that took place in Rwanda to secure another cease-fire after 6 April 1994. The study of the latter is useful in understanding the role of the U.N. as the massacres unfolded, as well as throwing some light on the attitude of the parties with respect of the massacres, the war itself, and the huge problem of the refugees.

The Goals of the "New Government"

In the aftermath of the murder of President Juvénal Habyarimana, on 6 April, and the murder of Prime Minister, Agathe Uwilingiyimana, the following day, several prominent and so-called Rwandese Hutu Power politicians tried to address the issue of the political vacuum. They met several times. On 8 April, Mr. Théodore Sindikubwabo, de facto head of the new government of Rwanda from 9 April to July 1994, went on national radio on behalf of the new ruling group and, quoting the Constitution approved on 10 June 1991, proclaimed himself the new President. During this same address, he announced the formation of an interim Government composed of the politicians from MRND and CND and their allies in other parties.

The UNAMIR Force Commander, Major-General Roméo Dallaire, visited the "new President." Their first meeting took place on 9 April at the Hôtel des Diplomates in Kigali. Based on the notes taken by a UNAMIR officer present at the meeting, there seemed to be three issues of critical importance to Sindikubwabo. He wanted the U.N. to fully endorse the new government, to help him establish contact with the RPF, and, finally, to help his government secure as soon as possible a cease-fire agreement. To support his plea for U.N. endorsement, Sindikubwabo claimed that his government was not in violation of the Arusha Peace Accords and, more importantly, it was of the utmost urgency that the institutional void be filled as quickly as possible.[1] General Dallaire listened cautiously and abstained from discussing the political issue.

The RPF also reacted rapidly to the announcement of the new Government. Like the position adopted at that time by the U.N. and many nongovernmental organizations, it did not recognize it. Moreover, it stated that it was contrary to the Arusha Accords and even racist (Verschave1994, 115). In November 1994, Paul LaRose-Edwards, wrote:

> The RPF meanwhile were angry that U.N. Special Representative Booh-Booh had made a failed attempt to set up a "transitional national authority" in Kigali. He had deemed it "national" despite the fact it had no RPF or Tutsi representation. (1994, 65)

> The RPF argued that it was pointless to negotiate with Sindikubwabo's government.

The legitimacy of the new government was also at the forefront of Major-General Dallaire's concerns. On more than one occasion, he wondered whether he had not simply witnessed a coup d'état by Hutu extremists. During his first meeting with the Senior Staff Officers from the Rwandese Government Forces (RGF) and the Gendarmerie in the early morning hours after Habyarimana's plane had been shot down, he witnessed how quickly all of the leaders present rejected, without any discussion, the idea of having Prime Minister Uwilingiyimana, who was then still alive, acting as the interim head of the Republic. According to his diary, the Force Commander gave the coup d'état theory more thought on 13 April. In the face of the RPF military advance, three days later the interim Government left Kigali to set up its headquarters in Gitarama, a fact that did not simplify the situation. Only the Minister of Defense stayed in the capital.

Without giving any formal recognition to the new Government, Major-General Dallaire was willing to act as an intermediary between the parties in an attempt to secure a cease-fire. However, in the days following the death of Habyarimana and the beginning of the massacres, he was mostly involved in the negotiation of truces, locally, in the demilitarized zone (DMZ) and in Kigali, in order to permit the extrication of his troops and the evacuation of U.N. people and several thousands of expatriates. Between 8 April and 11 April, UNAMIR contributed to the evacuation of 190 U.N. civilians. Having successfully negotiated two truces, the first one of forty-eight hours the second one of twenty-four hours, the Force Commander also rendered possible Operation Silver Back during which at least 3,000 expatriates were evacuated by approximately 1100 Belgian troops and 598 French troops.

The Preconditions to a Cease-Fire

The rapid advance made by the RPF and the need to re-establish control in Kigali and elsewhere soon reinforced the conviction of both the interim Government and the RGF that they had to secure a cease-fire as soon as possible. On 12 April, the same day the RPF troops from the North East linked-up with the RPF battalion quartered in the Conseil national de Développement building, located in Kigali, ten Colonels and Lieutenants-Colonels from the RGF handed a letter to Major-General Dallaire in which they asked him, on behalf of the commander of the RGF, to mediate a cease-fire between the two opposing forces.[2] This petition came as no surprise to the Force Commander because the Rwandese Minister of Defense, after the President, had made a similar request two days earlier. The rapid advance made by the RPF probably explains why the interim Government was so anxious to secure a cease-fire.

The problem, of course, was that the RPF did not recognize the Government and refused to negotiate directly with its members. For the Government, the answer was to try to convince the RPF to negotiate with the RGF and the Gendarmerie, with Major-General Dallaire acting as mediator. Such a task remained a very difficult one. The RPF, which was winning the war but had not yet reached its initial objectives, would have to be convinced to lay down its weapons and sign a cease-fire agreement when previous cease-fires in the past had been repeatedly undermined.

After several preliminary meetings, both parties finally agreed to meet on 14 April. Much to the disappointment of the U.N. and the RGF, the RPF did not appear at the meeting. The following day, however, the Force Commander, after having met again with both parties separately, succeeded in bringing them together at Hôtel Meridien. The Special Representative of the Secretary-General (SRSG) attended the meeting and when it was over, he was jubilant and issued a communiqué stating that "the first meeting between the two opposing military forces had occurred and that both sides agreed to discuss the conditions needed prior to establishing a cease-fire." What the communiqué did not say, however, is that the conditions required before the signing of any cease-fire agreement by the parties were incompatible. For the RGF, the cease-fire was a prerequisite to stop the massacres; for the RPF, the cessation of the massacres was a prerequisite to the signing of any cease-fire agreement.

Major I. Diagne, the UNAMIR officer responsible for taking notes during the subject meeting, summed up the RPF conditions as follows:

1. Stop the massacres carried out throughout the country;
2. Establish means of verification to ascertain whether the massacres were stopped;
   a. Installation of phone lines in the Conseil national de Développement;
   b. Patrols consisting of members from the RPF, RGF and UNAMIR;
   c. Journalists be granted free access to the Conseil national de Développement.
3. The Garde présidentielle would be dissolved :
   a. Military personnel responsible for war crimes would be charged accordingly;
   b. Public condemnation of the Garde présidentielle.[3]

The official RGF response to the RPF conditions were made known by Brigadier-General Marcel Gatsinzi on April 17. The letter stated that the RGF was prepared to stop the massacres being carried out by both sides on condition that the fighting stop first. No mention was made of the RPF condition concerning the Garde présidentielle.

Major-General Dallaire explained why the RPF was so firm in wanting the massacres to be stopped, as a preconditon to the cease-fire :

The Government forces wanted the cease-fire because they did not seem to be holding very well. They were weak militarily. The RPF did not want it because they were under the impression that a cease-fire would be a significant limiting factor in their endeavor to stop the massacres. If the cease-fire had happened, then we, the UN, would have been required to monitor the cease-fire lines and establish a series of rules for the cease-fire to be held: where, for example, the troops, ammunitions, weapons and that kind of stuff would be. The RPF naturally realized that these measures would stop their offensive, limit them in what they could do with their forces, also stop the Government troops where they were (giving them the advantage to regroup potentially), and, more importantly, compel the U.N. to force the RGF to go behind the lines to stop the militias, the rogue battalions and units of the Gendarmerie involved in the massacres. If we were going to do that, the RPF was fully convinced that the cease-fire will only reinforce those doing the killings and accelerate the massacres.

The Government side projected, for its part, that all that it needed to stop the massacres was a cease-fire, by which its troops will be released from combat duties against the FPR.[4]

The Security Council Adjusts the Mandate of UNAMIR

Following the signing of the Arusha Peace Agreement on 4 August, 1993, the Security Council resolved that the United Nations should, at the request of the Rwandese Government and the RPF, make its full contribution to the implementation of this agreement. Accordingly the Secretary-General recommended the establishment of a United Nations Assistance Mission to Rwanda (UNAMIR) with the mandate of "contributing to the establishment and maintenance of a climate conducive to the secure installation and subsequent operation of the transitional Government" (Security Council, S/26488, 24 September 1993).

After the incident in which President Habyarimana lost his life, the Secretary-General discussed with the Security Council possible ways of dealing with the new situation. He proposed three alternatives: a) an immediate and massive reinforcement of UNAMIR and a change in its mandate to allow it to coerce opposing forces into a cease-fire; b) a small group, headed by the Force Commander, to act as a mediator between the two parties to bring them to agree on a cease-fire; and, finally, c) the withdrawal of UNAMIR. (He did not propose maintaining the force at existing strength or using it to protect civilians.) On 21 April, the Security Council decided to reduce UNAMIR and adjust its mandate so that it would act as an intermediary between the parties to secure a cease-fire agreement and assist in the resumption of humanitarian relief operations to the extent feasible [Security Council, S/RES/912 (1994), 21 April 1994].

In doing so, the Security Council simply recognized or approved what UNAMIR was doing. Its strength had been reduced by the decision of the Belgian government to pull out its contingent and other countries were reconsidering their participation. Its Force Commander had been deeply involved in the negotiations of a cease-fire agreement and his peacekeepers that had not bunkered down when the fighting started were employed in humanitarian relief operations.

However, Major-General Dallaire, more concerned with the massacres and sufferings of thousands of civilians than the negotiations of a cease-fire agreement that appeared more and more distant, urged the Secretary-General to re-examine and adjust once more the mandate of his mission. This was done on 17 May, with the addition of the following responsibilities:

- To contribute to the security and protection of displaced persons, refugees and civilians at risk in Rwanda, including through the establishment and maintenance, where feasible, of secure humanitarian areas;
- To provide security and support for the distribution of relief supplies and humanitarian relief operations. (Cf. Security Council, S/RES/918 (1994), 17 May 1994)

Drafts of Cease-Fire Agreements

In spite of the setbacks, and his preoccupation with the massacres and the humanitarian relief, the Force Commander ordered the preparation of a plan to help implement an eventual cease-fire, should the parties finally come to an agreement. The final draft of the subject document was forwarded for comments to the Rwandese Government Forces and the Rwandese Patriotic Front on 18 April 1994. The document was deemed stillborn, however, when the RPF ignored it. Nevertheless the SRSG, remaining apparently firm in his belief that a cease-fire could be reached, and tried, for his part, to break the impasse by visiting Arusha where he met, on 24 and 25 April, with the Secretary General of the OAU and the Tanzanian Prime Minister. The meeting once more proved to be a disappointment. And to make things worse, the interim Government, now located in Gitarama, decided to propose its own set of pre-conditions. The list was made known on 28 April. It consisted of the following:

1. return of both military forces to their respective positions held on April 6th 1994;
2. stop the massacres;
3. return of all displaced persons to their homes;
4. formation of the Broad Based Transitional Government.
   (Meeting, Force Commander and Chief of Staff RGF, 28 April 1994)

Although he felt that these pre-conditions would not be agreed to by the RPF, Major-General Dallaire decided to go to Byumba to meet with

General Kagamé and inform him of their existence. General Kagamé's response was immediate and scathing. It can be summed up as follows:

> You (Major-General Dallaire) are the representative of the United Nations. You know who is doing what to whom. The RGF have participated in the massacres. Our forces had not yet moved when the massacres started. The Interahamwes are also taking part in the massacres. Who is controlling them? The idea of returning to the positions we held on 6 April 94 is a French idea. It was brought forward at a meeting organized by the French Ambassador in Kampala. I had a representative at the meeting.

> The U.N. wants to send an intervention force in Rwanda for humanitarian reasons. Its too late. Those who had to die have already been killed. Those who will now be protected are the perpetrators of the crimes. They now hold the reigns of power. If a U.N. force is deployed in Rwanda we will fight it.

> The U.N. must be blamed for not giving UNAMIR the appropriate mandate at the right time. Those who say stop the war and we will stop the massacres are using blackmail. The Special Representative is no longer welcomed to Rwanda. If he stays, we will stop all collaboration with the UN. (Meeting, Force Commander and Major-General P. Kagame, Byumba, 20 April 1994)

The meeting of the Force Commander with the commander of the RPF lasted about two hours. At the end it seemed clear to the U.N. officers that the chances for a cease-fire in the short term were nil. Still Boutros-Ghali decided to send two envoys to Rwanda, Mr. Iqbal Riza, Assistant Secretary-General for Peace-Keeping Operations, and Major-General J. Maurice Baril, the Military Advisor of the Secretary-General. Together, they held meetings on 23 and 24 May with the RGF and the interim Government in Kigali and Gitarama, in order to: (1) move the warring parties towards a cease-fire, (2) ascertain from them their views on and intentions towards the implementation of resolution 918 (1994); and (3) review with UNAMIR the modalities of the operations outlined in the Secretary-General report of May 13, 1994 (Security Council, S/1994/640, 31 May 1994).

On 31 May, the Secretary-General reported that the special mission had been able to obtain the agreement of the two parties to initiate the talks for the establishment of a cease-fire, as called for by resolution 918 (1994), and has found, "on the basis of the evidence that had emerged...that there can be little doubt that the killings in Rwanda constitute genocide.[5]

A draft document was prepared by the Special Mission and UNAMIR and sent to both parties on May 27. This working paper was, however, a source of considerable debate and writing of numerous amendments. It suggested, especially the French version, that the cessation of hostilities and even the signing of the cease-fire agreement, will take place before the massacres could end. On page 1 of the French proposal the following sentence appears :

> Le cessez-le-feu doit être précédé d'une trève, c'est-à-dire de l'arrêt des hostilités qui doit entrer en vigueur à minuit...

The equivalent of this sentence appears also in the English version. On page 2, paragraph 6 reads as follows:

> Immédiatement après la signature de l'accord, tous les actes de violence contre les civils seront arrêtés.Accord de cessez-le-feu entre les commandants militaires de la Force gouvernementale rwandaise et du Front patriotique rwandais. (Ébauche d'une entente de cessez-le-feu, 27 May 1994)[6]

The English text in this case reads as follows:

> Immediately upon the signature of this agreement, all violence against civilians will be halted.

Nevertheless, the meetings between the two groups, chaired by Brigadier-General Henry Anyidoho, the Deputy Commander of the Mission, started three days later at the UNAMIR headquarters located in Hôtel Amahoro. Two weeks later, 13 June, Anyidoho had this to say concerning the negotiations:

> I must say that the massacres are the primary reason from the very beginning of our discussions.... The massacres are slowing down, if not stopping altogether the process by which we hope to end the hostilities.[7]

The next day, representatives of the RPF headed by Andrew Rwigmana[8] had this to say:

> At the time of the signing of the agreement all violence against civilians will have ceased. In this connection the Garde présidentielle, all the militias, especially the Interahamwe and the self-defense groups were to be dismantled. Measures to carry out this dismantlement and the cessation of violence should occur before the new cease-fire can be signed. There will be no inflammatory radio broadcasts.[9]

In Search of a Demonstration of Good Faith

As the negotiations were under way, UNAMIR also tried to get the Government and the RGF to demonstrate their good faith. For the Force Commander it was essential that they demonstrate they could really influence the Interahamwe and the rogue units and have them stop the killings. However, they were never able to do it. They claimed they did not have enough troops to control the militias.

UNAMIR had Tutsi and RPF people and sympathizers behind the Government lines in Hôtel des Mille Collines, in Kigali, and also Hutu and Government people in the Amahoro Stadium, the Méridien Hotel and the King Faisal Hospital.[10]

A certain number of these internally displaced persons, among those who had taken refuge in Hôtel des Mille Collines, had expressed the desire to be transferred, when possible, behind the RPF lines. One of the means the Mission used to see if the RGF and the Gendarmerie could control the population, the Interahamwe and the rogue elements of the Government Army, and agree to do it, was the transfer of this group from the hotel. According to the Force Commander, everybody agreed to it: General Bizimungu, the Chief of Staff, the RGF and the RPF. "If things go smoothly," Dallaire later said, "that will be a sign of good will and permit us to attack the negotiations of a cease-fire. Unfortunately things did not go well. It ended up in a fiasco. Members of my garrison, that was responsible for the transfers, plus people they were protecting were beaten, others injured and my troops man-handled."[11]

The subsequent transfers of internally displaced persons in Kigali involved persons from both sides and were consequently more successful. Nevertheless, the explanations or excuses given by the RGF after the fiasco of Hôtel des Mille Collines did not convince the RPF of the good faith of their opponents and the impasse remained.

RPF Unilaterally Declared a Cease-Fire

The cease-fire finally took place, not with the signing of a formal agreement between the warring parties, but with a RPF unilateral declaration on 18 July 1994 ending the war. The United Nations, shocked by the ensuing large-scale violence in Rwanda, which has resulted in the death of approximately 800,000 men, women and children, the displacement of a significant portion of the population and an unprecedented increase of refugees in the neighboring countries,[12] spared no efforts to move the RPF and the RGF towards a cease-fire. Nevertheless, the attitude of the RPF towards this initiative remained negative from the beginning to the end. The RGF gave the appearance, at least during the first days of the war, that they were positively disposed towards a cease-fire. Later on, however, during the campaign, when they were forced to retreat, their interest in signing decreased considerably and finally vanished. The proposal made by the interim Government on 28 April is illustrative. Even if they kept saying "we want to stop the massacres, we want to sign a cease-fire agreement," they did not want it.

The opinion of Major-General Dallaire on this matter is worth quoting:

> Later on, during the war, I came to the conclusion, as the RGF continued to withdraw, withdraw, withdraw, taking with them large volumes of population (which they didn't have to do), that a strategic decision was taken by the interim Government to say: "right, we...will pull out and we will take as many people we can with us in order to regroup, reconstitute ourselves, and some day in the future come back." I truly believe that is what they had in mind.[13]

Notes

1. Meeting, President T. Sindikubwabo and Major-General R. A. Dallaire, 9 April 1994.
2. Communiqué from the Commander of the Rwandese government Forces, Kigali, 12 April 1994.
3. Meeting between SRSG, Force Commander, Mr, Kane, and representatives from both the RGF and RPF, 15 April 94, Hôtel Meridien, 1550 hrs.
4. Interview, Major-General R. A. Dallaire by J. Castonguay, 1 Nov 1994.
5. The United Nations and the Situation in Rwanda, Reference Paper, April 1995, Department of Public Information, 12.
6. Cease-fire agreement between the military commanders of the Rwandese Government Forces and the Rwandese Patriotic Army (proposed draft 27 May 1994).
7. Proceedings taken from the cease-fire meeting between the RPF and the RGF, held on 13 June 1994, 2.
8. A. Rwigmana is today "Chef du Cabinet" of the Minister of Defence. The author of the present paper had the opportunity to discuss this topic with him in Kigali, on 8 June 1995.
9. Translation of notes taken in French during a meeting held on June 14.
10. Approximately 25,000 persons took refuge in these public establishments during the war.
11. Interview, Major-General R. A. Dallaire by J. Castonguay, 14 November 1995.
12. Security Council, S/RES/912 (1994), 21 April 1994.
13. Interview, Major-General R. A. Dallaire by J. Castonguay, 14 November 1995.

14

Opération Turquoise:
A Humanitarian Escape from
a Political Dead End

Gérard Prunier

The Historical Background to Operation Turquoise

As the Rwandese genocide rolled on and as the world watched in passive horror, Paris decided to undertake a humanitarian intervention. A U.N. Resolution enabled Paris to intervene in Rwanda under a United Nations political umbrella, even though, for all practical purposes, France was acting alone. Why was this decision controversial and why did it cause, together with admiration and support, considerable malaise in international public opinion? In order to understand this question, we have to go back a bit in history.

Rwanda, together with its sister kingdom of Burundi, both parts of former Deutsche Ostafrika, had been given as mandate territories to Belgium by the League of Nations in 1919. After independence was formalized in 1962, the position of the former colonial power in these countries started to wane. The French President Valéry Giscard d'Estaing, personally fascinated by African affairs, pursued an aggressive policy in the former Belgian territories, as exemplified by the French military intervention in Shaba in 1978. In both Rwanda and Burundi, Paris adopted a position of benign but sustained interest. The first military cooperation treaty between Paris and Kigali was signed in 1974. President Habyarimana was received for the first time at the Elysée Palace in 1975. From that moment on, Rwanda became one of the so-called *pays du champ.*

As far as French-speaking Africa is concerned the distinction between *pays du champ* ("field countries") and the others is absolutely essential. The *pays du champ* are, in the French view of things, our own, part of the family so to speak, and the whole relationship between Paris and these states is special. Economic aid does not go through the normal Quai d'Orsay (Foreign Affairs Ministry) channels but through the *Ministère de la Coopération*. This is not a simple administrative distinction. Countries that deal with the *Ministère de la Coopération* have access to the special low-interest loans from the *Caisse Centrale de Coopération*, and military assistance is channeled through the Ministry of Cooperation. Most French foreign aid goes to *pays du champ*. A small country like Djibouti, for example, will get eight or ten times the amount of aid per capita as does its giant Ethiopian neighbor. Also, in political and cultural terms, the *pays du champ* retain close links with Paris. As Rwanda and Burundi became "absorbed" in this system, they acquired the rank of junior members in the francophone family.

The question of the francophone family may be hard to understand for non-French persons. The whole concept of a French Commonwealth is linked to the vision that the French have of their language. It is a special case among the world's cultures with the exception of the Arabic-speaking countries where the language, being God's own in the Muslim world view, is a sacred thing. Although secular, the French view of their language is almost as strong. In modern times, language has become a political marker as well. After 1918, France knew that it was not a major power any longer, but French had at least remained the world language for diplomacy and culture. When English took this place after 1945, it seemed to be the last blow. Moreover, as the United States was perceived as diabolical heir to the *perfide Albion,* a new concept was born: the English-speaking adversary—the Anglo-Saxons. In this scheme of things, the cunning Anglo-Saxons are seen to be everywhere, always conspiring with each other to harm French interests world-wide. Everything is a field of battle, whether commerce, military presence, diplomacy, and—more than anything else—language.[1]

The basic, unforgivable, and original sin of the Rwandese Patriotic Front when it invaded Rwanda on 1 October 1990 was that it came from a former British colony and that its leadership was English speaking and English educated. The invasion and the automatic politico-cultural connotations it caused in France in 1990 could be so directly linked to what several commentators described in terms of "the Fashoda syndrome," French reactions in Rwanda to the historical Franco-British rivalry. The reference was to a minor confrontation in Southern Sudan in 1898 at a miserable cluster of huts dignified with the name of "town," which resulted in the famous Fashoda incident that almost caused a Franco-British war.

In terms of both the level of violence and the pattern of foreign intervention, the Rwanda conflict can be seen as one of the first major post-Cold War conflicts. It is archaic in that its "native" element of violence stems from pre-colonial and colonial identity problems, while the French involvement arises from pre-Cold War European relationships.

The French Army in Rwanda

The decision to militarily support the Rwandese government in the face of the RPF attack was taken very early in October 1990, directly by President François Mitterrand himself. This was not exceptional; in all previous French military interventions in Africa the decision to commit French troops had always been the President's alone. The paratroopers—initially 150 but later increased to nearly 700—were sent from their base in the Central African Republic. Their mandate was very clear through the period of French military presence in Rwanda (October 1990 to December 1993): do everything to support the Rwandese Army in its struggle against the RPF short of actual fighting. The noncombat profile was intended to avoiding attracting attention and criticism, and in this it succeeded. A number of specialists were also brought in (helicopter mechanics, transmission experts, intelligence officers, staff officers, military administrators, artillery officers). They tremendously increased the level of expertise of the Rwandese Army.

The most vexing issue was undoubtedly that of training. After the genocide started, the French were accused in many quarters of "having trained the killer militias," as the newspaper *Liberation* wrote on 12 June 1994. Quite possibly, this occurred, but it is extremely doubtful that it was done deliberately. French instructors who were part of the expeditionary force did not carefully screen the men who were brought into the Military Training Program they were running. In part, this was due to the rapid expansion of the Rwandese Army—from slightly over 5,000 men at the beginning of the war in late 1990 to over 15,000 in 1992—which caused much confusion, corruption, and enormous administrative complications.

In general, the French response in 1990–93 was to "help our boys" against what seemed an obvious Anglo-Saxon plot: the invasion by

Ugandan-sponsored English-speaking guerillas. As it became clear that the Habyarimana forces could not win, France came to support the Arusha peace process. For lack of anything better, it seemed like an opportunity to incorporate the RPF—despite its alien nature—into "our" political system in Black Africa.

The genocide in 1994 took Paris completely by surprise. Given its past association with the Rwandese regime and obvious responsibility in the situation, the French Government decided to keep a low profile, which was initially possible. In April 1994 the French public was generally unaware that a conflict had been taking place in Rwanda for the last four years, and that France had been seriously involved. Media pressure started to build up slowly but steadily around the third week of April, building and went into a crescendo during May.

While the government was trying to maintain a facade of unconcern, behind the scenes there was considerable agitation to try to "save our men." Weapons and ammunition were being delivered secretly into the month of May, despite the official U.N. embargo (*Observatoire Permanent de la Coopération Française: Rapport 1995*, 157–59). On another level, confidential letters linked with some of the Secret Service circles tried to influence the French press by putting forward bizarre geopolitical arguments for justifying French presence through accusations against Uganda and the US.[2]

Deciding and Preparing for Intervention

By late May, a media offensive, NGO lobbying, and the public opinion climate had clearly put Rwanda back on the political agenda in Paris. One way or another, the government had to respond. What finally tipped the balance was a clarion call from Africa. Nelson Mandela's statement at the OAU summit on 13 June that "we must in action assert our will" to address the Rwandese situation was read as yet another challenge to the French role in Africa emanating from the Anglo-Saxon world.

Given the divided nature of French politics in the summer of 1994, the decision to launch what became know as *Opération Turquoise* was taken in a climate of mutual watchfulness. The 1993 legislative elections had brought to power a conservative majority, but Socialist President Mitterrand's term continued until 1995. Moreover, the conservatives were split between the followers of Prime Minister Edouard Balladur and the followers of RPR leader Jacques Chirac. As a result, no one involved in policymaking represented abstractly "France," but either Balladur, Chirac, or Mitterrand.

The President's Special Counsellor for African Affairs, Bruno Delaye, was at the OAU summit in Tunis. He was flanked by Prime Minister Balladur's Diplomatic Counsellor Bernard de Montferrand and by the Prime Minister's Africa-man, Philippe Baudillon. They watched each other as much as they watched their African partners. When they returned from Tunis, Mitterrand was quick to act: at the 14 June Cabinet meeting, he announced that France would intervene. He also asked the Ministers to keep the decision secret for a few days to avoid a media blitz. In the prevailing climate of political contest, this was too much to ask from the conservative cabinet. Foreign Minister Alain Juppé, a Chirac man, found the intervention idea too good to be left to the socialist President. The very next afternoon he talked about it on French TV, and the following day he wrote in a major newspaper:

> We have a real duty to intervene in Rwanda. The time to passively watch the massacre is over, we must take the initiative.... France is ready with its main European and African partners to prepare an intervention on the ground to put an end to the massacres and to protect the populations threatened with extermination.... France will live up to its responsibilities. (*Liberation* 16 June 1994)

From a moral point of view, it was a curious pronouncement. Having spent the last forty days silently watching its former pupils and proteges commit a massive genocide, the government discovered it had a conscience just as media pressure became irresistible and when South Africa threatened to intervene unilaterally.

The Ministry of Defense was to implement the decision, and was told to do so with a speed that the Army itself had grave doubts about. In fact, it was because the Ministry judged a hasty return to Rwanda dangerous that it asked this author to participate in the Crisis Unit which was preparing the intervention. The request came on 17 June and was unexpected.

My association with the Rwandese crisis had at first been only peripheral and mostly scholarly. It stemmed from a total failure of judgment on my part about the RPF's October invasion of Rwanda. During my long stay in Uganda in 1986, I met on many occasions young Banyarwanda soldiers who had fought with Museveni's guerrilla army and who did not hide their intention to one day fight their way back into their country of origin one day. I did not take them seriously and thought such an invasion would be impossible. October 1990 therefore came as a bit of a shock, and I started to seriously research the situation. Later, the small civilian massacres which had punctuated the war years led to my growing involvement with Human Rights NGOs concerned about the situation. My visits to Rwanda, whether with the RPF guerillas (1992) or on the government side (1993), had not met with much approval from the French authorities. Moreover, as a member of the International Secretariat of the Socialist Party, I had fairly easy access to various offices, and expressed some strongly-voiced criticisms of France's role in Rwanda. This did not exactly make me any more popular with the President's Office, the Secret Service *Direction Générale des Services Extérieurs* (DGSE) or with the Army. Thus, the call to serve in the Ministry of Defense Crisis Unit on Rwanda came as a surprise.

But the reason soon became apparent. Minister of Defense François Léotard was a Balladur-man, and the Prime Minister felt that the whole Rwanda operation was directed against him. Balladur is a typical financial technocrat, a pure product of the French bourgeoisie, with very little "feel" for the raw rough-and-tumble of African politics. He hoped to "multilateralize" France's relations with Africa, that is, to weaken the ties and make them less of a family melodrama. His preferred tools were the European Union and the World Bank. To him and his men in the cabinet, the Rwanda venture was dangerous. If it failed, the Prime Minister was bound to be blamed; if it worked, the initiators—Mitterrand and Chirac's man Juppé—would get the credit. In this political minefield, the Defense Ministry felt it should act with great prudence. To include an academic heretic in the Rwandese Crisis team could be a good idea as he might draw attention to some unforeseen difficulties.

This is what I immediately did. The first draft of the intervention plan had French troops entering Rwanda through Gisenyi. I considered this very inappropriate for a number of reasons:

1. Gisenyi was the heart of Hutu extremist land, the "blessed region" of the late President Habyarimana. French troops would be welcomed with open arms by the perpetrators of the genocide, a most embarrassing situation;
2. Geographically, the French entry point would be uncomfortably close to the fighting. The RPF was at the time laying siege to Ruhengeri, a few kilometers to the east, and we could count on our Interim Government "friends" to do everything in their power to push us eastward in the hope of engineering clashes between the French expeditionary forces and the RPF guerillas;
3. The official purpose of the mission was humanitarian, but there was precious little to do at that level in Gisenyi and Ruhengeri prefectures. As a local Hutu trader was later to tell a French journalist: "We never had many

Tutsi here, and we killed them all at the beginning without much of a fuss" (Aubenas 1994). The French forces would find no Tutsi to be paraded in front of TV cameras to justify the intervention.

Another question quickly came to mind. Was the humanitarian operation just a giant deceit? Were not the French troops in reality sent to bolster the Interim Government failing forces, just as the RPF suspected? In that case, I wanted no part of it. I decided that the question of troop entry point would be my litmus test: if the Army General Staff accepted a change of plans, it meant it was sincere about the purpose of the operation. If not, there was a hidden agenda. With the help of a number of the Defense Ministry permanent staff I fought for one of two solutions: a) fly our men to Bujumbura and enter Rwanda from the south; or b) land in Goma with heavy transports, transfer the loads on lighter twin-engine Transall planes, fly down to Bukavu and enter through Cyangugu. The first solution seemed preferable since going through Burundi might have a stabilizing effect on that country as well. But I had seriously underestimated the capacity of the RPF to use the mostly Tutsi UPRONA opposition party in Burundi as a relay for its positions. Demonstrations were organized in Bujumbura against French intervention, and FRODEBU Foreign Minister Jean-Marie Ngendahayo, whatever his personal views, had to refuse Paris the right of transit.

The alternate plan of going through Bukavu and Cyangugu was opposed by the military on financial grounds. Unloading in Goma, reloading, and flying to Bukavu would be costly.[3] The question was whether this opposition was genuine or whether it hid something else. After talking with General Mercier, who was in charge of the overall planning for the operation, I felt that he, at least, had no hidden agenda. But I was not sure about some of the other officers who were grumbling in the aisles about "breaking the back of the RPF."[4] The question was finally solved on Monday 20 June when Minister François Léotard made the decision to adopt the Cyangugu plan. My impression was that the decisive argument had been that at Nyarushishi Camp near Cyangugu we would find a large stock of surviving Tutsi who could be displayed to the TV cameras. A humanitarian intervention in a place where there was nobody left to save would indeed have been embarrassing.

As the intervention juggernaut gained momentum, everybody wanted to climb on board. President Mitterrand was irritated at seeing his idea hijacked by nearly everybody. To regain the initiative from Conservative Foreign Minister Alain Juppé, Mitterand made a speech while opening a Conference at UNESCO which had nothing to do with Rwanda.

Given the gravity of the situation, he proclaimed the urgency was extreme: "it was a matter not of days but of hours." This was on 18 June, after two months of brutal slaughter that had elicited no reaction from the Elysee.[5]

French professions to stop a genocide that had almost run its course were not taken at face value by many. The RPF had already vociferously condemned the intervention as a ploy by the French to save the "Interim Government" from eventual defeat. There were other, more unexpected rebuttals. Faustin Twagiramungu, Prime Minister designate according to the Arusha Agreement, also condemned the intervention from Montreal where he was on a visit. The OAU Secretary-General, Salim A. Salim, transmitted the protest of the OAU. In Kigali, UNAMIR General Roméo Dallaire referred to "the initiative launched by the French...which they describe as a humanitarian task" with a distinct lack of enthusiasm.[6] At the same time, all sorts of bad "revelations" were coming out about French participation in the training of men who were now part of the *Interahamwe* militias. Amnesty International had released a communique asking the French government to clarify its past involvement with the Rwandese Death Squads. A few days earlier, Colonel Dominique Bon, Military Attache at the French Embassy in Kinshasa, had practically admitted that there were still weapons deliveries to the FAR through Goma, a most embarrassing fact if the airport was now to be used for a humanitarian intervention (*La Lettre du Continent* 1994).

In this deleterious atmosphere, Prime Minister Balladur's enthusiasm for intervention waned even further. In a Parliamentary speech on 21 June he listed five preconditions for sending in the troops:

1. Get a U.N. Mandate.
2. Set a clear time limit to the intervention and stick to it.
3. No in-depth penetration of Rwanda; the operation should be carried from just outside the borders.
4. The operation should be purely humanitarian and have no exclusively military component.
5. Allied troops should be involved; France should not operate alone.

Condition three, of course, made no practical sense and could not be adhered to. As for condition five, Paris went ahead without being able to substantially fulfill it. The three others were met.

A problem which had not been much discussed in the planning of Colonel Dominique was how the Army would carry out a humanitarian operation in a warring country while managing to avoid armed confrontation. The French government had virtually no contact with the party most likely to shoot at them; that is, the RPF. There was in French official thinking a psychological resistance to the RPF, a mental stumbling-block against even proximity to the dreaded Anglo-Saxon enemy. When hearing on 20 June that the option of entering Rwanda through Cyangugu had prevailed, I took it upon myself to phone Jacques Bihozagara, the RPF European Representative, at his Brussels office. I learned that he had not been contacted by Paris. Through the Defense Minister's Cabinet, I urged the Foreign Ministry to make contact. When I called Bihozagara back to learn about the result of my efforts, I thought he would choke on the phone: he had received a telefax asking him to come to Paris to meet Mrs Boisvineau, Under-Director for Eastern Africa at the *Direction des Affaires Africaines et Malgaches* (DAM) of the Quai d'Orsay. We both knew that, although she was a very nice lady of good will, she had no political capacity for making decisions. Bihozagara was clearly angered:

> This is ridiculous. This is an insult. I have been in Europe for three years and I must have seen her six times at least. What good can I expect from seeing her once more? I won't come.

I got back on the phone and tried again to get some kind of a reasonable response from the Ministry of Foreign Affairs. By the next day, I had the pleasant surprise of learning through the press that the Foreign Minister was "in constant contact with the RPF." I called Jacques Bihozagara in Brussels to find him even more exasperated than the previous day. He had received a second telefax asking him to come to Paris to meet Secretary of State for Humanitarian Affairs Lucette Michaux-Chevry and DAM Director Rochereau de la Sablière. Bihozagara exclaimed:

> We are not asking for any bloody humanitarian aid, this is a political problem for God's sake! And as for Mr. de la Sablière, he can't decide about one thing. Either I see the Minister or else I won't bother to lose my time.

I relayed this answer to the Defense Minister's Cabinet where a certain irritation had become obvious. "God dammit! It is *our boys* going in there. And if they get their asses shot up because of those idiots at Foreign Affairs, there will be hell to pay," a Defense Ministry official told me. I do not know what kind of message was relayed between the Boulevard Saint Germain and the Quai d'Orsay, but the next morning of 22 June, the RPF representatives were in Paris and were received by Alain Juppé personally.

Managing later in the day to get the two RPF envoys inside the Defense Ministry was akin to carrying out a major military raid. Great precautions had to be taken so that they would not meet the "Hawks" on their way to General Mercier's office. Once there, we had two other problems. First of all the RPF was extremely surprised, to say the least, by the firepower that the French expeditionary forces wanted to take along on a humanitarian mission. They also grew very suspicious of the fact that the complete operational plans of the future *Opération Turquoise* were then written on only two sheets of paper. The RPF envoys were politely angry: how could we pretend that we were going to send 2,500 men all the way to Central Africa with masses of heavy equipment and with plans for the operation covering only two sheets of paper? Where were the hidden documents? We had to persuade them that there were none and that, yes, this was a bit flimsy, but that we would soon have more detailed plans.

As for the firepower, General Mercier explained, it was only contingency planning. He had just come back from Bosnia where he had learned a lesson: When he had no artillery, Serbian snipers would regularly shoot at his men. As soon as he received some artillery and tanks and used them—even just a bit—Serbian troops immediately became less aggressive. But in the Rwanda case, he emphasized, the heavy artillery, the armored vehicles and the aircraft would stay put in Zaire unless there was fighting involving his men. And to avoid such clashes, General Mercier continued, would the RPF host a French liaison officer at their Mulindi headquarters inside Rwanda?

There was a noticeable difference of attitude between the two RPF envoys, Jacques Bihozagara—who had grown up in Burundi as a refugee and spoke perfect French—and Théogène Rudasingwa, "the Ugandan." Jacques was by far the most accommodating of the two, and the worst suspicions of some of the officers in the Ministry of Defense were confirmed. "That one, the one who speaks English only, he is the sneaky one. He is Museveni's man, spying on the other," a Staff Officer remarked to me.

I asked Rudasingwa, who is by nature quite reserved, to at least try to smile. I was not very successful. But I could see that the earnest and open presentation of our positions by General Mercier had made an impact. The RPF refused the idea of a liaison officer, "a spy," as they put it, and their attitude in Paris remained defiant. But Jacques

Bihozagara and his "sneaky" colleague were not so sure any more that the French were entering Rwanda to fight them.

Reading into Prime Minister Balladur's mind, had it been possible, would have reassured them immediately. Balladur had been pushed into something he did not particularly want to do, and he was going to do it as quickly and cheaply as possible. On the same day that the RPF representatives met with General Mercier in Paris, the U.N. Security Council adopted Resolution 929 which authorized the French intervention under Chapter Seven of the U.N. Charter. On the 23rd at dawn the first elements of *Opération Turquoise* started to land in Goma.

The Intervention up to the Fall of Kigali

The surprise of the RPF delegates in Paris when they had learned about the amount of firepower *Turquoise* was planning to pack was understandable. For a maximum strength of 2,500 men, there were to be over one hundred armored vehicles, a battery of heavy 120 mm Marine mortars, two light Gazelle and eight heavy Super Puma helicopters plus air cover provided by four Jaguar fighter-bombers, four Mirage F1CT ground attack planes and four Mirage F1CR for reconnaissance. To deploy this armada, the Ministry had chartered one Airbus, one Boeing 747 and two Antonov An-124s to supplement a squadron of six French Air Force Lockheed C-130s and nine Transalls. The whole force was placed under the overall command of General Jean-Claude Lafourcade in Goma, and his subordinate General Raymond Germanos operating from Bukavu/Cyangugu. Still, the meeting in Paris had helped to mollify the RPF, and Colonel Frank Mugambage declared that he "was not opposed to a humanitarian mission by French troops" (SWB/Radio Muhabura 1994). This in turn softened the OAU, which passed a resolution in support of the French effort. Foreign Minister Alain Juppé declared that the French initiative was already reaping very substantial diplomatic benefits, though this was exaggerated optimism. Italy, the only European country which had briefly seemed ready to join Paris in its endeavor quickly backed out after the inexperienced Prime Minister Silvio Berlusconi was briefed by Foreign Ministry Officials. Apart from France's Black Africa clients, there were some vague supportive noises including a brief offer of Tunisian troops, rumors of forty Egyptian "observers", and the announcement of a Mauritanian Medical Team. In fact, Senegal was the only country which actually sent troops.

On the ground, the welcome given to the French troops by the *Interahamwe* and the local authorities of the former regime was enthusiastic. In Gisenyi, where the French only made a quick incursion, the Hutu extremist radio station RTLMC had been broadcasting for several days calling for "you Hutu girls to wash yourselves and put on a good dress to welcome our French allies. The Tutsi girls are all dead, so you have your chance." Elsewhere, enormous French flags were displayed, including on FAR military vehicles. This was particularly unfortunate because Tutsi, seeing the French flag, would come out of hiding only to be immediately killed by FAR soldiers or the militiamen. For French troops, it was a rude awakening as they began to realize the relationship France had entertained with the Rwandese authorities. As one French soldier said: "I am fed up with being cheered along by murderers" (de Saint-Exupéry 1994).

Efforts were made to justify the operation by "saving" as many Tutsi as possible. Nyarushishi camp near Cyangugu with 8,000 refugees was a good start. Apart from that, only small and scattered groups were found. On 27 June, French forces had gone up to Kibuye and eastward as far as Gikongoro. When Defense Minister Léotard and Secretary of State for Humanitarian Affairs Lucette Michaux-Chevry went to Goma two days later to inspect the situation, the limited life-saving effect of the operation was becoming clear. The only people *Opération Turquoise* could really help were those who were in the least danger (i.e., the ones in large concentrations such as Nyarushishi or Bissosero). For the many who were lost in the bush, nothing much could be done. The point was demonstrated by the situation around Kibuye, where the authorities were still killing at a fairly fast rate. Apart from Kibuye town itself and its immediate surroundings, the French forces were powerless to do anything. And not only were they few in numbers. The operation had been designed more for fighting than for providing humanitarian relief, as evidenced by the abundance of armored cars but lack of lorries to transport people. When finding small pockets of hunted Tutsi, the French would be unable to rescue them on the spot, but often said they would be back the next day with a lorry. By the next morning, the Tutsi were usually dead. Similarly, the French forces often stood by in medium size towns while the killing went on unabated in the hills a few kilometers away.

Meanwhile, the war between FAR units and the RPF continued. A group of moderate FAR officers led by General Leonidas Rutasira and Colonel Marcel Gatsinzi had organized themselves in Gikongoro inside the newly created French "safe humanitarian zone," from where they called for national reconciliation. Their initiative failed. Other FAR-officers hardly responded to their call. The French did not want to get embroiled in political affairs and gave no help. In some cases, French officers who sympathized with the former Rwandese regime even dissuaded moderate FAR officers from trying to get in touch with the RPF (Observatoire Permanent de la Coopération Française, *Rapport* 1995, 159). On the French side there were still extremist officers in the expeditionary force, despite General Mercier's careful weeding out. They were no doubt just itching for an occasion to get at the RPF and help their old friends.

In these circumstances, nobody knew what might happen in case of a clash between *Turquoise* troops and the RPF. The "Interim Government" that had taken power after Habyarimana's death was clearly trying to provoke a confrontation. In Cyangugu, for instance, the *Préfet* Emmanuel Bagambiki kept repeating that "the French Army must go into the RPF area and free our civilian population taken as hostages by the rebels," thus asking French troops to reconquer guerrilla-held territory (*Liberation* 25–26 June 1994).

In the absence of any agreed mechanism to defuse a crisis, I kept pushing for the creation of a telephone hotline that would enable the RPF General Staff to immediately get in touch with the Ministry of Defense in Paris and with General Lafourcade. The idea was not popular either with the Parisian diehard supporters of Hutu power or with some RPF elements who believed we would use the satellite telephone to electronically eavesdrop on them. I finally got a technician to explain to them that if we wanted to eavesdrop, we could easily do so from Goma anyway. We finally got the green light on 2 July and flew to Entebbe to enter the RPF zone and meet the RPF leadership. The telephone idea thus opened for political contact as well, something which had been sorely lacking since the beginning of the operation.

Earlier, on 23 June, the former French ambassador to Kigali, Jean-Michel Marlaud, and the former ambassador to Kampala, Yannick Gérard, had been received at RPF headquarters in Mulindi by Colonel Kanyarengwe. Marlaud was considered a diehard Habyarimana supporter and Ambassador Gérard was not really known to the RPF, which may be why General Kagame refused to see them. The choice of Kanyarengwe to meet them instead was a sign that the Front did not want to deal seriously with them. Now, our delegation met with part of the Political Bureau of the Front at Mulindi. We then drove down to

Kigali to find out that the city had finally fallen to the RPF. General Kagame was quite open to the telephone idea (we were carrying an Immarsat with us, complete with its regulation generator). We agreed to continue the discussion the next day in Mulindi, but things remained very fragile. As we sat down to talk the next day, General Kagame received a dispatch telling him of military preparations carried out in Gikongoro by the French former DGSE-man, now serving with *Turquoise* under the name of Colonel Thibaut.[7] "Colonel Thibaut" had publicly said that in case of a battle with RPF forces, no quarters would be given. General Kagame, who understands French but does not know it well, did not know the expression "pas de quartier." It was translated for him by a bilingual ADC: "Sir, it means they will kill the wounded." Kagame furrowed his brow, turned towards us and said calmly: "This is a hostile statement, isn't it?" It took a great deal of talking to persuade the RPF leader that at times French colonels could say foolish things without instructions from Paris. The misunderstanding was eventually worked out and Kagame promised not to attack French troops. To reciprocate, President Mitterrand and Admiral Lanxade declared on 6 July "the RPF is not our foe." Having taken Kigali probably helped the Front achieve this belated semi-recognition.

The Fall of the Northwest and the Refugee Explosion

As the "Interim Government" disintegrated, thousands of civilians were streaming out of Kigali *Prefecture*, moving on foot either towards the Northwest which was seen as the last government bunker, or towards the South where the French-proclaimed "safe humanitarian zone" seemed to promise physical protection against the RPF. Many of the people now moving had fled several times before during the RPF offensives in 1992 and 1993. For them, the RPF generated enormous fear and visions of devil-like fighters engaged in massive killings everywhere. But the fear was such that even some Tutsi were running away from their "saviours." Within a few days of the fall of Kigali, about one and a half million refugees had moved to the Ruhengeri and Gisenyi prefectures, and about the same numbers to the French zone.

The enormous crowd of at least 300,000 people was a mixture of many: dispirited *Interahamwe* who did not even bother any more to kill the few Tutsi who walked alongside them, civil servants and their families riding in a motley fleet of commandeered ministry vehicles, ordinary peasants fleeing from their own blind terror, exhausted FAR troops trying to keep a minimum of discipline, abandoned children with swollen feet, middle class Kigali businessmen in their overloaded cars, whole orphanages, priests, nuns, and madmen. If many were fleeing due to personal choice, the administrative authorities tried their best to get everyone to leave before the arrival of the RPF. In Ruhengeri, the *Prefet* had warned those who thought of staying that "the majority of the population will be massacred" (SWB/*Radio France Internationale* 1994). The extremist radio Mille Collines, which had stopped broadcasting from the capital on 3 July, restarted its poisonous propaganda from Gisenyi on 10 July.

On 11 July, General Lafourcade declared that the members of the Interim Government would be allowed to seek asylum in the French "humanitarian zone" if Gisenyi fell. This embarrassing political statement of course drew return fire from the RPF which said that it would pursue them, whatever the consequences (*Liberation* 13 July 1994). Evidently, there was imperfect coordination between the Ministry of Defense and the Quai d'Orsay because four days later the Ministry of Foreign Affairs declared that if ministers in the "Interim Government" entered the French zone, they would be interned (*Le Figaro* 16–17 July 1994).

French politicians were desperately squirming in the Rwandese mess, trying to glorify the humanitarian functions of the intervention in the hope of washing any genocidal bloodspots off their hands. On 12 July, Prime Minister Balladur declared at the U.N. in New York that:

> France has sent its soldiers out of a moral duty to act without delay in order to stop the genocide and provide immediate assistance to the threatened populations. (*Agence France Press* 1994)

He denied—contrary to the facts—that persons responsible for the genocide had been allowed to stay in France.[8] He promised cooperation with the Commission of Inquiry into the genocide, established by U.N. Resolution 935: "France was a co-author of this resolution and will put at the disposal of the commission all the information it will be able to gather" (*Le Monde* 13 July 1994). In fact, when the French government actually gave some documents to the Commission in charge of investigating the genocide and prepared the briefs of the international tribunal, these were so general as to be useless.[9]

The President displayed the same freedom of mind when he stated during an interview on French television that:

1. *Opération Turquoise* had saved "tens of thousands of lives."

2. In 1990, President Habyarimana had been in the process of democratiz-
ing Rwanda, following the principles of the La Baule summit.
3. France had nothing to do with the genocide since it happened after we
left.
4. France could not intervene in Rwanda during the genocide because this
was the job of the U.N.
5. If the present Rwandese crisis had produced a re-empowerment of President Mobutu Sese Seko, this was due to "unforseen circumstances."[10]

Slowly, such a process of truth rectification began to have an impact
on French public opinion. People began to forget that the French "safe
humanitarian zone" covered only 20 percent of the country and talked
as if France had secured all of Rwanda and made it safe. The actual
workings of *Turquoise* on the ground were overlooked. The genocide
began to recede into the misty past for millions of fast-zapping TV
viewers, and, with it, any responsibility France might have had. Rumors of RPF summary executions began to spread, giving birth to the
notion of "double genocide" that later would be more fully developed:
of "the Hutu killing the Tutsi and the Tutsi killing the Hutu," as U.N.
Secretary General Boutros Boutros-Ghali put it (1994, 88). All in all,
Rwanda was too much. Compassion fatigue began to set in.

The New Government and the End of *Turquoise*

Ruhengeri fell to the RPF on 13 July, Gisenyi less than a week later.
The human torrent of refugees swelled as hundreds of thousands crossed
into Zaire.

In Kigali, the new government was sworn in 19 July. For the first
time since 6 April, there was an attempt at some sort of normalization.
The last three months had seen a combination of genocide and civil
war which had killed over 10 percent of the population and forced another 30 percent into exile. Those who remained in Rwanda were in a
complete state of disarray. Many were displaced. A large number, especially among the Tutsi survivors, had lost everything, including their
houses. Many people were hiding in the hills.

The French intervention and presence had stabilized the situation in
the Southwest. However, the 1.2 million displaced persons could start
moving again at any time if they feared that their security situation was
about to change. Psychologically, most people were in various states of
shock and many women who had been raped were now pregnant with
unwanted children. Most of the infrastructure had been brutally looted,

as though a horde of human locusts had fallen on the country. Door and window frames had been removed, electric switches had been pried off from the walls and there were practically no vehicles left in running order except RPF military ones. There was no running water and electricity in the towns, and on the hills there was no one to harvest the ripe crops. The former Tutsi refugees who were returning from Uganda into the Mutara, or from Burundi into Bugesera, had plenty of room to pasture their cows.

This was the disaster scene which the new government was supposed to manage. But the "humanitarian" *Opération Turquoise* did not concern itself with this situation at all. The French did not even try to talk with the RPF and did not send an exploratory mission into RPF-held areas. The RPF was still perceived as the enemy, and helping the civilians now under its control was out of the question.

While the RPF-controlled government was partly derived from the Arusha concept, there were two major changes. First, the RPF had allocated to itself all the Ministries which under the Arusha formula should have gone to Habyarimana's MRND(D) party. Second, a new position of Vice-President had been created and given to General Paul Kagame so as to put him in a leading governmental position without making him President. The key issue was the relationship between the cabinet and the RPF, more specifically the Rwandese Patriotic Army (RPA), as the Front Army now became known. Conditions of almost total material dependence of one on the other did not further a healthy rapport. The French used the RPA's dominance of the government to confirm their judgment of "the Tutsi" and to completely separate *Turquoise* from political developments elsewhere in Rwanda. Soon, moreover, tales of RPF violence—partly reflecting the impact of RPA's hasty recruitment in the early summer of 1994—further inhibited a return to normal international relations with the new regime.

Across the border, disaster reigned as well. The human mass which had crashed on the shores of Zaire's Lake Kivu lacked everything: food, medicine, latrine pits (which were hard to dig in the volcanic lava ground), shelter and—most basic—clean water. A cholera epidemic broke out in the third week of July, and spread like wildfire. After a week, there were 600 deaths a day and after two weeks the 3,000 mark had been reached. The emergency catapulted the French *Turquoise* rear echelon in Goma into the forefront of the news. Almost overnight the soldiers were turned into grave diggers. In an article entitled "France must hold its head high," the Minister of Defense proudly wrote that "we have stopped the violence, cared for the victims and prepared the way for those who deserve the beautiful name of humanitarians" (*Liberation* 22 July 1994). The popular evening daily *France-Soir* reported more humbly: "The French military feel completely impotent in front of these uncontrollable events. They simply stand by, looking helplessly at this nightmare" (*France-Soir* 22 July 1994).

Bodies were lying everywhere. All available shelters were crammed with dying people and corpses kept falling into the lake, further polluting the water. Newspapers and TV reporters moved in with relish to document in horrendous details the grisly situation. This peculiar twist of fate, which now condemned many of the late killers to an atrocious death, had an important media and public opinion consequence that was well analyzed by the Secretary-General of *Médecins Sans Frontières*, Alain Destexhe:

> Yesterday the genocide of the Tutsi by the Hutu militia, today the genocide of the Hutu refugees by the cholera? This comparison, which one can see widely used in the press, puts on the same plane things which have nothing to do with each other. Through this confusion the original, singular and exemplary nature of the genocide is denied and the guilt of the perpetrators becomes diluted in the general misery. (*Liberation* 27 July 1994)

The point is important. The terrible sufferings of the Hutu refugees in Goma, with their "divine retribution" aspect, defused the intensity of feeling linked with the previous genocide. The genocide became weaker, more "diluted in the general misery," especially since it had much less media coverage than the latter event, and finally lost the exceptional nature which could have led to the quick constitution of an international tribunal.

In Kigali, the government affirmed that the perpetrators of the genocide had to be punished. Prime Minister Faustin Twagiramungu announced on 2 August that some 30,000 persons would be tried—a figure that appeared absurd at the time since there was not enough jail space in all of Rwanda to hold so many prisoners[11] and raised the prospect of carrying out death sentences on a massive scale. Nor did it make relations between Kigali and Paris any easier since the new government was simultaneously trying to get France to hand over the French zone after the planned departure of *Turquoise* forces on 21 August. Paris did not want to be involved in anything having to do with examining the genocide or judging its perpetrators, and for good reasons.

Mrs. Habyarimana and some of her relatives as well as close political associates were still in France.[12] In the "humanitarian zone," *Tur-*

quoise troops were discreetly ordered to let whatever former political leaders were still around go to Zaire without hindrance. Admiral Lanxade, Chief of Staff of the French Armed Forces, declared on 18 July that "France has no mandate to arrest the members of the former government" (SWB/*Radio France Internationale* 1994). Several of them had slipped into the French zone after the fall of Gisenyi and were negotiating with the French military authorities to obtain safe conduct out of the country. This obviously angered the RPF. General Kagame declaring that, even by letting them into the zone, "France had become an accomplice of the militiamen" (SWB/France 1 TV Channel 1994). The French retaliated by accusing—probably correctly—RPF soldiers of entering the zone illegally to kidnap people and loot property.[13]

The question of disarming soldiers and militiamen in the zone had been a vexing one from the start. France never had a clearly stated policy. As a rule of thumb, French officers would disarm obvious civilian militiamen, but only when they walked around openly with their weapons. No search was mounted to try to find hidden weapons. Regular FAR soldiers were not touched; psychologically it was difficult for French soldiers to disarm the very same Rwandese soldiers they had been arming and training for the past four years.

French forces in the zone were also regrouping civilian Hutu refugees in various camp locations where NGOs, the Red Cross and the U.N. were beginning to take care of them. This was a logical thing to do in the short run, but since *Turquoise* forces later withdrew without any further organization of the camps, these were left as festering sociopolitical sores which led to grave incidents, eventually culminating in the Kibeho tragedy of April 1995 when large numbers of civilians were killed as the Rwandese government dismantled the camp.

Towards the end of July, Paris finally recognized the need to talk to what it called the "de facto government of Rwanda." A delegation was sent to meet Premier Twagiramungu in Kigali on 22 July. The delegation had been carefully pegged at a medium diplomatic level, consisting of Mrs. Boisvineau, Under-Director for East Africa at the Ministry of Foreign Affairs, General Germanos, second in command for *Turquoise* and Bertrand Dufourq, Secretary-General of the Ministry of Foreign Affairs. As the talks moved forward, the RPF accepted on in principle that the "humanitarian zone" would be demilitarized after the departure of the French. Nobody in Paris had many illusions a bout how long this would last, but it was a face-saving mechanism and the

French ministries concerned still hoped to avoid a Goma-like panic when *Turquoise* withdrew.

Because they would indeed withdraw. In spite of various foreign appeals, mostly from the U.N. and the Americans, Balladur was resolutely sticking to the two months deadline imparted to French Forces by the U.N. Resolution 929, voted on 21 June. Incredible procrastination on the part of the United Nations left UNAMIR at a still desultory level of 1,000 men, with endless discussions still preventing the full 5,500 contingent from being deployed. Problems were obviously going to develop.

Refugees had started to trickle back into the RPF-controlled part of the country, albeit very slowly. By early August their numbers were estimated to be at around 100,000 (SWB/RTBF-Brussels 1994). But the movement was slowing down as the rumors of RPF exactions became more and more insistent. General Kagame had denied that these exactions were taking place; this scared everybody even more because it was taken as an example of sinister duplicity confirming the refugees' fear of the "Secret Tutsi Plan" that the MRND had always been talking about. Everybody "knew" that return would mean annihilation.

As the deadline for the French withdrawal in the Southwest drew closer, a new exodus got underway, out of the zone and towards Bukavu in Zaïre. The French were trying to reason with the displaced persons in their area, but nobody listened. The mixture of fear of the RPF and obedience to authority played up again, and long columns of refugees started to stream on foot towards the border. Desperate at seeing the flimsy zone structure collapse even before they had left, French military authorities swallowed their pride and brought Seth Sendashonga, the (Hutu) RPF Minister of the Interior, and his (Tutsi) Rehabilitation colleague Jacques Bihozagara by French military helicopter to Kibuye in order to try to calm the population. But increasingly there were also objective factors to civilian Hutu fears. Although the RPF did not pursue a policy of systematic persecution, some Tutsi did, especially the thousands of former refugees now streaming in from Burundi. Entering in the Southeast of Rwanda from Ngozi and Kirundo provinces on the other side of the now much-travelled border, the returning Tutsi evicted the Hutu from properties which they claimed had been theirs thirty years before.

As the deadline drew nearer and the panic grew in the "humanitarian zone," French defensive statements multiplied. Minister of Defense Léotard declared on 19 August that we did all what was possible to stabilize and reassure the population.... It is now up to the RPF to make the necessary gestures.... I don't think it is fair to say that our intervention has only saved people temporarily.... Let us not forget that the safe humanitarian zone now contains more population than all the rest of Rwanda put together. (*Liberation* 20-21 August 1994)

This strange defense and illustration of the intervention concept—about which, to be fair, the Minister of Defense had never felt very sanguine—rested on a factual error. The French zone sheltered around 1.5 million people, while there were around 3.2 million in the rest of the country. It was strange, also, that he such a statement was made forty-eight hours before the total withdrawal of French troops when thousands of refugees were streaming out of the area. The safety-and-stabilization process could definitely not be seen as having been more than temporary. Foreign Minister Alain Juppé, along with President Mitterrand a godfather of *Turquoise*—evidently recognized the point. On 22 August he defensively claimed in a radio interview that "we have taken all the necessary precautions. We did not simply leave during the night and put the key under the doormat" (SWB/*Radio France Internationale* 1994).

Although the exodus had been less catastrophic than in the Northwest, around half a million refugees had fled the French zone for Bukavu by the time the expeditionary force left on 21 August. As François Léotard had said, it was now up to the RPF.

Conclusions

When all has been said and done, what was the real meaning of *Opération Turquoise*? As discussed in the historical background, France felt it *had* to get involved in Rwanda when one its black francophone *proteges* was attacked by "the Anglo-Saxons," even if these "Anglo-Saxons" were black. Paris fought them (by proxy) for almost four years, but failed to achieve the hoped-for military victory. The Arusha Agreement seemed the next best thing to keeping a minimum of influence in the Central Great Lakes Area.

The genocide came as a complete surprise to the French political leadership. It is often said that this is very surprising: there had been so many signs, so many "small" massacres (October 1990, Bugesera in March 1992, Bugogwe in January 1993, and other smaller ones in between), surely the French had to know—they were *bound* to know. Wrong—and the reason is simple. The French were not dealing only with Rwanda in Africa. There had been rampant violence in the Ivory Coast, in Cameroon, in Togo, in Chad, in Gabon, and in Djibouti. None had "gotten out of control." In Paris, the Ministry of Cooperation, the Quai d'Orsay, the DGSE and the President's Office were all prepared for a certain "normal" level of violence. What was understood as a "few dozen" scattered dead was known to mean in fact a few hundred. As long as the media would not scream too loudly, as long as Bosnia, monetary problems and domestic unemployment figures stole the political headlines, no one really cared.

Up to April 1994, the French felt that Rwanda was just another one of these irritating but secondary African problems. When it blew up in our face, we were in good faith genuinely surprised. We had expected only some "routine bloodletting." Given the past history of our involvement, we did not know what to do. Intervening *during* the genocide in order to stop it (which we could easily have done) would have entailed two things: (1) fighting (and hence getting a few of our boys shot), and (2) fighting the FAR, our former allies. Both were impossible. Public opinion would not have allowed it, although—given its fickle, contradictory and incoherent nature—public opinion could very well have demanded both action to stop the genocide, but simultaneously refused to put white French soldiers lives on the line in order to save Africans. Moreover, an intervention at that point would have brought up past links with the FAR, and the government would have been strongly attacked for its policy incoherence. President Mitterrand, an old, experienced, and completely amoral political tactician, was very well aware of these probable developments. Finally, and most decisively, the French Army would in practice have refused to fight the FAR with which it had worked for years.

The President decided to wait and see. Once the FAR had almost collapsed and the genocide had run its course, while public opinion began to seriously demand that some action, he could launch the intervention with very few risks. *Turquoise* was a public relations device with some political undertones. It was sold to the public as a humanitarian operation, which of course it was not. This was recognized in the Security Council, where five members abstained on the vote authorizing the French intervention. Paris only got active diplomatic support from its faithful African retainers. Some were even a bit embarrassing in their clearly interested eagerness to see the French prop up whatever was left of the old Habyarimana regime, such as President Omar Bongo of Gabon who had asked for an interpositional force (*Liberation* 17

June 1994). Given the situation on the ground, this could only mean stopping the advance of the RPF.

The importance and efficiency of *Turquoise* in saving lives were greatly exaggerated for propaganda purposes. If we try to estimate the number of lives saved in Southwest Rwanda, and assume that all the Tutsi in the Nyarushishi camp as well as those picked up by French forces at smaller locations otherwise would all have been killed—which is unlikely given the speed of the advancing RPF units—a reasonable conclusion is that *Turquoise* saved around 10–13,000 lives.

The cholera epidemic in Goma was a godsend because through it we could kill several birds with one stone. First, *Turquoise* soldiers were on all TV screens, surrounded by heaps of corpses, among the dead and the dying. Their usefulness could not be put in doubt. They could be conventionally admired and pitied. Second, the presence of thousands of murderers among the refugees was conveniently blurred by their plight. They were suffering human beings whom we were helping. Who was going to bring back the stories of the genocide they had committed when their children were seen dying on the screen? Thus, our former regime friends moved from the status of murderers to that of fellow victims of the Tutsi they had killed. The best illustration of this intellectual confusion appeared in the Fall 1994 edition of the French encyclopedic dictionary *Le Robert*. On the 1994 Rwandese crisis it said: "The April shooting of President Habyarimana's plane by the RPF caused massacres which led to the flight of two million refugees out of the country."[14] Third, the war, the genocide, the refugees, and the cholera became mixed up: "suffering" became a pertinent category. Trying to dissect it to get at its political components was seen as obscene in the face of so much pain. French policy was the obvious beneficiary of this intellectual and political confusion. Finally, the composite crisis became a "natural catastrophe." The danger of a volcanic eruption looming over the refugee camps around Goma only reinforced this impression. The violence ceased being a political problem for most people. It became just "another of those things" in "another of those countries"—war, pestilence, volcanic eruptions, or barbaric tribal killings; just another local disease. With *Turquoise,* France took on the role of the courageous and gentle doctors trying to alleviate some of this dark, barbaric, incomprehensible pain.

One can say that, within its own public relations and diplomatic parameters, *Operation Turquoise* was a complete success. With time, details fade into the background and ambiguities are forgotten. Only cliches and simple images remain: French soldiers protecting Tutsi survivors at the Nyarushishi camp. French soldiers burying mountains of cholera casualties in Goma, wearing white kerchiefs over their noses to fight the stench. French doctors frantically trying to save dying babies and their mothers. This is what popular history and conventional wisdom will remember, rather than the complicated and ambiguous process which led to a late return of French troops to the desolate scene of their former involvement.

Notes

1. Lest the reader would think that this an exaggeration, remember the 1985 incident during which French frogmen put two bombs under the hull of the Greenpeace ship *Rainbow Warrior* in New Zealand, sank it, and killed one person on board. Greenpeace's "crime" had been to protest French nuclear tests in Polynesia. This author heard shortly afterwards a Foreign Ministry Official privately justify the action by saying that it was "legitimate resistance to New Zealand's imperialism."
2. See for example "Les enjeux diplomatiques de la tragédie rwandaise," *La lettre du Sud*, no. 27 (23 May 1994).
3. Large transport planes such as the Boeing 747s and Antonov 124s which the Ministry was planning to charter could only land in Goma since the Bukavu airport strip was too short for these wide-bodied aircraft.
4. Some of the French officers were quite aggressive. I came close to physical blows with a Colonel in the Defence Ministry Cabinet who called me a "traitor" and a "lout." This was not the result of personal enmity and conveys well the intra-army tensions.
5. The President was very sensitive about the press campaign revealing a compromising French role in Rwanda. On the morning of the 18 June speech, special couriers delivered by hand to all newspapers a communique from the Elysée Palace which read: "Every time it came to know about exactions and human rights violations, France immediately intervened, making all efforts to have the perpetrators sought out and arrested." Considering France's inactive human rights record during the mini massacres after 1990, the statement can only be seen as rather naive propaganda.
6. AFP News Agency, 19 June 1994. In private General Dallaire was even more severe. He knew quite well about the French secret arms deliveries to the FAR and when he learnt of the French intervention, he said: "If they land here to deliver their damn weapons to the government, I'll have their planes shot down"(Interview with a U.N. official, Geneva, 29 July 1994).
7. See SWB/ *Radio France Internationale*, 4 July 1994, and *Le Figaro*, 6 July 1994. The real name of "Colonel Thibaut" was Thauzin. He was also a former military adviser to General Habyarimana during the war and was itching to get the RPF. He was later recalled.
8. *Le Monde*, 13 July 1994. For the reality of the situation, see Observatoire Permanent de la Coopération Francaise: Rapport 1995, 165–67.
9. Author's interview with a member of the Commission. Kigali, 18 January 1995.
10. SWB/France 2 TV, 14 July 1994. This was a Bastille Day interview, and thus particularly determined to show *la gloire*.

11. In fact, eventually the prison population would increase to 120,000, but only after more jails had been built and many had died in the overcrowded prisons (Eds.).
12. Most were discreetly pushed out during the summer of 1994. Mrs. Habyarimana first went to Cameroun and then later to Kenya where she had a house.
13. SWB/*Radio France Internationale*, 6 August 1994. The accusation was perfectly true but reflecting the growing lack of control of RPF soldiers by their leaders rather than a deliberate policy by the new Kigali government.
14. This was corrected in a new edition after the RPF threatened court action.

15

Protection and Humanitarian Assistance in the Refugee Camps in Zaire: The Problem of Security

Kate Halvorsen

Introduction

With the massive outflows of refugees from Rwanda in the aftermath of the 6 April crisis, the rapidly worsening security problems in the camps in Zaire, and to a lesser extent also in Tanzania and Burundi, became a matter of great concern for the international community. The security issue affected all types of humanitarian assistance, at times seriously interrupting the relief programs. Working in an extremely inhospitable physical environment, international aid organizations faced a formidable challenge of providing humanitarian assistance and protection under conditions of violence, intimidation, and corruption in the camps. In Zaire, the difficulties were compounded by tense relations with the local authorities and Zairean soldiers.

Although UNHCR is not responsible for law and order in the camps—which is the primary responsibility of host country authorities—the High Commissioner has to address security issues when these prevent the organization from implementing its mandate. In the Zaire case, UNHCR took a leading role in calling attention to the security problem, proposing and even trying remedies. These problems and the eventual solution form the subject of this chapter.[1] The role of the humanitarian agencies and UNHCR with respect to other aspects of the humanitarian crisis was dealt with fully in the Part III of the Emergency Evaluation (1996).

Contingency Planning

The security problems were in part a result of unpreparedness, so the issue of contingency planning must be dealt with first. In response to the crisis in Burundi in October 1993 and the subsequent outflow of refugees to Tanzania, UNHCR undertook a mission to the Great Lakes Region to assess its preparedness for a larger refugee emergency. This resulted in regional contingency planning for refugee outflows from Rwanda and Burundi to Tanzania, Zaire, and Uganda. When the crisis struck in Rwanda on 6 April following the death of the presidents of Rwanda and Burundi, the first flow into Zaire was not as big as UNHCR had expected. Only around 7,000 persons came out to Goma, Zaire during this first period from 6 April to the middle of July. However, the flow into Tanzania was the fastest and largest movement UNHCR had experienced: some 250,000 persons arrived in Ngara, Tanzania in the course of only two days (28 and 29 April). That record was soon surpassed by the new inflow into Goma in Zaire. Starting on 14 July, around 1.2 million people crossed the border to Goma within four days (Goma II). The size and speed of the influx was unprecedented in UNHCR's history and caught the international community by surprise and in total disbelief.

In retrospect, many observers wondered why the early warning systems apparently failed. This was also noted by UNHCR's own staff. As one said: "Why was it not possible, even in Geneva where an inter-agency task force was monitoring the evolving situation inside Rwanda with a view to foreseeing population movements, to predict more reliable figures than the 50,000 upon which contingency planning was based?" (UNHCR 1994). Several early warning signals and predictions of refugee influxes had been made and constituted the basis for UNHCR's regional contingency planning that commenced in late 1993. UNHCR had two sources of information about the situation in Rwanda. One was ICRC, which by May/June estimated that there were 250,000 internally displaced persons (IDPs) in the northwest of the country, but had no indication as to whether they were on the move. The other source was UNREO (United Nations Rwanda Emergency Operation), the Nairobi-based field operation of the U.N. Department of Humanitarian Affairs (DHA).

On 10 June, UNREO called a meeting in Nairobi for contingency planning in case of a major outflow of refugees from Rwanda. UNHCR among many other agencies and organizations were present at the meeting where UNREO presented a document containing various scenarios with different numbers of refugees, ranging from one half to one and a half million persons. According to UNHCR there was nothing in the meeting or document which indicated clearly how many to plan for and where and when they would actually cross the border. UNHCR therefore made no changes to the contingency plan which at that time was being developed by UNHCR Goma. It was a modular plan based on an initial arrival of 50,000, with allowance for subsequent increase in numbers. The contingency plan included concrete plans for choice of implementing partners (CARE, UNICEF, MSF-H, Oxfam, WFP, among others), for the stockpiling of foods and medicines, and plans for staffing and camp sites, including water, sanitation, health, road construction, and rehabilitation.

UNHCR's modular plan also noted several limitations that might come into play in case of a large influx in Goma. One factor was the limited implementing capacity of NGOs, and another was the limited cooperation from the Zairean government, especially the local authorities (UNHCR 1994). UNHCR's own emergency response capacity was stretched to its limit by the sudden and large Ngara influx in late April.

Another major concern in the planning process was the hostile attitude in the Goma area towards receiving Rwandese refugees. The Kivu region of Zaire is the most densely populated area of the country; it is also one of the most remote and underdeveloped areas, administered in irregular ways by local authorities, and politically in opposition to President Mobutu. The region has been troubled by ethnic conflicts involving earlier inflows of Rwandese migrants and refugees. During the 1950s, several thousands of both Hutu and Tutsi from Rwanda settled in the fertile areas in North Kivu, and during the 1960s more Tutsi came to settle both here and in other countries in the region. The refugees were industrious and many established prosperous business ventures. While many became Zairean citizens, the prominent economic position of many Tutsi gave rise to considerable tensions and conflicts with the local population, who still considered them as foreigners. During the 1980s, and as late as 1993, several clashes occurred between ethnic Rwandese and the local Zairians, in the process displacing some of the local population. The arrival of the new refugees in April 1994— even though few at the time—was regarded by local people and authorities as a reinforcement of the ethnic Rwandan presence and a further threat to Zairean territory and resources (Interview, UNHCR, September 1995).

The issue of camp sites arose from the beginning of Goma I as the initial three sites were overcongested and not suitable. During April and May and into June alternative sites were sought both for the present refugee population and for contingency planning. The local authorities, however, did not cooperate. UNHCR thus had to make plans within this restraint as well as the physical limitations imposed by a difficult volcanic terrain. Three areas were finally identified as the only suitable ones, and these formed the basis for further contingency planning.

When the large inflow occurred—more than 1 million persons in only a few days—total chaos and disorder initially prevailed. Apart from the physical conditions, which resulted in disease, a cholera epidemic and high death rates, the large and sudden inflow made it impossible for UNHCR to screen or register the refugees. Partly as a result, the camps started off with a highly mixed and difficult population structure.

The Camps: Security and Protection Problems

The refugee flow consisted of civilians as well as many members of the former government, the civil administration, the militias, and defeated government forces. Many were implicated in the massive human rights violations of the regime before 6 April, and in the genocide which unfolded afterwards. As the Rwandese communities sought to re-establish their preflight structure and social organization in the camps, the former leaders and the military were able to take control over much of the camps. This is in itself not unusual in refugee situations. What distinguished the Rwandese situation, however, was the extent of control by former soldiers, leaders, and militia and the intensity of the security problems, coupled with the virtual absence of host government law enforcement.

The security problem had many dimensions. The refugees, as well as foreign relief workers, were frequently harassed by local Zairean soldiers, especially early on. Of more enduring concern were the Rwandese militias, former soldiers and leaders who mixed with the general refugee population. Widely believed to be responsible for the killings and harassment of refugees, these militant groups sought to control the large exile population and prevent repatriation on terms other than their own. Finally, the close proximity of the camps to the Rwandan border created another form of insecurity by facilitating military activity across the border.

The Zairean Context

Maintaining law and order, and ensuring that refugee camps have a humanitarian and civilian character, is formally the responsibility of the national government. In the case of Goma II, however, the Zairean law enforcement body was either part of the security problem or lacked the capacity to provide control. The police force was virtually nonfunctional. The local military was ill trained and seriously underpaid; the soldiers had not been paid for months and survived from theft and corruption, feeding also on the refugee relief supplies.[2] The local authorities had little control over the local military units. The central government evidently exercised little control over anyone, but seemed generally favorable to the militants in the camps; this was also evident on the level of local authorities. The Zairean government had been a main ally of the Habyarimana government in Rwanda; the remnants now filled the camps. Consequently, during 1994, the lack of action by the Zairean armed forces was one of the main constraints in providing adequate protection to refugee in the Zairean camps.

But if there was political support for the refugees on one level, tension rapidly mounted on another level. The huge refugee influx brought chaos to the little town of Goma, causing new health hazards, a rapid increase in crime, and distortions in the local economy. The presence of the refugees and the international aid community pushed up the cost of housing and reduced the cost of labor, especially round the area of Goma. Working for wages far below the local level, especially in agriculture and domestic services, Rwandese refugees took jobs from the local population. There was also damage to public buildings, cattle rustling, increased banditry, and a proliferation of automatic weapons. Aid supplies created a surplus of maize on the local market and led to a decrease in local maize production (Pottier 1995). In addition, the local population witnessed how the international community assisted the refugees with food, shelter, and other items, and gave some of them jobs with good salaries, which further aggravated tension. One local official in Goma described a common sentiment: "the refugees are of different cultural ethics and behavior. Carrying weapons and killing are quite common among them; the same goes for stealing and squatting on other people's property. The refugee population has overwhelmed Zairean resources, destroyed our environment, introduced uncontrolled inflation into our market and abused our hospitality. We want them out of here soon" (UNHCR 1995:37). As a result some locals staged road blocks and took international staff as hostages, or occupied their offices and cars.

The Camps: Control and Distribution

An estimated 230 Rwandese former political leaders were in Zaire (1,200 with their families), most lived comfortably outside the camps with links to the camps. The militia was believed to be mainly responsible for the security problems in the camps (UNHCR 1995). Many arms were confiscated when the refugees crossed the border, but some of these were subsequently returned and new supplies evidently were flown into the area (Human Rights Watch, 1995). While in North Kivu the former soldiers and leaders initially lived in the refugee camps, in South Kivu (Bukavu area) there were two separate camps for the military. Mostly, the military camps were not assisted by the international relief community, but at least one NGO (Caritas) gave some aid in Bukavu to prevent the military from raiding the regular camps. Moreover, the military were often fed by family and community members in the refugee camps, moved freely in and out of the camps, took whatever else they needed and recruited from among the refugees. Reports indicated that, directly or indirectly, the refugee camps became a source of attacks on the Kigali government. On 18 November, the Secretary UN General reported that there were indications of preparations for an armed invasion of Rwanda and stockpiling and selling food for this purpose (UNSG 1994).

The result was the disruption of humanitarian assistance from very early on during Goma II and continuous acts of physical abuse, harassment, threats, rape, extortion, killings, and gang warfare. Security incidences were constantly reported by UNHCR personnel in the camps. For instance, on 10 August one refugee was beaten to death for talking about repatriation; on 11 August two refugees were beaten to death during food distribution for objecting to the quantity of food; on 24 August five refugees were killed in a gang fight (UNHCR 1994: no.17). A report on 3 September noted that "not a day passes without several persons killed either by angry mob against robbers or by gangs who sometimes also attacks Zairians" (UNHCR 1994: no.18). On some days, food distributions had to be stopped. "Young militiamen and general thuggery" were behind the violence, concluded another UNHCR report (UNHCR 1994: no.17).

There was also incitement to ethnic hatred and violence against the Tutsi. On 22 November Reuters reported the establishment of an exile administration in the refugee area, which worked with the defeated armed forces and the militia to stop repatriation and prepare for revenge against the new government in Kigali. The group disseminated a pamphlet entitled "Le peuple Rwandais accuse..." to all camps in Bukavu and held "information meetings" (UNHCR 1994: no.35).

At the outset, when food had to be distributed as quickly as possible, only one distribution site was established per camp, and the old leadership could easily take control over the distribution. Large amounts of food and nonfood items were diverted. It is standard UNHCR practice to use existing community structures in the organization of distributions, and the restoration of old communities during a time of chaos is important also from a refugees perspective, as many Rwandese affirmed (Pottier 1995, 33). The system nevertheless served to strengthen the negative elements in the camps. The situation improved somewhat during September and October when more distribution points were established in each camp (Pottier 1995).

Although most of the camp population as well as the relief workers were affected by the security and protection problems, the vulnerable groups among the refugees were most severely affected. Vulnerability and security must be broadly understood as not only exposure to physical abuse: the absence of an accountable authority in the camps, the threat or use of violence and the corruption also affected access to services in the camps and distribution of food and other basic materials. Among the vulnerable groups were a relatively large group of unaccompanied minors and female heads of households in addition to physically and mentally disabled, chronically ill and traumatized persons who all suffered acutely from the insecure and unstable situation. These groups were especially affected by the disruption and diversion of food distribution which resulted in high levels of malnutrition and related problems (UNHCR 1995).

Repatriation

The security situation seriously affected the repatriation, but conditions within Rwanda were also important. Immediately after the mid-July influx to Goma, people started to return to Rwanda, evidently because of the conditions in the camps. By 11 August a total of 115,000 had returned. Pressures against repatriation from the old leadership in the camps mounted, however. On two occasions in August UNHCR had to halt repatriation because of security incidents. On 24 August, for instance, 300 refugees were prevented from returning by thugs who seriously wounded one of them, detained five others and damaged a UNHCR vehicle (UNHCR 1994: no.17). By August and September reports from Rwanda were circulating among the refugees that returnees were being subjected to severe human rights abuses and also had difficulties recovering their properties. By the month of September repatriation had stopped completely.

Towards the end of the month, UNHCR sent a mission to Rwanda to look into the situation of the returnees with the hope of making plans for accelerated returns. The (Gersony) mission reported, however, that the RPF was engaged in systematic killing of Hutu in Rwanda and that serious human rights abuses were still happening (UNHCR interview, July 1995). The findings were subsequently disputed and the report remained very controversial. As a result of the uncertainty about the safety of the returnees, UNHCR did not start planning a comprehensive organized repatriation but continued to facilitate spontaneous voluntary returns.

By the end of 1994 it was clear that the largest return had taken place in July and August with estimates of the total varying from 100,000[3] (U.S. Committee for Refugees, 1995) to 600,000 (Government of Rwanda 1995), while UNHCR and the UNSG operated with an in-between number of 200,000. Repatriation slowly continued with 2000 in January, increased to 10,000 in February, but declined in March as reports again reached the refugees about increased human rights abuses of returnees. The movement came to a full halt with the Kibeho incident in April 1995, when thousands of internally displaced were killed in encounters with the Rwandan army as the government closed down IDP camps. (Adelman and Suhrke, 1996) After a few weeks, repatriation again started at a slow pace and by June 1995 a total of approximately 25,000 had returned since the beginning of the year (Rwanda Evaluation, Study IV, 1996).

Addressing the Security Problems

In the case of the Rwandan refugees, the question of eligibility for protection raised a serious moral dilemma which affected the whole international community. Everybody involved in the refugee emergency was painfully aware of the fact that the perpetrators of genocide and human rights abuses were being fed and assisted in the refugee camps. The OAU Convention recognizes that the need for protection is not limited to those fleeing persecution, but also includes victims of war and generalized violence. In mass influxes resulting from war, all people are, therefore, according to the OAU Convention on Refugees, prima facie refugees. However, the exclusion clause of the 1951 Refugee Convention can be applied if there is reason to believe that someone is responsible for serious war crimes or crimes against humanity. It was known that there were large numbers of people who should be excluded, but the problem was to identify them, collect evidence against them and to actually separate them from the bona fide refugees in the camps.

Apart from the legal issues, it was evident that the negative elements in the camps also had to be dealt with because of the deteriorating security situation. Since security problems hampered the delivery of humanitarian assistance, UNHCR could legitimately take the leadership in addressing these issues as well. On the field level, UNHCR had at the outset established a coordination group with NGOs led by a Security Officer, which monitored the security situation and discussed remedies. At the same time discussions were going on at other levels.

In the first round, involving numerous meetings with UNHCR, various U.N. agencies, the Zairean government and NGOs, the major focus was on proposals for separating the former soldiers, militia, and refugee leaders from the camps. This meant moving an estimated 60,000–100,000 militia and former soldiers with their family members. In early September, a joint UNHCR/Government of Zaire mission was sent to the camps to consider the feasibility of separation based on a proposal by the Government of Zaire to the Rwandan refugee leaders in Goma and Bukavu to discuss alternative sites for this group (UNHCR 1994: no.18). In practice, however, it would be very difficult, if not impossible, to identify the militants or extremists who in principle were excludable from refugee protection, and get people to serve as witnesses against them. Even if they could be identified, it was doubtful that they would leave peacefully, as demonstrated by the so-called Gatete incident in Ngara camp in Tanzania. Gatete, a refugee leader and known killer, was promised protection from the Tanzanian police in exchange for leaving the camp. When Gatete ignored the agreement and remained in the camp, UNHCR attempted to throw him out, which resulted in riots and security threats against UNHCR and NGO staff members (UNHCR interview, July 1995). Moreover, a UNAMIR technical team concluded that it would take six months to complete the move to alternative sites and the move would be both complicated and extremely costly. As a result, the option was abandoned.

Instead, UNHCR proposed to the U.N. Secretary General in September to establish a security contingent consisting of Zairean military personnel with support from international technical experts. While the Secretary General's Task Force on Rwanda meeting in New York on 27 October supported UNHCR's proposal and suggested that UNHCR produce an overall strategy combining security in camps with modalities of return to Rwanda (UNHCR 1994: no.30), the Secretary General wished to pursue other options including the deployment of separate peacekeeping forces in the camps. He was reluctant to collaborate with President Mobutu and Zairean soldiers because it could be regarded as the U.N. training and strengthening of Mobutu's forces, and because it involved UNHCR far beyond its scope and mandate (Jones 1995).

The option of deploying peacekeeping forces had a mixed reception in UNHCR. Some welcomed the idea, while others argued that "UNAMIR is seen by refugees as supporting the Kigali Government, and its image, particularly after a clumsy attempt to promote repatriation through leaflets, is substantially tarnished to make an extension of its services to Goma viable" (UNHCR 1994). An alternative option put forward by DPKO (U.N. Department of Peacekeeping Operations) to hire a private company to provide security in the camps was also rejected on the grounds that it would be too costly and complicated to implement.

After a series of bad security incidents in the Goma area, fifteen NGOs issued a communique on 3 November which emphasized the urgency of the situation. Citing an "untenable" situation with "unacceptably dangerous" living and working conditions for refugees as well as aid workers, the NGOs threatened to withdraw unless there was "an immediate and tangible effort to bring about positive change in the camps" (UNHCR 1994: no.32). Shortly thereafter, five out of the eight NGOs working in the Bukavu areas issued a similar memoranda to UNHCR and suggested ways of addressing the security problems.[4] The large Medecins sans Frontieres (MSF) decided to cease its activities: "the situation has deteriorated to such an extent that it is now ethically impossible for MSF to continue aiding and abetting the perpetrators of the Rwandan genocide." MSF also feared an offensive would be launched against Rwanda from the camps and lead to "another round of genocide" (UNHCR 1994: no.34).

On 18 November the Secretary General presented a report with three major military options on how to deal with the security problems in the camps to the Security Council. These included deploying a regular U.N.

peacekeeping operation, a U.N. force set up specifically to separate the former military and militia from the ordinary refugee population, or a multinational force not under U.N. command to do the same. Another measure which was recommended in combination with any of these options was to set up a group of foreign police and military experts to train and monitor local security force(s) (UNSG S/1994/1308). A joint UNHCR/DPKO assessment mission went to Goma in December to evaluate the situation and concluded that the most realistic measure was to deploy international security experts to work alongside Zairean forces. In the meantime, the Secretariat's canvassing for troops to peace-keeping forces received insufficient response and this alternative had to be abandoned. Finally, on 10 January 1995 the Secretary General asked UNHCR to pursue the option of a Zairean security contingent with international advisors, as first suggested by UNHCR three months earlier (UNHCR 1995).

As this was an innovative solution to an increasingly common problem, and a first of its kind in UNHCR's experience, it is important to consider its structure, functions and results in some more detail.

The Zairean Camp Security Operation

While the process of finding a solution was slow, the establishment of the two camp security contingents went very quickly. On 27 January UNHCR and the Government of Zaire signed an Memorandum of Understanding and an appeal went out to donors for money and personnel. The Dutch government promptly offered sixteen policemen. The Zairean government agreed to provide an elite group of soldiers to be trained and supervised by the international group of military experts. UNHCR agreed to support the Zairean authorities with an incentive allowance for each individual and provide additional support for uniforms and security posts, light and heavy vehicles, telecom equipment, office furniture, and equipment for a crisis cell in Kinshasa. In addition, UNHCR field offices in Goma and Bukavu would administer and supervise the group of international security advisors, with the Zairean military command, and also supervise, monitor, and train the Zairean contingent in refugee protection matters. The objectives of the security contingents were to: (a) improve law and order in the refugee camps; (b) seek to end intimidation and violence against candidates of voluntary repatriation; (c) protect installations and humanitarian personnel; and (d) provide escorts to convoys for voluntary repatriation from refugee camps to the border. The contingent was separated into two major areas of operation, Goma and Bukavu (UNCHR 1994: no.42).

The Zairean government selected soldiers from the elite presidential guard who were disciplined and well trained. The first group of 100 soldiers arrived on 11 February to form the Zairean Camp Security Contingent (ZCSC) which increased to a total of 1,513 by the end of April 1995. The first twelve international Liaison Officers arrived in Goma on 23 February to form the Civilian Security Liaison Group (CSLG) which increased with a few more members from Europe and ten each from four West-African countries, making a total of forty-five. UNHCR rapidly deployed one staff member to Goma, who arrived on 13 February, to be responsible for the overall coordination of the operation. In addition, five UNHCR staff members were deployed to assist the functions of Head of Operations. The Operation was first planned for five months, but was later extended to the end of 1995 (UNHCR 1995).

Both the CSLG and the ZCSC were trained by UNHCR protection staff in the principles of refugee law and doctrine. The security liaison officers trained the Zairians in riot control and diffusing conflict by nonviolent methods, and police versus military patrolling. They were also provided with riot gear, such as helmets, batons, and rubber bullets. The CSLG also monitored the work of the ZCSC by participating in night patrols on a regular basis and during daily activities. Both contingents had offices in close proximity of each other (UNHCR 1995).

Contrary to much apprehension among international relief workers, by July 1995 the operation had a significant positive impact according to UNHCR and NGOs, as well as the refugees themselves. The cooperation between the Government of Zaire and the Zairean soldiers had been good, with the exception of a few incidents of theft and corruption, which were dealt with effectively. In the camps, the number of killings, theft, banditry, rapes, beatings, and other security incidents were greatly reduced, as was the general level of tension. Relief workers reported they could more easily perform their duties. Food and non-food item distributions evidently were no longer controlled by the militias and reached the family level. Riots and demonstrations at food distribution points were effectively dealt with, as were a few serious incidents during repatriation operations. The refugees themselves reported that security had improved after the contingent became operational, and they especially noted that their presence during distribution and the ability to diffuse tense situations had a great effect (Pottier 1995).

Importantly, the previously prevailing situation of impunity was corrected. People were taken to jails and courts and punished for theft, violence against other refugees, possession of small arms, and in one instance, rape. Disarming the refugees was not a part of ZCSC's mandate because the contingent was heavily outnumbered by armed refugees; nevertheless, some small arms were seized and arrests made, including members of the Rwanda army who made political speeches in the refugee camps.[5] By July 1995, other positive achievements were noted: the ZCSC had investigated mine explosions involving both refugees and locals; they had arrested a gang of armed robbers; had intervened against another local military unit which had been terrorizing refugees and stealing their belongings; and they had successfully escorted refugees who wanted to return to Rwanda (UNHCR 1995). As the security situation improved, so did other areas of protection and assistance because relief workers could function more effectively. Only some were manifestly displeased: on February 23 some local Zairean soldiers exploded grenades close to the UNHCR office as a reaction to the fact that other Zairean soldiers were being paid by UNHCR.

Although the general security situation in the camps steadily improved, the situation remained volatile. A number of cross border incidents were reported in the region—e.g., on 11 April thirty Hutu refugees in one of the refugee camps were killed and another fifty-six wounded by Rwandans coming across the border. The militias were still in the refugee camps; military training was still going on; and military operations from the camps into Zaire were being conducted. By mid-1995 UNHCR had received many reports of soldiers and militia in Zaire still receiving military training and supplies and that they conducted low-level intense operations.[5]

Policy Implications

All contingency planning for refugees is subject to the limitations of the pull effect and cooperation from local authorities. In the Zairean case, UNHCR operated under several restraints in this respect. Nevertheless, one lesson is that—to the extent possible—contingency preparations should include plans for separating out soldiers from the civilian population, as well as alternate security arrangements if no effective local national entity exists. A contingency plan for security should include measures to disarm refugees, and prompt registration and eligibility determination.

Another lesson learned is the need to compile accurate information on security incidents so as to quickly identify the nature and seriousness of the problem. In this case, inadequate documentation was a problem, although it did not hinder action to be taken. Both UNHCR and the NGO community should institute procedures to document security incidents in a systematic and thorough manner.

Initially, it was believed that the innovative solution to the security problem involving an international military/police contingent would provide a model for the future, but the subsequent performance of the ZCSG, when it became more or less allied with the Hutu militants, as the next chapter documents, raises questions about the model. The Zairean case set another precedent. While UNHCR's primary role is to provide legal protection and humanitarian assistance, the High Commissioner took a lead role also on security issues when this was necessary to implement its mandate and when a vacuum was left by Security Council inaction.

Notes

1. This chapter draws heavily on data collected through interviews with UNHCR staff members in Geneva (July 1995–96) and the study of UNHCR documents. It also draws on substudies and reports made by other members of the Rwanda Evaluation teams, and other U.N. documentation. These are cited when appropriate.
2. The local Zairean soldiers were also a security threat. Being unpaid, many survived by theft and extortion. The huge quantities of relief items delivered to the refugee camps gave them a new source to exploit. Several incidents involving Zairean soldiers were reported by UNHCR. During the month of November, for instance, fighting erupted between Zairean soldiers and refugees, on one occasion, twenty-four refugees and three Zaireans were killed and seventy-seven wounded. Zairean soldiers also looted and razed villages and ordered refugees living in the surrounding communities to move into the camps (UNHCR, 1994f: no. 37).
3. These and subsequent numbers of repatriated all refer to so-called new caseload refugees (i.e., those who fled Rwanda after 6 April 1994), of whom the majority were Hutu.
4. Measures suggested by NGOs in Bukavu included: (a)separation of nefarious elements from the refugees; (b) elimination of arms in camps; (c) urgent and complete registration, and (d) establishment of security and protection in the camps (UNHCR, 1994c: no.34).
5. By the first week of June 1995, for instance, arms had been seized on seventy-one occasions, including twenty-three rifles or pistols, thirty grenades, four mines, and various amounts of ammunition.

16

The Rwandan Genocide and the Collapse of Mobutu's Kleptocracy

Abbas H. Gnamo

Introduction

Changes and transformations of societies and states could be the result of internal dynamism, external factors, or the combination of both. For a long period of time, the Marxist school emphasized internal contradiction as an underlying cause of social and political change. In contrast, although internal development is important, in some cases internal factors are insufficient to account for change. Perhaps that is why Otto Hintze privileged external influence on the evolution and transformation of European states: "We must stress that in the life of peoples, external events and contradiction exercise a decisive influence upon internal constitution" (Nairn 1977, 11).

Throughout its post-colonial history, external forces played a critical role in the Zairean domestic political arena, perhaps more than elsewhere in the region. However, the most dramatic political event in the Great Lakes region had the most significant impact—the genocide in Rwanda in 1994. Temporarily, this tragedy and its aftermath rehabilitated Mobutu's declining power, at least vis-à-vis France, but undermined his shaky authority and legitimacy in the long term. The consequence of the Rwandan crisis, together with the evolution in the geopolitical vision of the major powers in the post-Cold War era and a strong desire for change within Zaire itself, combined to bring about a much awaited change—the departure of Mobutu.

Political analysts, diplomats, and Zaireans believe, correctly, that in the post-Cold War era Mobutu's autocratic and patrimonial rule, as the ideological and philosophical basis of his government, are anachronistic and a "leftover" of history. Mobutu did not want to relinquish power, despite internal and external pressures coming from his friends and adversaries. He continued to divide and manipulate the opposition that permitted him to prolong the transitional period (starting in 1992) and his decaying reign until May 1997.[1] So, the overthrow of Mobutu was not the surprise of the century; many people expected that Mobutu would either transmit power to a democratically elected leadership or that he would be ousted through a coup. They did not imagine, however, that the force would be an Alliance coming from the far remote eastern region.

On the other hand, perhaps no one in the Great Lakes region or elsewhere imagined that the Rwandan tragedy would affect the whole region in general, and, in particular, its very much larger neighbor, Zaire. But history frequently produces unexpected results. The international community, including the U.S., took too long to recognize that the massacre in Rwanda was first a human rights disaster and then a genocide (Braeckman 1994; Prunier 1995; Adelman and Suhrke 1996). It was simply perceived as a classical tribal war (la lutte tribale). The spiral of violence in Rwanda-Burundi, between the Hutu and Tutsi, over the last four decades persuaded many observers to consider that the Rwandan massacre was one among many others or a repetition of history.[2] However, this is a very simplistic approach to this complicated human tragedy. As René Lemarchand wrote:

> The Rwandan genocide is neither reducible to a tribal meltdown rooted in atavistic hatred nor a spontaneous outburst of blind fury set off by shooting down of the presidential plane on April 6, as officials of the Habyarimana regime have repeatedly claimed. However widespread, both views are travesties of reality. What they mask is the political manipulation that lies behind the systematic massacre of civilian populations, planned annihilation, not the sudden eruption of long-simmering hatreds, is the key to the tragedy of Rwanda. (Lemarchand 1995, 8)

Above all, France, then the influential power in the Great Lakes region, and Zairean authorities failed to realize that the ethnopolitical crisis in this tiny and poor republic would alter the status quo and geopolitical alignment in Central Africa. Moreover, it is doubtful whether the Rwandan Patriotic Front (RPF) and its leadership, coming from Rwandan Tutsi refugees of three decades ago, imagined that their invasion would lead to such a tragedy, although they were determined to oust the Hutu-dominated government and reconquer state power. Neither could the RPF have predicted that the calculated risk of launching a war would affect the lives of millions in neighboring countries. But it did, radically and unalterably, as Africa Confidential underlined (Africa Confidential 9 May 1997, 38:10).

In this chapter, we will try to grasp the broader dynamics of the conflict by examining the domestic political situation and ethnonational factors in Zaire. Mobutu's strained diplomatic relations with most of his neighbors, in particular, his amicable ties with the former Rwanda government and president Habyarimana, his hostility towards the current Tutsi-dominated government since 1994 and the Ugandan leader, Yoweri Museveni, made him many enemies. The massive refugee presence in Zaire, including many who perpetrated the genocide—the génocidiaires as they are called—as well as his support to the various guerrilla insurgents operating from Zaire in neighboring states, also constituted key factors. In the aftermath of the Rwandan genocide and the beginning of the war in eastern Zaire in the fall of 1996, all Mobutu adversaries in the region united against him in order to solve "four conflicts in one," i.e., the problems of Rwanda, Burundi, Uganda, as well as the Zairean domestic crisis (Prunier 1997). In addition to the four conflicts, the crisis in Angola could be added; Angola joined the anti-Mobutu front to settle its UNITA problem.

The war which led to the overthrow of the Zairean government started in eastern Zaire. The conflicts in North-Kivu and South-Kivu were different, though they were ethnonational in character. First, the conflict in North-Kivu was between the authochtones and the Banyarwanda (people of Rwandan origin, both Tutsi and Hutu). The second was between the Hutu refugees including the ex-FAR—Forces Armées Rwandaises—and the Interahamwe ("those who attack together") and the authochtones on the one hand, with the Banyamulenge, i.e., Zairean Tutsi, on the other. The conflict escalated when the Hutu refugees perpetrated ethnic cleansing against the Zairean Tutsi (Banyamulenge) with the understanding and encouragement of Zairean authorities and soldiers. The threat of expulsion loomed over the Zairean Tutsi community. The Banyamulenge took up arms against the Hutu and their backers, the Mobutu regime; the latter had deprived the Banyamulenge of Zairean citizenship rights almost two decades earlier. The Zairean Tutsi received the support of their Tutsi or pro-Tutsi regimes in the region. The Banyamulenge revolt was joined by traditional revolutionary elements hostile to Mobutu's rule. This brought Laurent Kabila, a long-time opponent of Mobutu, into the political scene, and resulted in the formation of the Alliance which easily overran this huge country.

As has often been the case, the major powers were not absent in such a conflict, though their role does not appear critical to the outcome. The two post-Cold War major powers for Central Africa, and Africa in general, are the U.S. and France. The two democracies were allied as partners against the Communist threat. However, with the end of the Cold War they became rivals. However, contrary to what many observers believe, Kabila's takeover and the departure of Mobutu were largely planned, orchestrated, and executed by African leaders without direct participation of foreign powers, though with the apparent understanding and even encouragement of the U.S.

The Diffusion of the Conflict:
Refugees and Ethnonational Problems in Eastern Zaire

The total victory of the RPF in July 1994 resulted in two major developments: the end of genocide and the massive displacement of refugees. Instead of a message of reconciliation and mutual trust, rumors of massive executions by the RPF of the Hutu spread throughout the country, inducing the population to leave in great numbers for the neighboring countries of Zaire, Tanzania, Burundi, and Uganda. At the same time, "Old Refugees," the Tutsi, living in exile for more than three decades, returned to Rwanda. Most of the estimated up to two million Hutu refugees were concentrated in eastern Zaire (Goma = 850,000, Bukavu = 332,000 and Uviru = 62,000), although the spread of cholera in the refugee camps of Goma caused the death of no less than 30,000 people.

The ethnonational conflict in eastern Zaire was of two types. The first was the decades-long interethnic relations between those who lived together both in harmony and conflict. The second was the problem created by the massive refugee presence. Among the refugees were 50,000 ex-FAR, various Hutu militias largely responsible for the massacre of 1994, and the Hutu guerrillas from Burundi led by Leonard Nyangoma.

The current population of eastern Zaire is composed of various ethnic groups. Some of them migrated from Rwanda about two hundreds years ago. Above and beyond this migration, which included both Hutu and Tutsi, because of the overpopulation and shortage of land in Rwanda/Burundi, the Belgian colonizers continued to bring immigrants of Rwandan origin to colonial Congo where there was a need for manpower. To these groups, one has to add the displaced Tutsi refugees from Rwanda by the Hutu revolution and government from 1959 to 1963. Moreover, there was an illegal but continuous immigration from Rwanda-Burundi to eastern Zaire after the colonial period. Needless to say, in precolonial Africa the notion of fixed borders did not exist even when there was some form of centralized authority. Even in Europe, until the French Revolution and the subsequent rise of nation states, borders were fluid. Post-colonial African borders are "artificial" in the sense that they were traced by European colonizers without any respect to ethnic composition and the definition of the local social universe, language and culture. Neither the colonial state nor the sovereign states could strictly control population movements from one country to another where they have relatives, kinsmen, affinities or potential opportunities—in Africa the reference is genealogy more than borders. Most particularly, the sovereignty of many African states is nominal, and states lacked full control over their own territory. Because of administrative weaknesses, the states hardly registered births and deaths, let alone imposed visas. The implication: it is difficult to distinguish between those who lived there for centuries or arrived only years ago, particularly where the people are of the same ethnic group.

The last and the best known population movement to eastern Zaire was related to the Rwandan genocide in 1994 when very large numbers of Hutu refugees arrived and altered century-old interethnic relations. The Hutu refugees constituted a unique kind of refugee flow since it included the armed ex-FAR and the Interahamwe militias responsible for the genocide and planning to return with force to Rwanda to oust the Tutsi dominated government. Their massive presence affected the local population in many ways. It resuscitated the dormant conflict between the various ethnic groups, each struggling for access to resources in Kivu, the poorest and the most densely populated region in Zaire. Above all, the Hutu influx broke a centuries-old Tutsi-Hutu alliance in Zaire. Until the Spring of 1993, the two communities had fought together against indigenous Hunde and Nyanga even when the Hutu were involved in ethnic cleansing against the Tutsi in Rwanda. Finally, the circulation of a considerable number of weapons created a climate of insecurity and even anarchy in the region.

Of course, until the crisis of the 1990s, the integration of Banyarwanda into the community was relatively easy due to broad social contacts and a common intermarriage process which, over the years, intertwined the population to the point where it was nearly impossible to distinguish the ethnic identity of individuals. The Hutu of North-Kivu were

particularly "Tutsized" and lived in harmony with Tutsi, whereas in
South Kivu, the Banyamulenge remained more or less "pure-Tutsi."
The Banyarwanda community had done well economically, particularly in commerce, but economic envy and jealousy of the authocthones
was one result (Prunier 1997, 195). Moreover, the influence of the Hutu-
Tutsi intelligentsia in the political and economic life of northern Kivu
was resented by other ethnic groups as was the domination of the
emigrés. The indigenous populations claimed they were marginalized
by the newcomers throughout the Mobutu era. The Banyarwanda were
accused of putting in place a secret and hierarchical structure exclusively composed of the immigrants to promote their economic and political power at the expense of Hunde-Ngaya. The latter, whose leaders
were close to Mouvance présidentielle (or Mobutu's supporters), even
claimed that their land ownership rights in the hills were jeopardized
by the Hutu-Tutsi elite. For its part, in many of the inter-ethnic conflicts, the Mobutu clan perpetually sided with one of the protagonists
according to circumstances and opportunity. For instance, in earlier
periods Mobutu supported the Banyarwanda against the authochtones
who contested his authority, but later he encouraged the anti-
Banyarwanda sentiment of the local ethnic groups during the national
conference[3] and particularly after the Rwandan genocide. As Thomas
Turner wrote:

> The crudest examples of divide-and-rule tactics involves incitement of ethnic vio-
> lence. In North Kivu, Hunde, Nyanga, and other "local" peoples attacked immi-
> grants from Rwanda, with obvious encouragement of Mobutu and his supporters.
> In mineral-rich Katanga (as Shaba Region was known once) local people attacked
> Kasaians as a direct result of Mobutu's rule. (Turner 1996, 257)

Mobutu always used the sentiment of frustration, real or imaginary,
of different communities, frustration emanating largely from competition for economic resources and political power. In this conflict, where
the indigenous population accused newcomers or immigrants from another province of sabotaging, profiting, exploiting, and oppressing the
original inhabitants, Mobutu did not adopt a responsible position. His
attitudes were dictated by the political advantage he would obtain from
the conflict. Instead of being an arbiter, he incited ethnic violence. In
addition, he took controversial measures which aggravated the conflict. For instance, in 1992 he abrogated a principle of non-assignment
of soldiers in their own province of origin, as well as in North-Kivu.
The result was that every soldier mistreated the civilian population of

his ethnic enemy. A case in point was the torture of the Hutu-Tutsi by the soldiers of FAZ (Forces Armées Zairoises) under the order of Hunde-Nyanga notables. In spite of strong protests to local political and judicial authorities, this case was never even investigated (Bakajika 1997, 19). This, added to other conflicts of an economic and ethnopolitical order, exacerbated tensions which led to the recent war in eastern Zaire.

The massive arrival of Hutu refugees in the summer of 1994 altered interethnic relations in many ways. First, the Banayarwanda (Hutu and Tutsi of Rwandan extraction), who largely intermarried and expressed solidarity during different conflicts with other ethnic groups in eastern Zaire, lost their cohesion after the Rwandan genocide because both the conflict and the Hutu refugees in Zaire set the two communities in opposition. Generally speaking, the reaction to refugees in Zaire varied. It seems that there was a general consensus that the refugees should be sent home, though many Zaireans in the east sympathized with the Hutu of Burundi and Rwanda. It was in this context that the politicians in Kivu envisaged the expulsion of the Zairean Tutsi—Banyamulenge—from the region. Since a 1981 law requiring proof of their ancestry, the judicial condition or the citizenship rights of this community was in doubt. In 1982, the government revoked the citizenship of the people of Rwandan origin, the Banyamulenge and Banyarwanda, and officially branded them as "strangers" who could not hold public office. In so doing, this measure was a flagrant human rights violation, but also politically absurd. In effect, how was it that the state, created some three decades previously, could deny the citizenship rights of a people who had lived there for 200 years? However, as Peter Rosenblum noted, "corruption and political instability also prevented the conflict over citizenship from being addressed in a legitimate forum, encouraging the search for alternative solutions, such as mass expulsion" (Rosenblum 1997, 200–05).

The massive arrival of anti-Tutsi refugees, combined with the local anti-Tutsi sentiment fermented by local authorities and the Zairean government, largely contributed to the escalation of the conflict. The ex-FAR and the Interahamwe established de facto minirepublics over more than one million Hutu refugees and the local people with the full understanding of the Zairean government and the FAZ (Forces Armées Zairoises). One has to bear in mind that the former Rwandan authorities and the ex-FAR did not come empty-handed; they were not ordinary refugees induced to leave their country. They had the necessary time to transfer whatever could be transferred from Rwanda to Zaire.

For instance, they shipped 20,000 tons of coffee estimated at 50 million dollars which they stocked in the stores belonging to Mobutu's family (Verschave 1994, 160).[4] They had also brought with them 17 billion Rwandese francs, most of which was put under the direct control of Mobutu (Prunier 1995, 321). Above all, they made use of the constant flow of humanitarian aid from the UN and NGOs. For instance, it is reported that:

> since 1994, these displaced people, as well as those in Tanzania, had been fed, clothed and housed by the UN High Commission for Refugees (UNHCR) at a cost of more than $1m a day. Little attempt had been made to return them to Rwanda, mainly because the hard-line Hutu militias and the former Rwandan Army threatened anyone wanting to return home. (Strategic Survey 1996/1997, 214)

Further, the number of refugees was deliberately inflated to get more resources which went to those who controlled the camps. The refugees were also supplied with arms by different dealers and perhaps by some states. Hence, they controlled the camps, preventing innocent refugees from going back home for at least four reasons. Firstly, if the refugees returned home, the militants would be cut off from lucrative humanitarian aid. Secondly, the refugees served as pawns for propaganda. Thirdly, they were buffers to prevent their own arrest. Finally, the return of refugees would thwart their long term plan to organize themselves, overthrow the-RPF dominated government and restore Hutu supremacy.

For the hard-liners, the dream of terminating the "work" (genocide) remained alive. According to a document allegedly left behind during the war and found in one of the refugee camps, the plan of invading Rwanda from Zaire was on the agenda. The extremists undertook many small-scale incursions into Rwanda from their refugee camps. In fact, many observers were conscious of the necessity of separating the criminal elements from the majority of refugees, but no country was ready to engage in a conflict with the ex-FAR and armed militias. The host government did not take any measures to control the situation because of Mobutu's sympathy with the Hutu and due to antipathy to the current RPF leadership; nor did the Zairean government have any of its own means to do so given the state of his unpaid and undisciplined soldiers. Further, the latter developed a friendship with the ex-FAR and the Interahamwe, who were more resourceful and rich thanks to relief aid and smuggling. The Tutsi-dominated government was always irritated by repeated incursions and violations of its border from the west.

Rwanda warned the international community that if nothing was done, it would attack the camps. Paul Kagame, Minister of Defense and vice-president of Rwanda, informed the U.S. about his intentions (Rosenblum 1997, 201–02).

Moreover, the militia and the ex-FAR did not behave like conventional refugees. Their presence had a profound effect on the life of many Zaireans in the region. Bakajika summarizes the social, political and economic consequences of Rwandan refugees on the Zairean populations as follows:

> The start of school for Zairan schoolchildren was jeopardized, the teachers preferring to offer their services to nongovernmental organizations (NGOs) for US$4 per day. Almost all of the civil service drivers became day laborers with these NGOs; the Rwandan refugees regularly committed acts of appropriation, intimidation, even violence against the natives, but also against the long-settled Tutsis in Zaire, insecurity supported by the Interhamwé, FAR, and FAZ. (Bakajika, 1997:20)

However, the most affected were the Tutsi pastoralists living in the region for many centuries. In the face of the ethnic cleansing launched by the ex-FAR and Interahamwe in collaboration with other local ethnic groups who used this opportunity to "settle" their own conflict with the Tutsi, they forced some of the latter to abandon their houses in order to return to Rwanda, where their kinsmen were in power and where they would be better protected. However, many of them decided to take up arms to defend themselves. As opposed to their cousins, Banyarwanda in the North-Kivu, who suffered in 1993 and 1994 without any external support, the Banyamulenge of South-Kivu believed that the time had come to put up strong resistance as they could count on the regime in Kigali and eventually those of Bujumbura and Kampala. The two could help not only due to ethnic solidarity, but also to ensure the safety of their own borders and states.

Having foreign support from friendly neighboring countries was important but was not sufficient in itself; there had to be a suitable internal climate in Zaire if the war had any chance of success. The Zairean state was on the verge of collapse after thirty years of dictatorial and inept rule under Mobutu, who continued to suffer from cancer and was usually abroad for treatment. The inconclusive democratic transition with different competing institutions and individuals claiming legitimacy further destabilized the country as did the acute economic crisis that paralyzed the administration, the health and educational sector. Above all, the completely disorganized army, which was rarely paid, and was inadequately trained and armed, was not capable of putting up much resistance as was seen in the seven-month war.

The Armed Rebellion and the Zairean Crisis

Without taking into account previous skirmishes, the war started in October 1966 in eastern Zaire. Naturally, the cause of this war was local, but its implications were both regional and geopolitical. As Gérard Prunier argued, "If the catalyst of the conflict was local—the persecution of the Banyamulenge by a Kinshasa-supported South Kivu tribal coalition—the reasons why it broke out, and especially why it broke out on such a large scale, involved the entire region" (Prunier 1997, 197). One has to analyze, therefore, why the war broke out and why it involved both the Zairean armed opposition and most of Zairean neighbors such as Rwanda, Burundi, Uganda, and Angola. Although all these countries have their own explanation for involvement in the war, the trigger was associated with the legacy of the Rwandan genocide of 1994.

In the summer of 1966, the conflict in eastern Zaire began. It gathered momentum in the fall of 1996 through the combination of two related factors. The first was the increasing harassment of the ethnic Tutsi—Banyamulenge—estimated at 300,000 people, in Kivu; they had already been denied their citizenship rights since 1982. Then they received a serious threat of expulsion from their homeland by the Zairean army and regional authorities, in this case the Deputy Governor of South-Kivu, Lwasi Ngabo Lwabanji. The Banyamulenge decided to put up armed resistance against the Hutu militia and the Zairean army. Second, this resistance corresponded with a strong desire on the part of Rwanda, which was irritated by a massive presence of Hutu refugees, among them the Interahamwe and the ex-FAR, on its border in eastern Zaire from which the Hutu armed elements continued to destabilize its western regions through repeated incursions. The armed elements took the refugees hostage in order to obtain continuous relief aid and eventually to use them as a shield in the case of attack from Rwanda. In the absence of any reaction from the international community towards this situation, Rwanda thought that the only way to solve the problem was to join the war of the Banyamulenge, not by a simple ethnic solidarity, but as an effective means to end the incursions and to nip in the bud plans for the reconquista by the refugees. The former Rwandan soldiers and the militia had made no secret about their intention to invade

Rwanda when they were once again strong. Internal security of Rwanda had deteriorated in the summer of 1996, although some aspects of this insecurity emanated from "the violence linked to struggles within the RPF and among Tutsi returnees from different countries" (Rosenblum 1997, 201). Furthermore, although the concerns of other neighboring countries of Zaire—Uganda and Burundi—were not as strong as those of Rwanda, they shared the same interest with the latter since Zairean soil was used as rear bases for the opponents to their regimes (Strategic Survey 1997, 213–18).

At the start, the war appeared spontaneous with the Banyamulenge spearheading the fight against the refugee camps and the FAZ. But later, it became clear that the uprising of the Tutsi was far from sponta- neous, though the reasons for the revolt were justified. This was mainly because the fighters were prepared, armed, and trained to act according to a well-established strategy and objectives far beyond the organiza- tional and military capacity of the Tutsi community (Banyamulenge). The plan was said to have been organized by strategists from Rwanda and Uganda. The first strategic goal was to destroy Hutu refugees camps in Eastern Zaire. The second was the conquest and control of the min- eral-rich South and Central provinces. Finally, the rebellion was to tar- get the major cities before marching on Kinshasa. This presupposed the participation of well-trained Rwandan, Ugandan and perhaps Burundian soldiers (Leymarie 1997, 12).

The attacks started in September 1996. On 13 October, the first group of Hutu refugees started to flee the rebel incursion into the eastern Zairean town of Uvira. On 18 October, the fighting intensified around Uvira which was captured on 24 October. This was followed by the fall of Bukavu and Goma on 30 October and 1 November respectively; the conquest covered about 300 miles of eastern Zairean territory. At this point the war changed its nature, attained its climax and attracted wider media coverage because of the refugee and humanitarian crisis.

The defeat of the ex-FAR and the militias and the lack of humanitar- ian aid meant the refugees were forced to return to Rwanda. Others were cut off from all aid and were caught in the war. The war induced no less than 600,000 refugees to return to Rwanda, whereas others, who were not willing to return, estimated as high as 300,000,[5] fled west deep into the Zairean jungle. These refugees suffered from lack of food, medical aid and persecution from the ADLF (L'Alliance des Forces Démocratiques pour la Libération du Congo-Zaire—ADLF-CZ) fight- ers. Many of them, the exact number is not known, were said to have

been systematically massacred, and some commentators even characterized these killings as another "genocide."[6] The U.N. also accused
the rebels of systematically exterminating Hutu refugees in several
places. Kabila denied these accusations. In any case, the repatriation of
the other refugees to Rwanda was completed by the end of the summer
of 1997.

One has to bear in mind that the fighting commenced by Banyamulenge had considerable support from Rwanda/Uganda, although it
is difficult to quantify the assistance. The sweeping victory shows the
importance of this aid, although Rwanda, Burundi and Uganda resolutely denied any involvement until the last stage of the war. But their
role was evident to all. As Newsweek wrote: "The rebels quick conquest of territory shows how deeply foreign troops are involved in the
offensive. Despite Mobutu's weakness, it never made much sense that
a ragtag army composed from the Tutsi tribe could march alone across
a huge country" (Newsweek 12 March 1997, 41).

However, as soon as the war began, Laurent-Désiré Kabila, the leader
of L'Alliance des Forces Démocratiques pour la Libération du Congo-
Zaire (ADLF-CZ) became involved. Kabila is neither Hutu nor Tutsi,
but originates from "pure" Zairean roots—the Mluluba ethnic group.
Although the Banyamulenge are Zairians, they were perceived as Tutsi,
and the emergence of Kabila and his friends "Zairianized" the conflict
or provided the war with a national dimension. This became more evident when he became a spokesman and leader of the rebellion. However, the question of who really commanded and fought in the rebellion
remained shrouded in mystery, particularly until the beginning of 1997.
According to Peter Rosenblum, who visited the zone of the conflict
during Christmas of 1996:

> The mysteries surrounding the rebellion remain, no doubt intentionally. Little is
> known about who is actually fighting or what authority Kabila really has. Are the
> fighters Ugandan? Rwandan? Angolan? Zairean? Who is pulling strings? Is Kabila
> "Zairianzing" the rebellion as it sweeps through the country or simply winning
> the battle of appearances necessary for popular support? (Rosenblum 1997, 201)

Such questions had been raised by Zaireans and many observers
throughout the war. In the beginning of the war, as in latter periods
when the FAZ was losing one battle after the other without putting up
any resistance, the Zairean public was shocked and felt humiliated by
what was perceived as external aggression. Kabila was considered a
simple "puppet" or stooge of Uganda/Rwanda. Whatever his real au-

tonomy vis-à-vis these countries, it is certain that Kabila was propelled by Uganda/Rwanda not only to form the Alliance with the Banyamulenge and other small fronts, but to recruit and arm thousands of dissatisfied Zairean ethnics who live in Bukavu in eastern Zaire. He also recruited from other regions as the war went on and he expanded his zone of influence.

Until the recent crisis, little was known and written about Kabila, although he has a reputation as an eternal foe to the Mobutu regime.[7] He was born at Moba, around Lake Tanganyika, in Shaba province. He belongs to the Luba ethnic group. In the late 1950s, he studied in Paris and then in Eastern Europe. As many young men of his generation of Africans of that time, he came back with socialist ideas of Third-World militancy. Upon his return to the Congo, he became a deputy in a newly-independent Congo.

In 1960, Kabila gave his support to Patrice Lumumba, the father of Congo's independence, who was arrested, tortured, and killed in 1961. He then returned to Eastern Europe (Belgrade), and in 1963 he took part in the Lumumbist insurrection led by Gaston Soumaillo and supported by the USSR. At the time, Kabila was fiercely anti-imperialist and anti-American. In 1965, along with Che Guevera, he tried without success to give support to an anti-Mobutu revolt led by Pierre Mulele. Disappointed, Che Guevera left Eastern Zaire, South Kivu, six months later. In 1967, Kabila founded "le Parti Révolutionaire du Peuple" which formed the current Alliance with four other small parties on 18 October 1996 at Memera, South Kivu. Between 1967 and 1996, he lived an ordinary life in Kivu with fellow combatants. Generally, he was said to have combined political militancy of the Marxist inspiration of Che Guevera with commercial adventures (Le Monde 1997, 2). The coalition he formed (ADLF-CZ) included people from the Muluba ethnic group (Shaba and Kasai regions), the Munyamulenge ethnic group (South Kivu), the Banyamulenge (Zairean Tutsi) in Kivu (Masisi) and South-Kivu regions, and the Mukungo ethnic group of the Shaba region. The factions composing the Alliance were far from having a coherent political and ideological orientation.[8]

Militarily speaking, there was hardly a battle, perhaps with the exception of Lubumbashi and Kenge, where strong resistance was carried out for many days by the Republican Guard. Initially, there was a collective belief that the well-trained, armed, and paid Garde Républicaine could save Mobutu's power or could resist, but it did not. The demoralized, poorly equipped and trained, undisciplined, and above all unpaid soldiers were not up to the ADLF fighters. The FAZ were no longer soldiers, but anarchic bands. The support they received from the ex-FAR, the Interahamwe and UNITA did not make a difference. Indirectly, the UNHCR backed the FAZ by financing a Zairean Security Contingent (CZSC) to protect refugees. This desperate attempt did not work either. The FAZ, instead of protecting the population, engaged in unbelievable banditry and looting before escaping from the battlefield. As such, they did more damage than the ADLF fighters. Many people in the region, therefore, were openly hostile to the FAZ and were waiting for the arrival of the rebels to end the anarchy.

During this crisis, the Zairean dictator was abroad, first in Switzerland and then in France, to treat his prostate cancer and recuperate from surgery. Mobutu invented a clever but manipulative political formula known as "Mobutu or Chaos" (cf. Young and Turner 1985—"avant moi le chaos, après moi le déluge"; see also Braeckman 1992, 357–61). Perhaps he believed that the defeat of his army and the humiliation of his country in his absence would mean that he was needed back in Zaire. This, more than ever, could have restored his fading internal legitimacy. In fact, many Zaireans thought that with his presence things would not have gone as badly. Many disillusioned Zaireans expressed their discontent against the Kengo government that was accused of not doing enough to defend the country. Some tried to connect this weakness to his Tutsi ancestry. Many also believed and hoped that the return of Mobutu would permit the restoration of the prestige and image of Zaire that had been "tarnished" by its small neighbors. It was with this in mind that many Zaireans gave him a triumphant welcome upon his return from France on 18 December 1996. Mobutu vowed to annihilate the enemy and recover the occupied Zairean territory; he named new military commanders, mobilized his famous Republican Guard, and he even employed mercenaries from France, Belgium, and Serbia. But he was unable to reverse the tide. The highly expected counter-offensive did not take place. His Republican Guards and mercenaries lost one battle after the other. With the fall of Kisangani, the third largest Zairean city, to the rebels, all analysts, as many Zaireans, concluded that a counter-offensive was no longer possible. The occupation of the whole territory became a question of time.

One can ask why the Alliance won an easy victory. The first explanation for the success is attributed to the strength, discipline, training, and determination of the ADLF fighters. The second explanation resides in the collapse of the Zairean state, which had already lost all credibility and legitimacy through corruption and inept rule over the last three decades. In spite of their initial hostility towards the rebels who were perceived as instruments of foreign aggression, there was an increasing awareness—prise de conscience—of the Zairean people that the time for change had come even if it was brought by the ADLF supported by foreigners. So they welcomed Kabila's men, or at least understood them. Thirdly, the army, including the Republican Guard, did not fight as it should have, not because of lack of motivation or cowardice, but because it wanted change as well. As Colette Braeckman wrote: "Moreover, if Mobutu's army didn't fight, it was not simply due to cowardice or lack of motivation: it was also because the majority of the soldiers were themselves waiting for the change, and they were no longer worried too much about defending a discredited regime that had forgotten to giver them their pay. (Braeckman, 1997: 12–13)." (Braeckman 1997, 12–13). On the contrary, those who fiercely resisted the ADLF were the Hutu militias, the ex-FAR and UNITA fighters, who had everything to lose with the overthrow of the Mobutu regime; because of this, they saw the war as their own.

On the other hand, upon his return from Europe, Mobutu attempted some cosmetic changes. In fact, the reshuffling of the cabinet was largely expected to at least give a new élan to his counter-offensive, if not to solve the underlying socioeconomic crisis of the country. He also surprisingly re-appointed the extremely unpopular Kengo wa Dondo as the head of the crisis government. The rationale for this was that Kengo appeared to be France's favorite to succeed Mobutu. The ailing dictator could not resist French pressure, given that France was his only important friend after he was abandoned by the U.S. Kengo was unsuccessful in solving the crisis militarily or politically, and was forced to resign. Mobutu replaced him with Etienne Tishesekedi, his long-time political foe and rival. In the cabinet he formed, the latter practically excluded Mobutu's supporters, whereas he reserved key portfolios for the ADLF in the hope of sharing power with the Alliance. Kabila, however, declined since had already decided not to share power with anyone save his friends. Not surprisingly, Mobutu replaced Tishesekedi with General Likulia Bolongo three days after his nomination.

This does not mean, however, that Tshisesekedi himself did not make mistakes during the long period of democratic transition and the recent conflict despite his political courage and resolute opposition to dictatorial rule. During the democratic transition, he was unable to provide leadership although Mobutu's divisive and manipulative mechanisms were partly responsible for this handicap[9] (Rosenblum 1997, 203). Furthermore, in the beginning of the war, Tishesekedi and other members of the opposition parties and civil society, seem to have forgotten their differences with the dictator in the nationalistic fervor against what was considered as external aggression. He went too far when he visited Mobutu in Nice, asked the population to pray for the health of ailing president and accepted to be Prime Minister in a situation where the government and the dictator were on the brink of collapse (Braeckman 1997, 13).

An African Revolution? Regional States and Major Powers in the Zairean Crisis

Although the dialectic for change and many other factors united to end Mobutu's thirty year dictatorship from within, the momentum in fact came from outside. In fact, many commentators underlined the role played by some Zairean neighbors—in this case Rwanda/Uganda/Burundi/ Angola, in the Zairean crisis. At the same time, they emphasized the role of the U.S. and France behind the scenes. Some tended to reduce the war to Anglo-Saxon/Francophone rivalry to promote their economic, geopolitical, and cultural interests. It is true that there has been an intense competition between the U.S. and France, the only two major powers with considerable influence in Africa in the post-Cold War era, and their divergence gave rise to some controversies and polemical exchanges between the officials of the two nations. In the Great Lakes region conflicts they adopted different attitudes; France cannot be happy with the way the situation evolved. The U.S. turned out to be a great beneficiary whereas France is generally considered the loser.

Nevertheless, African leaders played the key role in the Zairean crisis or what many termed the "Zairean Revolution." Many observers, journalists, and even some scholars tended to conclude that the Zairean conflict was an "African Revolution." For instance, Julius Nyerere, a senior African statesman, said, "the transfer of power in Zaire from the beginning to the end was an African affair; the West was powerless" (Le Monde 21 May 1997, 3). Gérard Prunier arrived at the same conclusion when he stated: "The Great Lakes crisis and the Zairean civil war into which it developed are perfect illustrations of the fact that, for better or worse, Africa is now an independent historical actor. Recognizing this will have to be the first step in any attempt at conflict resolution in the future" (Prunier 1997, 199). Both French and Anglo-Saxon commentators agree. For instance, Africa Confidential wrote that, "the overthrow of Mobutu was overwhelmingly organized and achieved by a coalition of Africans not given to taking outside orders. Just as Africa is trying to move on from the 1884 Berlin Conference; the West should move on from the 1898 Fashoda incident" (Africa Confidential 38:10, 1997, 3; also Le Monde Diplomatique, juillet 1997, 12–13).

The question then becomes: which African states were involved in the Zairean conflict? For what purpose? Those who took part can be divided into two categories: key actors and sympathizers. Their objective was to attain short-term and long-term objectives. The majors actors, perhaps with a varying degree of involvement, were Rwanda, Uganda, Burundi, and Angola.

First, as analyzed earlier, the Rwandan government did not feel secure with the massive presence of Hutu refugees, estimated at 1.5 million if one includes those of Burundi, among whom were tens of thousands of armed militia and the ex-FAR. These militias not only did not renounce armed struggle, but made a number of incursions into Rwanda, the western préfectures being the most affected. With the génocidiaires not disarmed, the spectrum of another war and massacre loomed over Rwanda. Internally, steps to open the government by including Hutu moderates into the Tutsi-dominated RPF government did not work out when three of four ministers forced to resign were Hutu, and the government became, or at least appeared to become, more and more purely Tutsi than ever before.

Rwanda asked the international community to disarm the militia and separate them from other refugees. Paul Kagame informed the U.S. that if nothing was done, Rwanda would attack the camps in order to ensure a secure border and buffer zone. In addition, the RPF felt that it had a moral obligation to help and protect Tutsi minorities in Eastern Zaire who had been denied citizenship by the Zairean government, been mistreated by local authorities and were even threatened with expulsion from Zaire. The situation was aggravated by the arrival of the former Rwandan army and militia who perpetrated ethnic cleansing against the Banyamulenge.

Secondly, Uganda, an important ally of Rwanda, shared the same strategic and political interests. One has to bear in mind that the Tutsi fighters largely contributed to the success of the National Resistance Movement-Army (NRM-A) of Uganda and Museveni's takeover of state power in Uganda in January 1986. In return, Museveni helped the RPF, a movement created by Tutsi exiles of 1959–1962, in the invasion of

Rwanda. The two regimes are not only allies but also interdependent. Beyond this understandable solidarity with Rwanda, Uganda had its own problem with Zaire because of guerrilla incursions from Zaire. Although Museveni brought relative stability and prosperity to his country compared with his predecessors, the war staged by two guerrilla movements (the West Bank Liberation Front and the Holy Spirit Movement) continued in the northern part of the country (Oloka-Onyango 1997, 212–16). Thus, he decided to seal his border from the west in order to cut the fighters off from their base in Zaire.

Further, one should not forget that Museveni and Mobutu had always disliked and distrusted each other. This hatred was based on ideological and personal grounds. However, Museveni was accused, by the Hutu politicians and their sympathizers of trying to build a Tutsi-Hima Empire/hegemony in the Great Lakes region. Likewise, France accuses him, since the invasion of the RPF and in the current crisis, of political machination backed by Anglo-Saxon interests, and of being a coordinator of a grand American plan in the region (Schraeder 1997, 206–11 Leymarie 1997, 12–13). Whatever motives he may have had in the Zairean crisis, Museveni, with Paul Kagame, played a key role in the overthrow of Mobutu's dictatorship. Many states started to see Museveni in the garb of a "kingmaker," and there were even comparisons to Otto von Bismarck of Germany. Although this comparison is extravagant, Museveni was an informal leader of the anti-Mobutu coalition regrouped behind the ADLF.

Third, another actor, perhaps less involved compared to Rwanda and Uganda, was Burundi. Burundi is a twin state of Rwanda and has its own version of the Hutu-Tutsi conflict. In July 1996, the Tutsi army ousted the president and brought to power Major Pierre Buyoya, a former Tutsi leader who was defeated in the democratic election of 1993. Since the assassination of a Hutu democratically elected president, Melchoir Ndadaye, in 1993, Burundi's troubles have grown deeper and deeper; when the power sharing mechanism failed, the former Hutu interior minister, Leonard Nyangoma went into exile and formed a political organization called the National Council for the Defense of Democracy (CNDD) and its armed branch, the Democratic Defense Front (FDD). He went to South Kivu, Zaire where the Hutu guerrillas launched their operations into Northern Burundi. The Tutsi-dominated government in Burundi was condemned by the international community and neighboring countries that imposed an embargo. But it joined the war on the basis of security imperatives and to maintain Tutsi supremacy in

Burundi. Just as with Rwanda and Uganda, Burundi wanted to cut off the Hutu warriors from their rear bases in order to have a secure border. It is possible that it joined the two groups because of ethnic solidarity, but Rwanda and Uganda refused to help Burundi against the Hutu rebellion.

Finally, another important actor, but a relatively newcomer to the conflict, was Angola. Angola, on the other side of Zaire, does not share the same ethnic composition with Burundi/Rwanda/Uganda, but it does share political and strategic interests. During the Cold War, Mobutu was the most important American ally in Africa in its policy of containment of Communism. After Angolan independence from Portugal, the Soviet-supported Movimento Popular de Libertaçao de Angola (MPLA) triumphed over J. Savimbi's Uniao National para independencia Total de Angola (UNITA), supported by the West and South Africa. Zaire was the major ally of Savimbi. Upon the departure of Cuba from Angola, the end of the Cold War and the consequent democratization process in that country, the West reconsidered its massive support to UNITA, progressively ending support since the reasons they helped both Mobutu and Savimbi were no longer applicable. But Mobutu and Savimbi, the two leftovers of the Cold War, continued to support each other; Zaire allowed UNITA to illegally export diamonds amounting to $500 million a year (U.S.) in exchange for food, arms, and fuel to ensure its survival, although UNITA was politically marginalized. From the point of view of the Angolan government, peacemaking, and a power sharing mechanism with UNITA, were not possible or potentially lasting unless UNITA could be completely disarmed and annihilated as a military organization. The dispersal of UNITA was only possible when Mobutu was overthrown and Angola decided to join, relatively late in February, the War of the ADLF orchestrated by Uganda and Rwanda. The Katangese fighters, under the command of General Delphin Mulanda, were shipped to the zone of the conflict, Bukavu, and contributed considerably to the victory of the Alliance. The victory of the Alliance and the overthrow of Mobutu represents, therefore, a serious, and perhaps a final, blow to UNITA, which lost a precious regional political ally. As Africa Confidential noted:

> Jonas Savimbi must feel that the earth has moved; but not because he has any closer to quenching his passion to become president of Angola. The tremors running from northern Angola down to Savimbi highland redoubt in Bailundo are the aftershocks of the political earthquakes in Central Africa and the fight of last significant foreign ally, Mobutu Sese Seko. (Africa Confidential 38:11, 1997, 3–4)

Consequently, perhaps thousands of UNITA combatants joined, as did the ex-FAR and Interahamwe before them, the ranks of Zairean soldiers—not only as a way to pay tribute to the dictator for his past unconditional support, but also to ensure their own survival:

> The stiffest resistance Kabila confronted came not from the Zairean army but from the Angolan rebel group, UNITA, led by Jonas Savimbi, a cold war ally of the U.S.'s and great friend of Mobutu's. One of the hardest-fought battles of the civil war was two weeks ago in the southern town of Kenge between Kabila's troops and UNITA rebels who have long depended on Zaire as pipelines for weapons and other supplies. UNITA fighters were also among the last defenders of Kinshasa's international airport. (Time 26 May 1997, 22)

In brief, Uganda, Rwanda, Burundi, and Angola came together against Mobutu's Zaire to bring about stability in the region and ensure the security of their respective governments by cutting off their opponents from their rear bases in Zaire. Incontestably, the overthrow of Mobutu would settle a part of their problem since it would weaken their adversaries and possibly induce them to negotiate. From the point view of these states and of the U.S., the current development,—the Alliance's victory—will stabilize Central Africa, whereas France and its Francophone allies maintain, a contrario, that it will destabilize the whole region.

The transfer of power from Mobutu to the Alliance cannot solve the underlying political problems in all these countries. The Angolan government needs to find a way to transform UNITA into a political party, though futile attempts have been made in the past to share power. In Angola, the fighting between MPLA and UNITA forces started with the offensive of the government, although it is difficult to sense the magnitude of this confrontation. In Rwanda and Burundi, there must be a serious effort at reconciliation, power sharing and negotiation, as well as institutional reforms to bring about lasting peace and harmonious co-habitation between and the Tutsi and Hutu (Adelman et al, 1997). In Burundi, the Tutsi army and the Hutu rebels are at war and there is no solution in sight. Likewise, the precarious peace and stability in Rwanda may not last forever after the massive repatriation of refugees; among the returnees there are militia, ex-FAR and many gangs. In Uganda, there is renewed fighting in the northern provinces that might force Museveni to find a political solution to his problem rather than a military one. In other words, although the conditions for regional stability are united more than ever before, one should not underestimate the dynamic of internal conflicts of these states and the challenges ahead—the departure of Mobutu cannot in itself solve a decades-long political problems in neighboring countries (cf. The Economist, 21 June 1997, 48–49). Thus, the belief in solving "five conflicts in one" is illusory unless there is a coherent and workable mechanism for conflict resolution in each state mentioned above.

The members of the anti-Mobutu coalition achieved their immediate goal. With the change of the regime in Kinshasa (the removal of an enemy—Mobutu—and replacing him by a friend—Kabila), Rwanda achieved one of its long-term objectives. This vision was shared by many leaders, particularly in English-speaking Africa (Tanzania, Zambia, Zimbabwe, South Africa) and other countries with strong ties with the U.S., such as Ethiopia and Eritrea. The leaders of Ethiopia, Uganda, Angola, Eritrea, and Rwanda formed, more or less, a contact group and adopted the same political position vis-à-vis the conflict (Cf. Jeune Afrique 1892, 9–15 avril 1997, 5). What all these regimes have in common is that they are the product of a coup d'état or guerrilla warfare and, as such, they are characterized by a special kind of leadership described as "reconstructing autocracies": "These were states which had been in an advanced condition of collapse, and where power had been seized—usually by guerrilla warfare, sometimes by military coup d'état—by an efficiently organized though militaristic regime with a commitment to construction, even at the cost of continuing autocracy" (Clapham 1996, 204–05).

It has to be noted that Museveni preached a "Zero-Party" political system not only for his country but for the whole Africa, whereas other victorious fronts in Ethiopia, Rwanda and Eritrea transformed themselves into a mono-party system/ruling party (Oloka-Onyango, 212–16). As opposed to Museveni, who rejects liberal democracy as a western concept non-transferable to pre-industrial societies,[10] other "constructing autocrats" are not against multipartyism in principle, but they are less committed to political pluralism and fair and free elections, in which they may lose power. Until now, they easily resisted external pressure for democratization and they argued that they were doing well both in economic and human rights terms as compared to the regimes they ousted. They tend to give more priority to economic recovery and stability than democratic issues and strict respect for the rule of law. In spite of this, they have enjoyed the full support of the U.S. and international financial institutions which seem to have been more interested in efficient economic management and political stability than in political pluralism. Throughout the conflict, the "reconstructing autocrats" gave considerable support to the ADLF and Rwanda. They were also convinced that the liberation of Zaire from dictatorial rule, though not democrats themselves, would liberate Africa in general and Central Africa in particular. To quote the Economist on this point:

> Many other African countries, themselves hovering between relapse and recovery, depend on Congo future stability. If Laurent Kabila, the new ruler, can get his huge country to function properly, the economy of the whole Central Africa would be galvanized. If he fails, and the nation implodes, the disaster could suck the neighbors into a black hole of chaos. (The Economist 24 May 1997, 43)

It is true that the young generation of African leaders have always disliked Mobutu for ideological reasons. For them, he embodied all negative images of post-colonial Africa: corruption, inept, and irresponsible rule, patrimonial conception of authority, bad governance, and above all embezzlement. During the Apartheid era, when the blacks in South Africa and the "Front Lines states" suffered and the OAU fought to the best of its capacity, Mobutu entertained good relations with the discriminatory regime. Secondly, many of these leaders were radical socialists, Pan-Africanists, militants of the Third World and even Marxists, whereas Mobutu represented a conservative political spectrum usually in the service of multinational companies and his own interests. They seem to share the point of view of a Zairean scholar, who wrote: "Zaire was one of the first countries to experience the bitter realities of the unresolved conflict between the demands of national liberation—genuine independence and economic development—and the strategic interests of the major powers in post-colonial Africa" (Nzongola-Natlaja 1994, 219; M'Bokolo, 1997). For most of them the model was Nyerere, a former Tanzanian president and highly respected African political figure. Many of them met in Tanzania in the 1970s and some, like Museveni, studied at Dar University. For his part, Kabila spent many years of his life in Tanzania where he took Nyerere as his political guru. Therefore, Kabila has a distinct advantage of obtaining not only the support of a young generation of leaders, but also the sympathy and the blessing of senior statesmen like Mandela and Nyerere. In different conferences and interviews, the latter clearly defended the position of the Alliance and Kabila (Le Monde 21 May 1997).

The most important, but discrete support, for the Alliance and the countries supporting it came from South Africa—Mandela. Before the beginning of the war in eastern Zaire, South Africa armed the RPF—arms sales that were highly criticized as one of the contributing factors to the escalation of the war; the arms sales were subsequently suspended. During the war and particularly during its last stage, Mandela attempted mediation between Mobutu and Kabila. He worked hand in hand with American diplomats, with Bill Richardson, special envoy of President Clinton, as well as with the U.N. and OAU representative, Mohamed Sahnoun. (The OAU did little except offer its best wishes in different summits such as Nairobi I and Nairobi II.) The efforts were aimed at avoiding bloodshed and a "soft landing" of the rebels in the Zairean capital or to facilitate an orderly transfer of power. South Africa, as all countries forming the anti-Mobutu coalition, believes that a well-governed and managed Zaire will stimulate the economy of Central Africa and lay the basis for the creation of an African Free Market. South Africa and Zaire have abundant human and material resources and, as such, a dynamic Zairean economy is likely to stimulate the economic growth of South Africa. Consequently, the two countries can be engines for the development of the African economy for the century to come.

Although I stressed the important role played by African leaders and states in the Zairean Revolution, one has to concede that without the encouragement, understanding and accommodation of the U.S. in this revolution engineered by Africans, Mobutu would not have been overthrown as easily. They U.S. favored the anti-Mobutu coalition. First all, the U.S. abandoned Mobutu—the man the U.S. discovered, put into power, and protected from his enemies on the way to helping him become one of the wealthiest people in the world (Kelly 1993). This was mainly because, as one spokesman of Department of State was quoted as saying, "the reason for being a friend with him came to an end with the Cold War." Secondly, Mobutu embodied the opposite of what the U.S. tries to promote in Africa or elsewhere in the world: a market economy, good governance and liberal democracy. The U.S. characterized Mobutu, their "useful tyrant," as a "caricature of history." Thirdly, there is a renewed interest in Africa in the U.S., despite the Somalia syndrome of 1993, as the remaining great potential market for American capital, although the U.S.'s current imports from Africa are only 1.9 percent of its total imports. Thus, President Clinton was quoted as saying: "Our efforts to help Africa in order to develop itself will create more opportunity to export American goods and services as well as more jobs at home (U.S.). These efforts will reduce also in the future the cost of American humanitarian aid of a great magnitude" (Roussin 1997, 17). America losing its "Afrophobia" began with a number of initiatives which look like a second "Marshal Plan," and which concerns almost all sectors of development: economy, infrastructure, health, education. and governance. This economic and strategic interest is based on an active and dynamic diplomatic role throughout Africa, including Francophone countries, in this case Rwanda and Zaire. In addition, the U.S. president plans to visit Africa in 1998 (The Economist 26 April 1997, 23–24).

As far as the current crisis in Zaire is concerned, there are some indications that the U.S. gave material and logistic support to Kabila's forces (Newsweek 21 May 1997, 40–42). However, its diplomatic and political aid and understanding largely contributed to the success of the Alliance; it did not condemn its allies (Rwanda and Uganda) for intervening in Zaire and helping the ADLF. It systematically opposed all diplomatic initiatives calling for military-humanitarian operations, particularly coming from France, which would have altered the momentum and even blocked the Alliance's war. In fact, initially it supported, though reluctantly, the Canadian initiative to rescue the refugees in distress, but when most of the refugees returned the mission became less relevant and lost its raison d'être. Canada itself abandoned it, though there were many refugees still to be rescued, because of lack of political will of many states, problems of logistics and, above all, because of the opposition of regional states. Moreover, the U.S. was said to have dissuaded the King of Morocco from sending his soldiers to help Mobutu, whom it persuaded to step down. It also attempted, in collaboration with Mandela, to facilitate the non-violent transfer of power in Kinshasa. After the takeover of state power by the ADLF, the U.S. administration provided a clear understanding and recognition for the victors, although many would have preferred the sharing of power between the opposition parties and the Alliance which formed an exclusive transitional government for two years. As Bill Richardson, special envoy of President Clinton, said: "The jury is still out on Kabila. But he has potential; we should give him a chance" (Time 26 May 1997, 22). The American influence on the cultural, political, and economic agenda of the new government, which turned away from France and Belgium, proved very strong. Thus, the American influence on Zaire, located in the heart of Africa and endowed with a considerable material resources, added to many other pro-American governments of the region, including Eritrea, Uganda, Ethiopia, and Rwanda. This reinforces the supremacy of the U.S. in Africa more than ever before.

In contrast, this incontestable American diplomatic and political triumph represents a humiliating defeat for France, its only rival in Africa. The French failure in Zaire was highly resented in Paris and, in light of this, many French commentators used various adjectives to characterize the event: "désastre," "effacement," "isolement," "fiasco," and so on (Leymarie 1997, 12–13). Many African regimes, which heavily depend on France for protection and survival, could say the same thing; they doubt if they can still count upon France or if the latter will be in a position to protect them from foreign-supported insurgents like the Alliance of Kabila. It is true that French influence is declining and shrinking from year to year, due to several different factors and in the face of the rising American influence, particularly after the end of the Cold War paved the way for competition between the two democracies. Even during the Cold War period, despite its Alliance with the U.S., France tried to have an independent voice in international politics as a medium economic power and as a nuclear one. The U.S. and other western powers recognize France's special role and interest in French-speaking Africa, perhaps with the exception of Zaire, where America exercised a tremendous influence. This gave rise to the notion of la chasse gardée (exclusive hunting ground) of France. With the end of the Cold War and hence of a bipolar world, France and the U.S. are no longer partners but rivals. In effect, the U.S. contests the notion of la chasse gardée as an outmoded concept, whereas France is attached to its diplomatic, political, and cultural pre-eminence in Francophone countries; in other words, the status quo. Perhaps the following statement of Warren Christopher, the former U.S. Secretary of State, in response to another polemical statement from a French cooperation minister, Jacques Godfrain, summarizes the situation: "All nations must cooperate, not compete, if we are going to make a positive difference in Africa's future. The time has passed when Africa could be carved into spheres of influence, or when outside powers could view whole groups of states as their private domains."[11]

Therefore, as far as France and the U.S. are concerned, the Cold War has been replaced in Africa by a "cold peace." If France blindly supported the Habyarimana regime and the Hutu-dominated government, it was because it thought that the RPF was supplied and supported by the Anglo-Saxons and their "representative" in the region, Yoweri Museveni; the whole project was perceived as a ploy to humiliate France. After the genocide, France realized that it lost Rwanda and continued to treat the Tutsi-dominated government as agents of Anglo-Saxons. Since Opération Turquoise of the summer of 1994 in Rwanda, the French government rehabilitated Mobutu, who was highly criticized and hated in France, Belgium and the U.S. since the speech at La Baule in 1990 by President Mitterand.[12] When the war began in Eastern Zaire, France reacted much the same way as it did in 1994; the war was launched by Washington agents in the region. In the eyes of French policymakers, the Banyamulenge, which referred to Kabila as well as Rwandan forces, were all in the service of the U.S. which aimed to undermine France's influence (pré carré) in Africa. By fixing its eyes on the external power, France underestimated the local roots of the conflict.

Since France thought that the collapse of Mobutu and his replacement by pro-American rebels would jeopardize their pré carré in West Africa, it decided to stand by the dictator. Militarily, France could do little. In effect, as opposed to many other African countries, France did not sign a defense agreement with Zaire. Even if it had a defense pact, France did not have adequate soldiers to protect the dictator against a veritable war machine put in place by the ADLF and its supporters; the old pattern of sending of hundreds of commandos to defend a government of a small country against its opponents/insurgents was irrelevant. Moreover, French authorities could not convince the French public to support an African engagement where French vital interests are not at stake; French economic interest in Zaire is generally exaggerated and less important compared to Congo, Gabon and Cameroon.

In the face its incapacity to do something alone, France launched its diplomatic initiatives in favor of humanitarian-political intervention. Its initiatives were rejected by Rwanda, Uganda and the U.S. However, the U.S. agreed to send soldiers when Canada offered to lead an international military force to bring aid to starving refugees on 11 November 1996. Although Canada rallied world support on 12–13 November, the massive return of refugees (more than 600,000 in a few days), thwarted the plan; weeks later Canada abandoned its plan. But France continued to call for military intervention that no one wanted. At the same time, France proved to be the only supporter of Mobutu until the end, along with its Francophone allies and some Anglophone countries such as Nigeria, the Sudan and to some degree, Kenya. All the leaders are dictators trying to rescue an autocrat hated at home and abroad. What is striking, however, is that when Mobutu practically lost the war and power as well as whatever legitimacy and credibility he had in March, French diplomats continued to play Mobutu's card and maintained that Mobutu was "incontournable," that is he cannot be ignored, in the words of French Foreign Minister, Hervé de Charette (Leymarie 1997, 12–13). After everything was over, French authorities were trying to maneuver and find a place for Mobutu's men in the transitional government, perhaps as a means of retaining some influence. It was in the context of this vain attempt to save the face of Mobutu (la sortie honorable), that the summit of Libreville took place and came up with irrelevant resolutions. The irony embedded in the history of this political alignment is that the French ended up as the last defender of the dictator created and maintained, but finally abandoned, by the US, whereas the latter allied itself with the "revolutionaries" of yesteryear— their principal enemy who had converted to the rhetoric of liberal democracy and a market economy.

In Zaire, the "second largest Francophone country in the world" as it used to be called, the French lost diplomatically, politically and perhaps culturally—English will now be an official language along with French. This became evident on the occasion of the Francophonie summit in Hanoi, Vietnam, in November 1997; Zaire not only boycotted the summit, but also announced its withdrawal from the organization. This, combined with other conflicts where French presence was challenged, as in Central Africa, "small" Congo and elsewhere, will have great repercussions on French politics in Africa. France not only needs to rethink its policies towards Africa in light of the new reality in international relations, but it also must take account of the aspiration of African peoples. There are some who even call for a "second round of decolonization" in order to establish a more balanced and equal relationship instead of the paternalistic one instituted by de Gaulle and continued by his successors of the fifth Republic, including the late socialist president, François Mitterand.[13] In other words, traditional French politics and ties vis-à-vis Francophone Africa have become more and more untenable for a variety of reasons which Peter J. Schraeder summarized in the following terms:

> Most important, regardless of what special ties French policymakers ideally would like to pursue, French freedom of action is increasingly constrained by a variety of factors and developments: France's responsibilities and interests outside Africa; the evolving structure of the international system; declining military capabilities during a period of growing domestic constraints; and, most important, the emergence of new elites in Francophone Africa less willing to accept the same types of ties enjoyed and permitted by their predecessors. (Schraeder, 211)

Conclusion

The Rwandan tragedy of 1994 and the fall of Mobutu's kleptocracy were intimately interconnected. Internal political, economic and social crises provide other explanatory factors. Whatever the final balance of internal and external forces might have been, Mobutu is now gone and a new era has begun in Zaire with the ADLF's takeover of state power. Incontestably, the challenge ahead is tougher than was the sweeping military victory: reconstructing the economy, the infrastructure, and a state destroyed by a thirty-year-long dictatorial rule. The process of democratization, strict respect for human rights and the rule of law as a basis for a political system and culture are other substantial challenges. In all these domains, the measures taken by Kabila so far are ambiguous and partial, leading many observers to pessimism as much as optimism with regard to the future of the Democratic Republic of Congo (DRC). It is too early to make a reasonable political judgment on whether Kabila and his associates have the capacity and the will to accomplish the enormous tasks that face them, but there are also few enough reasons to feel sanguine.

On the other hand, the overthrow of Mobutu will normalize the diplomatic relations between Zaire and its neighbors, a condition sine qua non for the stability of the region. At the same time, it must be stressed that the changes in Zaire cannot in themselves end decades-long ethnonational and political conflicts in neighboring states—one can mention the Hutu-Tutsi conflict as an example. The Tutsi and Hutu have to find imaginative methods and mechanisms to resolve that conflict and build lasting peace. The major powers and the international community must help in an attempt to achieve this goal which, is ultimately the only way regional stability, human security and harmony can develop in the Great Lakes region.

Notes

1. At the height of power struggle between the opposition parties and the dictator, Georges Nzogola-Ntalaja wrote: "Mobutu cannot negotiate giving up power, or even sharing it. More than any other player in the Zairean political arena, he understands that the present conflict between the forces of change and those of the status quo is above all concerned with state power and access to the resources that the state controls. Since losing power is likely to diminish, if not eliminate the access he and his entourage used to have to such resources, he is prepared to do everything possible to block peaceful resolution of the conflict" ("Zaire I: Moving Beyond Mobutu," 93:583, May 1994, 193–97; see also Shawn H. McCormick, "Zaire II: Mobutu, Master of the Game?" in ibid., 223–27).

2. During the Rwandan genocide and ethnic cleansing, the Western media and the majority of commentators dismissed the dynamic of the conflict as "tribalism," whereas they treated the same kind of conflict in the former Yugoslavia, Bosnia, as nationalism. This is a reflection of old views using "tribalism" in reference to Africa and "nationalism" when referring to Europe.

3. Prunier (1997) noted: "National conference delegates from Kivu fought each other in Kinshasa according to complex and shifting patterns of ethnic rivalries,

but they all agreed on one point: Kivu's Kinyarwanda speakers were to be politically eliminated and possibly forced back physically into Rwanda."

4. François-Xavier Verschave also indicated that the arms confiscated from ex-FAR went to the benefit of Mobutu. The arms would be sold back to the ex-FAR when they were ready to reconquer Rwanda or the arms could be used to reinforce UNITA in return for a financial payment to Mobutu.

5. Note that although the original estimates of refugees in Zaire totaled 1,200,000, the total was now 900,000, and some contend that the figure of 300,000 who fled into the bush was exaggerated (Eds.).

6. The controversy between the U.N. and the new authorities in Zaire about the massacre of Hutu refugees by the Tutsi elements of the ADLF continues. One has to wait for the result of the U.N. commission of inquiry. But some humanitarian organizations characterized this massacre as another genocide.

7. For the details see two issues of Africa Confidential, 28 March 1997, 38:7 and Africa Confidential, 9 May 1997, 38:10.

8. Africa Confidential (28 March 1997, 38:7) provides the list of factions and individuals comprising the ADLF. Like the political parties, the armed opposition, L'Alliance des Forces Démocratiques pour la Libération du Congo-Zaire (AFDL-CZ), is far from homogeneous in ethnic origins and in political-ideological orientation. It includes the Parti de la Révolution Populaire (PRP) of Laurent Kabila; the Alliance Démocratique des Peuples (ADP); the Mouvement Révolutionnaire pour la Libération du Zaire (MLRZ) led by Masau Nindaga; the Conseil National de Résistance pour la Démocratie (CNRD) led by André Kisase Ngandu, who was killed in January under unknown circumstances, and the Front de Libération National du Congo (FLNC).

9. Rosenblum 1997, 203. He underlined, "Tshisekedi's impetuous and unpredictable behavior, including long period of silence during which he has refused to meet with other political figures or foreign diplomats, has alienated much of the intellectual class and most other opposition politicians. Although Tshisekedi remains popular, the opposition itself is badly splintered and largely ineffectual. It remains reactive and without creativity or depth, guided by old-generation politicians who rarely leave the capital."

10. For the debate about the relevance of liberal democracy in Africa, see Makinda, 1996, 555–73.

11. Schraeder 1997, 210. For an extensive analysis of the international politics of Francophonie see Clapham 1996, 88–103.

12. In his speech, the President of France made aid to Africa conditional on the democratization process and respect for the rule of law. In fact, France did press the poorest countries (Benin, Mali, Niger, etc.,) to democratize themselves, whereas it maintained the status quo in Afrique utile, i.e., where French interest is considerable, such as Cameroon, Gabon, Togo, Côte d'Ivoire. So, Paristroika appeared more as a means of disengaging France from the poorest countries than a commitment to democratization in all French speaking Africa. See Toulabor, 1995, Ch. 8.

13. For various analyses, see, among others: Chipman 1989; Bayart 1983; and Bach 1986, Chapter 5.

Glossary I
Personal Names

Aideed, Mohamed Farah.
> Former General in the Somali armed forces who became leader of the United Somali Congress (USC) and, in alliance with other clan-based political parties, led the overthrow of the Barre regime in January 1990 when Aideed captured Mogadishu and took control of the Ministry of Defense and the Presidency ushering in two years of further civil war until Barre fled in May 1992; it was Aideed's June-October 1993 confrontation with UNOSOM II culminating in 18 dead and 78 wounded U.S. servicemen on 3 October that led to the withdrawal of U.N. peacekeepers and the new resolve of the U.S. to restrict its support for U.N. peacekeeping in Africa, an action that would have tragic consequences for Rwanda in general and the just-launched UNAMIR peacekeeping force.

Allen, Ron.
> ABC correspondent.

Amin Dada, Idi.
> Assumed power in a military coup in Uganda in January of 1971 and was overthrown in 1979.

Amin, Mohamed.
> Reuters bureau chief in Nairobi.

Annan, Kofi.
> U.N. Under-Secretary General and head of DPKO during the creation of UNAMIR and the genocide in Rwanda; appointed Secretary General of the U.N. in 1997.

Anyidoho, Brigadier-General Henry.
> The Deputy Commander of UNAMIR during the genocide.

Aurillac, Michel.
> French Minister for Cooperation under Chirac from 1986–88 and part of the French pro-Habyarimana and pro-Mobutu group.

Bagaza, Lt. Col. Jean-Baptiste.
> Cousin of President Michel Micombero of the First Republic of Burundi whom he overthrew on 1 November 1976; President of the Second Republic until 1987.

Banyingana, Major (Dr.) Peter.
> A leader of the RPF and the invasion force who was killed alongside Major General Fred Rwigyema on 2 October in suspicious circumstances.

Bagambiki, Emmanuel.
> A Hutu extremist Préfet who called on the French to reconquer the RPF held territory and "free" his fellow Hutus.

Bagaragaza, Thadde.
> A one-time speaker of the National Assembly under Habyarimana who joined the opposition MDR

Bagosora, Colonel Théoneste.
>Director of Services in the Ministry of Defence under Habyarimana and believed to be the coordinator of the 6 April coup and genocide; now under indictment at Arusha.

Balladur, Edouard.
>Prime Minister of France when the allied conservative parties came to power in the March 1993 French elections and, therefore, during the genocide.

Bandi, Kaggwa.
>Baganda commander of the National Resistance Army (NRA) allegedly targetted by the NRA's death squad because of opposition to Museveni.

Barahinyura,
Jean Shyirambere.
>Author of Le Général-Major Habyarimana: Quinze ans de tyrannie et de tartufferie au Rwanda (1988) attacking the President, of Rwanda: Trente-deux aux aprés la révolution sociale le 1959 (1992) attacking the RPF, and a founder of the CDR.

Barayagwiza, Jean-Bosco.
>CDR founder and leader.

Baril, General Maurice.
>Made head of the Canadian armed forces in 1997, but during the Rwandan crisis and genocide, military adviser to the UNSG in U.N. headquarters in New York in the DPKO and the contact person for his fellow Canadian, General Romeo Dallaire, Force Commander of UNAMIR.

Barre, Mohamed Siad.
>Major General in Somali armed forces whose October 1969 coup ushered in twenty-one years of authoritarian military dictatorship.

Barril, Captain Paul.
>Head of the special antiterrorist unit in the Groupement d'"Intervention de la Gendarmie Nationale (GIGN) in the Elysée Palace in Paris until 1983 when he resigned for tampering with evidence in an IRA court case; subsequently, he became a freelance military adviser, officially appointed by Habyarimana's widow on 6 May 1994 to investigate her husband's assassination, and who reappeared on French television on 28 June 1994 accusing the RPF of shooting down President Habyarimana's plane and attacking the government, accusations based on his claimed possession of the voice recorder of Habyarimana's plane, satellite photos, and the launchers of the rocket; in the accusation, he alleged that the rockets had been fired from Masaka hill, which, on 6 April, was held by the Presidential Guard and not by the RPF.

Baudillon, Philippe.
>French Prime Minister Balladur's Africa-man.

Bayingana, Dr. Peter.
>A member of RANU who later became a leader in the RPA.

Béliard, Jean-Christophe.
>French charge d'affaires in Tanzania and representative at the Arusha talks.

Bemeriki, Valerie.
>Member of the CDR and a broadcaster on RTLM.

Bernard-Meunier, Marie.
>Assistant Deputy Minister for Global Issues in the Department of Foreign Affairs and International Trade (DFAIT) who wrote the Foreward to Proceedings—Conflict Prevention: African Perspective for the International Francophone Meeting, Ottawa, September 1995.

Berlusconi, Sylvio.
> Prime Minister of Italy who originally agreed to participate and then backed out of the French Opération Turquoise intervention in June of 1994.

Bertello, Msgr. Giuseppe.
> Papal nuncio in Kigali after 1990 until the genocide, dean of the diplomatic core in Rwanda.

Bicamumpaka, Jerome.
> An extremist member of the MDR and the Foreign Minister in the genocidist government of Rwanda that took power on 7 April 1994 who was invited by the UNSG to address the U.N. General Assembly where he duly misinformed the assembled delegates about the situation in Rwanda; he then went to Paris on 27 April to be received by Mitterand, Balladur and Juppé; he with others failed to obtain Mobutu's backing for a government in exile in Zaire after the genocidist government fled Rwanda.

Bihozagara, Dr. Jacques.
> A Tutsi, the RPF European Representative who had grown up in Burundi as a refugee and spoke perfect French and became Minister of Rehabilitation in the new RPF government of Rwanda in July 1994, and subsequently became Minister for Youth and Sport.

Bizimana, Maj-Gen Augustin.
> Defence Minister from August 1993 and part of the extremist plot.

Bizimungu, Casimir.
> Foreign Minister in the Habyarimana regime and head of the minority northern Ruhengeri faction in rivalry with the majority Gisenyi faction; travelled to Paris in October 1990 to get French military intervention to assist the Rwandese government to fight the RPF invasion; an alleged instigator of the genocide.

Bizimungu, Pasteur.
> A Hutu and prominent Rwandese businessman active against the MRND who fled to Uganda in 1990 and told the RPF that the Rwandese government was ready to collapse; he became President of Rwanda after the RPF victory.

Boisvineau, Mrs.
> Direction des Affaires Africaines et Malgaches in the the Quai d'Orsay; and Under-Director for Eastern Africa under President Mitterand.

Bolongo, General Likulia.
> Prime Minister of Zaire appointed by Mobutu after Tishesekedei was removed.

Bon, Colonel Dominique.
> French Military Attache at the Embassy in Kinshasa.

Bona, Seguya
> Baganda. Commander of the National Resistance Army (NRA) allegedly targetted by the NRA's death squad because of opposition to Museveni.

Booh-Booh, Jacques-Roger.
> A Cameroon who served as the U.N. Special Representative to Rwanda after the Arusha Accords were signed and who arrived in Kigali in November.

Boutros-Ghali, Boutros.
> Secretary-General of the U.N. during the Rwanda genocide.

Broadbent, Ed.
> Head of the International Centre for Human Rights and Democratic Development—a Canadian government funded organization in Montreal.

Bucyana, Martin.
> Head of Papeterie de Zaza and a founder and secretary general of CDR; assassinated in February of 1994.

Bunyenyezi, Major Chris.
> A military leader in the RPF 1990 October invasion who took overall command when Major General Fred Rwigyema was killed on 2 October; Bunyenyezi was himself killed in an ambush on 23 October.

Buyoya, Major Pierre.
> Tutsi leader defeated in the 1993 Burundi election who later returned to power after the June 1996 coup.

Bwanakweri, Chief Prosper.
> A noble and a liberal leader of the Tutsi in the 1950s.

Byegyeka, Lieutenant.
> A Tutsi Rwandese leader in the NRA.

Chalker, Lynda.
> British Minister of Overseas Development.

Charette, Hervé de.
> French Foreign Minister.

Chirac, Jacques.
> Secretary-General of the neo-Gaullist party in France, and the presidential successor to François Mitterand in April 1995.

Choffray, Capt.
> Sector headquarters Belgian officer in UNAMIR.

Chollet, Lieutenant-Colonel.
> Nominated on February 1992 to head the Détachement d'Assistance Militaire et d'Instruction (DAMI) in Rwanda; he took on the role of advisor to both President Habyarimana and the Chief Commander of the Rwandese Armed Forces, and was, de facto, in charge of counterinsurgency operations.

Christopher, Warren.
> U.S. Secretary of State during the Rwandan genocide.

Claes, Willy.
> The Belgian Foreign Minister who made the decision to withdraw the Belgian contingent from UNAMIR after ten Belgian peacekeepers were killed.

Classe, Msgr. Léon.
> A priest who arrived in Rwanda in 1907 and stayed until 1945, eventually rising to Bishop; he supported the Tutsi as the natural rulers of Rwanda.

Cohen, Herman (Hank).
> Under Secretary of State for African Affairs under President George Bush, and, after retirement, President of the Global Coalition, an African lobby agency.

Cussac, Colonel.
> Military attaché and head of the French Military Assistance Mission in Rwanda.

Dahinden, Philippe.
> Reporter for Swiss Radio who founded Radio Muharo with support from Reporters sans Frontieres and Rwandan human rights activists.

Dallaire, Brig. General Romeo.
> Canadian general, the first Force Commander of UNAMIR who sent the famous 11 January 1994 cable to U.N. headquarters detailing the planned coup and genocide.

Debarge, Marcel.
> French Cooperation Minister during the RPF offensive in February 1993.

Delaye, Bruno.
> President Mitterand's Special Counsellor for African Affairs.

Dennis, Cecil.
> Liberian Foreign Minister.

d'Estaing, Valéry Giscard.
> French President who pursued an aggressive policy in the former Belgian territories and authorized the French military intervention in Shaba in 1978.

Destexhe, Alain.
> Secretary-General of Médecins Sans Frontières and a Belgian Senator who has devoted considerable effort to the analysis of the Rwandan genocide.

Dewez, Lt.-Col J.
> Battalion commander of the 2nd Battalion of Belgian troops constituting the KIBAT battalion of UNAMIR.

Diagne, Major I.
> The UNAMIR officer responsible for taking notes for Dallaire.

Dijoud, Paul.
> Director for Africa and the Maghreb in the Quai d'Orsay in the early nineties.

Diria, Ahmed.
> Tanzanian Foreign Minister who attempted to mediate the delays in the formation of a broad-based government in Rwanda in early 1994.

Dufourq, Bertrand.
> Secretary-General of the French Ministry of Foreign Affairs.

Dumas, Roland.
> French Foreign Minister in 1991.

Dussault, Bernard.
> Named Canadian Ambassador for Central Africa in the Spring of 1994, later High Commissioner to Kenya.

Edwards, Lucie.
> Preceded Dussault as Canadian High Commissioner to Kenya.

Foccart, Jacques.
> A secret service agent appointed by Jacques Chirac as special adviser on Africa.

Foley, Mark.
> ABC News assignment manager in London.

Fuller, Carol.
> U.S. State Department's desk officer for Rwanda during the Arusha negotiations.

Gaspard, Gihigi.
> Member of the CDR and a journalist on RTLM.

Gatabazi, Félicien.
> Secretary-General of the PSD who was assassinated in February 1994 and succeeeded by Félicien Nagago.

Gatsinzi, Brigadier-General Marcel.
> Moderate RPA officer in charge of negotiating a cease-fire after the coup and who called for national reconciliation in the newly created French "safe humanitarian zone."

Gaspard, Gihigi.
> A member of CDR and broadcast journalist on RTLM.

Gérard, Yannick.
> Former ambassador to Kampala who travelled to RPF headquarters in Mulindi with Ambassador Marlaud to meet with Colonel Kanyarengwe before Opération Turquoise was launched.

Germanos, General Raymond.
    Subordinate commander of Opération Turquoise and headquartered in Bukavu/Cyangugu.
Gillet, Eric.
    Belgian lawyer and human rights activist who, in 1991, reported involvement of the French in interrogating RPF prisoners and was part of the international human rights delegation in January 1993 that first labelled the killings in Rwanda as genocide.
Gitera, Joseph.
    A populist demagogue businessman, founder of APROSOMA in 1957 and elected president of the Provincial Council in 1960, dismissed from the post in 1961, later became a member of PARMEHUTU and the delegate from Butare.
Godfrain, Jacques.
    French Cooperation Minister.
Gore, Al.
    Vice President of the U.S. in the Clinton administration.
Habyarimana, Jean-Baptiste.
    Tutsi préfet of Butare who prevented genocide there until replaced by Sylvain Ndikumania on 20 April 1994.
Habyarimana, Juvenal.
    An original member of the Committee of Nine who was made head of the Ministry of the National Guard and Police in 1965, and became president of Rwanda through a coup on 5 July 1973 on the basis of a new constitution centralizing power in the Presidency and legalizing only his own MRND party; he was elected President on 24 December 1978 beginning a succession of five year terms which ended when his plane was shot down on 6 April 1994 setting off the extremist coup, the genocide and the renewal of the war with the RPF.
Hangimana, François-Xavier.
    The founder of the Rwandese newspaper, Ijambo, who was arrested in May of 1991 for insulting government ministers and military officers and released on 24 September of that same year.
Hansen, Peter.
    Undersecretary-General for Humanitarian Affairs in the United Nations (DHA) during the Rwandan genocide.
Hervé, Ladsous.
    Assistant French Permanent Representative to the United Nations.
Huchon, General.
    In charge of the Mission Militaire de Cooperation and Assistant Commander-in-Chief to General Lanxade in the Elysée Palace.
Hunter, Dorothea.
    Oxfam representative who reported on the Rwandese refugee situation in Uganda in 1968.
Joxe, M. Pierre.
    French Minister of Defense in the early 1990s.
Jennings, Peter.
    ABC News network anchor.
Juppé, Alain.
    Foreign Minister of France during the genocide.
Kabila, Laurent-Desirè.
    Led the Alliance des Forces Dèmocratiques pour la Libèration du Congo-

Zaire (AFDL) in the civil war in Zaire in 1996-97, overthrew Mobutu in 1997, became President and renamed the country the Democratic Republic of Congo.

Kabuga, Félicien.
Wealthy businessman, whose daughter was married to a son of President Habyarimana, and a member of the President's inner circle, the AKAZU , who helped found the propaganda radio station RTLM.

Kagame, Maj.-General Paul.
Currently Vice-President and Minister of Defence of Rwanda; a Tutsi refugee raised in Uganda who fought for seven years with Museveni's guerillas, he became head of military intelligence for the Uganda National Revolutionary Army (NRA) when Museveni became President of Uganda; he was enrolled in the U.S. General Staff College in Fort Leavenworth, Kansas at the time of the October 1990 invasion and became head of the RPF when both Rwigyema and Bunyenyezi were killed in October 1990.

Kajuga, Robert.
A Tutsi who was the Commander of the Interahamwe who turned out to be a notorious extremist killer targetting Tutsi.

Kaka, Sam Major.
Commanding Officer, Military Police in Uganda.

Kalimuzo, Frank.
A Tutsi refugee highly placed in the Obote Ugandan government who joined the Hutu in pressuring the Obote regime to clamp down on the Tutsi refugee warriors in the sixties.

Kamutu, E.
Leading member of and minister in the "scientist" wing of Obote's Uganda People's Congress who tried to protect the Banyankole in Ankole by distinguishing between them and Museveni's refugee warrior supporters.

Kanyabugori, Fidele.
The lawyer representing the Rwandese human rights organization, Kanyarwanda, who was arrested on 29 March 1992 for submitting a petition demanding an independent investigation of the Bagogwe massacre.

Kanyarengwe, Colonel Alexis.
A Hutu Rwandan Minister of Internal Affairs forced into exile in 1980 when accused of plotting against President Habyarimana who joined the RPF and became President and spokesperson in November of 1990.

Kanyarushoki, Pierre-Claver.
Rwandan Ambassador to Uganda in the Habyarimana regime and negotiator at Arusha.

Katano, Habimana.
A member of MRND(D) and extremist broadcaster on RTLM.

Kayibanda, Grégoire.
Founder of the Mouvement Social Mahutu, editor-in-chief of the Catholic newspaper Kinyameteka in 1956 which documented Tutsi abuses, an original member of the Committee of Nine, leader of PARMEHUTU and Rwanda's first President until overthrown by Habyarimana in 1973; he was imprisoned and died in prison in 1976.

Kayira, Dr. A.
Leader of the Uganda Freedom Army (UFA), the Buganda insurrectionist rival to Museveni's NRA in the early eighties.

Kazinga, Agathe.
Wife of President Habyarimana, a heir of a Hutu northern royal lineage and

leader of the AKAZU; nicknamed Kanjogera after the terrible mother of the king.

Kengo wa Dondo.
> Prime Minister of Zaire and head of a crisis government appointed by Mobutu when Kabila marched across Zaire to overthrow the Mobutu regime.

Kennedy, Senator Edward.
> U.S. Senator, advocated jamming the RTLM genocidal broadcasts.

Khan, Mohamed Shahryar.
> U.N. Special Representative to Rwanda who succeeded Jacques Roger Booh-Booh after the genocide.

Kigeri IV, King.
> Unwami (King) of Rwanda deposed after the elections in Rwanda in 1961.

Kigeri V, King.
> Jean-Baptiste Ndahindurwa, younger brother and, at age twenty, successor to King Mutara Rudahigwa III of Rwanda after the latter's mysterious death in 1959; overthrown in the Hutu revolt of 1959.

Kigongo, Moses.
> Vice-Chairman of the National Resistance Army (NRA) of Uganda.

Kitare, Captain.
> A Tutsi leader in the NRA.

Kyaligonza, Tom.
> A Tutsi Brigade Commander in the NRA.

Lafourcade, General Jean-Claude.
> Head of Opération Turquoise and headquartered in Goma.

Lanxade, Admiral.
> Chief of Staff of the French Armed Forces during Opération Turquoise.

Lavigerie, Charles Martial.
> French Catholic missionairy, founder of the Société des Missionaires d'Afrique, or the Père Blanc, the White Fathers, in Algiers in 1868; courted traditional Rwandese officials to induce conversion.

Léotard, François.
> French Minister of Defense in Prime Minister Balladur's government.

Lemaire, Lt.
> An officer in the Belgian unit of UNAMIR in charge of ETO ("Beverly Hills").

Levesque, Georges Henri.
> A Canadian Dominican priest, Dean of the faculty of Economic and Social Sciences at Laval University in Quebec City, and founder and Rector from 1963 to 1971 of the National University of Rwanda at Butare.

Lizinde, Colonel Théoneste.
> A Hutu and Security Chief from the northern district of Bugoyi, the rival to Habyarimana's home base in Gisenyi, who had been used by Habyarimana to kill dozens associated with the former Kayibanda regime, and with others was arrested in 1980 for allegedly plotting a coup in April, but freed in 1991 by the RPF in the capture of Rihengeri; he became a member of the RPF.

Lotin, Lt.
> Headed the Belgian platoon of UNAMIR sent to escort the Prime Minister, Mme Agathe Uwilingiyimana, from her residence to the radio station on 7 April; he was murdered along with other members of his platoon.

Lumumba, Patrice.
> The father of Congo's independence; arrested, tortured, and killed in 1961.

Lwabanji, Lwasi Ngabo.
> Deputy Governor of South-Kivu who threatened to expel the estimated 300,000 Banyamulenge (Tutsi) whose citizenship had been cancelled in 1982.

Malecela, John.
> Prime Minister of Tanzania who served as a mediator between the RPF and the Government of Rwanda during the Arusha talks.

Mandela, Nelson.
> After being imprisoned for decades, Mandela emerged from prison to lead the ANC; he was elected President of South Africa in 1994 just as the genocide in Rwanda was getting underway; he tried to mediate the civil war in Zaire.

Mapuranga, Dr. M. T.
> OAU Assistant Secretary General for Political Affairs appointed by the OAU as Special Representative to Rwanda in 1993.

Marchal, Colonel Luc.
> A Belgian, head of the Kigali sector of UNAMIR; court-martialed in Brussels in 1996 for failing to protect his men, a military trial which ended in acquittal.

Marlaud, Jean-Michel.
> French ambassador to Kigali and successor to Georges Martre.

Martre, Georges.
> French ambassador in Kigali at the time of the RPF invasion in 1990.

Maurin, Lieutenant-Colonel.
> Assistant to the military attaché, Lieut.-Col. Chollet, and took over his functions when news broke in France concerning Chollet's activist role in Rwandan anti-RPF military operations.

Mayjambere, Silas.
> Founder of the UPR in 1990 and fled to exile in Belgium that same year.

Mayuya, Colonel Stanislas.
> A close associate of President Habyarimana who was allegedly killed by the AKAZU because he threatened their monopoly control over Habyarimana.

Mercier, General.
> French officer in overall charge of Opération Turquoise.

Michaux-Chevry, Lucette.
> French Secretary of State for Humanitarian Affairs.

Micombero, Michel.
> A Tutsi-Hima, a Captain in Burundi who led the defeat of the Hutu army mutineers on 19 October 1965, became Prime Minister and Minister of Defense and then, as Head of the National Revolutionary Council, was President when the First Burundi Republic was proclaimed on 28 November 1966; he was President until 1976 when he was overthrown on 1 November.

Miller, Reid G.
> Nairobi bureau chief for the Associated Press.

Mkapa, Benjamin.
> Prime Minister of Tanzania; Tanzanian Minister for Higher Education during the Rwandan genocide.

Mobutu, Sese Seko (Joseph-Desire).
> Chief of staff under Lumumba in the Congo, staged a coup when the government party split into two factions led by Lumumba and Kasavubu, and formerly declared himself President in 1965, renaming the Congo Zaire in

1970; overthrown in a Rwanda-backed rebellion led by Laurent Kabila in 1997.

Moi, Daniel Arap.
:   President of Kenya.

de Montferrand, Bernard.
:   Prime Minister Balladur's Diplomatic Counsellor.

Mortehan, Monsieur.
:   Catholic missionary in Rwanda associated with divisive colonial church politics.

Moussali, Michel.
:   UNHCR special envoy to Rwanda in 1994 who argued that Rwanda would experience "a bloodbath of unparalleled proportions" if efforts were not made to salvage the peace process.

Mubarak, Hosni.
:   President of Egypt.

Mugambage, Colonel Frank.
:   The RPF's second ranked officer after Paul Kagame and its prime diplomat who negotiated with Colonel Marcel Gatzinzi of the FAR on a ceasefire following the coup, and with the French over Opération Turquoise.

Mugenzi, Justin.
:   Leader of the PL.

Mugesera, Léon.
:   A graduate of Rwandan and Canadian universities, ideologue of extremism of considerable repute, vice-president of the MRND(D) in Gisenyi, who, in his famous speech of 22 November 1992 at an MRND meeting in Gisenyi, not only declared all other political parties, other than MRND and CDR, accomplices of the enemies of Rwanda, but advocated extermination of the ibyitso; he obtained refugee status in Canada; the Canadian government is currently attempting to extradict him to Arusha.

Mukeshimana, Agnes.
:   A seventeen-year old Tutsi survivor of the genocide at Mugombwa in Muganza.

Mulanda, General Delphin.
:   Commander of the Kantangese fighters in the Zairian alliance against Mobutu.

Mulroney, Brian.
:   Canadian Prime Minister in the early nineties.

Muntu, Mugisha, Maj. Gen.
:   Rwandan Army Commander.

Mussa, Amr.
:   Foreign Minister of Egypt;1993 Chairman of the OAU Council of Ministers.

Museveni, Yoweri.
:   Ugandan Minister of Defense, the leader of the anti-Obote guerilla movement, who became President on 29 January 1986 following his victory and the defeat of the Okello regime that had replaced Obote in 1985.

Mulele, Pierre.
:   Co-leader with Kabila of the 1965 anti-Mobutu opposition in Zaire

Mutesa, Kabaka (King) E.
:   King and President of Buganda in 1961 during the overthrow of the Rwandese monarchy.

Mwinyi, Ali Hassan.
:   President of Tanzania who convened a regional summit of the leaders of

Burundi, Kenya, Rwanda and Uganda in Dar-es-Salaam on that fateful day, 6 April 1994, to obtain an agreement on a broad-based government for Rwanda.

Nahimana, Ferdinand.
Head of ORNIFOR, and a founder of CDR, held to be responsible for the 3 March 1992 broadcast which led to the Bugesera massacre and the displacement of 15,000 Tutsis; he was transferred to become first counsellor in the Rwandese embassy in Bonn.

Ndadaye, Melchior.
Elected president of Burundi on 1 June 1993 by almost a two-thirds majority; he was assinated in October of that year.

Ndayamaje, Innocent.
Founder of the Front national de resistance, the National Resistance Front, in 1986; he was sentenced to five years in prison for organizing an illegal party.

Ndayambaje, Emmanuel.
Bourgmestre in Muganza, now in prison in Belgium charged with genocide.

Ndikumania, Sylvain.
Made préfet of Butare on 20 April 1994 when the genocide commenced there.

Ndugate, Major Stephen.
A Tutsi leader in the Ugandan NRA.

Nepomuscen, Nayinzira.
Leader of the PDC.

Ngabolwabanji, Lwagi.
Deputy Governor of South Kivu during the Zaire civil war.

Ngango, Félicien.
Successor of Félicien Gatabazi as leader of the PSD; his entire family was slaughtered on 7 April when the Belgian UNAMIR protectors were forcefully separated from them.

Ngendahayo, Jean-Marie.
FRODEBU Foreign Minister in Burundi who refused France the right of transit in Opération Turquoise.

Ngeze, Hassan.
Editor of Kangura, an anti-Tutsi and antimoderate newspaper founded in 1990; arrested in June of 1991 with many other editors as a demonstration of balance and released on 12 September 1991; arrested after the genocide and put on trial before the ICTR in Arusha in 1997.

Ngulinzira, Boniface.
Rwandese Defense Minister under Habyarimana who signed the Military Defense Agreement with France.

Nsabimana, Col. Deogratius.
Chief of Staff at Byumba in 1993 and advocate of extremism.

Nsambimanc, Sylvain Georges.
Prefect of Butare during the genocide and put on trial for crimes against humanity before the ICTR in Arusha in 1997.

Nsamwambaho, Fredrick.
Leader of the PSD founded in 1991.

Nsanzuwera, François-Xavier.
Public prosecutor in Kigali.

Nsanzimana, Sylvestre.
Member of the MRND and Minister of Justice in 1991 when he was appointed Prime Minister on 10 October 1991, but his appointment to head the new transitional government was rejected by the opposition parties.

Nsengiyaremye, Dismas.
> A veterinarian who became Prime Minister of the Rwandan coalition government in 1992.

Nsengiyumva, Thadée
> A liberal Catholic priest who became Primate of Kigali and urged the Church to distance itself from the Habyarimana regime; he was well known for his December 1991 manifesto, died alongside Archbishop Vincent Nsengiyumva on 3 June 1994 in Kabgayi.

Nsengiyumva, Vincent.
> Catholic Archbishop in Rwanda and a prominent member of the Central Committee of the MRND until ordered to resign by the Pope in 1989; was allegedly murdered by RPF soldiers on 3 June 1994 in Kabgayi.

Nsthamihigo, Bishop.
> Anglican Bishop of Kigali during the genocide, now living in exile in Nairobi and widely suspected of being involved in the genocide.

Ntabakuze, Aloys.
> FAR battalion commander put on trial before the ICTR in Arusha in 1997.

Ntabonvura, Emmanuel.
> A Tutsi fourteen-year-old genocide survivor at Mugombwa in Muganza.

Ntaryamira, Cyprien.
> The President of Burundi, killed in the plane crash with President Habyarimana on 6 April 1994.

Nyangoma, Leonard.
> Hutu Burundi leader who went into exile in Zaire in July of 1993 and founded the guerilla movement in opposition to the Tutsi military regime in Burundi.

Nyerere, Julius.
> Former President of Tanzania and mediator in the Rwanda conflict and subsequently in the Burundi conflict.

Nyiramutarambira, Félecula.
> An opposition member of Parliament from Butare killed in 1989 in a suspicious accident just after she accused the government of corruption in road contracts.

Nzirorera, Joseph.
> Secretary General of MRND, Public Works Minister under Habyarimana, who, with Casimir Bizimungu, represented the minority Rihengeri faction of northerners in rivalry with Habyarimana's wife's Gisenyi faction.

Obote, Milton.
> President of Uganda in 1966 after overthrowing the Kabaka government; overthrown in turn by Idi Amin in January 1971, but overthrew Amin in 1980 in a Tanzanian-backed war, but ousted on 27 July 1985 in a coup by Brigadier General Basillio Okello.

Oduho, J. H.
> Leader of the Sudanese African National Union (SANU).

Ogata, Sadako.
> U.N. High Commissioner for Refugees.

Okello, Brigadier General Tito Basilio.
> Overthrew Obote in a 27 July1985 coup and became President until overhtrown by Museveni in 1986.

Rawson, David.
> American Ambassador to Rwanda before and during the genocide.

Riza, Iqbal.
> Assistant U.N. Secretary-General reporting to Kofi Annan in DPKO.

Rudahigwa III, Mutara.
>King of Rwanda, whose mysterious and abrupt death in Burundi in July of 1959 triggered the Tutsi attempt at independence and the Belgian-backed revolt of the Hutu in November against the Tutsi and the new King, King Kigeri V.

Rurangaranga, Major Edward.
>A prominent Banyankole minister and close associate of Obote who exerted pressure on the Banyankole to denounce Museveni's NRA as a "foreign" or Tutsi operation and advocated the eviction of the Tutsi refugees from Ankole.

Rucogoza, Faustin.
>A Hutu leader of the MDR founded in 1991 who, as information minister, had threatened to close down Radio Télévision Libre Mille Collines and who also became one of the first victims of the genocide.

Rudasingwa, Théogène.
>General-Secretary of the RPF during the Arusha negotiations; met officials in the Ministry of Defense in Paris to discuss Opération Turquoise; the Rwandan Ambassador to the U.S.

Rutasira, General Leonidas.
>FAR moderate officer; called for national reconciliation during the genocide.

Rwabukwisi, Vincent.
>Editor of the periodical Kanguka arrested in June 1991 for publishing seditious material and released on 12 September 1991.

Rwakasisi, Chris.
>A prominent Banyankole minister and close associate of Obote who exerted pressure on the Banyankole to denounce Museveni's NRA as a "foreign" or Tutsi operation and advocated the eviction of the Tutsi refugees from Ankole.

Rwanyarare, Dr. E.
>Leading member of and minister in the "scientist" wing of Obote's Uganda People's Congress who tried to protect the Banyankole in Ankole by distinguishing between them and Museveni's refugee warrior supporters.

Rwema, Bisengimana.
>Opponent of the first President of Rwanda and cabinet director of the Mobutu government in Zaire from 1970–1980.

Rwigmana, A.
>RPF contact when the U.N. attempted to arrange a ceasefire after the Rwandan April 1994 coup; currently "Chef du Cabinet" of the Minister of Defence.

Rwigyema, Major General Fred.
>Fought in Museveni's rebel movement and was appointed deputy army commander and deputy minister of defence when Museveni took power; became head of the RPF and leader of the 1 October 1990 RPF invasion; he was killed on 2 October.

Sablière, Rochereau de la.
>DAM Director.

Sagatwa, Colonel Elie.
>A cousin of Habyarimana's wife and married to one of his sisters, a prominent member of AKAZU, Habyarimana's principal private secretary and co-owner of the rabid anti-Tutsi newspapaer Kangura.

Sahnoun, Mohamed.
>International diplomat and mediator; former Algerian representative to the U.N. who had served as assistant secretary-general of the OAU.

Salim, Salim A.
> OAU Secretary-General.

Savimbi, Jonas.
> Leader of UNITA in Angola.

Sendashonga, Seth.
> A Hutu, Minister of the Interior in the first RPF cabinet in 1994; currently in exile in Kenya.

Serubuga, Colonel Laurent.
> A prominent member of AKAZU, Habyarimana's brother-in-law, army chief of staff and co-owner of the rabid anti-Tutsi newspapaer Kangura.

Silberzahn, Claude.
> A former DGSE high-ranking official who implied that his intelligence service had foreseen the genocide (*Au coeur du secret*, Paris: Fayard, 1995).

Simard, Father.
> Canadian Catholic missionary to Rwanda who was murdered in October 1994.

Simpson, O.J.
> The American football player and television personality who was accused of murdering his wife and her friend; television coverage of the story and the trial far surpassed the time devoted to coverage of Rwanda and the genocide.

Sindambiwe, Father Silvio.
> A journalist critical of government corruption in the Habyarimana regime who was killed in 1989 in a very suspicious road accident.

Sindikubwabo, Théodore.
> Member of the MRND(D) from Butare, Speaker of the Assembly in the coalition government, and President of the interim government of Rwanda from 9 April to July 1994; allegedly instigated the genocide in Butare after replacing Jean-Baptiste Habyarimana as préfet by Sylvain Ndikumania.

Soumaillo, Gaston.
> Leader of a Lumumbist insurrection in 1963 in which Kabila took part.

Streiker, Gary.
> CNN correspondent in Nairobi.

Swinnen, Johan.
> Belgian ambassador in Kigali before the genocide; one of the last diplomats to be evacuated.

Tiberonda, Dr. Adonia.
> Leading member of and minister in the "scientist" wing of Obote's Uganda People's Congress who tried to protect the Banyankole in Ankole by distinguishing between them and Museveni's refugee warrior supporters.

Tishesekedi, Etienne.
> Opposition politician surprisingly appointed by Mobutu as Prime Minister after Kengo was removed, but was himself removed after three days in office.

Twagiramungu, Faustin.
> Rwandan Prime Minister designate according to the Arusha Agreement who condemned Opération Turquoise from Montreal, but met the French delegation in Kigali in July.

Uwilingiyimana, Agathe.
> A Hutu, member of the MDR, Minister of Education in the first genuine coalition government in April 1992, Vice President and Prime Minister of Rwanda in the 17 July 1993 cabinet authorized to sign a peace agreement,

and, with members of her family (excepting her five children, who were flown out on a French plane), murdered on 7 April 1994.

Valerie, Bemeriki.

A member of CRD and extremist broadcaster on RTLM.

Vandriessche, Capt.

An officer in the Belgian unit of UNAMIR.

Wasswa, Lt. Col. Adam.

Second-in-command of the RPF; killed in a car crash in Uganda in July 1991.

Xavier, François.

Editor of *Ijambo*, founded in 1990; detained in May 1991 and charged with slandering military officers and demoralizing the army.

Glossary II
Foreign and Technical Words and Phrases

Abadehemuka.
> The name of the political party of Unwami (King) Kigeri IV of Rwanda during the fight for independence.

Abakutsi.
> Traditional work obligations, usually of Hutu farmers to local Tutsi nobles, which later referred to any work obligations of Rwandese citizens to the state.

Akazi.
> An evolved form of abakutsi, but as forced labor done for the colonial authorities.

AKAZU or akazu.
> "Small house"—the phrase, taken from the reference to the inner court of the King in pre-colonial Rwanda, but herein referring to the inner group close to President Habyarimana with the connotation of abuse of power and privileges; since the group was made up largely of family members of Habyarimana's wife who controlled most of the big enterprises in the country and influenced internal and external policy; it was also nicknamed Clan de Madame.

Amasasu.
> See isusu.

Amahoro.
> Both the name of a modest hotel in Kigali, which was made into UNAMIR's HQ, and the name of a large stadium nearby where many of the Tutsis who were saved fled where they were protected by the Bangladeshi battalion.

Amwizero.
> Literally "hope"; the name of a radio station in Burundi funded by the E.U. in 1996.

Anglo-Belgian Protocol.
> Dated 14 February 1914, it brought part of the Mufumbiro region and Kigeatuczi district in what is now Uganda together in what was called Kabale.

Arusha Accords.
> The peace agreement signed on 4 August 1993 between the RPF and the Rwandese government establishing the demobilization of parts of both armies and the integration of the rest, the provision for the return of the Tutsi refugees who left in 1959-1962, and, most importantly, the power-sharing agreement among the various parties within Rwanda and the RPF.

Assemblée nationale de transition.
> Transitional National Assembly, the official name for the renamed parliament provided for in the Arusha Accords.

367

ATS Don Bosco.
>Technical school run by Franciscan monks in the center of Kigali and used to house a platoon of UNAMIR soldiers.

Authochtones.
>Those considered to be the indigenous population of an area and in contrast to migrants who may have lived in an area for two centuries or even more.

Bafumbira.
>A subgroup of the Banyarwanda living in Uganda, Rwanda, and the Congo.

Bagogwe.
>Sub-group of traditionally nomadic Tutsi living in the northwest of Rwanda.

Bahutu Manifesto.
>The full title was the Notes on the Social Aspect of the Racial Native Problem in Rwanda, a document signed by the Group of Nine in March 1957 to present to the U.N. trusteeship mission documenting the economic, social, and political oppression of the Hutu under exclusive Tutsi rule within the Belgian trusteeship.

Bairu.
>See Hiru.

Banyamulenge.
>A Tutsi ethnic group in Zaire.

Banyarwanda.
>The Hutu, Tutsi and Twa inhabitants of Rwanda; used also to refer to the approximately 17 million inhabitants of Rwanda, Burundi, Uganda, Zaire, and Tanzania who speak Kinyarwanda.

Bourgmeistre.
>The mayor of a town or city, or head of a commune who replaced the traditional chiefs in the municipal elections in Rwanda in 1960.

Bugesera Massacre.
>The pogrom and massacre of approximately 300 Tutsis on 4 March 1992 following a Radio Rwanda broadcast that members of the Parti Libéral planned to kill twenty prominent Hutus seen in retrospect as a trial run for the eventual genocide; it produced about 15,000 homeless, some of them becoming refugees in Burundi; Bugesera is a province in southeastern Rwanda with the largest percentage of Tutsis

Caisse, Centrale de.
>A banking facility of the Ministry of Cooperation in Paris through which low cooperation interest loans are administered to favored nations in the developing world.

Chiga.
>Numerically the dominant group in Kigezi, most of the present day Kabale district of Uganda, who put up a determined and protracted resistance against centralized autocracy and foreign trusteeship under the League of Nations.

Cellule.
>Division of a commune, the lowest echelon in the Rwandan administrative structure.

Constitution.
>Refers to the 24 November 1962 first constitution of Rwanda, first proclaimed in the coup d'état de Gitarama, 28 January 1961.

Corvée.
>Customary work obligations of Hutu for Tutsi nobility (see abakutsi).

Coup d'etat.
>Overthrow of a government—in Rwanda: (1) 1961 Gitarama—a peaceful

meeting of local Hutu political leaders voted to abolish the monarchy, create a republic and elect a president—recognized by the Belgium government on 1 February 1961; (2) 5 July 1973 military but non-violent northern Hutu coup led by Major General Juvénal Habyarimana against the previous regime dominated by Hutu from the central and southern regions; (3) 6–7 April 1994 Hutu extremist violent overthrow of the Hanyarimana transitional coalition government.

Committee of Nine.
The signatories to the Bahutu Manifesto (cf. Manifeste des Bahutu) of 1957, and included J. Habyarimana, G. Kayibanda, C. Mulindahabi, S. Munyambonera, C. Ndahoyo, M. Niyonzima, I. Nzeyimana, G. Sentama, J. Sibomana.

Commune.
A division of a subprefecture itself divided into cellules.

December Massacre.
The 1963 massacre of an estimated 10,000 Tutsi following the abortive attempt of Tutsi rebels invading from Burundi to overthrow the Hutu government.

Garde Républicaine.
Mobutu's Republican Guard.

Fashoda Syndrome.
Named after a minor confrontation in southern Sudan in 1898 that almost caused a Franco-British war; used to explain French reactions in Rwanda in terms of the historical Franco-British rivalry.

Frodebu.
The party of Melchior Ndadaye, elected president of Burundi on 1 June 1993; the party itself won 65 of 81 parliamentary seats in the 29 June 1993 elections.

Fronasa.
Front for National Salvation, Museveni-led rebels against the Amin regime.

Génocidiaire.
A genocidist, someone who commits genocide.

Hima.
A group akin to the Tutsi living in northern Rwanda and southern Uganda (Ankole).

Hiru.
A group living in Ankole, Uganda, also called the Bairu, allied with Rwandese Hutu.

Hutu.
Abahutu and Bahutu, the singular and plural terms respectively for the majority (85 percent) of the Rwandese who are largely farmers, though some raise cattle.

Ibyitso.
"Accomplice" referring to Tutsi within Rwanda accused of supporting the RPF.

Igihinahiro.
Literally "the time of uncertainty," the period between the signing of the Arusha Accords on 4 August 1993 and the date when the BBTG would be installed, an event aborted by the 6 April 1994 coup.

Ijambo.
The name of a Rwandese newspaper founded in 1991 by François-Xavier Hangimana in the new spirit of press freedom.

Imprimerie Nationale du Rwanda.
>Government-owned and Habyarimana-controlled publishing house.

Impuzamugambi.
>"Those with a single purpose," the CDR youth wing and militia.

Interahamwe.
>Literally "those who work together," the name of a militant publication of the MRNDD as well as the youth wing and militia of the MRNDD established in 1992 who were given paramilitary training and armed with the sole aim of dealing a blow (in whatever manner) to anyone opposed to the regime; later used to identify all the militias that were the main perpetrators of the genocide.

Inkotanyi.
>A Kinyarwandan word meaning the "indefatigable ones" referring to the RPF invaders of 1990 onwards and their tenacity.

Inyangarwanda.
>"Those who hate Rwanda," applied first to the Hutu who rebelled against the monarchy, then to the Tutsi rebels against the Hutu government, and finally referring to anyone who disagreed with the Habyarimana regime.

Inyenzi.
>Literally cockroaches in Kinyarwanda, the name initially intended as an insult for the Tutsi invaders in the early 1960s because cockroaches were seen as dirty and attacked at night, but was adopted by those same invaders and then applied to the 1990 invaders, and finally to all Tutsis targeted by the genocide.

Isusu.
>"Bullet," the name of a secret extremist organization in the Rwandese army which supplied arms to the militias.

Kbaka Yekka.
>Kabaka Alone, Kabaka (King) Mutesa's political party in Buganda, Uganda at then end of the colonial period.

Kanguka.
>A periodical founded in 1991 by Vincent Rwabukwisi.

Kangura.
>"The voice which seeks to awaken and defend the majority," a newspaper founded in 1990 to counter the influence of the other newspapers in the opening towards freedom of speech and became notorious for its venom directed against the Tutsi; the editor was Hassan Ngeze and it was owned by Habyarimana's principal private secretary, Col. Segatwa, and the army chief of staff, Col. Serubuga.

Kanyarwanda.
>A human rights organization in Rwanda founded by Fidele Kanyabugori.

King Faisal Hospital.
>Hospital in Kigali which became a sanctuary for Rwandese protected by UNAMIR.

Kinyarwanda.
>A Bantu language spoken by the Rwandese.

Mandate.
>The placement of Rwanda and Burundi under Belgium jurisdiction by the League of Nations and confirmed in 1946 as a United Nations Trustee Territory.

Manifeste des Bahutu.
>Bahutu Manifesto issued by the Committee of Nine on 24 March 1957.

Meridian Hotel.
>A hotel in Kigali that served as a sanctuary for foreigners after the 6 April 1994.

Midaille Nyiramachibiri.
>An extremist newspaper.

Minimi.
>Semi-automatic gun.

Ministère de la Coopération.
>French Ministry for foreign aid, but also used to support Francophone countries in Africa and as a conduit for military assistance.

Mouvance présidentielle.
>The designation for Mobutu's supporters.

Mpororo.
>A centralized state from the sixteenth to the nineteenth centuries inhabited mainly by the Bahororo, and encompassing most of the counties of Western Ankole and most of Kigezi district in contemporary Uganda and a portion of northern Rwanda.

Muluba.
>An ethnic group which lives in the Shaba and Kasai regions of the DRC or Zaire and which joined the Alliance to overthrow Mobutu.

Mukungo.
>An ethnic group in the Shaba region of the DRC or Zaire and which joined Kabila's Alliance to overthrow Mobutu.

Munyamulenge.
>An ethnic group in South Kivu in the DRC (Zaire) which joined Kabila's Alliance.

Network Zero.
>Death squads linked to Habyarimana and purportedly responsible for many assassinations and killings between 1992–1994.

Operation Hope.
>Launched in December 1994 by humanitarian organizations, UNHCR, UNAMIR and the Rwandese government to empty the internally displaced persons camps.

Operation Noroît.
>Name of military operation sent to Rwanda by France following the 1 October 1990 RPF invasion, officially to protect the French expatriates present in Rwanda; the original force consisted of 150 soldiers drawn from the French forces stationed in the Central African Republic; increased to 350 in November and to 700 in February of 1993 following the RPF offensive.

Operation Retour.
>The name given to the concerted effort to empty the refugee camps in Zaire and Tanzania.

Operation Silver Back.
>The name of the Belgian military operation which landed in Kigali on 10 April 1994 to rescue Belgian citizens and other ex-patriots from the renewed war in Rwanda.

Opération Turquoise.
>The French-launched humanitarian military mission sent to Rwanda in June 1994 perceived by the RPF as an attempt to create a haven for the FAR or, at the least, cover the escape of the killers.

Parachute journalist.
>Generalist reporter or anchor parachuted into a story who is usually unfa-

miliar with the history and culture of the area to which he or she has been assigned.

Parti Révolutionaire du Peuple.

A revolutionary party founded by Laurent Kabila in Zaire in 1967, and which, with four other small parties, on 18 October 1996 at Memera, South Kivu, combined to form the ADFL, otherwise known as the Alliance.

Pays du champ.

"Field countries"—states considered part of the family in which the whole relationship between Paris and these states is special entitling such states to special low-interest loans from the Caisse Centrale de Coopération and military assistance through the Ministry of Cooperation.

Pegasus.

A Belgian UNAMIR post in Kigali.

Pré carré.

The term for French influence in Africa.

Préfecture.

The major administrative sub-unit of the state in Rwanda.

Presidential Guard.

The elite battalion of the Rwandan armed forces (FAR).

Quai d'Orsay.

French Foreign Affairs Ministry.

Radiodiffusion de la Republique Rwandaise.

State-owned radio in Rwanda.

Radio Muhabura.

Literally "leading the way," the RPF radio founded in mid-1992 and ended when the RPF-led government took power in July 1994.

Reconnaissance Batallion.

Constituted the Presidential Guard of the FAR.

La sortie honorable.

Honorable departure, term for Mobutu to save face, resign and go into exile.

Sous préfecture.

A subprefecture, a division of a prefecture, the major political administrative unit in Rwanda.

Ten Commandments.

Commandments published in 1990 in the rabid anti-Tutsi paper, *Kangura*, which were intended to appeal to and guide the supporters of the Habyarimana regime in how to deal with their "enemy," the Tutsi, as well as provide a philosophy justifying exclusive power for the Habyarimana regime.

Tusagusazisha.

Literally, "we can make you old" or we can eliminate you.

Tutsi.

Abatutsi and Batutsi, the singular and plural forms respectively of an identifiable group in Rwanda related to the Hima and from whom the ruling class in Rwanda was drawn until the Hutu revolution in 1959–1962.

Twa.

Abatwa and Batwa, the singular and plural forms respectively of the original indigenous population of Rwanda currently constituting 1 percent of the population, said to be pygmies, but their size was likely a result of their hunter-gatherer diet.

Ubuhake.
>   Derived from guhakwa meaning to pay one's respect to a superior in his court; abolished by the Belgians in April 1954, the term referred to a contractual service in traditional Rwandese society which in later interpretations became either a happy cohesion or a form of slavery; a powerful person provided protection and the client would work for the patron—cut lumber, take care of him in old age, etc.

Umubyeyi.
>   Literally means the parent, the provider and the one above everything; title bestowed on Habyarimana by his followers.

Umurangi.
>   A newspaper published by MDR extremists.

Umurwanashyaka.
>   Another extremist paper.

Umuzungu.
>   Abazungu is the plural, the name for Caucasians.

University National du Rwanda.
>   Canadian Dominican Catholic Order founded this university in the 1960s at Butare; Habyarimana created a branch in the north in Ruhengeri in the 1980s.

Usumbura.
>   The former name of Bujumbura.

Viking.
>   Code name for Lt. Lotin's Belgian UNAMIR unit in Kigali, located in the Kimihurura district of Kigali, which first reported the systematic "cleansing" of opposition figures by the Presidential Guard and gendarmes.

Glossary III
Abbreviations and Acronyms

ACP.
>   Group des sept pour la cooperation du secteur prive European avec l'Afrique, les Caribes et le Pacific, the Group of Seven for European Private Cooperation with Africa, the Caribbean and the Pacific formed in 1975; on 20 February 1992 ACP passed a resolution urging the RPF and Rwandese government to negotiate and sign a cease fire, the Rwandese government to respect human rights, and France to withdraw its troops from Rwanda.

AFDL (ADFL English).
>   Alliance des Forces Démocratiques pour la Libération du Congo-Zaire, the rebel forces led by Laurent-Desiré Kabila that overthrew the Mobutu regime in 1996–97.

AFP.
>   Agence France-Presse—a French press bureau with an office located in Kigali.

AGCD.
>   Administration General de la Cooperation au Developpement—the Belgian overseas aid agency primarily assisting former colonies of Belgium.

AHG.
>   OAU Assembly of States and Governments.

AI.
>   Amnesty International; international human rights organization headquartered in London.

AICF.
>   Action Internationale Contre la Faim, International Action Against Famine, an international humanitarian agency.

AML.
>   Armored car.

APC.
>   Armored personnel carrier.

APROSOMA.
>   Association pour la promotion sociale de la masse (Association for the Social Promotion of the Masses)—primarily Hutu political party started in the November 1957 by Joseph Gitera.

ARP.
>   Agence Rwandaise de Presse—a Rwandese press agency.

ARD.
>   Alliance pour le Renforcement de la Démocratie—Alliance to Strengthen Democracy, a conservative coalition developed in 1993 which included the dominant political party, the MRNDD, the extremist Hutu nationalist party, the CDR, and three other minor parties (PDR, PARERWA and PECO), or-

ganized on 11 November to oppose the Arusha Accords and the devolution or sharing of power with other groups; believed by many to be responsible for coordinating the violence which undermined the Arusha Accords, but by others (Prunier) to be only a paper organization.

BBC.

British Broadcasting Corporation, Britain's state-owned broadcasting company.

BBTG.

Broad-Based Transitional Government as provided for in the Arusha Accords.

BUYBAT.

The name of the Ghanaian unit in UNAMIR.

CARE.

International NGO providing humanitarian assistance to Rwandese refugees.

CAP.

Centre d'analyse et de Prévision, a French intelligence agency.

CBC.

Canadian Broadcasting Corporation, the Canadian state-owned broadcasting company.

CDR.

Coalition pour la défense de la république, Coalition for the Defense of the Republic, the most extreme Hutu party formed in 1992 and adamantly opposed to the Arusha Accords.

CEPGL.

Communaute Économique des Pays des Grands Lacs, the Great Lakes Economic Community, a transnational economic group which includes Burundi, Rwanda and Zaire (also called CPGL).

CIDA.

Canadian International Development Agency, Canada's overseas aid agency.

CND.

Conseil National de Developpement (also NCD), the National Council for Development, the parliament from 1978 until August 1993 made up of 70 representatives elected for five year terms by universal suffrage from 140 candidates nominated by the MRND.

CNDD.

Conseil National pour le défense de la democratic, National Council for the Defense of Democracy, a political organization formed by Leonard Nyangoma in 1993 when he fled Burundi after the murder of its first Hutu elected President, Melchoir Ndadaye; the guerilla group and militant arm of CNDD was called the FDD, the Democratic Defense Front.

CPGL.

See CEPGL.

CSLG.

Civilian Security Liason Group, the organization to coordinate the protection (and evacuation) of employees of international organizations and agencies and their families from Rwanda; subsequently, the same name was given to the 45 international Liaison Officers first deployed in Goma on 23 February 1995 to help train the ZCSC.

DAM.

Direction des Affaires Africaines et Malgaches, a unit in the French Ministry of Foreign Affairs.

DAMI.

Detachment d'assistance militaire et d'instruction, the French military mis-

sion to Rwanda which was accused of helping train FAR soldiers and
Interahamwe militia members.

DART.

Disaster Assistance Response Team of the Canadian military capable of
rapid deployment for humanitarian emergencies.

DAS.

Delegation aux affaires strategiques created in 1992 by Pierre Joxe, Minister of Defense.

DFAIT.

Canada's Department of Foreign Affairs and International Trade.

DGSE.

Direction Générale des Services Extérieurs, President of France's Secret
Service.

DHA.

U.N. Department of Humanitarian Affairs (recently renamed the Office for
the Coordination of Humanitarian Affairs—OCHA).

DMZ.

Demilitarized zone between the RPF and the FAR determined by the
ceasefire agreement.

DPA.

U.N. Department of Political Affairs.

DPKO.

U.N. Department of Peacekeeping Operations.

DRC.

Democratic Republic of the Congo, the new name of Zaire under Kabila.

ESM.

Ecole Superieure Militaire, headquarters of the FAR located 200 meters
from Camp Kigali.

ESO.

External Security Organization.

ETO.

A technical school in Kigali housing Belgian peacekeepers and code-named
Beverly Hills.

FAR.

Forces Armées Rwandaises—Rwandese Armed Forces under the
Habyarimana regime.

FAZ.

Forces Armées Zaire—Zairean Armed Forces under Mobutu.

FIDH.

Federation International des Droits des Hommes which produced a report
in 1993 which linked the Rwandese slaughters to the U.N. Convention on
Genocide.

FDC.

Force Democratique du Changement, the Democratic Force for Change,
the coalition of MDR, PSD and the PL formed in January 1993 in opposition to the ARD and in support of a cease fire, political inclusion, compromise, and peace.

FDD.

The Democratic Defense Front, the Burundi Hutu guerilla group and militant arm of CNDD formed by Leonard Nyangoma in Zaire after he went
into exile in 1993.

FRODEBU.

The ruling Tutsi party in Burundi at the time of the Rwandese genocide.

FNC.
> An automatic rifle.

FNR.
> Front national de resistance, the National Resistance Front organized by Innocent Ndayamaje in 1986 who was sentenced to five years in prison, since the ruling MRND was the only legal party permitted at that time under President Habyarimana.

GDP.
> Gross Domestic Product.

GOMN.
> Groupement des Observateurs Militaires Neutres, the OAU Neutral Military Observer Group (also NMOG) set up in 1993 to observe the cease fire signed between the RPF and the Rwandese government and the border between Uganda and Rwanda, and to report on any supply of logistics to the RPF; subsequently became part of UNAMIR.

GOR.
> Government of Rwanda.

GP.
> Garde Présidentielle—Presidential Guard.

HRWAP.
> Human Rights Watch Arms Project.

ICHRDD.
> International Centre for Human Rights and Democratic Development—a Canadian government funded agency located in Montreal which helped organize the international commission on human rights which visited Rwanda in January 1993 and first reported that the violence in Rwanda was planned, systematically organized and, in legal terms, constituted genocide.

ICRC.
> International Committee of the Red Cross, an international, Geneva-based humanitarian organization dedicated to the protection of and assistance to civilian victims of armed conflict, political and military prisoners; ICRC serviced the food and health needs of the almost one million Rwandese displaced by the civil war until the signing of the Arusha Accords, and was one of the two organizations to continue to operate in Rwanda when the civil war was resumed and the genocide was perpetrated.

ICTR.
> International Court Tribunal for Rwanda in Arusha, Tanzania to try perpetrators of the genocide in Rwanda.

IDC.
> International Christian Democrats.

IDP.
> Internally Displaced Person.

IFRC.
> International Federation of the Red Cross and Red Crescent Societies.

IMF.
> International Monetary Fund.

INF.
> International Neutral Force, original phrase for what eventually became UNAMIR.

ISO.
> International Security Organization.

JPMC.
> Joint Political Military Commission, a mechanism established under the Arusha peace negotiations to which GOMN or NMOG reported on violations.

KIBAT.
> The Belgian battalion of UNAMIR stationed in Kigali; ten soldiers of this battalion were brutally murdered by the FAR on 7 April 1994.

KWSA.
> UNAMIR's Kigali Weapon Secure Area located within ten km. radius of the center of Kigali.

MDR.
> Mouvement démocratique républicain, Democratic Republican Movement, founded in 1991 as the successor to the first President, Grégoire Kayibanda's MDR-PARMAHUTU; it became the main opposition party under Faustin Rucogoza.

Mi.5.
> Semi-automatic weapon.

MIGS.
> Montreal Institute for Genocide Studies.

MP.
> Member of Parliament (Canada).

MPLA.
> Movimento Popular de Libertaçao de Angola in Angola, originally supported by the Soviet Union and which defeated J. Savimbi's Uniao National para Independencia Total de Angola (UNITA) in an election.

MRND.
> Mouvement Révolutionnaire National pour le Développement, National Revolutionary Movement for Development, President Habyarimana's party, founded in 1975, which became the MRNDD in 1991.

MRNDD (formerly MRND).
> Mouvement Révolutionnaire National pour le Développement et la Démocratie, the new name of MRND in July 1991.

MSF.
> Médicins Sans Frontières, Doctors Without Borders, a medical humanitarian agency initially founded in France, and, along with the ICRC, the only humanitarian agency to stay in Rwanda after the 6 April 1994 coup and instigation of genocide.

MSF-H.
> Médicins Sans Frontières, Doctors Without Borders from Holland.

MSM.
> Mouvement Social Mahutu, a Hutu party created in 1957 founded by Grégoire Kayibanda, Rwanda's first president.

NASA.
> National Security Agency in Uganda under Obote.

NGO.
> Non-Governmental Organization.

NMOG.
> Neutral Military Observer Group (see GOMN).

NRA.
> National Resistance Army (Uganda), the rebel group founded in February 1981 and led by Museveni until 1986 when victory was achieved; approximately one third of the force was made up of Rwandese refugees.

NRC.
    National Resistance Council, the political wing of the NRA.
NRM.
    National Resistance Movement (see NRA and NRC above).
OAU.
    Organization of African Unity.
OECD.
    Organization of Economic Cooperation and Development, an agency of nineteen donor countries.
ORC.
    Open Relief Centres where accommodation, food and protection would be provided for returning IDPs and refugees.
ORINFOR.
    Rwanda Office of Information, a parastatal organization created by Habyarimana in 1974 to control the media, including Rwandan television, radio and two government newspapers.
PADE.
    Parti Démocratique, Democratic party, a creation of the MRND.
PALIPEHUTU.
    The principle Hutu Burundi opposition party.
PAPERWA.
    Parti Révolutionnaire Rwandais, Rwandan Revolutionary Party, a creation of the MRND.
PARMEHUTU.
    Parti du Mouvement de l'Emancipation de Bahutu, the party of Grégoire Kayibanda, the first President of independent Rwanda.
PDC.
    Parti Démocrate Chrétien—the Christian Democratic Party, the smallest of four opposition parties to the Habyarimana regime founded in 1991 and led by Nayinzira Nepomuscen.
PDD 25.
    Presidential Decision Directive (U.S.) issued by President Clinton on May 1994 restricting U.S. financial and logistic support and the use of the U.S. military for humanitarian interventions.
PDI.
    Parti Démocratique Islamique, initially an MRND organized party representing the Rwandese Muslim community which joined the 1994 RPF-led coalition government.
PECO.
    Parti Ecologiste, a MRND-created party and part of the genocidal government in Rwanda.
PL.
    Parti Libéral, the Liberal Party in Rwanda, led by Justin Mugenzi, the third largest opposition party with many Tutsi and business-minded members.
PRA.
    Popular Resistance Army which became the NRA.
PSD.
    Parti Social Démocrate, the Social Democratic Party, the second largest opposition party, one which entered the 1994 RPF-led coalition.
PSR.
    Parti Socialiste Rwandais, the Rwandan Socialist Party, a very minor party, but one which entered the 1994 RPF led government.

RADER.

La Rassemblement Démocratique Rwandais, the Rwandese Democratic Union, created in September 1959 by Chief Bwanakweri and supported by moderate Tutsi and Belgium.

RANU.

Rwandese Alliance for National Unity, the successor to the RRWF in 1980 and precurser to the RPF formed in 1988.

RGF.

Rwandese Government Forces (see FAR).

RoE.

Rules of Engagement interpreting the mandate of a peacekeeping force; draft rules written by the Force Commander, General Dallaire were never formally approved by New York.

RIF.

Reduction-in-Force.

RPA.

Rwandese Patriotic Army, the army of the RPF.

RPF.

Rwandese Patriotic Front, the political arm of the RPA, and the dominant coalition partner after the RPF victory in 1994.

RRWF.

Rwandese Refugee Welfare Foundation, created in June of 1979 and replaced by the more political RANU in 1980.

RTLM or RTLMC.

Radio-Télévision Libre des Mille Collines, One Thousand Hills Free Radio, the private radio station of the extremist founded in mid-1993 that broadcast hate propaganda against the Arusha Accords and the Tutsi population.

RUTBAT.

The Rutongo Battalion, the poorly equipped and inexperienced Bangladeshi battalion named after its place of deployment just outside Kigali; it included a logistics unit and was assigned UNAMIR's armored vehicles.

RWANDEX.

A large state agency that operated three depulping mills to process coffee; the Kigali warehouse was used as the logistical base for UNAMIR.

SAP.

Structural Adjustment Program (World Bank/IMF), a liberal trade economic policy imposed on Rwanda at the end of the eighties.

SANU.

Sudanese African National Union.

SPLA.

Sudan People's Liberation Army.

SRSG.

Special Representative of the Secretary-General of the U.N.

TGE.

Transitional Government of Ethiopia.

TMAA.

Technical Military Assistance Agreement between France and Francophone African states.

TNA.

Transitional National Assembly.

UDPR.

Union Démocratique du Peuple Rwandais, the Democratic Union of the

Rwandese People, set up by the MRND but which went over to the opposition and joined the coalition government formed by the RPF after their victory.

UFA.

Baganda Uganda Freedom Army, an insurgency group in Buganda, Uganda against Obote.

UNAMIR.

United Nations Assistance Mission to Rwanda, a U.N. peacekeeping mission launched in October 1993 as part of the Arusha Accords.

UNAR.

Union nationale rwandaise, National Rwandese Union, a pro-monarchist anti-Belgian political party which emerged in 1959 largely supported by Tutsi to promote independence.

UNDP.

United Nations Development Program.

UNESCO.

United Nations Educational, Scientific, and Cultural Organization.

UNHCR.

United Nations High Commission for Refugees.

UNICEF.

United Nations Children's Fund.

UNITA.

Uniao National para Independencia Total de Angola organized by Jonas Savimbi in Angola.

UNITAF.

United Nations International Task Force.

UNOC.

United Nations Operation in the Congo.

UNOMUR.

United Nations Military Observer Force for Uganda and Rwanda; worked alongside NMOG until latter disbanded; then UNOMUR was folded into UNAMIR.

UNOSOM.

United Nations Operation in Somalia.

UNREO.

United Nations Rwanda Emergency Operation under DHA and responsible for coordinating humanitarian aid in the Rwandese crisis.

UNLA.

Ugandan National Liberation Army.

UNSG.

United Nations Secretary General.

UPC.

Uganda People's Congress.

UPR.

Union du Peuple Rwandais, the Rwandan People's Union, a political party established on 9 November 1990 by Silas Mayjambere.

UPRONA.

Tutsi opposition party in Burundi.

USAID.

United States Agency for International Development.

USIA.

United States Information Agency.

VOA.
> Voice of America, the U.S. international broadcasting organization

WFP.
> World Food Program which supplied food and other humanitarian supplies to refugees.

YMCA.
> Young Men's Christian Association.

ZCSC.
> Zairian Camp Security Contingent set up to provide security for the refugee camps in Zaire.

Contributors

Howard Adelman, a Professor of Philosophy at York University in Toronto since 1966, was the founder and Director of the Centre for Refugee Studies and editor of Canada's periodical on refugees, *Refuge* until 1993. He has authored and edited eighteen monographs and edited volumes, as well as numerous chapters in edited books and refereed journals. He has written extensively on the Middle East, humanitarian intervention, membership rights, ethics, refugee policy, and early warning. Recent books include *Immigration and Refugee Policy: Australia and Canada Compared* (University of Melbourne and University of Toronto 1997) and *African Refugees* (Westview 1994) and, with Astri Suhrke, *Early Warning and Conflict Management: the Genocide in Rwanda* (1996).

Agnes Callamard currently is the Research Policy Coordinator in the International Secretariat of Amnesty International in London, United Kingdom. Born in France, she holds a Ph.D. in Political Science from the New School for Social Research in New York. She has been a post-doctoral fellow at the Centre for Refugee Studies in Toronto where she conducted research on refugees with a particular focus on those in Africa. She has also been a consultant to the U.N. and has done field work in eastern and South Africa. She is the author of many articles on refugees and is currently preparing her manuscript, *Mozambique Refugees in Malawi* for publication.

Frank Chalk is a Professor of history at Concordia University and Chair of the Montreal Institute for Genocide Studies. He is co-author of *The History and Sociology of Genocide: Analysis and Case Studies* (1990) and has published numerous other articles and book chapters on genocide.

Jacques Castonguay holds a doctorate in psychology from the Univeritè de Montrèal. He is a member of the Order of Canada, was Head of the

Department of Military Psychology and Management at the Collège Militaire Royal de Saint Jean, and has taught at the Dominican University College in Ottawa and at York University in Toronto. Author of several books and numerous papers, his most recent book, *Green Berets in Rwanda*, was published in Paris in 1998.

Todd Eachus graduated in Political Communication from George Washington University and is currently Community Affairs Director at Adelphia Communications. He has researched and authored a number of articles on the effects of modern television news media on US foreign policy and, in particular, the role of the news media on the US involvement in Rwanda.

Shally B. Gachuruzi currently teaches in the Department of Sociology and Anthropology at the University of Ottawa. Born in North Kivu, Zaire/Congo, he received his Ph.D. in sociology from Laval University, Quebec. He has specialized and published on forced migration, environmental, and development issues. He was a Post-Doctoral Visiting Fellow at the York University (1994–1997), where he coordinated two international symposia on Rwanda and Zaire.

Abbas Haji Gnamo is currently a Research Associate at the Centre for International and Security Studies in York University. Born in Ethiopia, he received his Ph. D. in Anthropology from the University of Paris, where he also earned his DEA (diplome d'Etudes apporfondies) in political science/African Studies. In addition to his book, *La Etate et les Crises d'Integration Nationale en Ethiopie Contmporaine* (CEAN-IEP 1993), he has published many articles and chapters in books. He is currently working on ethnicity in relation to current conflicts in Africa.

Kate Halvorsen graduated in sociology from the University of Bergen (Norway) and worked for UNHCR in Thailand and Mozambique from 1991–94. She has been a researcher at the Chr. Michelsen Institute in Bergen and is currently Director for the Vietnam Project of Norwegian Church Aid in Hanoi. She has published articles on human rights, gender issues, and refugees.

Bruce Jones is currently Hamburg Fellow on Conflict Prevention at the Centre for International Security and Arms Control at Stanford University, and Associate, Conflict Analysis and Development Unit at the

London School of Economics. He has also been a consultant to U.N., European, and African humanitarian, development, and conflict resolution organizations. He has written a number of book chapters, articles, and reports on Rwanda, Somalia, complex emergencies, and conflict management, including, most recently, a report to the U.N. Standing Committee on Strategic Coordination on the Great Lakes region of Africa.

Joan Kakwenzire, originally from Rwanda, has taught history at Makerere University in Kampala and has been a human rights activist. She was a contributor to the report on the Genocide in Rwanda by the U.S. Committee for Refugees and currently works as a consultant in Uganda to aid and development agencies.

Dixon Kamukama, born in Uganda, currently teaches at Makerere University in Kampala and has been involved in the study of the social relations between the Bairu and Bahima of Ankole, who are closely related to the Bahutu and Batutsi of Rwanda, respectively. He is the author of *The Rwanda conflict: Its Roots and Regional Implications.*

Turid Laegreid has a graduate degree in political science from the University of Bergen and was a research fellow at the Norwegian Institute of International relations (NUPI). From 1996 she worked for the Norwegian Refugee Council as Head of the Latin American section, and since 1998 has been the Council's resident Representative in Colombia.

Steven Livingston received his Ph.D. in political science from the University of Washington and joined the Political Communication faculty at George Washington University in 1991. His research focuses on media, international affairs, and U.S. foreign policy. In 1992–93, he was a Social Science Council Senior Research fellow in Foreign Policy Studies and in 1996 was a fellow at the Joan Shorenstein Center on Press, Politics, and Public Policy at Harvard University. He is author of *The Terrorism Spectacle* (Westview 1994) as well as numerous articles focused on the media effects on defense and foreign policy processes, particularly in regard to humanitarian emergencies.

Ogenga Otunnu, educated at Makerere University, Dalhousie University, St. Mary's University, and the Technical University of Nova Scotia, received his Ph.D. in History from York University. He was a research scholar at the Centre for Refugee Studies, York University (1991–1996) and is currently a Visiting Professor in Third World Politics in the Department of Politics and School of Public Administration, Ryerson Polytechnic University, Toronto and a Research Associate of The Lamarsh Centre for Research on Violence and Conflict Resolution at York University. He has published on refugees and environmental issues in Africa and is currently preparing a manuscript, *Political Violence in Uganda, 1890–1997* for publication.

Gérard Prunier, after receiving degrees in Political Science and Sociology, earned a Ph.D. in African History. He spent several years in East Africa in the 1970s (Uganda, Tanzania, Ethiopia) and joined the French Centre National de la Recherche Scientifique (CNRS) in 1984 as a Researcher in Modern and Contemporary African History. His latest book was *The Rwanda Crisis: History of a Genocide* (Columbia UP 1995) and is presently completing a work on *Rwanda in Zaire: from Genocide to Continental War* (Hurst & Co 1998).

Astri Suhrke has a Ph.D. in international relations and has published widely on social conflict and population movements. She is a co-author of *Escape from Violence* (OUP 1989) and, with Howard Adelman, co-author of Vol. 2 of the *Joint Evaluation of Emergency Assistance to Rwanda* entitled *Early Warning and Conflict Management* (1996) as well as a number of other articles related to the issue. She is currently a Senior Fellow at the Chr. Michelsen Institute in Bergen and Research Associate at the Carnegie Endowment for International Peace in Washington, D.C.

Amare Tekle earned a Ph.D. in international relations from the University of Denver in 1966 and has served the Ministry of Foreign Affairs in Ethiopia. He was the Commissioner for the national referendum in Eritrea in 1993, which confirmed that country's independence. Dr. Tekle has taught in the U.S. and has written widely on conflict and conflict resolution in the Horn of Africa.

Bibliography

Books and Theses

Adelman, H., H.A. Gnamo, and B.S. Gachuruzi (eds.). *A Framework for Conflict Resolution: Peace-Building and National Reconciliation in the Great Lakes Region of Africa.* (Toronto: Centre for International and Security Studies, York University: 1997).

Africa Rights. *Rwanda: Death, Despair and Defiance.* (London: Africa Rights:1994).

Africa Watch. *Beyond the Rhetoric: Continuing Human Rights Abuses in Rwanda.* (New York: Africa Watch: 1993).

Ajala, A. *Pan-Africanism.* (London: Andre Deutsch: 1974).

Allard, Kenneth. *Somalia Operations: Lessons Learned.* (Washington: National Defence University Press: 1995).

Aldritch, Robert and John Connell. *France in World Politics.* (London: Routledge: 1989).

Alexandre, Laurien. *The Voice of America: From Detente to the Reagan Doctrine.* (Norwood: Ablex Publishing: 1988).

Andereggen, Anton. *France's Relation with Sub-Saharan Africa.* (Westport, CT: Praeger: 1994).

Bayart, Jean François. *La Politique Africaine de François Mitterand.* (Paris: Karthala: 1984).

Bayart, J. F. *L'état en Afrique.* (Paris: Fayard: 1989).

Boutros-Ghali, Boutros. *An Agenda for Peace.* (New York: United Nations:1992).

Braeckman, Colette. *Le Dinosaure: le Zaire du Mobutu.* (Paris: Fayard: 1992).

Braeckman, Colette. *Rwanda, histoire d'un génocide.* (Paris: Fayard: 1994).

Central Intelligence Agency. *The World Factbook:1994–1995.* (Washington: Brassey's: 1994).

Chrétien, Jean-Pierre, Jean-François Dupaquier, Marcel Kabanda, and Joseph Ngarambe with Reporters sans frontières. *Rwanda: Les médias du génocide.* (Paris: Éditions Karthala: 1995).

Cervenka, Z. *The Unfinished Quest for Unity: Africa and the OAU.* (London: J. Friedman: 1977).

Chalk, Frank and Jonassohn, Kurt. *The History and Sociology of Genocide: Analyses and Case Studies.* (New Haven: Yale University Press: 1990).

Chipman, John. *French Power in Africa*. (London: Blackwell: 1989).

Clarke, John F. and David E. Gardiner (eds.). *Political Reform in Francophone Africa*. (Boulder: Westview Press: 1996).

Clapham, C. *Africa and the International System: The Politics of State Survival*. (Cambridge: Cambridge University Press: 1996).

Clay, Jason W. "The Eviction of Banyarwanda: The Story Behind the Refugee Crisis in Southwest Uganda." (Cambridge University M. A.: no date).

Cohen, Samy. *La défaite des généraux*. (Paris: Fayard: 1994).

Destexhe, Alain. *Rwanda: Essai sur le génocide*. (Bruxelles: Editions Complexe: 1994).

Edel, M.M. *The Chiga of Western Uganda*. (London: Oxford University Press: 1957).

Essack, Karrim. *Civil War in Rwanda*. (Dar es Salaam: Forem Litho Printers: 1993).

Glaser, Antoine and Stephen Smith, *Ces Messieurs Afrique*. (Paris: Fayard: 1995).

Goffin, Alexandre *Rwanda, 7 avril 1994: dix commandos vont mourir*. (Brussels: ASBL 1995).

Guichaoua, Andre (ed.). *Les Crises politiques au Burundi et au Rwanda*. (Lille: Université des Sciences et Technologies: 1995).

Guisnel, Jean. *Les Généraux: enquète sur le pouvoir militaire en France*. (Paris: La Découverte: 1990).

Hazoumé, Alain and Edgar Hazoumé. *Afrique, un avenir en sursis*. (Paris: l'Harmattan: 1988).

Helle-valle, Jo. *Banyarwanda in Uganda: Ethnic Identity, Refugees Status, and Social Stigma*, Masters Thesis. (University of Oslo: 1989).

Hempstone, S. *Mercenaries and Dividends: The Katanga Story*. (New York: Frederick A. Praeger: 1962)

Himmelstrand, Ulf, Kinyanjui Kibiru, and Edward Mburanga (eds.). *African Perspectives on Development*. (London: James Currey Ltd.: 1994).

Joyaux, François and Patrick Wajsman. *Pour une nouvelle politique étrangère*. (Paris: Hachette Collection Pluriel: 1989).

Kanogo, T. *Squatters and the Roots of Mau Mau*. (London: James Currey: 1987).

Karugire, A. *A Political History of Uganda*. (London: James Currey: 1993).

Kamukama, Dixon. *Rwanda Conflict: Its Roots and Regional Implications*. (Kampala: Fountain Publishers: 1993).

Kelly, S. *America's Tyrant: the CIA and Mobutu of Zaire*. (Washington: American University Press: 1993).

Kirk-Greene, Anthony and Daniel Bach (eds.). *State and Society in Francophone Africa since Independence*. (London: Macmillan: 1995).

Kitching, G. *Class and Economic Change in Kenya*. (New Haven and London: Yale University Press: 1980).

Krop, Pascal. *Le Genocide Franco-Africaine: faut-il juger les Mitterand?* (Paris: J. C. Lattès: 1994).

La Brosse, Renaud de and Reporters sans frontières. *Les médias de la haine.* (Paris: Éditions La Découverte: 1995).

Lemarchand, René. *Rwanda and Burundi.* (London: Pall Mall Press: 1970).

Lemarchand, René. *Burundi, Ethnocide as Discourse and Practice.* (Cambridge: Cambridge University Press: 1994).

Lena, Antaine. *Africa Divided: The Creation of Ethnic Groups.* (Sweden: Lund University Press: 1993).

Linden, Ian. *Church and Revolution in Rwanda.* (Manchester: Manchester University Press: 1977).

MacGaffey, J. et al. *The Real Economy of Zaire: The Contribution of Smuggling and other Unofficial Activities to National Wealth.* (Philadelphia: University of Pennsylvania Press: 1991).

Mamdani, M. *Politics and Class Formation in Uganda.* (London: Heinemann: 1977).

Mamdani, M. and J. Oloka-Onyango (eds.). *Uganda: Studies in Living Conditions, Popular Movements and Constitutionalism.* Vienna and Kampala: JEP Series, 1983.

McEwen, A.C. *International Boundaries of East Africa.* (London: Oxford University Press, 1971).

Minear, Larry and Thomas G. Weiss, *Humanitarian Politics.* 36 (New York: Headline Series, Foreign Policy Association: 1995).

Muhanguzi, Justice. *The War in Rwanda: The Inside Story.* (Mbarara: Media Station Ltd: 1992).

Museveni, Y. K. *What is Africa's Problem?* (Kampala: NRM Publications, 1992).

Mutesa, E. *The Desecration of My Kingdom.* (London: Constable, 1967).

Mutesa, E. *Sir Mutesa's Appeal to the Secretary General of the UNO: Uganda's Constitutional Crisis.* (Mengo: Department of Information: 1966).

Nairn, T. *The Break-up of Britain: Crises and Neonationalism.* (London: Brydone Printers: 1977).

Ndarishikanye, Barnabé and Jean-François Dupaquier with Reporters sans frontières and the Commission Européenne. *Burundi, le venin de l'intolérance: Étude sur les médias extrémistes.* (Paris: Reporters sans frontières: 1996).

Newbury, Catharine. *The Cohesion of Oppression: Clientship and Ethnicity in Rwanda, 1860–1960.* (New York: Columbia University Press: 1988).

Nicholson, Frances (ed.). *Evolving International Concepts and Regimes.* (Cambridge: Cambridge University Press: 1997).

Nzongola-Ntalaja, K. (ed.). *The Crisis in Zaire: Myths and Realities.* (Trenton, N. J.: Africa World Press: 1986).

Obote, A. M. *Myths and Realities: Letter to a London Friend.* 1970.

O'Halloran, Patrick J. *Humanitarian Intervention and the Genocide in Rwanda*. (London: Research Institute for the Study of Conflict and Terrorism: 1995).

Péan, Pierre. *Affaires Africaines*. (Paris: Fayard: 1983).

Polhemus, J. H. *The Organization of African Unity and Interstate System Conflict Management, 1963–1968*. (PhD. dissertation, Duke University: 1971).

Prunier, Gérard. *The Rwanda Crisis: History of a Genocide*. (New York: Columbia University Press: 1995).

Reyntjens, Filip. *L'Afrique des Grand Lacs en crise, Rwanda-Burundi: 1988–1994*. (Paris: Edition Karthala: 1994).

Reyntjens, Filip *Trois jours qui ont fait basculer l'histoire*. (Brussels: 1996).

Richards, A.I. ed. *Economic Development and Tribal Change: A Study of Immigrant Labour in Buganda*. (Cambridge: Heffer and Sons: 1952).

Rotberg, R.T. and A.A. Mazrui (eds.). *Protest and Power in Black Africa*. (New York: Oxford University Press, 1970).

Scott, R. Feil, *A Rwandan Retrospective: Developing an Intervention Option*. (Washington: Carnegie Commission on Preventing Deadly Conflict: 1996).

Serre, François de la; Leruez, Jacques, and Wallace, Helen (eds.). *French and British Foreign Policies in Transition*. (New York: Berg Publishers: 1990).

Sesay, Amadu (ed.). *Africa and Europe: From Partition to Independence or Dependence?* (London: Croom Helm: 1986).

Silberzahn, Claude. *Au Coeur du Secret*. (Paris: Fayard: 1995).

Stigand, C.H. *Equatoria: The Lado Enclave*. (London: Frank Cass: 1968).

United Nations. *The United Nations and Rwanda 1993–1996* (New York: U.N. Publications: 1996).

Verschave, François-Xavier. *Complicité de Génocide: La politique de la France au Rwanda*. (Paris: Éditions la Découverte: 1994).

Watson, Catherine. *Exile From Rwanda: Background to an Invasion*. (Washington: US Committee for Refugees: 1991).

Young, C and T. Turner. *The Rise and Decline of the Zairian State*. (Madison: University of Wisconsin Press: 1985).

Zarembo, Alan I. *Explaining the 1990 Invasion of Rwanda: Domestic Pressures or Foreign Policy Interests?* (Hanover: Dartmouth College Senior Honours Thesis: 1992).

Zolberg, Ari, Astri Suhrke, and Sergio Aguayo, *Escape from Violence: Conflict and the Refugee Crisis in the Developing World*. (New York: Oxford University Press: 1989).

Papers, Articles, and Book Chapters

Abaka, E. and Gachugi, J.B. "Forced Migration from Rwanda: Myths and Realities," *Refuge* 14:5, 9–12, 1994.

Abaka, E. and Woldu, S. "The International Context of the Rwandan Crisis," *Refuge* 14:5, 15–17, 1994.

Adelman, Howard and Astri, Suhrke. "Early Warning and Response: Why the International Community Failed to Prevent the Genocide," *Disasters: The Journal of Disaster Studies and Management,* 20:4, December 1996.

Adelman, Howard. "Refugees, the Right of Return and the Peace Process," *Economics of Peace in the Middle East,* Bashir Al Khadra, ed., Yarmouk University, 1995.

Adelman, Howard. "Modernity, Globalization, Refugees and Displacement," in Alastair Ager, ed., *Refugees, Contemporary Perspectives on the Experience of Forced Migration,* London: Cassell Publishers, 1997.

Adelman, Howard. "Crimes of Government as Causes of Mass Migration," in Alex P. Schmid, ed., *Migration and Crime,* Milan: ISPAC, 1997.

Amaza, Ondoga. "Rwanda and Uganda—Post-War Prospects for Regional Peace and Security," unpublished, Pan African Congress Paper, Jan. 1995.

Bach, C.D. "France's Involvement in Sub-Saharan Africa: A Necessary Condition to Middle Power Status in the International System," chapter 5 in Sesay (ed.) 1986.

Bakajika, B. "De la manipulation ethnique au Zaire au conflit des pays des Grands Lacs," paper presented at the Workshop: *Beyond the Crises: the Prospect for Peace and Sustainable Development in the Great Lakes Region of Africa,* Centre for International and Security Studies, York University, 31 January 1997.

Barber, J.P. "The Moving Frontier of British Imperialism in Northern Uganda, 1898–1919," *Uganda Journal* 29:1 (1965):27–40.

Barnett, Michael. "The Politics of Indifference at the United Nations: The Professionalization of Peacekeeping and the Toleration of Genocide," unpublished paper, August 1995.

Batsch, C. "L'Afrique noire plus proche que jamais," *Cosmopolitiques,* December 1987, 67–78.

Bennett, James. "Zur Geschichte und Politik der Rwandischen Patriotischen Front" in Schurings, Hildegard (ed.), *Ein Volk Verlaesst Sein Land: Krieg und Volkermord in Ruanda,* Cologne: Neuer ISP Verlag: 1994.

Berkeley, Bill. "Sounds of Violence," *The New Republic*: 22 and 29 August, 18–19, 1994.

Block, Robert. "The Tragedy of Rwanda," *The New York Review of Books,* 20 October, 3–8, 1994.

Bloed, Arie and Pascale, C.A.E. de Wouters d'Oplinter. "Jamming of Foreign Radio Broadcasts," in *Essays on Human Rights in the Helsinki Process ,* ed. A. Bloed and P. Van Dijk, 163–80, Dordrecht: Martinus Nijhoff: 1985.

Bourmaud, Daniel. "La France en Afrique: Politique Africaine and Politique Etrangère," conference paper, "Brazzaville plus 20," Boston University, October 1994.

Brazier, F.S. "The Incident at Nyakishenyi, 1917," *Uganda Journal,* 32, 1 (1968): 17–27.

Braekman, Colette. "Comment le Zaire fut libéré?" *Le Monde Diplomatique,* July 1997.

Bugingo, J. "After Living in Uganda for Three Decades, the Rwandese Refugees have yet to find a secure home, 1991," unpublished paper deposited at the Refugee Studies Programme, Oxford University.

Burkhalter, Holly J. "The Question of Genocide: The Clinton Administration and Rwanda," *World Policy Journal* 11 (Winter): 44–54.1994.

Chalk, Frank. "Hate Radio versus Democracy Radio: Lessons from United Nations and United States Experiences in Cambodia, Mozambique, Rwanda, and Somalia." A paper presented at the First Annual Conference of the Association of Genocide Scholars, The College of William and Mary, Williamsburg, Virginia 14 June, 1995.

Chaigneau, Pascal. "Afrique: De l'Effectif au Rationel," Joyauz and Wajsman (1989).

Chipman, John. "French Military Policy and African Security," *Adelphi Paper* 201: London: International Institute for Strategic Studies, summer 1995.

Chrétien, Jean Pierre. "La Crise Politique Rwandaise," Genève: *Afrique*: 30:2: 121–42: 1992.

Cohen, Samy. "Prospective et politique étrangère: Le centre d'analyse et de prévision du ministère des affaires étrangères," *Revue française de science politique* 6: December 1982.

Cohen, Samy and Michael Clarke. "Decision-Making in Foreign Policy," in Serre et al. 1990.

DesForges, Alison. "Rwanda: The Politics and History of a Genocide," Lecture at the First Annual Conference of the Association of Genocide Scholars, The College of William and Mary, Williamsburg, Virginia, 14 June 1995.

Dexter, Gerry L. "Africa's Shadow Voices," *Africa Report*, Sept./Oct., 84–86, 1986.

Ellis, Stephen. "Tuning Into Pavement Radio," *African Affairs:* 88:352 (July): 321–30, 1989.

Fein, Helen. "Prediction, Prevention, and Punishment of Genocide: Observation on Rwanda and Future Policies," *Refuge* 14:5, 1–4, 1994.

Ferney, Jean-Christophe. "La France au Rwanda: Raison du prince, dé-raison dEtat?," *Politique Africaine*. October 1993.

Foucault, Michel. "Le pouvoir, comment s'exerce-t-il?" in H.L. Dreyfus, Paris, Gallimard, 313–14, 1984.

Gachuruzi, B. Shally, "Le rapatriement des réfugiés rwandais: un véritable dilemme," *Refuge* 14:5, 21–25, 1994.

Gasana, James K. "Qui est responsable de l'attentat contre le président Juvénal Habyarimana?" in Guichaoua (1995): 689–93.

Ghai, D.P. "The Baganda Trade Boycott: A Study in Tribal, Political and Economic Nationalism," in Rotberg and Mazrui, eds. (1970) 755–70.

Golan, Tamar, "A Certain Mystery: How can France do everything that it does in Africa—and get away with it?" *African Affairs* 80:318. January 1981: 3–12.

Guichaoua, Andre. "L'Hotel des 1000 collines en otage," in Guichaoua 1995.

Hägglund, Gustav. "Peacekeeping in a modern war zone," *Survival,* May/June 1990, London: IISS 1990.

Heintze, Hans-Joachim and Howard H. Frederick. "International Legal Prohibitions Against Media Content Advocating War, Racism and Genocide: Indisputable Principles, Varying Enforcement," *Media Law and Practice.* September: 91–97, 1990.

Hopkins, E. "The Nyabingi Cult in Southwestern Uganda," in R.I. Rotberg and A. A. Mazrui, eds., *Protest and Power in Black Africa.* New York: Oxford University Press, 1970: 258–336.

Jones, Bruce. "Intervention Without Borders: Humanitarian Intervention in Rwanda, 1990–1994," a paper presented to a London School of Economics Workshop on *Humanitarian Intervention,* 28 January 1995.

Kabongo, I. "Myths and Realities of the Zairian Crisis, in Nzongola-Ntalaja (1986) 27–50.

Karhilo, Jaana. "Case Study on Peacekeeping: Rwanda," Appendix 2C SIPRI Yearbook 1995. *Armaments, Disarmament and International Security.* Oxford University Press: Oxford 1995.

Kiapi, A. "The Legal Status of Refugees in Uganda: A Critical Study of Legislative Instruments," paper presented at the Makerere Institute of Social Research, December 20, 1993.

Leitenberg, Milton. "Rwanda, 1994: International Incompetence Produces Genocide," *Peacekeeping and International Relations.* 23:6, 1994.

Lemarchand, René. "Managing Transition Anarchies: Rwanda, Burundi, and South Africa in Comparative Perspective," *The Journal of Modern African Studies.* 32:4: 581–604, 1994.

Lemarchand, René. "Rwanda: the Reality of Genocide," *Issue*:xxiii:2, 1995.

Leymarie, P. "Sous le choc de la révolution congolaise," *Le Monde Diplomatique,* July 1997.

Leurdick, Dick A. "Proposals for Increasing Rapid Deployment Capacity: A Survey" in *International Peacekeeping,* 2:1, Spring 1995.

Livingston, Steven. "Sustaining Press Attention: A Comparison of the Cases of Somalia and the Sudan, in The Media," *Humanitarian Crises and Policy Making,* Robert Rotberg and Thomas Weiss (eds.). Brookings Institution Press, 1996.

Livingston, Steven and Todd Eachus. "Humanitarian Crises and U.S. Foreign Policy: Somalia and the CNN Effect Reconsidered," *Political Communication,* October–December, 1995, 413–30.

Lwanga-Lunyiigo, S. "Uganda's Long Connection with the Problem of Refugees: From the Polish Refugees of World War II to the Present." Paper presented at the Makerere Institute of Social Research, 20 December 1993.

Makinda, M. Samuel. "Democracy and Multi-Party Politics in Africa," *The Journal of Modern African Studies*, 34:4 (1996): 555–73.

Mateke, P. "The Struggle for Dominance in Bufumbira, 1830–1920," *Uganda Journal*, 34:1 (1970): 35–47.

M'Bokolo, E. "Aux sources de la crise zaroise," *Le Monde Diplomatique*, May, 1997.

Mushemeza, E.D. "Refugees and International Relations: A Case of Uganda and Her Nieghbours, 1960–1990." Paper presented at the Makerere Institute of Social Research, 20 December 1993.

Muwanga, Lance-Sera. *Violence in Uganda: What is inside Museveni's Uganda.* 1983.

Muwanga, Lance-Sera and Gombya, *The Pearl of Africa is Bleeding.* 1986.

Nabuguzi, E. "Refugees and Politics in Uganda." Paper presented at the Makerere Institute of Social Research, Makerere University, 20 December 1993.

Nzogola-Ntalaja, G. "Zaire I: Moving Beyond Mobutu," *Current History*, 93:583. May 1994:193–97.

Oxfam. "International co-ordination in the Rwandan crisis." Paper presented at Wilton Park Special Conference *Aid Under Fire: Redefining Relief and Development Assistance in Unstable Situations.* 7–9 April 1995.

Oloka-Onyango, J. "Uganda's Benevolent Dictatorship," *Current History*. 96:610. May 1997:212–16.

Otunnu, O. "Refugee Movements from the Sudan: An Overview Analysis," *Refuge* 13:8. January, 1994:4–8.

Prunier, G. "The Great lakes Crisis," *Current History*, 93:383. May 1994: 193–99.

Romano, Sergio. "Le Regard de l'Autre," *Politique Etrangere.* 51: 1986: 35–41.

Romano, Sergio. Aldrich and Connell, 1986, 35–41.

Rutanga, M. "People's Anti-Colonial Struggles in Kigezi under the Nyabingi Movement, 1910–1930," in M. Mamdani and J. Oloka-Onyango, eds., *Uganda: Studies in Living Conditions, Popular Movements and Constitutionalism.* Vienna and Kampala: JEP Series, 229–49.

Rutayisire, Wilson. "Genocide in Rwanda—An Overview of the Causes, its Systematic Conception, Planning and Execution," unpublished paper, November 1995.

Schabas, William A. "Atrocities and the Law," *Canadian Lawyer.* August/September: 33–36, 1993.

Schraeder, J. P. "France and the Great Game in Africa," *Current History*, 96:610. May 1997:206–11.

Sekiki, A. R. "The Social Problems and Political Predicament of Refugees." Master's thesis, University of Dar es Salaam, March 1972.

Smith, Steven. "France-Rwanda: Lêvirat colonial et abandon dans la région des Grands Lacs," in Guichaoua, 1995.

Suhrke, Astri. "A Crisis Diminished: Refugees in the Developing World," *International Journal*, XLVIII:2, Spring 1993, 215–39.

Toulabor, C. "Paristroika and One-Party System," in Kirk-Greene and Bach, 1995.

Turner, T. "Zaire Flying Above the Toads," in Clarke and Gardiner, 1996, 246–64.

Whiteman, Kaye. "President Mitterand and Africa," *African Affairs* 82:328, July 1983.

Zolberg, Aristide. "Tribalism Through Corrective Lenses," *Foreign Affairs*, July 1973.

Reports

Adelman, Howard and Astri Suhrke with Bruce Jones. *Early Warning and Conflict Management: Genocide in Rwanda.* (Copenhagen: DANIDA: March 1996).

Amnesty International, *Rwanda: Persecution of Tutsi Minority and Repression of Government Critics, 1990–1992.* (London: May 1992).

Africa Confidential, *Rwanda-Zaïre*, 36:4. (February, 1995).

Africa Watch, *Rwanda: Talking Peace and Waging War.* IV:3: 7–23. (February 27, 1992).

Compte rendu analytique, Brussels, 2 volumes, originally published as the reports of the proceedings of the *Commission d'enquête parlementaire concernant les événements du Rwanda* established under the President of the Belgian Senate. (Brussels, 1997).

Department of Foreign Affairs and International Trade (DFAIT). *Proceedings—Conflict Prevention: African Perspective*, for the International Francophone Meeting, Ottawa, September, 1995.

Human Rights Watch. *Rwanda: Talking Peace and Waging War.* 4:3 (27 February 1992).

Human Rights Watch Africa, *Rwanda: A New Catastrophe.* 6:12 (December 1994).

Human Rights Watch Arms Project, *Arming Rwanda: the Arms Trade and Human Rights Abuses in the Rwandan War.* New York and Washington, D.C. (January 1994).

Human Rights Watch Arms Project. *Rwanda/Zaire: Rearming with Impunity—International Support for the Perpetrators of the Rwandese Genocide.* 7:4. (May 1995).

International Commission of Jurists, *Uganda Human Rights.* Geneva: ICJ: 1977.

International Organization for Migration (IOM), *Rwanda Emergency Update*, 8 (September 7, 1994).

The International Institute for Strategic Studies, *Strategic Survey 1996/1997*, "Africa: The Arc of Conflict and Crises," 1997.

IOM, *Rwanda Emergency Update*,12 (October 6, 1994).

IOM, *Rwanda Emergency Update* (January 31, 1995).

IOM, *Rwanda Emergency Update*,19 (February 1, 1995).

KIBAT: Chronique 06 avr-19 avr 1994, unpublished log of the KIBAT battallion of UNAMIR (the 2nd Battalion of Belgians). (Brussels, September 1995).

LaRose-Edwards, Paul. *The Rwandan Crisis of April 1994: The Lessons Learned*. (Ottawa: Department of Foreign Affairs and International Trade: 1994).

Rapport de la commission internationale d'enquête sur les violations des droits de l'homme au Rwanda depuis 1er Octobre 1990 (7–21 janvier 1993). Rapport Final. 1993. Federation Internationale des Droits de l'Homme (Paris), Africa Watch (New York), Union Interafricaine des Droits de l'Homme et des Peuples (Ouagadougou), and the Centre International des Droits de la Personne et du Développement Démocratique (Montréal, Mars 1993).

Rapport de l'enquête sur les violations massives des droits de l'homme commises au Rwanda à partir du 6 avril 1994. Commission d'enquête Cladho-Kanyarwanda Kigali: Comité de Liaison des Associations de Défense des Droits de l'Homme et Associations pour la Promotion de l'Union par la Justice Sociale,1994.

Red Cross and Red Crescent, "Rwanda," *Red Cross and Red Crescent*, 2:3–6 (1994).

République Rwandaise. Accord de Paix d'Arusha entre le Gouvernement de la République Rwandaise et le Front Patriotique Rwandais. 1993. *Journal Officiel de la République Rwandaise*. Année 32:16 (15 août, 1993).

République Rwandaise. *Etude sur le terrorisme au rwanda depuis 1990*, Gendarmie Nationale: Centre de Recherche Criminelle et de Documentation, Kigali, 1993.

Rudasingwa, Theogene. "The Balance Between the Necessity for Justice and the Imperatives of National Unity and Reconciliation and Democratisation," unpublished. (Kigali, 1995).

Uganda Government. *Report of the Commission of Inquiry into the Recent Disturbances Amongst the Baamba and Bakonjo People of Toro*. (Entebbe: Government Printer: 1962).

Uganda Government, *Uganda, 1962–1963*. (Entebbe: The Government Printer: 1964).

Uganda Government, *Uganda, 1964*. (Entebbe: The Government Printer: 1965).

Uganda Government, *Report of the Commission of Inquiry into Violations of Human Rights.* (Kampala: 1994).

Uganda Printer. *Proceedings of the Legislative Council.* (Entebbe: Government Printer, September, 1959).

Uganda Printer. *Report of Inquiry into Disturbances in the Eastern Province, 1960.* (Entebbe: Government Printer: March 1962).

Uganda Protectorate. *The Cattle Disease Ordinance, 1902, The Cattle Disease (Amendment) Ordinance, 1913.* CO 612/6.

Uganda Protectorate. *The Refugees (Control and Expulsion) Ordinance, 1947.* CO 684/6.

Uganda Protectorate. *An Ordinance to make Further and Better Provision for Regulation of Immigration into the Protectorate, No. 33 of 1947. CO 684/6.*

Uganda Protectorate. *An Ordinance to amend the Immigration (Control) Ordinance, 1947, No. 18 of 1949. CO 684/7.*

Uganda Protectorate. *An Ordinance to provide for the Registration and Control of Aliens, No. 23 of 1949. CO 684/7.*

Uganda Protectorate. *Report of the Commission of Inquiry into the Disturbances in Uganda during April 1949* (Entebbe: Government Printer, 1950).

Uganda Protectorate. *An Ordinance to amend the Immigration (Control) Ordinance, No. 8 of 1953. CO 684/9.*

Uganda Protectorate. *An Ordinance to Amend the Immigration (Control) Ordinance, No. 7 of 1954. CO 684/9.*

Uganda Protectorate. *An Ordinance to Make Provision for the Registration of Persons of the Kikuyu Tribe of Kenya,* 22 February, 1954. CO 684/9.

Uganda Protectorate, *Uganda Order in Council, 1902.* Part III. Entebbe: The Government Printer, 1956:82–96.

Uganda Protectorate. *The Aliens (Batutsi Immigrants) Rules, 1959 (Legal Notice No. 311 of 1959),* Proceedings of the Legislative Council. (Entebbe: The Government Printer, 29 February 1960).

Uganda Protectorate, *Proceedings of the Legislative Council.* (Entebbe: The Government Printer, 29 February, 1960).

Uganda Protectorate. *Report of the Commission Appointed to Review Boundary between the Districts of Bugishu and Bukedi.* (Entebbe: Government Printer: 1962).

United Nations Department of Public Information, *The United Nations and the Situation in Rwanda.* Reference Paper, April 1995.

United Nations. Department of Public Information. The United Nations and the Situation in Rwanda. (New York, August 1994).

United Nations. Department of Public Information. *The United Nations and the Situation in Somalia.* (New York, March 1994).

United Nations Department of Peace-Keeping Operations (DPKO), *Report of the Reconaissance Mission to Rwanda: Political Aspects,* August 1993.

United Nations Secretary-General. *"Special Report of the Secretary-General on the United Nations Mission for Rwanda* UN Doc. S/1994/470, April 20 1994.

UN Doc. S/1995/297 *Progress report of the Secretary-General on the United Nations Assistance Mission for Rwanda.* 9 April 1995.

UN Doc S/1995/411, 23 May 1995. *Report of he Independent International Commission of Inquiry into the Events at Kibeho in April 1995.*

UN Doc. A/50/60 *Supplement to an Agenda for Peace.* (New York, January 1995).

UNHCR, *Rwanda and Burundi: Emergency. Special Unit for Rwanda and Burundi,* (31 August 1994).

UNHCR, *Rwanda Emergency Crisis* (20 June 1994).

U.N. Reconnissance Mission to Rwanda. (New York: September 1993).

United States Congress. House. Committee on Foreign Affairs. Subcommittee on Africa. *Recent Developments in Somalia.* 103rd Cong., 1st Sess. (Washington, D.C.: Government Printing Office, 1993).

United States Congress. Senate. Committee on Foreign Relations. Subcommittee on African Affairs. *Crisis in Central Africa.* S. Hrg. 103-785, 103rd Cong., 2nd Sess. (Washington, D.C.: Government Printing Office 1994).

United States Congress. Senate and House. Committee on Foreign Relations and Committee on International Relations. *Country Reports on Human Rights Practices for 1994, Report Submitted by the Department of State,* S. Prt. 104–12, 104th Cong., 1st Sess. (Washington, D.C.: Government Printing Office 1995).

United States Information Agency. Bureau of Broadcasting. Office of Strategic Planning. *Report on the Mass Media Climate in Sub-Saharan Africa.* (Washington, D.C.: USIA: March 20, 1995).

D. Waller. *Rwanda: Which Way Now?* Oxford: Oxfam (UK and Ireland: 1993).

Wamba-Dia-Wamba. "The State of all Rwandese—Political Prescriptions and Disasters," Unpublished, (Dar es Salaam, 1994).

News Reports, Press Releases, and Government Statements

Adolph, Carolyn. "Public Is the Key to U.N. Reform: General," *The Gazette.* Montreal, 24 February, 1995, A7.

Africa Confidential. "Uganda: A Man in No Hurry," 31:19: 2–4 (28 September, 1990).

Africa Confidential. "Rwanda/Uganda: A Violent Homecoming," 31: 20:1–2, 12 October 1990.

Agence France Presse. "Lancement de Radio Minuar [UNAMIR] au Rwanda," AFP dispatch, Kigali, 16 February 1995.

Agence France Presse, 1 April 1997.

Associated Press. "11 Arrested in Rwandan Killings," *The Gazette.* Montreal, 2 April 1996, B1.

Bayart, Jean-François. "Le Rwanda comme un révélateur," *La Vie*, 7 July 1994.

Berkeley, Bill. "Rwanda: Those Who Started the Slaughter," *The Washington Post*, 18 April, 1995, A17.

Boston Globe, June 1, 1997.

Broadbent, Ed. "Media, Even in the West, Partly to Blame for Rwanda Massacres'" *The Gazette* Montreal, 3 May 1995, B3.

Carter, James. "Tough Job Done, NBC is Looking Ahead," *The New York Times*, 4 March 1993, A20.

Corry, John. "Assignment Africa on 13," *The New York Times*, 24 November 1986, C17.

Darton, John, "France in Africa: Why few raise a fuss," *New York Times*, 27 April 1994.

The Economist. "Try Words, They Come Cheaper," 3 September 1994, 47.

Gattegno, Hervé. *Le Monde,* 22 September, 1994.

The Gazette. "Wind It Up and It Plays," Montreal, 17 August 1995, B1.

Girard, Renaud. "Rwanda: Les Faux Pas de la France," *Le Figaro*, 19 May 1994.

Kalfleche, Jean-Marc. "De l'abus du domaine reservé," *l'Express*, No. 1948, November 1988, 56.

Kaplan, Peter W. "Famine is Chronicled in 'African Calvary'," *The New York Times*, 11 April 1985, C26.

Le Monde, "Neuf accords militaires entre Paris et Kinshasa," 22 June 1994.

Le Nouvel Observateur, 26 May-1 June, 1994.

Hilsum, Lindsey. "Settling Scores," *Africa Report.* May/June, 1994.

Holmes, Steven A. "Africa, From the Cold War to Cold Shoulders," *The New York Times*, 7 March, 1993, 4.

Houston Chronicle, November 9, 1996.

Houston Chronicle, November 16, 1996.

InformAction. "30 témoignages pour le Rwanda: Soleil dans la nuit." Press release. Montreal, 4 May.

International Herald Tribune, 12 June 1995.

Jehl, Douglas. "Officials Told to Avoid Calling Rwanda Killings 'Genocide'," *The New York Times*, 10 June 1994, A8.

Jennings, Christian. "Peace Radio Station Licensed in Burundi'" Reuters dispatch, Bujumbura, 15 February, 1996.

Kangura, Rwanda: 1990–1994 issues.

Kalfleche, Jean-Marc. "De l'abus du domaine reservé," *L'Express*, 148; November 1988.

London Times, April 30, 1997.

Lorch, Donatella, "Refugees Trying to Flee a War Settle for Limbo," *The New York Times*, 8 July, 1993, A4.

Lorch, Donatella. "Bodies From Rwanda Cast a Pall on Lakeside Villagers in Uganda," *The New York Times*, 28 May 1994.

MacGuire, James. "Rwanda Before the Massacre," *Forbes Media Critic*, Fall 1994.

Marks, John. "Letter to Friends of *Search for Common Ground*," (Winter, 1995).

Monitor, 6: Kampala, Tuesday, May 17–20, 1994.

Mugesera, Léon. "Respect des droits de la personne au cours de l'agression imposée au Rwanda depuis octobre 1990 par des éléments issus de l'armée Ugandaise." Kigali: L'Association des Femmes Parlementaires pour la Défense de la Mère et de l'Enfant, 1991.

Newsweek, "Zaire: Washington's Africa Move," 21 May 1997.

New Vision, Kampala, Monday, June 6, 1994: 1–2, 4.

New Vision, Monday, June 8, 1994: 1.

New Vision, June 11, 1994: 2.

New Vision, "Goma Insecure," Tuesday, August 16, 1994: 1–2.

The New York Times, "Accord Ends 3-year Civil War in Rwanda," 5 August, 1993, A12.

The New York Times, "U.N. Approves Troops for Rwanda,", 6 October, 1993, A17.

New York Times, May 22, 1997.

New York Times, June 1, 1997.

The New York Times Magazine, "Rwanda's Aristocratic Guerillas," 17 Jan. 1993, 10.

The New York Times Magazine, "Bodies appear in an explosion of spray," 5 June 1994, 40–47.

Norris, Alexander. "Ex-Rwandan Official Not War Criminal, Lawyer Tells Hearing." *The Gazette* A7: Montreal, 22 June, 1995.

Norris, Alexander. "Immigration Tribunal Hears Tape of Speech of Ex-Aide to Rwandan Dictator." *The Gazette* A6: Montreal: 23 June, 1995.

Péronnet, Valérie. "Poste sans frontières," *L'Express*, 24 June, 1994.

Rieff, D. "God and Man in Rwanda," *Africa Report* 142–43, May/June 1994.

Roussin, M. "De notre préence en Afrique," *Le Monde*, 28 June 1997.

Rwandese Review 2:3, Feb. 1993; 2:4 April 1994.

Reuter News Report, 20 April 1995.

Saint-Exupéry, Patrick de. "Rwanda: les assassins racontent leurs massacres," *Le Figaro*, 29 June 1994.

Saint-Exupéry, Patrick de. "La France lachée par l'Afrique," *Le Figaro*, 22 June 1994.

Schell, Jonathan. "War on the Air: Radio Is Used to Spark a Massacre." *The Gazette*, B3, Montreal, 12 August, 1994.

Simons, Marlese. "France's Rwanda Connection," *The New York Times*, 3 July 1994, A6.

Spicer, Keith. "Bloody Ideas: Media and National Mythologies in the Global Marketplace," Speech text, 22 August 1994a.

Spicer, Keith. "Propaganda for Peace," *The New York Times,* 23, 10 December, 1994b.

Steele, Scott and Luke Fisher. "Eye of the Storm," *McLean's*, 58–59, 6 June, 1994.

Sunday Vision. "Defeated Rwanda army regroups to attack RPF," 1–2, 28 August 1994.

Zarembo, Allan. "Rwanda: What Apartheid Wrought." *Wall Street Journal* 12:115, 1994

Films

Les oubliés de Kigali produced for the Belgian French-language television corporation (RTBF) by Frederic François.

Forsaken Cries: The Story of Rwanda, Amnesty International.

Index